FAMILY CASEWORK DIAGNOSIS

FAMILY CASEWORK

DIAGNOSIS

ALICE L. VOILAND AND ASSOCIATES

COLUMBIA UNIVERSITY PRESS

NEW YORK AND LONDON 1962

COMMUNITY RESEARCH ASSOCIATES, INC.

Board of Directors and Officers

MILTON H. GLOVER, *President*

MRS. FREDERIC R. KELLOGG, *Vice-President*

CRAIG R. SMITH, *Secretary*

J. CORNELL SCHENCK, *Treasurer*

GEORGE H. HILL

WILLIAM H. MITCHELL

ROBERT S. NEBLETT

GEORGE E. PERRIN

ROY SORENSON

HERBERT A. WOLFF

BRADLEY BUELL, *Executive Director*

Staff

FOREWORD

Family Casework Diagnosis marks the conclusion of one aspect of a series of research and experimental projects which Community Research Associates, Inc. (CRA) has been conducting since 1947. The particular research on which this book is based was financed by the Louis W. and Maud Hill Family Foundation of St. Paul. Throughout this period The Grant Foundation of New York has provided basic financial support for the CRA program.

Historically speaking, these various undertakings were triggered by the findings of the St. Paul study. In this study pertinent statistical data concerning problems and services were collected by CRA in cooperation with the Greater St. Paul Community Chest and Council during the month of November, 1948. Of particular significance were the assembled facts which documented the heavy concentration of agency services in a relatively small group of seriously disorganized multiproblem families who presented two or more of three basic problems: dependency, ill-health, and maladjustment. The program implications of these findings were developed and interpreted in *Community Planning for Human Services,* by Bradley Buell and Associates in 1952.

At that time it was recognized that the systematic identification of these multiproblem families served no clinical purpose, except perhaps to emphasize the need for a thorough diagnostic analysis of the reasons for their failures in social functioning. It was also clear, however, that this clustering of problems and services was a point of sufficient epidemiological import that its significance should be taken seriously by the planners and administrators of the community's health and welfare services. Underscored also, was the need to coordinate and integrate the numerous services given to the same families by different agencies. Equally obvious was the desirability of using the *total family* as the primary base in formulating plans for better organizing these community services.

The research and experimental projects subsequently launched by CRA in 1952 through 1958 represent the effort to cope with the program-planning and operational problems along the lines suggested by these findings. Two approaches were employed. Both were initiated and proceeded concurrently. One approach involved the conduct of three experimental projects at the level of agency operation. The cooperation of the key agencies in widely separated geographic areas was secured. Focus was upon prevention and control of dependency in Winona County, Minnesota; indigent disability in Washington County, Maryland; disordered behavior in San Mateo, California. All three operational experiments were ended by 1958; findings were published during that year.[1]

The other approach to prevention and control resulted in this book. It was conceived as a companion piece of research to supplement the purposes of the experimental projects; namely, a study designed to delineate and formulate the basic essentials of family casework diagnosis. A pilot study was launched in 1952 to see whether clinically useful hypotheses might be developed in this regard. Paul T. Beisser of CRA, then Associate Director for Adjustment Services, and one of its founders, was the Director. The study team was headed by Mrs. Mildred Kilinski, now Director of Family Services, Community Service Society of New York, and included Richard Magraw, M.D., a practicing psychiatrist, now Assistant Dean of the College of Medical Sciences, University of Minnesota, and Robert Mooney, M.D., a practicing internist of St. Paul. A random sample of cases of multiproblem families identified in the original 1948 St. Paul study and known to Family Service of St. Paul was selected for exploratory analyses. The preliminary findings were provocative and suggestive. Therefore, a second project, with a broader purpose, was undertaken in 1953. New family case data

[1] Consult Community Research Associates, Inc., 124 East 40 Street, New York 16, N.Y., for reports.

of greater variety and depth were assembled from seven voluntary family service agencies in accordance with a well-worked-out plan. The participating agencies were: Brooklyn Bureau of Social Service and Children's Aid Society; Family Service of Cincinnati and Hamilton County; Family and Children's Bureau, Columbus, Ohio; Family Service of Milwaukee; Family and Children's Service, St. Louis; Family Service of St. Paul; and Family and Child Services, Washington, D.C.

The findings of this later phase constitute the main source from which the materials in this book are drawn. However, the family research project and experimental projects mutually benefited from a process of cross-fertilization and were, in fact, dual aspects of a single research operation and objective. As this is written, CRA is entering a new phase of operational research based on the combined results of these endeavors. The diagnostic tools and methods developed therefrom are either in actual use or in process of installation in county public welfare departments of the states of Minnesota and Pennsylvania, and in the cities of San Francisco and Omaha.

Mr. Beisser was Director of the family research project and continued in this capacity until his retirement. He was assisted throughout by Alice L. Voiland whose long and distinguished experience in family casework practice was of inestimable value to the staff. Upon her shoulders rested the main task of clinical analysis of case data, formulation of concepts, development of methods suitable to research objectives, interpretation of findings, and writing the manuscript. In this she was greatly aided by continuous consultation from F. Stuart Chapin, Emeritus Professor of Sociology, University of Minnesota.

To Miss Voiland, Mr. Beisser, Dr. Chapin, and all others associated in this undertaking CRA wishes to tender its grateful acknowledgment.

New York   BRADLEY BUELL
January, 1962   *Community Research Associates*

ACKNOWLEDGMENTS

I WANT TO GIVE particular thanks to my friends and colleagues for their guidance, constant support, and forebearance during the years this book was in preparation.

I am especially grateful to Paul H. Gray, M.D., and to Mildred Kilinski, both of whom read the manuscript and offered many valued suggestions; to Erminie C. Lacey for her efficient tabulation of statistical data; and to Ruth L. Parker for her editing of the preliminary draft of the manuscript.

My last words of acknowledgment go to Dorothy M. Swart in appreciation of her editorial skill and perceptiveness, which made easier the final task of bringing this book to successful completion.

ALICE L. VOILAND

CONTENTS

Foreword by Bradley Buell   vii
Acknowledgments   xi

PART ONE

Introduction   3
I. An Approach to Family Diagnosis   5
II. The Determinants of Social Behavior   33
III. Healthy Family Functioning   70

PART TWO

Introduction   93
IV. A Classification of Psychosocial Disorders   95
V. The Perfectionistic Family   115
VI. The Inadequate Family   156
VII. The Egocentric Family   193
VIII. The Unsocial Family   234
IX. Framework for Family Diagnosis   290
X. Interpretation of the Diagnostic Framework   303
XI. Application   333
Bibliography   349
Index   359

Part One

INTRODUCTION

TODAY, as in the past, the vast majority of social caseworkers practice in the setting of community-supported welfare agencies. In large measure, their basic responsibility is to help persons who come to these agencies with problems in some area of social functioning. This is the human material with which most social casework deals.

From these simple truths stems the great and immediate challenge now clearly facing the field. How can social casework better diagnose these problems and direct its rehabilitative efforts in behalf of individuals and families already known to these agencies? Experimentation with selected groups of cases within a given agency followed by a reformulation and sharpening of concepts and methods is one essential way of trying to meet this challenge. It enhances skills, and contributes to an enrichment of casework knowledge as it gets into the main stream of teaching and practice.

It would also seem, however, that this challenge calls for something more basic and intrinsic to social work as a profession. It demands the development of concepts and methods that may be meaningfully and realistically related in an integrated way to the total spectrum of social casework and agency operational needs.

This book articulates an approach to family casework diagnosis which is a beginning effort in the direction of this kind of integration. The materials derive from the experience and findings of an eight-year research project related to the study of family casework as practiced in a variety of community-supported agencies. It is dedicated to the social casework practitioners and to the community agencies which support their endeavors. Each, in its own way, copes with the many issues and problems attendant upon insuring professional help to troubled families who need their services.

I. AN APPROACH TO FAMILY DIAGNOSIS

SEVERAL DYNAMIC factors and interests gave impetus to the launching of this research. Foremost among these were Community Research Associates' (CRA) broad research objectives as conceived in 1954; namely, to formulate concepts and experiment with procedures for the prevention and control of dependency, indigent disability, and disordered behavior in agencies that deal with these problems. A diagnostic classification of disordered families was necessary to the implementation of these goals. This grew logically out of the previously demonstrated need (32) to use the family as the unit of count for collection of community-wide social data as well as for the focus of diagnostic study and community planning. Practically speaking, also, the prospect of conducting a series of experimental projects underscored the need for a tool that could be consistently applied by agency personnel. A diagnostic classification of families would further these goals and objectives by providing:

1. A systematic method for analyzing and classifying family pathology at the practitioner's level, that was also consistent with statistical methods of assembling data to show the epidemiological characteristics of the total community's problem case load.

2. A system of counting families, which also classified them according to behavior patterns that had some diagnostic significance as to the causes and treatment of dependency, indigent disability, and disordered behavior.

Early in the conduct of the three experimental projects another aspect of these basic research objectives began to emerge. It became increasingly evident that there was considerable confusion among the casework staff about what did and what did not constitute a "family diagnosis." As contrasted to the present, casework literature in 1953 and 1954 contained little or no material which clearly articulated concepts of family diagnosis within a framework that enabled the systematic identification of healthy and pathological family functioning. Ackerman (2) had made a beginning in this direction in the field of psychiatry, and his work was subsequently published in 1958. In the field of social work, Pollak and Ormsby (139) developed "Design of a Model of Healthy Family Relationships," published in 1957; Weiss and Monroe (159), "A Framework for Understanding Family Dynamics," in 1959, to mention but a few. At that point, however, it was essential that CRA develop a usable approach to family diagnosis.

A final and equally impelling reason for undertaking this research was more akin to the larger interests and problems confronting the field of casework. This concerned the formulation of concepts and principles from raw case data that would enhance and forward family casework practice and knowledge. CRA supported and continues to support the belief that for practical purposes social casework at the present time offers the most solid foundation on which to build a community program for prevention and control of problems in social functioning. The casework members of CRA had also come to believe that social casework, as then taught and practiced, lacked precision and an orderly approach in the diagnostic process. It was thought that casework could, and should, do much better. This seemed to be especially true of family casework diagnosis, although by its very nature it has many facets and is extraordinarily complicated. It did seem, however, worth a try.

Thus, at the time this research was launched in 1954, there were two specific objectives: (1) the development of a diagnostic classification system which identified disordered family types; and (2) the articulation of concepts and principles of family casework diagnosis, if this seemed warranted as we proceeded. Both, obviously, are different aspects of a total process and purpose. The final report is appropriately titled, "Family Casework Diagnosis."

RESOURCES AND SETTING

At the beginning of the research there was available the experience and findings of a pilot study (37) conducted by CRA in 1952. Ten types of disorganized families were classified according to the interaction patterns—marital axes—of the marital partners.

By the fall of 1953, the cooperation of the seven voluntary family casework agencies had been enlisted to assemble new and more complete family data than were available to the pilot study. From these data the validity of the marital axis as the presumed key to the causes of family dysfunctioning was to be explored as one aspect of developing more precise classifications of disordered family types.

The agencies' active participation in the collection of data extended from January, 1954, to September, 1955. In each agency the director of casework supervised the research project and served as the liaison with the CRA staff assigned to the study. The selection of project caseworkers was made by the local agency executive and casework director. The seven agencies had a collective total of fifty caseworkers in the project at the outset. This figure remained relatively stable throughout the eighteen-month period, although at termination a total of sixty-two caseworkers had participated. In some agencies there was no loss of project workers resulting from resignation or for other reasons. In a few there were no replacements when losses occurred; in others, replacements were immediate. All participants had graduate degrees from an accredited school of social work and had had at least three or four years' experience. Eighteen different schools had provided the professional training. Most prominent in order of frequency were Smith College, New York School of Social Work, Ohio State University, Washington University, and the University of Chicago.

This phase was largely devoted to implementing the collection of data. A family case analysis schedule, forty-two pages in length, and divided into thirteen sections, was the main research tool. It was also designed to serve as the case record and covered the following areas considered vital to a comprehensive psychosocial history:

1. Identifying data
2. Problems as seen in the application process by the client and by the worker
3. Adaptive capacities of adult heads with respect to:
   Employment and work adjustment
   Income and income management
   Marital relationships
   Parent-child relationships
4. Adaptive capacities of children
   Under six years of age
   Six to eighteen years of age or over
5. Health (physical and mental)
6. Intelligence
7. Premarital relationships of partners
8. Personal history and background of partners
9. Psychosocial diagnostic formulation of case, including marital axis designation
10. Psychiatric and supervisory consultation reports
11. Treatment plans and aims
12. Summary of contacts with family
13. Evaluation of treatment results

Two important features of this schedule were that it was generically conceived insofar as family functioning was concerned and that it required descriptive data to substantiate diagnostic judgments and check items entered in each section. Moreover, at the point of intake, throughout the life of the case, and at its termination, the caseworker was expected to indicate whether or not his judgments remained consistent. In addition, he was to indicate according to the degree of certainty whether or not any of the ten identified marital axes was identified in the case, and seemed to be demonstrated in the marriage. A classification manual of the ten marital axis disorganized family types was used by each caseworker as a guide in this process.

The CRA staff took responsibility for in-service research training as well as for planning and implementing certain administrative procedures related to the assembling of data. This was done through the use of written instructions and periodic workshops. For example, the first workshop of casework supervisors was devoted to a careful review of the family case analysis schedule developed by CRA, following which revisions were made and agreed upon. Workshops were also conducted by CRA in each of the seven family agencies on an average of three to four times annually, from November, 1953, through June, 1955. Casework, supervisory, and administrative staff participated, depending upon what issues were paramount. Use of the schedule and questions as to the meaning of case data usually involved only the casework staff and case supervisors. Matters relating to methods of case selection, collection of problem data with respect to total agency case load, and other administrative considerations usually concerned only the executive and the casework supervisor. In general, these workshops served to keep the project agencies functioning as an integrated unit throughout the data collection period. September, 1955, marked the termination of the operational phase, and all schedules had been returned to CRA. A preliminary report of findings was subsequently released to the seven agencies in March, 1957, for their criticisms and suggestions. The first draft of the manuscript of this book was sent to each of the agencies in June, 1960. This was studied by the executive director, by the casework supervisor, and, insofar as time permitted, by the casework staff who had participated in the research. In October, 1960, the casework supervisors or executive directors of six of the original agencies attended a workshop session conducted by CRA to discuss these materials. Although considerable time had elapsed between the termination of the project in the agencies, the release of the preliminary report, and the preparation of the manuscript, the response of this agency group was remarkable and their criticisms invaluable. This kind of cooperation is essential in any research project based on the study of live case materials from an ongoing agency. This latter fact alone, however, makes the undertaking anything but simple.

SAMPLING METHODS

A strictly random selection of cases from the agencies proved impractical. Neither the volume nor the flow of applications could be controlled or reconciled with the need to build a project case load within a limited period of time. The following criteria for selections were therefore applied by the director of casework in each agency:

1. Only new or reopened continued-service cases of families applying to the agency during the period of January 1, 1954, through June, 1956, were to be included.

2. Both marital partners should be present, preferably with their children.

3. If the marital partners were separated, divorced, or one had deserted, periodic contact with the absent partner should be likely or possible.

4. Marital partners should be under sixty years of age.

5. A minimum of five interviews was required in order to include a case in the final sample.

The general purpose was to secure data about families with young children as well as with adolescents. The sixty-year age limit of marital partners was arbitrarily selected with this in mind. There was no requirement as to type or seriousness of psychosocial problem presented. However, each casework director was given the responsibility of making certain that the range of problems occurring in the total agency case load should be present in the final sample, if only by the inclusion of one case for a single problem category. The problem listings of the Family Service Association of America (FSAA) were used as a guide for classification, both for the project cases and for the total agency continued-service case load. These problem data provided the basis for determining representativeness of the project sample to the individual agency's total continued-service case load, to the seven-agency project sample, and to the larger group of agencies annually reporting to FSAA on a national scale.

The formula for determining each agency's quota of schedules was based upon the number of project caseworkers, and the number of cases the particular agency casework supervisor believed could reasonably be assigned, scheduled, and treated during the eighteen-month period. In general, twenty cases per worker, assigned at the rate of two cases per month, provided the base from which each agency quota was projected. Eight hundred and eighty-eight schedules, out of a total of 900 returned by the seven agencies, were accepted as the final sample.

ANALYSIS OF COLLECTED DATA

In analyzing the 888 schedules, two basic types of data were studied by two methods:

1. The general characteristics and representativeness of the 888-case sample and of a 100-case sample, by statistical methods of analysis
2. The symptoms of social functioning and dysfunctioning in a 100-case sample, by casework analysis through inspection supplemented by statistical analysis.

The general characteristics of the families were determined by the tabulation of purely factual data recorded on the schedules. Some of these findings are summarized as background for understanding the kinds of families typical of the sample subjected to clinical analysis.

Ethnic characteristics show that in the group of 888 families, 63 percent were acknowledged Protestants; the remainder, Catholic, Jewish, or of other faiths. Though these were predominately white families, also present were families of Negro, Asiatic, Arabic, Japanese, Indian, and Mexican extraction.

The spouses were living together as legally married couples in 82 percent of the famiiles. The remainder were apart in the current union by reason of separation or divorce, but were still in the family picture. There had been previous marriages for one or both partners in 26 percent of the families. Over half the male heads and three fourths of the female heads were under forty years of age at the closing of the project. Over two thirds of the families had a weekly income of $75 to $100 or more. A total of 258 children was present in 92 percent of the families, one third of them under six years of age.

The following facts throw some light on the quantitative aspects of family data collected. Of these 888 cases, 87 percent had a total of more than five interviews. In 62.7 percent of this group, both husband and wife had been seen; in 3.6 percent, the husband only;

and in 33.6 percent, the wife only. Thus, in the majority of instances, it was possible for the caseworker to evaluate and weigh the significance of data obtained from more than one source.

Duration of casework contact with the project families, an important factor in securing adequate data, also presents an assuring picture. Under agency treatment for four months to one year were 46 percent of the 888 cases; for eighteen months or longer, 23 percent; for three months, 28 percent; length of time unknown, 3 percent. Of the agencies' total continued-service case load, only 40 percent had five interviews or more during the same period, whereas, by comparison, in 87 percent of the project cases five interviews or more were held.

Thus, we find that these are predominately families in their childbearing and income-producing years, the vast majority of which have young children of school age or older, or both. Length of contact per case assured adequacy of data, as well as time for diagnostic and therapeutic effort.

In brief, there is statistical evidence of an empirical sort which indicates that we may provisionally generalize that the results from an analysis of the sample 100 cases are probably also true of the 888. There is further evidence, for a provisional set of conclusions, that the sample 100 cases are not only representative of the 888 total, but that the 888 cases are, in fact, geographically representative of cases treated among fifty family agencies reporting annually to FSAA during the same period.

CASEWORK ANALYSIS OF MARITAL AXIS DATA

Methods involve research instruments and processes. To a large extent, both evolved from the reading and rereading of raw case materials for purposes of diagnostic analysis and evaluation. With each succeeding stage, greater precision and clarity were achieved in research instruments and processes.

The methods used in the initial stage of data analysis related to establishing a relationship between the kind and degree of pathology found in the marital relationship and the type and degree of maladaptive behavior present in the family and its individual members. In other words, the marital axis identified in each case needed to be examined with respect to the possible presence of other problems of family functioning which could be considered typical of the family type.

Two kinds of casework analysis of marital axis data were undertaken on 282 cases randomly selected from the total 888. This sample was later enlarged to 400. The case materials were analyzed and tabulated by inspection according to six defined problem categories: financial; marital; parent-child; adult personality; child behavior; and health. The first three referred to the various ways in which the adult heads of the families met their responsibilities as family wage earners and providers, the compatibility of the spouses in their marital relationship, and their effectiveness as parents. The remainder pertained to the emotional stability of the adult family members, the socially adaptive behavior of children, and the physical well-being of all family members.

When such problems were identified, classified, and tabulated by the ten axis types in the case sample, the results disclosed no significant relationship between the particular marital axis present and the kind of psychosocial pathology revealed in family members. Generally speaking, the problems denoting dysfunctioning were diffusely scattered over all marital axis types. Inevitably, these findings raised doubt about the marital axis concept as a base from which to classify problems symptomatic of family malfunctioning, and about the reliability of the problem categories used.

The first problem was further explored by the use of a three-point value scale by which to determine the degree of compatibility in the marital relationship as this related to problems in other areas. The areas covered: (1) emotional, which related to the affectional relationship of the spouses and the ways they maintained their self-esteem; (2) homemaking, which concerned the shared values and agreement between spouses and that which they expected of themselves and of their partners as wage earners and family heads responsible for conduct of domestic affairs; (3) sexual, which included the shared values and interests of the spouses with respect to the form and frequency of the sexual act; (4) social, which covered the shared values and agreement of spouses with respect to religious, cultural, and leisure interests, and contact with relatives. A value of "1" denoted normal, or an emotional rapport that supported a healthy marital relationship. A value of "2" denoted some alienation, but not sufficient seriously to disrupt the relationship. A value of "3" denoted marked alienation clearly disrupting to the relationship.

Application of this rating scale to 400 cases by inspection and hand sorting yielded two results:

1. Serious incompatibility (value 3) appeared in all axis classes indiscriminately, with no clusterings of any kind in single or combined areas of emotional, homemaking, sexual, and social areas.

2. Serious incompatibility (value 3) also appeared in one or two areas simultaneously, with compatibility between the spouses in other areas. Shared values and agreement between partners existed particularly in regard to the wage earner's job performance and adequacy as provider, but not necessarily in the sexual area. It also became evident that although the marital partners could be satisfied with the emotional rapport between them, psychosocial pathology, particularly in children, was observed. In other words, the fact that the two spouses got along well together did not make the family invulnerable to other types of problems.

There was clinical evidence, but inconclusive statistical evidence, that the character of the relationship between the two partners somehow related to the functional capacity of the total family. There did not, however, seem to be any correlation between the nature of the marital emotional tie and the presence or absence of typical psychosocial pathology in other areas of adult behavior, such as child rearing, earning a living, or in the adjustment of children.

Insofar as methodology was concerned, it appeared that the use of the ten marital axes as the main points of focus for the analysis of family data had not yielded significant results. Moreover, it was increasingly clear that the marital axis did not provide a broad enough base from which to proceed. The pilot study team had recognized that this might occur. Nonetheless, they decided that the soundest way to approach the initial problem of family classification was to proceed from the biological foundations of the family as represented in the male-female relationship of the marriage. Their next planned step was to expand the field of inquiry to the realm of all interpersonal relationships of family members. This later phase could not be undertaken because of time limitations and insufficient case data. With this knowledge, and the results obtained by the casework analyses and statistical analysis of marital axis data just described, a reformulation of concepts, methods, instruments, and processes followed.

REFORMULATED CONCEPTS

Inevitably, method reflects concepts and premises. In retrospect, it is indeed difficult, if not impossible, accurately to reconstruct the extent to which original concepts influenced method, and the data produced by the method demanded a reformulation of concepts and premises.

In other words, conceptualization and the devising of method inescapably proceed simultaneously, at least at this stage of family casework research. In our case, this problem was compounded by the fact that there was then no known method of analyzing family data which was so conceived that it would result in a product clearly suitable and appropriate to social casework. For these reasons, the research method had to be flexible to deal adequately with emerging, unforeseen factors. We did, however, have the benefit of sound guiding research principles. In this we were fortunate in having the help of Dr. F. Stuart Chapin, who was also able to adapt statistical methods for testing the validity of the findings derived from a strictly clinical approach.

The most significant premises that were eventually formulated give some insight as to the soundness of the methods, the character of the findings, and the foundations on which they rest.

Social casework as practiced in community-supported agencies is presumed to direct its primary efforts to the diagnosis and treatment of social functioning impairments of families and individuals; in other words, social dysfunctioning. Therefore, it is necessary to know what constitutes normal functioning.

In general, healthy social functioning for any individual is considered to involve two psychosocial processes:

1. Mastery of the tasks and requirements of everyday living, in approximate accordance with the cultural values of the society in which the individual finds himself
2. Alleviation of the anxieties caused by such social tasks and by inner pressures in ways that promote mental health as well as satisfy society's expectations for social behavior.

These processes of social functioning have two additional implications:

1. A social milieu within which the individual functions, to which he reacts, and which in turn acts upon him
2. Social tasks and social expectations which the individual must meet, and in relation to which he must handle his own emotional needs.

The foregoing basic concepts provide the foundation for the more precise and definitive aspects of family functioning.

The "family" refers to the father and mother, related through their own or adopted children, or the nuclear family. Two primary objectives are required of the family by society: the rearing of children so that they become psychosocially mature personalities; the maintenance of psychosocially stabilized behavior in the adults. Against this background, the social functioning and dysfunctioning of the family and its individual members need to be examined according to the attitudes and behavior they manifest in meeting their responsibilities of:

1. Child rearing
   Parental functioning
   Child development
2. Marital functions
   Reciprocity in gratification of emotional and biological needs
   Helpful concern
   Problem-solving orientation
3. Financial functions
   Income production
   Income management

Our concept of pathology or social dysfunctioning is relative. Consequently, the degree factor poses an inescapable problem in assessing and differentiating the normal from the abnormal. In all people the fundamental needs that require gratification from the environment are largely the same. Therefore, evidence of all human needs will be reflected to some extent in the behavior of all family members, irrespective of the adequacy or inadequacy of their capacities for social adaptation. Everyone needs to feel self-respect, to be dependent upon another, to achieve some form of sexual gratification, feel loved and valued, have some outlet for his creative urges, express his aggressions, and so on.

This premise scarcely needs justifying. Distinctions as to health and pathology are therefore based upon: which needs dominate behavior; how many of these needs are urgent; the behavior technique used in gaining satisfaction of these needs from the environment; the exaggeration and flexibility of the defenses used; which and how many family members or other individuals are deprived or damaged in the process.

Within this context, family social dysfunctioning in one or more of the three family functional areas is determined. It is further presumed that family dysfunctioning is present only when defined psychosocial disorders are identified by an agency, acting in behalf of both the community and the family or individual. These psychosocial disorders are considered to be of two general types—Level A and Level B.

Level A psychosocial disorders consist of behavior that is prohibited, restricted, or represents a failure to perform obligatory social duties in accordance with specific laws or with the rules and regulations of agencies that have the force of law. These disorders are always defined in relation to official agency action which is undertaken as a result of their identification.

Level B psychosocial disorders consist of behavior or conditions representing failures in social role responsibilities that do not fall into the Level A categories. That is, they have not been identified by action of the court or by a legally designated agency. Such failures, however, in order to be considered Level B psychosocial disorders must have been identified as such by some community health or welfare agency to which the family member goes voluntarily or involuntarily.

Thus, a differentiation has been made between deviant behavior and failures in social functioning which have been identified by community agencies and those which have not. In other words, there are many families whose social functioning might be considered pathological from a clinical point of view, but they are never known to a community agency. Definitions used here, and the findings, therefore, reflect this orientation.

The general relevance of family social dysfunctioning both to the causes and to the resolution of identified psychosocial disorders is considered to be of sufficient significance to make family diagnosis a prerequisite to most rehabilitative programs.

Within the context of the foregoing fundamental principles, "family diagnosis," as differentiated from other types of diagnosis, refers to the intellectual process of assessing specific factors which, taken in the aggregate, are seen as having or not having a bearing upon the social dysfunctioning of the family and hence on the presence of identified psychosocial disorders:

1. The social setting
2. The kinds of object relationships formed by adults and children
3. The degree of self-reliance they have achieved
4. The kind of social conscience they have developed
5. The predisposing sensitivities within the personalities of family members
6. The physical and intellectual capacities of each which render him vulnerable to the pressures of social and family living.

This concept of family diagnosis embraces the normal as well as the abnormal.

The last premise, systematization of casework procedures, is considered a part of sound casework practice. These procedures refer to a sequence of related activities and ideas already known to the field of casework: problem identification; diagnosis; prognosis; treatment planning; and evaluation of data. As here conceived, these five casework processes have a dual meaning. In the first instance they refer to steps undertaken by the caseworker which also serve as a basis for systematic case management useful not only to the caseworker but also to the supervisor and administrator. In the second, they denote the processes followed by the caseworker which involve what he must perceive and think about, in identifying the psychosocial disorder, in making a diagnosis and prognosis, in planning treatment, and in evaluating his case data.

In general, therefore, we are saying that at this point in the development of professional social work, casework, as practiced in community-supported health and welfare agencies, is considered to be a method for dealing with the pathological aspects of social functioning, the results of which have become troublesome, either to the individual family member, to other family members, to society, or to all three. Society delegates to these agencies the responsibility of carrying forward an effective rehabilitation program in the family's and community's behalf. As time proceeds and social work develops, this function of social casework may be changed. However, our findings derive from these current concepts.

RESEARCH TOOLS AND METHODS

Following the marital axis analysis a new 100-case sample was so selected that the number of schedules that each agency returned was proportionately representative of the total 888. Depending upon the number of schedules that each agency contributed, every third one, fourth, and so on, was chosen until the proportionate figure was reached. These cases were read and reread for purposes of intensive diagnostic analysis. Four features of the methodology eventually evolved can be generally described.

A diagnostic framework was developed within which data pertaining to family social functioning were organized, examined, and reexamined by inspection and later by statistical analysis. This involved the use of a series of large work sheets on which were recorded, case by case, typical behavior patterns observed in five basic areas: (1) family composition; (2) psychosocial disorders and precipitating stress; (3) family social functioning; (4) individual intellectual, physical, and emotional characteristics of adult and child; and (5) family of origin history of the marital partners. This framework contains the same basic elements as those of the case analysis schedule. It was, however, reorganized, modified, and expanded during the research, depending upon findings. Its conceptual base was also developed with greater depth.

A second feature of methodology was the use of the classification of psychosocial disorders—a newly developed part of the framework. This enabled the systematic classification of the general areas of family and social dysfunction of concern to the community, the family, or both. Only with the use of this classification was it possible uniformly to compare the problems of one family with those of another and begin the process of sorting out similarities and differences.

The third feature was an extensive list of some 130 defined symptom factors of behavior relating to family and psychosocial functioning, by which the predominant patterns of social adaptation among various family members were described within the framework for family diagnosis. These items and their definitions derived directly from the examination of raw data. They were necessary not only to isolate common and distinctive patterns of family functioning, but also to prepare syndrome tables for statistical analysis of clinical judgments.

The last feature is actually a process in which prognosis is used as a research tool to facilitate the initial sorting of the 100 families into groups, all of which had certain resemblances. The predictive base originally used was the statistically defined Level A psychosocial disorder classification.

In brief, it may be said that the systematic use of a defined framework for family diagnosis, and prognostications made with respect to the probable course or occurrence of Level A psychosocial disorders within each family, proved to be the methodology which first got us off the ground, so to speak, in the direction of classification.

Prognosis—a Research Tool

Experience in this research demonstrates that the construction of a diagnostic classification scheme for clinical application based upon a strictly logical arrangement or list of pathological conditions is doomed to failure. To be useful to the clinician, any classification must be sufficiently descriptive and extensive to assure that pathology can be identified with certainty and with some idea as to causation. Prognosis, a basic part of any scientific diagnostic procedure, was consciously used as a research tool to facilitate the discovery of significant family patterns. In so doing we introduced the disciplined use of casework knowledge about the psychodynamics of behavior within a constant and statistically defined frame of reference; namely, predictions with reference to Level A psychosocial disorders.

The value and importance of prognosis as a research tool, or as an integral part of any diagnostic process, scarcely need justification (103, pp. 175–89). All caseworkers implicitly or explicitly employ prediction in their work with individual clients and families. In order to know what needs to be done in a given family, the caseworker must try to anticipate what might happen in regard to the family's handicapped status.

In substance, this is the sort of intellectual process that took place in data examination. Moreover, we were constantly forced to evaluate and reevaluate the relevance of the psychosocial data at hand to the assumptions made. In so doing, the areas in which we were on firm ground were delineated and those in which knowledge was scanty were exposed. Correctness or incorrectness of any specific prognosis was not the point at issue. Rather, it was the use to which these prognoses were put that was important in suggesting further areas for exploration in the search for new clues, in assessing those previously overlooked, and in reevaluating judgments already made.

The first task in this new phase of analyzing the 100-case sample was to identify the range and variety of Level A psychosocial disorders found in these families. The ultimate objective was to discover the relationship of their presence or absence to the kind and degree of social dysfunctioning existent in the family members in child-rearing, marital, and financial functional areas.

In tabulating the current Level A disorders, and those that appeared within a year prior to the last application to the agency, the following categories [1] were used:

1. *Financial disorders,* including irregularities in income production and/or management, that required financial assistance

---

[1] These categories were subsequently reorganized into the classification of psychosocial disorders used in this book.

2. *Adult disorders,* including physical, emotional, and mental impairments, resulting in antisocial acts, commitments to mental or correctional institutions, charges of neglect and nonsupport

3. *Child disorders,* including physical, emotional, and mental impairments that resulted in acts of youthful unsocial behavior, probationary status, commitments to mental or correctional institutions

4. *Family dissolution disorders,* as measured by separation, desertion, divorce, and placement of children.

Level A psychosocial disorders were identified in 57 percent of the 100 families. These problems appeared singly or in combinations within a given family during or immediately preceding the period of agency contact. In other words, in over half of these 100 families there were single or multiple problems of: income interruption necessitating partial or total financial assistance; mental illness requiring hospitalization; crime, neglect, nonsupport, or other illegal activity resulting in incarceration or probationary status; physical illness requiring hospitalization; youthful unsocial behavior resulting in correctional commitment or probationary status; separation, desertion, or divorce, accomplished or in process; placement of children in foster homes under supervision of a community agency.

At the same time, a careful examination of recorded data on the 43 percent of the 100 families with no Level A psychosocial disorders revealed severe maladjustments in parental functioning and child development, as well as distorted concepts of marital relationships. The reasons for these differences in problem symptomatology required explanation.

The next step was the use of prognosis with the Level A disorder categories as the base for prediction. Briefly, this meant making a critical assessment of each family member and the influence of one upon the other. Under two conditions, one of three decisions had to be made:

1. *If no Level A psychosocial disorders were present,* was the probability (*a*) strong; (*b*) moderately strong; or (*c*) remote, that one or more such disorders would develop in the family in the foreseeable future?

2. *If one or more Level A psychosocial disorders were present,*

was the probability (*a*) strong; (*b*) moderately strong; or (*c*) remote, that such disorders would be resolved, persist, or assume new forms in the foreseeable future?

In actual application to the sample cases, these prognostic levels were designated as: poor (strong probability); fair (moderately strong probability); and good (remote probability).

The occurrence of incidents or events can never be accurately predicted. However, it is possible to predict, as though the future were known, by assuming the possibility of typical situations or problems and picturing how the adult or child might meet them. This was the approach taken. For example, certain properly evaluated clues pertaining to a five-year-old's developmental progress might logically lead to the expectation that upon entering school he would have trouble sharing with other children, adjusting to the routines of the classroom, and so on. In everyday language, this use of prognosis can be compared to what the average caseworker might do if asked by his supervisor to take his case load and, upon study of each case record, make a professional "guess" as to the likelihood of a ten-year-old's becoming delinquent in the foreseeable future, to the possibility of a father's resuming his role as wage earner and provider, to the chances of a marriage ending in divorce.

Although validation of prognostic judgments was not an end in itself, still, after completion of the prognostic process, these predictions were compared to the actual course and the final outcome of the case. When agreement was found to exist between prediction and outcome, reasons for this were examined more fully; the same process was followed in those instances in which there was a disparity between the two.

Once these predictions or prognoses were made, the 100 families were divided into two major classes:

Class A families included those wherein no Level A psychosocial disorders existed and the probability was remote that they were likely to develop; if present, the chances were good that they would be resolved. This class was generally designated "no poor prognosis families."

Class B families encompassed those wherein at least one Level A psychosocial disorder was present, and the probability was strong that at least one would worsen or recur—or a new one develop. If no Level A psychosocial disorders currently existed, the probability was strong that at least one would occur in the foreseeable future. This class was generally designated "poor prognosis families."

The main distinctions between the two classes of families lay in their seemingly different degrees of vulnerability to the types of problems that reach Level A psychosocial disorder status. In other words, the second class of families appeared to be more likely than the first to become dependent, be broken by divorce or desertion, place their children, require hospitalization for mental illness of adult or child, incline toward juvenile delinquency or other anti-social acts, and so on. Did this necessarily mean that Class A families had less serious problems of social adjustment? If so, what constituted this difference in adaptive potential?

These findings led to the practical application of hypotheses evolved during the process of this research; namely, that there should be some relationship between the prognostic level assigned to Level A adult disorders and that assigned to financial, child, and family disorders.

Following this line of reasoning, the 100 sample cases were then resorted into three major groups by placing together all cases which had been assigned to the same prognostic level with respect to adult disorders:

Group I consisted of families in which the development of Level A adult disorders was not probable; if present, resolution of the problem was likely (good prognosis).

Group II included families in which there was a moderately strong probability that Level A adult disorders would develop; if present, a fair chance that these would continue or new ones occur (fair prognosis).

Group III identified families in which there was a strong probability for the continuance of existent adult disorders, the development of additional disorders, or intensification of those already present (poor prognosis).

Diagnostically, these groupings yielded significant information when subjected to clinical inspection. In our judgment, neither partner in Group I families was likely to succumb to psychotic illness requiring hospitalization or become involved in antisocial activities leading to apprehension and/or incarceration in the foreseeable future. We judged these eventualities to be unlikely in the adults of Group II families but more probable than in the families of Group I. The adults in Group III were seemingly much more vulnerable to psychotic illness and to behavior bordering on the antisocial. This further told us that the particular adult disorders of Group III families appeared to be of a more serious nature and less susceptible to modification than those of the other two family groups; that is, more severe in that they required or would require more stringent measures for their treatment and control (poor prognosis).

However, unexplained contradictions resulted from this method of classifying families. There was a favorable prognosis for the wage earner's continued adequate support of his family coexisting with an extremely high possibility that a child in the family would become delinquent, but with no indication that either parent was likely to engage in antisocial acts or be committed to a mental institution in the foreseeable future. On the other hand, the likelihood of family dissolution in the form of child placement was coexistent with little indication that the child would develop Level A psychosocial disorders of delinquency or truancy, or conditions requiring commitment to a mental institution. Nor was there the probability that the father or mother would be committed for mental illness or engage in antisocial activity demanding legal intervention.

With this general insight, the next step consisted of examining each one of these three major family groups independently of the others. The prognosis for adult disorders was compared with the prognosis for disorders in the categories of: financial disorders, or dependency; child disorders, or delinquency, truancy, and psychotic illness; family disorders, or divorce, separation, child placement. The comparison was undertaken by first identifying the specific nature of the Level A adult disorders present or probable in family groups I, II, and III.

The following will illustrate the differentiating process which ensued case by case. The degree of likelihood that a husband or wife would be hospitalized for mental illness or mental deficiency, or be apprehended for antisocial acts, was compared with the prediction made for each child in the family as this related to youthful unsocial behavior, truancy, hospitalization for mental illness or deficiency. In the case of financial disorders, this process involved a comparison by type of adult disorder and the prognosis made with respect to it, with the likelihood that the family would remain or would become dependent. Family dissolution disorders consisting of legal separation, desertion, and divorce and the prognoses made with respect to them were compared with the prognostic levels assigned to the various types of adult disorders.

This approach began to give needed perspective to the relationship between the marital partners' emotional stability and the effectiveness of their adaptive capacities in meeting the family functional tasks. Similarly, child behavior became more understandable when viewed against the background of parental functioning. The Level A psychosocial disorders, as such, also began to take on more precise diagnostic meaning.

At this point, a systematic clinical analysis of all psychosocial data pertaining to the family was undertaken group by group. The purpose was to consider in depth the psychodynamic aspects of each family's behavior patterns in their relevance to the specific types of Level A psychosocial disorders present, or likely to occur. The "simplest" group was examined first; namely, Group I, or those families in which there was only a remote probability that the family heads would develop Level A disorders (the good adult prognosis group). This procedure was repeated for Group II families in which there was a greater possibility than in Group I that the husband and wife might become involved in a Level A disorder (fair adult prognosis group); and Group III families in which there was marked evidence that a current Level A disorder would worsen or that one would develop (poor adult prognosis group).

When a case did not seem to belong in Group I, II, or III, it was temporarily laid aside. This aspect of the sorting process is illustrated by a family placed in Group III because there was a strong probability that the father would need to be hospitalized for psychotic illness (poor prognosis). Although the designated prognosis for this adult disorder correctly placed this family in the "poor prognosis" Group III, certain things were not conclusive. The total constellation of factors characterizing the family's social functioning did not bear sufficient resemblance to that of the majority of other families in this group to justify its being retained. There were more strengths and the problem of psychotic illness was being coped with in a more constructive fashion than in the other families. Consequently, this case was withdrawn from this group of families to be reevaluated.

The reverse situation prevailed in other families logically placed in Group I (good prognosis) because there was little likelihood that either adult family head would develop Level A adult disorders. Hypothetically, it could be assumed that the prognosis for the adjustment of the family in other areas would be favorable. The contrary was true in some instances. When viewed in their totality, the adjustment syndromes of certain families revealed severe psychosocial pathology in child rearing and in child development. This was accounted for by the particular type of personality maldevelopment of the adults. In social functioning, however, this pathology did not appear in a form that became a matter of community concern, such as hospitalization for mental illness or apprehension for antisocial behavior, a Level A psychosocial disorder. Nonetheless, the children in these families were or might become so involved. In other words, when viewed in its totality, this family's adjustment was inconsistent with the majority of other families in Group I. Therefore, cases such as these were laid aside for reexamination and reclassification.

Once the shift was made to sorting the 100 cases according to the prognosis assigned to Level A adult disorders, more distinctive family behavior patterns gradually began to emerge. Previously formulated definitions descriptive of social attitudes and behavior were carefully reexamined, redefined, and reclassified within the conceptual framework presented in Chapter IX.

It was at this stage that the symptomatic behavior factors referred to earlier were developed for each area of family functioning. The general principle followed in formulating and defining these items was that they should reflect what the individual consciously says or demonstrates that he expects from himself and from others in meeting the psychosocial tasks for which he is responsible. From this, certain unconscious motives of behavior were inferred. As stated previously, all clinical data were tabulated and classified for each individual member of the family on work sheets by the casework analyst, and in all instances the family was used as the basic unit of count. A comprehensive report prepared by Dr. F. Stuart Chapin includes the tables of psychosocial syndromes, arranged according to family types, which resulted from this process. An appraisal and interpretation of the statistical significance of these tables, as well as of all others important to the research findings, are presented in this document. The report, under the imprint of CRA, is available to libraries and educational institutions interested in social casework research.

The clinical description chapters of each family type presented in this book contain the factors comprising the psychosocial syndromes that are either key or distinctive to each of the four disordered family classes. From these the reader can identify the general nature of the symptom factors used as one aspect of differentiating and classifying families for diagnostic purposes.

DISORDERED FAMILY TYPES

The disordered family types have been titled the perfectionistic family, the inadequate family, the egocentric family, and the unsocial family. The names reflect a reformulation of the marital axis concept with respect to family social functioning; namely, that the dominant characteristics of the emotional tie between husband and wife definitely color the clinical picture of the interpersonal behavior patterns of all family members and their social adjustment. However, these disordered family types, in contrast to the marital axis family types of the pilot study, have a somewhat different base. Rather we have generalized what we considered to be the more basic aims or goals of the object relationships formed by the marital partners and have identified the various ways in which these may express themselves; in the marital relationship, child rearing, child development, and financial functions of the family.

In other words, the classification system of the disordered family types is not based on the identification of a series of interaction patterns among family members. It is a system of classification whereby the innumerable interpersonal behavior patterns may be identified according to the more fundamental aims of object relationships. Moreover, it rests on the psychosocial syndrome principle. In family diagnosis, psychosocial functioning and dysfunctioning have meaning only when such behavior is evaluated as a total unit within the context of all family functional areas. That is to say, the key psychosocial symptoms typical of a given family, when viewed collectively, group themselves in a way that lends distinction to one family as contrasted with another. These syndromes, however, to have any diagnostic meaning, must be related to the known psychodynamics of family behavior and the nature of the physical, intellectual, and emotional attributes of individual family members.

This approach to family classification is best illustrated by the following comparison:

The need to be loved, valued, and dependent is apt to be particularly urgent in the male partner of the unsocial family type. The pressure of these needs for gratification dominates all his personal relationships and social functioning. The means by which he attempts to secure love and respect and to be looked after within his environment are: childish appeals for sympathy; demands for unwarranted praise as master of his house and for his job performance; bursts of anger when this is not forthcoming, or when his clothes are not neatly laid out by his wife; intolerance of his children except when he wishes to play with them on his own terms. This is considered to represent a "severe" degree of pathology in social functioning.

From the standpoint of family diagnosis, the psychosocial syndrome that characterizes this behavior and results in the unsocial family, and not some other, is determined by certain specific factors. All areas of family functioning, including the child-rearing, marital, and financial, are similarly and adversely affected. The male partner's adjustment in the community at large also is apt to be unsuccessful. In addition, he usually has a wife who is psychotic or one who alternately indulges and hostilely denies his insatiable needs for love and dependency. This renders him even more help-less and incompetent to deal with life's problems at home or abroad. The maladjustment of the children also is notably evident in this family, thus adding another dimension to the degree of pathology and the syndrome characteristic.

By contrast, in the inadequate family the same basic needs are evident in the male partner's behavior but they are neither of the same quality nor as pervasive. His wife usually has similar characteristic needs, and to about the same degree of intensity. A further differentiating factor is that his method of getting these needs met from his environment serves social adjustment better than is true of the male of the unsocial family. The characteristic technique of the inadequate family male is to rely upon others for encouragement. However, as long as such reassurance and confidence are continuously forthcoming from wife, relative, employer, children, and others, he may keep going. Work adjustment, for example, is apt to be reliable and steady. He feels better if the employer shows a personal interest in him, but in any case is not apt to quit in a fit of anger. This male usually wants children but reacts to their presence by feeling his dependency status to be threatened. Therefore, children are often felt to be intruders. Often this is shown by his desertion at the time of the birth of the children.

This picture of the inadequate family is similar to, but not identical with, that of the unsocial family. The husband in the latter often admits that he does not wish for children. To him, anyone is an interloper who in fact or fancy interferes with gratification of his infantile wishes to be the sole recipient of all love, affection, and consideration. The male of the inadequate family does not default as completely and in as many areas, despite the same needs. Effects upon the children, although handicapping, usually do not result in forms of maladjustment that are as consistently difficult or inaccessible to treatment as is apt to be the case with children of the unsocial family.

These comparative examples illustrate how degrees of pathology and the syndromes are determined. They also give a picture of the characteristic ways in which individual family members meet the responsibilities of their family functions.

Thus, where manifest behavior is similar in two or more families, its distinctive qualities will derive from the particular area of social dysfunctioning at issue, the extremity of the pattern employed for coping with the problem, and the persons adversely affected thereby. Family behavior diagnosed within this context represents a composite, not a segmented aspect of social functioning or personality functioning in any one individual.

Insofar as possible, psychosocial terminology is used in the clinical descriptions of family types. In order of arrangement the classes represent a continuum in the direction of the family's decreasing capacities for mastering adaptive tasks. The numerical distribution of the 100 sample families according to family type is as follows: perfectionistic families, 20; inadequate families, 18; egocentric families, 31; and unsocial families, 31.

Statistical and diagnostic analysis revealed a steadily increasing degree of vulnerability in family members to a multiplicity of problems, particularly in the two vital areas of child rearing and child development. However, numerical concentrations had to be consistent with the clinical findings. There also appears to be a correlation between the dominant character traits and ego capacities of the adult partners in the continuum of family types, and the diagnostic categories of psychopathology with respect to gradients of severity.

Thus the disordered family types identified in this research are dynamic descriptions of syndromes of psychosocial functioning. These types are not considered "pure" in the sense that they present the total picture. The specific factors in the life histories of the family and its individual members will be highly individual. It is the caseworker's job to determine these case by case. The point remains that the classifications provide a consistent framework within which to test meaning and to differentiate, in a more orderly way, behavior noted.

Moreover, the classes are not presumed to be the only possible groupings. Their validity as a classification system, with its own integrity, however, has been established empirically by statistical method. In all probability these family types appear in the case loads of most family agencies in varying distributions.

To date, the testing of the classifications has been confined to CRA's projects. They were first applied in the three public welfare demonstration projects in San Mateo, Winona, and Washington counties on a total of 672 families; more recently, in a study of the Hartley-Salmon Child Guidance Clinic in Hartford. In each, their use produced results which were diagnostically consistent with what was known about the family. Currently, also, in the public welfare departments of Pennsylvania and Minnesota, and in the cities of Omaha and San Francisco, the framework for family diagnosis and the classification of psychosocial disorders have been adapted to operational needs with relative success. Much remains to be done. However, there is accruing statistical and diagnostic evidence which suggests that the integrated use of these findings can tell us a number of significant things important to social casework at the practitioner and administrative level, as well as in the area of community planning of health and welfare services. Testing the reliability of all findings and further exploration of their practical usefulness in a variety of agency settings are currently in the planning stage.

II. THE DETERMINANTS OF SOCIAL
BEHAVIOR

FAMILY CASEWORK diagnosis, as here conceived, shows that no single group of factors may be held responsible for the social dysfunction of a family or its members. Not the constitutional inheritance alone, nor the total personality, the specific nature of the immediate environment, the social standards of group living, nor the roles played by family members, can wholly account for psychosocial pathology. Rather it is presumed that these factors in varying combinations are most likely to mold basic patterns of individual adjustment, thus providing the explanation for social dysfunctioning.

In part, these are unique for each case. In part, however, these factor combinations also have uniform features that are typical for the society with which the individual is identified.

In recent years, cultural and sociological forces as etiological factors in social maladjustment have gained widespread acceptance in the field of social casework. We shall attempt to indicate the probable significance of these larger factors to social casework diagnostic evaluation of the specific features of behavior patterns and the immediate environment and make-up of individual family members. It may also assist the worker in noting significant cultural trends in individual cases, knowledge of which will be useful to social planners and those concerned with the prevention of social dysfunctioning through social reform.

It is not presumed that knowledge of cultural influences, per se, increases the diagnostic and therapeutic skills of the social caseworker. As a clinician the practitioner basically needs to understand the individual as a human being in relation to his own social setting. This understanding must be in specific terms.

The fundamental ideology of a society rarely changes unless the social structure is also altered. Thus, ideals and customs intrinsic to the organization of a society constitute the fabric of social life, the actual basic values and standards by which people live. These may be modified and reinterpreted under the stimulus of new knowledge, events, and a variety of factors. The specific form in which they are expressed will also vary with the individual, at any given time, in any given culture.

Regardless of these variations, of supreme importance to the survival of any society is the perpetuation of the race. From society's standpoint, therefore, the first obligation of its adult members is to create and maintain a family, and thereby to assume their procreative, educational, and economic responsibilities.

All societies must demand, too, an additional something from their adult members, over and above such elementary responsibilities. The male is expected to put his talents and abilities to work for the benefit of the larger society as well as for achievement of his purely personal and utilitarian goals. Similarly, in addition to the mother's primary responsibility for bearing and rearing the children, the feminine role in administration of domestic affairs is of particular importance if the stability of society is to be maintained.

All societies have laws or customs which govern a wide range of personal, social, and economic relationships. Many of these pertain to the civil rights and liberties of the individual; others are concerned with rights to property and inheritance, protection against theft, and the like. Still others deal with contractual obligations, both personal and business.

While the philosophy of jurisprudence and the legal system through which it is expressed will vary from society to society, respect for law is essential. Laws and legal rulings thus represent a method of control used by society to motivate its members to meet its basic requirements.

Almost all societies distinguish between the social requisites that apply to adults and those that apply to children. Certain legal protective rights are exercised in behalf of the child. For example, there are usually rules that prescribe for his care should his parents die or abandon him and, in sophisticated civilizations, that guarantee him a minimum education. Furthermore, a child's behavior outside his family circle is not held to be wholly beyond the jurisdiction of the courts. In most societies, procedures for dealing with the juvenile offender tend to take into account his emotional immaturity and lack of considered judgment.

Some provision for the handicapped person—the emotionally ill, the mentally defective, the physically disabled, the aged—is commonly made in most societies today. The behavior of such individuals is not considered to be outside legal jurisdiction. The particular emphasis varies considerably among contemporary societies. In Western civilization law and custom are shaped to deal with the condition itself as well as with the social circumstances which ensue.

CULTURAL TRENDS IN THE UNITED STATES

The most characteristic feature of our cultural life is its great emphasis on the individual. The complex structure of our society, its highly diversified functions, and the rapidly changing scene are additional features reflected in social life today (4, p. 434). Consequently, social adaptation is not a simple matter.

A successful democracy, as defined in the United States, requires a high degree of personal maturity of its citizens. It calls for clear judgment, expressed through the channels of representative government. Its ideologies embrace consideration for the rights of others and acceptance of restrictions and postponements, even renunciation of personal desires, to safeguard the welfare of others. Obviously, no single individual does more than approach such a standard of personal maturity. But if any degree of pleasure is to be derived from living in this culture, the hard facts of learning how to live responsibly within the wide range of possibilities offered and, in some instances, to conform to strict regulations, must be faced.

Thus implicit in the social structure of our society are the values toward which the behavior and strivings of the individual will be oriented: the ideal of individual worth, independence, personal achievement, and a moral and ethical conscience. To these concepts all persons are exposed, and to these each individual reacts in his own fashion.

Individual Achievement

Out of the great emphasis upon individual worth and responsibility has grown the high premium placed on achievement and personal enterprise. The supreme ideal is that of the self-reliant, self-made man. This individualistic spirit was typified in the exploits of the American frontiersman. In an expanding country, the boundless opportunity for individual enterprise, endurance, and initiative sparked the development of new lands in the unexplored West.

The philosophy of the frontiersman still persists, both in appropriate and in distorted forms. Today, however, with the advent of the space age, the nature of the opportunities for such independent action, achievement, and endurance obviously has changed.

Nevertheless, competitive spirit, personal efficiency, prestige, and independent action continue to stand high in the scale of values for judging the individual. The implications of this ideal of personal initiative, in their relevance to individual adjustment, are important factors in producing certain psychosocial disorders. Erikson (50, p. 186) points out, however, that within the network of a culture's values, initiative is probably the key element upon which the psychosocial health of any personality and of any society seems to depend. For without some form of initiative, no effective personality could develop, no economy could exist, no value would make sense.

Social Status

Another evidence of the stress on self-determination appears in the equality of political and economic rights accorded to men and women. Here, the power of husband over wife, a concept inherited from our European background, has undergone certain subtle changes. The women of the frontier were dowerless, in contrast to those in other countries. Consequently, a man had to select his wife on her own merits—and frontier life demanded wives with spirit and initiative. Women who had strength of character and ability to manage the family's affairs independently for weeks at a time gained in acceptability as helpmates; at the same time, they were expected to be even more attractive and womanly by virtue of having been chosen for personal qualities alone.

As the years passed, many tasks never expected of European women became of necessity feminine responsibilities in the rougher setting of a developing continent. A new way of expressing aesthetic and moral values was open to them. The woman crusader, flouting the dictates of decorum, campaigning for "the right," for social reforms, became a familiar figure, recognized as a valid part of the country's culture. Despite this tacit approval, men still hoped that *their* wives would not receive "the call," and that the so-called "good" and necessary works would continue to be the prerogative of widows and spinsters.

Meanwhile, the masculine role was undergoing a change which influenced profoundly the sterotyped patterns of male behavior observable today. In a young and growing country, the harsh realities of competition demanded that man make a living and, in many instances, cut corners to do so. Success was measured in terms of money, possessions, power. The specific qualities of their male or female roles were underemphasized in both men and women. Rather, "success" as husband or wife, father or mother, and which of the two was doing a better job, became the criterion for judging social adjustment.

Independent Choice

In our culture, the individual has always been personally responsible for making his own choices. This is particularly evident with respect to his marriage partner. Tradition encourages men and women to marry for personal reasons, especially for attractiveness and romantic love. Society does not insist that a man have a job or even the prospects of one; that a woman have a knowledge of cooking, marketing, sewing, or caring for children. Nor is there any hint of an investigation of possible histories of mental illness or commitment to correctional institutions. There is limited orientation to the essential factors in male and female sexual activity.

The concept of individuality and independent judgment also is markedly evident in the tendency to avoid interference with young people's marriage plans, to refrain from offering the prospective couple any kind of advice as to what the creation of a family and life as a member of a family group mean, sexually and socially. As a result of this cultural pattern we have one of the most difficult forms of marital living devised by any society. The trouble, however, does not rest wholly in the ideal, per se, of individual choice. Rather, the lack of a sensitive and realistic interpretation of this ideal from parent to offspring constitutes a critical problem.

The current emphasis on "freedom" as well as upon "equality" of the sexes is one important influence contributing to this difficulty. As now interpreted in our culture, this emphasis fails to take into account the fact that sexual maturity is achieved by the male and by the female at somewhat different stages, related to the differing personality structures of the male and female. As boys and girls are reared to be more and more alike, learning the same skills, appropriate sex identity becomes more and more difficult to achieve. Children and youths turn to their peers, their everyday companions, to learn values and to find models for their behavior. They seek guidance from those whose judgment is as untested and immature as their own. Earlier and earlier dating occurs. However, except in unusual cases, this does not represent a longing for a sexual partner, despite a normal upsurge in glandular activity. Rather, under the guise of sexually emphasized interests, dating takes on meaning only as it demonstrates membership in an appropriate sex group. It is an assumption of adult sexuality which carries little recognition of its true significance (116, pp. 206–19).

There is evidence that parents still expect that the degree of freedom allowed in the sexual relationship outside marriage will be controlled by the girl. Thus, although in many instances the male is a willing participant, he consciously or unconsciously tends to deprecate the girl who frankly acknowledges or seeks sexual satisfaction without benefit of marriage.

The subject of sex is discussed with greater freedom than it was even a generation ago. Much has been written on the subject and is available to the average person. Nevertheless, condemnatory attitudes tend to prevail toward the young unmarried woman who engages in sexual intercourse. While petting and love-making are accepted by most parents, it is usually with the qualification that full consummation of the sexual act should not take place. Out-of-wedlock pregnancies continue to be viewed as socially undesirable in this country. For the young person, these attitudes, seemingly permissive on the one hand and prohibitory on the other, may create an irreconcilable emotional situation.

In an emotional sense, the implications for male and female differ widely in our culture. The male has less to lose, socially speaking, if he chooses to have sexual intercourse outside marriage. However, the fact that the female is permitted to participate premaritally in a sexually stimulating relationship, but only up to a point, frequently creates an attitude that is difficult for her to modify after marriage (132, p. 345).

Since today's rules of social behavior are not clearly defined, they give no clear guidance to the prospective bride and groom. Therefore, it is difficult for them to anticipate what it means to live together as man and wife in a way that will enable them to meet realistically their own or society's expectations of ideal family living. Legally speaking, any unmarried man and woman who are of age can marry if they have secured a marriage license; some states also stipulate a medical examination and/or a three-day waiting period. Although life may be easier later if the parents have given consent, there is no social or legal requirement that this sanction be obtained, if age requirements are met—in most jurisdictions age eighteen for the girl, twenty-one for the boy. Nor is there usually social disapproval of the marriage if the parents do object. Typically, the new husband and wife place a premium on being independent of their parents. Most newly married people expect to make their own decisions, have their own home, and manage their lives without advice from relatives—and, in time, to beget children and to carry on the cultural traditions.

It is apparent that the cultural ideology of the United States requires of the individual two basic personality ingredients. The first of these is the capacity to exercise independent moral choice and judgment; the second, individual initiative and achievement. This implies the acquisition during the formative years of the ability to initiate action for self-satisfying accomplishment within the framework of a normally functioning conscience. The result in adult adjustment should be the most rewarding form of human self-expression; it is also the most difficult to achieve.

Social Change

The problem of deciding what is wrong, what is right, and where and how the individual should direct his energies is extraordinarily complicated because of rapid and manifold changes taking place in our social, economic, and political life. If he is to be reasonably informed, the individual must have knowledge not only of local and national trends but also of world-wide happenings. He must keep pace, psychologically and practically, with the shifting values these social changes bring.

For each individual, essentially this means reconciling the discrepancies between the old and the new values and standards of personal and family living. Unfamiliar values, untried in a person's own life experience, seem peculiar and illogical. Conditions of living and ways of behavior to which the individual is unaccustomed inevitably create anxiety and therefore become difficult to evaluate. When clarity of judgment is impaired, confusion results, followed by further anxiety and, frequently, by disorganized behavior. Although social and economic shifts are inevitable, they are in a sense forced changes, which in turn impose forced readjustments. By its very nature the human organism does not easily relinquish behavior once learned. The innate tendencies and psychological urges toward conservation of energy, the adherence to behavior that is automatic, operate strongly to resist the necessity of making compromises and learning new ways of meeting life's tasks. These factors alone make for tension and anxiety in social adjustment.

The situation is compounded by the frequency and swiftness with which these shifts occur. Reconciliations with past, present, and future, which must be made quickly and often, place undue strain upon the most flexible of personalities. An emotional equilibrium can scarcely be reestablished without an increase in emotional tension and the development of neurotic symptoms.

Social adaptation is further complicated by the infinite number of patterns from which the individual may select. The behavior and personality of each person in the United States are composites of many different models, lacking any group style or stereotype. The possibilities offered by the culture are endless—in choice of occupation, residence, model for behavior. Just what is selected is a matter of opportunity, individual need, and emphasis, the latter largely determined by childhood experiences within the family circle (4).

THE FAMILY

We now turn to the ideals and customs of our society which emphasize the form and general characteristics of the family and influence the nature of the familial responsibilities. There are four basic aspects of family life to which both universal and specific social values apply.

In all cultures, the biological or nuclear family is the universal key to the preservation of the race and the transmission of its cultural ideals and objectives. From society's standpoint, legal marriage followed by parenthood is commonly approved and desired. Even though sexual union without legal sanction may not be forbidden, it does not, in any society, constitute of itself a marriage (100, p. 4). This holds true, socially speaking, despite the fact that in the United States common law marriages are recognized in a number of states (132, p. 390).

Sexuality and the Family System

Regardless of the varying practices of courtship and marriage rites, all societies recognize the inclination toward incestuous relationships. Thus sexual activity universally is prohibited between all individuals in the biological family except the husband and wife (95). Since a primary task of family living is to keep all members working together in some sort of cooperative effort, it is obvious that if all the men of the family were sexually competitive for all the women the result would be fatal to fulfillment of their roles as providers and protectors for their wives and children. Doubtless the prohibition of incest became a social device reached through trial and error over the centuries, to assure the organized procreative and integrated functioning of the family as a unit (100; 136). From these basic cultural necessities arose another requirement exceptions to which are social rarities; namely, that a mate must be selected outside the biological family group.

A third prohibition which is invoked by most societies is the banning of homosexuality (136, p. 103). Undoubtedly, this is a direct consequence of the immense importance attached to the marriage relationship, to the place of the nuclear family in the social structure, and to its role in the socialization of the child. From society's point of view, such a prohibition serves to prevent personal alliances which are in competition with, and thus undermine the motivations to, marriage and establishment of families. From the point of view of individual personality development, it very strongly reinforces appropriate sex identification.

The biological factor of sex differences is responsible also for a fourth universal psychological phenomenon; namely, the oedipal situation (119, p. 411). The human aspects of the familial setting stimulate an emotional attraction between children and parents of the opposite sex, accompanied by jealous hostility between children and parents of the same sex. The exact form in which this psychological theme expresses itself varies from culture to culture, from family to family, and within a single family. A male child, for example, may form a strong attachment to an older sister rather than to his mother. The point to be made, however, is that the emotional attraction between parents and children of the opposite sex, described by Freud as the "oedipal complex," is considered intrinsically normal to the familial situation and appears in some form in all families irrespective of culture (100, p. 5). The psychological manifestation of the oedipus complex undoubtedly would be subject to change if the institution of the family were to change (55).

Equally common is rivalry among children of the same family. This too may express itself in a variety of ways; for example, the competitive feeling may be directed toward a male cousin rather than toward a brother. But sibling rivalry as described by Freud is a normal psychodynamic characteristic of family life in all cultures (100, p. 5).

Marital Functions

An enduring relationship in marriage is an ideal goal of every known society. Regardless of how frequently the mores may permit marriages to be dissolved, the assumption always is that the union between man and wife is to be long-term. Societies that compel marriage for life, regardless of the degree of harmony between the spouses, make an extreme application of the universal concept of enduring marriage. Even where divorce is permitted by law, a certain amount of social disapproval continues to exist.

Each society sets its own standard of attributes that are desired in a marital partner. Many preferences are products of economic or situational factors. All have a tendency to persist long after the institution or original circumstance which gave them value has disappeared. While some cultural patterns are more rigid or stylized than others, all societies have traditions, customs, laws, which in one way or another permit, restrict, or give direction to sexual activities and the circumstances under which they may take place. Broadly speaking, the general purpose is to assure that life is devoted neither to continuous sexual activity nor to prevention of propagation.

Every society is faced with the problem of setting ideals and customs which will help its members to maintain a continuously satisfying sexual relationship in marriage. Such customs as do exist derive from and reflect the specific biological and psychological differences between the male and female. In view of their contrasting characteristics, male and female in every culture must learn to regulate their sexual urges to their inherent patterns and to the pattern of their total marital relationship.

The need for social regulation of sexual activity outside the marital union also is commonly recognized by all societies, to the same general end of maintaining a balance. In the United States, for example, no such system as concubinage or the employment of mistresses is socially sanctioned and prostitution is not legalized. In countries where marriage is entered into primarily by family arrangement, prostitution often is recognized and legally supervised.

Although there have been a few societies in which two or more men might be married to one woman, claims for the existence of a socially accepted complete promiscuity, or of "group marriages," have not withstood close scrutiny (100, p. 3).

Child-rearing Functions

Customs and traditions involving the responsibilities of parents are universal among all known peoples. Parenthood is held in such esteem, in fact, that in some societies men are refused full status unless they marry and become fathers. In others, they are retired from active citizenship if they produce only girl children. Still other societies reward parents for each child by means of state grants, regardless of the family income.

It is elementary, therefore, that the survival of any society depends upon the desire of its members to become parents. This willingness or unwillingness is subtly determined by, and superimposed upon, the biologically determined sexual qualities. As a result, most men wish to become fathers, and most women to become mothers.

The extent to which adults emphasize the importance of begetting and rearing children is greatly influenced by both cultural and familial influences. But, universally, fathers and mothers nurture and protect their offspring and inculcate the personal and social values that will produce in these offspring the wish to become, in their turn, parents who will carry on the cultural traditions. These two parental functions form the core which is vital to the preservation of the race.

In all societies, there is some division of labor between the male and the female parent in order to assure to their children the food, clothing, training, and other measures necessary for their upbringing. In some cultures, however, the respective responsibilities of the father and the mother are not too distinct.

Traditions as to who normally assumes the indispensable responsibility for physical care may vary from culture to culture. In most instances it is the natural mother who cares for the infant and toddler and continues to watch over the health needs of the child as he grows older. The father provides the physical necessities.

This traditional division of parental responsibility is not a chance social emphasis, but stems from the unalterable fact that the biological attributes intrinsic to the male and female better equip each than the other (physically and psychologically) for certain functions. The whole anatomical structure of the female bears this out. Although the biological foundations of fatherhood are less well defined, the preponderance of aggressivity in the male might be said to give him superior equipment for developing the paternal patterns of protector and provider.

The particulars of what each society expects parents to teach their children about its ethical and social values also vary with the culture. In general, the parents are charged with interpreting to the child what it means to be a member of his or her own sex. They must define what personal and social privileges childhood enjoys; what limitations are placed upon them; what obligations and added privileges may be looked forward to upon reaching adulthood. The child must be taught specific behavior appropriate to his sex, what it means to be a socially functioning male or female, if he is to attain the full rights and duties which society will grant him as an adult.

The parent himself may accept, reject, evade, or distort the intended meaning of a particular social custom or ethical value. Nonetheless, he does communicate to his children patterns of behavior which are basic to his culture. These patterns will differentiate his children's behavior from that of children reared in other societies.

Financial Functions

The masculine task of providing the family with food, shelter, and other necessities has become, in modern Western societies, primarily a matter of earning the money with which to purchase them. For that reason, this text uses the term "financial functions" to denote the responsibility entailed in acting as "provider." While variations may and do occur—occasioned by the father's death, for instance—this male responsibility continues to be of utmost significance in the social life of most cultures. The division of labor between male and female may be worked out in numerous ways, but the core remains the same—a home shared by a man and his female partner, into which the male brings the food which the woman prepares.

At various times among nations, the state has abrogated the

male's function of economic provider for his offspring. An example of this was Nazi Germany, where illegitimacy was rewarded and mothers and children were cared for in government nursing homes. However, this breaking of the tie between the breadwinner and his family has not yet persisted long enough in the history of the world to become an accepted custom.

THE FAMILY IN THE UNITED STATES

Any attempt to identify significant values which are distinctive to the family in the current social scene in the United States is indeed difficult. Some idea of their diversification is gained with respect to religious affiliations. The Protestant faith alone is comprised of 258 different denominations. Catholics constitute 25 percent and Jews less than 4 percent (161, p. 259) of religious groups. In 1960, of 45,000,000 families in the United States, 27,620,000 were living in cities and 17,000,000 in rural areas, with 3,800,000 of the latter on farms—another significant picture of cultural diversity (154, p. 39). Most family studies confine themselves to the white, middle-class, Protestant, dominantly urban family group (132, p. 390). Admittedly, to describe the particular habits and customs of this segment as if they represented the total cultural pattern is to distort perspective, since each stratum of society has its own variations from universal norms. Nonetheless, the urban middle class undoubtedly is America's most dominant group; certainly, it is the one most written about. Perhaps for that reason, the cultural pattern of this class tends to set the ideal toward which others gradually converge. Undeniably, these circumstances have influenced our point of view, but the customs and habits which are described here are believed to be typical of at least a substantial portion of our society, and to provide a background for diagnostic understanding of these factors by social caseworkers.

Structure

In the United States in recent decades, the traditional family as a larger kinship group has been declining in influence. Accompanying this change has been the rise to prominence of the family of procreation—father, mother, children—as an independent unit. This primary family group has, indeed, become the structural norm of our culture. There are many manifestations of this fact. A clear illustration appears in the markedly altered responsibility which the family assumes for the care of its aging members. Legislation increasingly removes financial responsibility for the aged from the family to the state. Old age insurance, federal housing projects designed for the older couple or single aged person, and a variety of community projects—recreational and guidance—attest to this trend. Providing for the physical and emotional needs of aged relatives is no longer considered a typical family function.

The March, 1960, census estimate was that only 2.16 percent of all married couples in the United States were living with relatives (154, p. 37). The nuclear family was estimated to average approximately 3.65 persons in 1960 (154, p. 40). There has been a decrease in the number of childless and one-child families, from 69.4 percent in 1950 to 61.5 in 1960; families with four or more children increased from 6.3 percent in 1950 to 9.4 percent in 1960 (154, p. 38). When the surviving parent of one of the spouses or a brother or a sister lives with the family, sociologists call it a "bilateral" family. In the 888 families included in this study in 1954, a slightly higher proportion—4.6 percent as compared to 3.5 percent in the total population (132)—were so living. However, in all instances, the related person was a father, brother, or sister of one of the spouses.

Experience gained in the diagnosis and treatment of the whole array of psychosocial disorders in three experimental projects has shown CRA that a somewhat new type of family association is developing among the group of aged persons who receive a large share of health and welfare benefits. In many instances there is no relative nor anyone else with whom the individual has continual face-to-face contact. At the same time, there may be some friend or a remotely related kinsman who actually represents the aged person's "family" and his personal relationship ties (48). Therefore, CRA has added the "substitute family" to the other forms of family structure which need to be considered in a family approach to casework diagnosis and treatment. The "substitute family" is defined as including one member of a family of origin (father, mother, brother, sister, aunt, or uncle of one or both of the spouses) living with, or in close association with, relatives outside the immediate family or with friends who perform the family supporting functions. Other substitute family forms can, of course, be defined, particularly with respect to children separated from an own parent or parents.

A further important feature of the family is the extent to which it has declined in importance as a focal point and a stimulus for creative activity. Today, practically every emotional, physical, and social need can be realized (although not completely fulfilled and socially approved) outside the bonds of marriage and the home. Those who wish it can obtain sexual satisfaction on a more or less casual basis outside marriage without necessarily having recourse to prostitution, the more usual practice being to select a sexual partner on a personal basis without the assumption of social, financial, or legal responsibility. Food, entertainment, recreation, laundry service, medical care, and clothing come "ready made"; one needs only to have money to buy them.

These developments of themselves are neither good nor bad. The problem posed is the degree to which these economic and social developments have served either to stabilize goals of family living and marriage or to crystallize a state of confusion or uncertainty. The latter would seem the predominant result at present.

Marital Functions

Marriage is highly valued in the United States. In fact, this country has one of the highest marriage rates of any nation, and the proportion of the population that is married is also among the highest. There is evidence too that the proportion of persons who marry at an early age has been increasing in the last half century. This condition results from a favorable age distribution of the population, plus a favorable sex ratio on the one hand and unusually favorable economic conditions on the other.

For those concerned with family living, divorce has always been a choice subject for analysis. While permanence of the marriage relationship is heavily stressed in this country, the United States has one of the highest divorce rates (132, p. 395). Since there is no uniform divorce or marriage registration, few data are available at the national level. Many states do not even have centralized marriage and divorce reporting (97, p. 15). Although the divorce rate, based on information from the National Office of Vital Statistics, showed a decline from 10.6 to 9.3 percent over the years 1949–59, conclusions drawn from this fact alone are not definitive in terms of a relationship to the total cultural pattern of family stability. There is no way of knowing, for example, what proportion of the persons obtaining a divorce over a ten-year period represents a recidivist count. Prevalence rates, on the other hand, would have more epidemiological import than incidence. The recidivist aspects of divorce would have especial psychosocial meaning. Since many divorced spouses in the sample studied did remarry, it would be interesting to know to what extent repetitive dissolution of marriage is indicative of a particular type of family malfunction. It is also of real importance to know whether the tendency toward divorce is more typical of one type of adaptive pattern than of another. In 26.2 percent of the 888 family service case records examined in connection with this study, the husband or wife or both had been married at least once before. In 32.5 percent of this group of 236 marriages, one or both spouses had children by a previous marriage. By definition, all of these were families who had sought professional help from a social agency.

The general cultural attitude toward divorce may be summarized by the fact that it is neither socially sanctioned nor socially forbidden. In representing a failure to make a success of married life, it remains a subject of community disapproval. The partners concerned are thus, to some extent, branded as failures, not so much because they are unsuited to each other, but because they have erred in selection of a mate. None of these social attitudes, however, takes into account the fact that remarriages in many instances are successful.

Thus, while theoretically this country embraces monogamy as its legal marriage form, actually plural marriage is not restricted, provided neither spouse is no longer legally bound to another. Although monogamy is the accepted form in that marriage is allowed to only one spouse at a given time, probably the more accurate designation of the marriage form sanctioned in the United States would be "serial monogamy."

Certain other limitations are imposed by law as well as by the sanctions or prohibitions of religious groups. In accord with universal practice, marriage of parent and child, brother and sister, grandparent and grandchild, uncle and niece, aunt and nephew, is prohibited by law. One half of the states prohibit marriage between stepparents and stepchildren and other affinal relationships. All jurisdictions ban marriage of the insane (132, p. 391).

The exceptional freedom accorded young persons in the choice of a mate has further implications for confusion or stability in the ensuing marriage relationship. The very personal responsibility attached to the selection of a mate "to love always" places a heavy emotional burden on both spouses. Success or failure depends completely upon the partners. In these circumstances, when dissolution threatens the marriage it is understandable that unwarranted feelings of personal failure or of loss of status and self-esteem are likely to be engendered. On the other hand, some marital partners approach marriage with the feeling that disagreements, whims, and demands can be indulged, and they have no strong motivation to resolve their differences. Such husbands and wives have little tolerance of the hostilities and resentments that are always present as counterparts of positive feelings and affection. Even the partner who is less inclined to give way to doubts and disappointments may be plagued by fears of desertion, or by anxiety over whether he himself should secure a divorce.

Thus, the choice of a spouse, and the ability to evaluate what love, companionship, and reciprocity really mean, increasingly determines whether husband and wife will be disappointed in marriage, in themselves, or in the partner. The lack of any firm system of values and standards, by which the development of this capacity for choosing wisely may be guided during the "growing up" period, plays an important role.

Despite all evidence to the contrary, the deeply bred tradition of individual choice accompanied by morality, in social and marital relationships, still exerts a powerful influence. The family agency cases of newly married couples, studied in detail in connection with

this research, offer documentary evidence of this fact. Marital difficulties were present in a high proportion of cases but had not been
anticipated by the partners. They had expected *their* marriage to be
successful. Generally speaking, and within the limitations of their
personal capacities, their intent had been to make it so. But there
was abundant evidence of uncertainty regarding the right thing to
do and feel in their marital relationships and in the discharge of
other family functions. All this became evident quite early in the
casework relationship.

The very fact that these insecurities were so readily discovered by
the caseworker reflects the inconsistencies between our cultural
ideals for a happy married life and the actual responsibility which
today's family takes to assure the achievement of this goal. It is
evident that these particular partners found it easier to turn to an
outside source for help and guidance than to their own families.
Indeed, a thorough study of the experience of family casework
agencies in identifying the discrepancies between the ideal values
stressed for marriage and actual marital experience would throw
realistic light on the problems faced by husbands and wives. A
study of this kind might well provide a background against which
could be formulated new patterns of premarital relationships better calculated to point the way toward the American ideal in family
adjustment.

One of the most conspicuous characteristics of the marriage relationship is the stress placed on equality of husband and wife. Only
to a secondary degree do ideals and customs emphasize that which
more clearly delineates the ideal, personal, male-female qualities.
This lack of sex differentiation is evident in many other aspects of
our culture, irrespective of age or social status. It is only in the occupational sphere that differentiation between the sexes is patterned
according to more generally dominant male-female values, with
preference given to the male.

Not only does the necessity of sex differentiation have biological
foundations, but its prominent emphasis in our recent past attests
to its importance. It testifies also to the need for such reformulation
of social values and customs as will reinforce these natural differences.

As it is reflected in marital living, the social ideal of equality between the sexes is based on a distorted concept of what constitutes healthy male-female relationships. There are many reasons for this. The greatest single contributing social factor is the fact that occupational status is given primary value (134, p. 368). Such an emphasis is both sound and contradictory for sex role differentiation as it now is patterned.

It is indeed desirable that the adult male have a job. It is fundamental both to his psychological well-being and to his social status. It is not too much to say that only in exceptional cases can a man be genuinely self-respecting and enjoy the respect of others if he does not earn an acceptable living (134, p. 367). This involves not only his own economic support but also the primary financial support of his wife and children. However, in this country his occupation tends to absorb a large proportion of a husband's time and energy, thus diminishing his use of masculine energies in other areas. This also has repercussions in the sexual aspects of the marital relationship, in the common interests he shares with his wife, and the nature of his parental role. The diffused authority and so-called "shared" leadership of the contemporary middle-class family strongly reflect the consequences of this situation, especially in decision-making.

Marriage itself determines the social and personal status of the female partner. In a society where strong emphasis is placed upon individual achievement, many women find in marriage the single outlet in which their personal qualities and efforts play a decisive role (134, p. 370). Thereafter, their life goals are not so much a matter of gaining personal prestige through a career, but of organizing their lives about the responsibilities of housewife and mother.

However, the relatively unstable character of the role of housewife, the strong inclination to view household tasks as drudgery, and consequently the tendency to employ servants wherever financially possible, all affirm the fact that in terms of prestige domesticity is still ranked lowest of all types of work. Advertising continuously reinforces this social concept by appealing to the housewife to save herself from "degrading" chores, to keep her hands as "petal soft" as her daughter's, and so on. It is notable that many women who go through the motions of performing domestic tasks psychologically dissociate them from their total personality. They do not find in such work the elements of self-preservation and ego interests that his occupation affords to the male. Another factor involves the tendency to deprecate any kind of work that has no immediate gain. This is indeed unfortunate with respect to the domestic role. When the opportunity to derive some satisfaction from household duties is denied a wife, she is deprived at the same time of a socially constructive and psychologically sound channel for expression of *normal* feminine masochism—a must, with respect to her healthy personality functioning.

Although many wives concern themselves with secondary interests, such an adjustment is likely to produce a high level of insecurity for the woman as an individual and as a wife. As a result, we see in America a rather unstable oscillation of married women between domesticity and a career, between glamorous prestige and the "good companionship" relationship with men, with sexuality a secondary factor. This all reflects the lack of clear-cut definition and acceptance of femininity on the part of women, and on the part of men with respect to women. It also indicates the unsureness of the male with respect to his own masculine role. It is not surprising that strains and insecurities arise in the average marriage.

The emancipation of women has played a particular part in determining the male-female roles in the marital relationship. The political and economic equality granted the sexes in the early part of the century has been so construed that today it embraces almost the total personalities of male and female, in all areas. Buttressed by the cultural stress on materialism and the prestige of work for immediate gain, the "well-adjusted" woman has emerged as one who is emancipated from her biologically endowed feminine tendencies—domesticity, the nurturing role, and her receptive, understanding, affection-giving capacities. The paradox is that at the same time no other *completely* satisfactory fulfillment is available to her.

Without question, the emancipation of women has also made available additional channels through which the female personality has thereby been enriched. Emancipation from the rigid taboos formerly attached to pleasurable participation in the sexual act, expression of personal attractiveness in dress, appreciation and culti-vation of cultural interests and educational tastes, and so on, are notable examples. Woman find the social welfare field particularly suited to feminine participation, linked to their traditional relation-ship with children, the sick, the emotionally or socially handicapped. Such undertakings are naturally congenial to the normal woman, because of her natural receptivity and enduring qualities.

The goals in marriages today have a common quality, with only the details at variance. Although love may seem to dominate the early period, disillusions, anxieties, and fears tend to come to the fore when the young couple settle down to the day-in, day-out process of living. The average marriage does not necessarily end in divorce, but it reflects a distorted emphasis on achievement and prestige, as well as confusion in each partner's own sex role orienta-tion, this latter a facet of the emphasis on equality.

Materials from CRA's case studies as well as data from other sources indicate what happens under these circumstances. It is not uncommon for a vague uneasiness to pervade the relationship. One or both partners fear that the other no longer loves him; that life is passing him by; that he is not all he should be. At the same time, both are usually in agreement as to the husband's need to succeed, and the wife urges him along and encourages his efforts. The wife frequently wishes that the husband would help more with the household tasks, take more responsibility in the care of the children, show more concern for her as an individual. The husband, on the other hand, hoping for relief from his daily chore of having to be a "successful" person, resolves the problem either by avoiding all home responsibilities or by taking over certain traditionally femi-nine tasks on a part-time basis or as "recreation." For example, it is not uncommon for a husband regularly to do the dishes. Often the preparation of food, concocting specialties, and cooking meat are among his domestic interests. To be sure, there is nothing unmascu-line in these activities per se, and under certain circumstances they may be necessary to keep the family together. At the same time, there is a real question why such traditionally feminine duties should be assumed by the male, thus confusing further the mascu-line-feminine identifications.

Against this background, what of the sexual adjustment of marital partners? The impact of knowledge regarding the role of sex in the development of the human personality, concomitant with its franker discussion, has contributed to the belief that sexual intercourse in marriage is for pleasure as well as for procreation. These factors, combined with the growing emphasis upon sexual attraction and interest, provide a strong incentive to spontaneity and satisfaction in the sexual act. However, today's freedom in acknowledging sexual urges is also complicated by a feeling that sexual relationships must *always* be enjoyed, and that at all costs, failures must not occur, or at least must not be admitted. In other words, success, again, must be achieved or there is "maladjustment." This becomes complicated, partly as a consequence of the customary premarital sexual relationship in which the girl assumes the initiative in saying "yes" or "no." In marriage, if the wife continues to be withholding rather than giving, in many instances either frigidity results or she is unable to realize her full sexual potentialities.

For the male, in our achievement-oriented society, sexual potency is inordinately valued and can be said to equate in importance with the prestige of gainful work. However, the ego or self-preservative interests which the male finds in his occupation are sometimes at odds with his sexual interests so that his economic endeavors constitute the foremost competition with direct sexual gratification. These occupational interests foster sublimation, but they also consume energy and therefore to a certain extent lessen sexual spontaneity. For the male with a predisposition to passivity, the social emphasis upon success and prestige fits in well with his neuroticism in the sexual sphere. Nonetheless, the social emphasis on occupation, which psychodynamically involves the diversion of sexual energies from their original aims, plays an important part in furthering a balance between too great and too little sexual activity.

Child-rearing Function

In the United States, attitudes toward, and methods of, child rearing indicate that pressures are brought upon parents to pose as better and more complete representatives of their culture than they really are (117, p. 659). They are continually presented on all sides with the "ideal" picture of how children should be brought up. Each child is viewed as a "potentially achieving personality" who must have the best chances in life, get the best education, secure the best job, wear the best clothes, receive the best habit training. All must be physically perfect, filled with vitamins, swim at age three, answer the telephone at four, count to 100 by age five, and, in general, acquire, as early as possible, competence in adult behavior.

Discipline tends to be permissive and children are both seen and heard (132, p. 394). Also, families have shown a growing disposition inappropriately to apply the democratic principle of government to child rearing by giving children a voice in the family council, even though they are not of an age to assume this responsibility. For husband and wife to share mutually their child-rearing responsibilities, for husband and wife to consult each other when important decisions are to be made, has become the norm.

When it is properly interpreted, such an orientation to child rearing is sound. However, the pitfalls far outweigh the advantages. Foremost is the fact that most of the teaching, supervision, and disciplining falls to the mother, with the father taking a minor role even with adolescent male children. For both boys and girls, identification with their parent of the same sex as a model for adult behavior thus becomes more and more tenuously anchored.

Frequently, the boy turns to his mother for support and guidance. From her he receives praise when he makes good grades, eats the right food, shows aggressivity and independence in his everyday relationships. In return he is loved, approved, and allowed unrestricted access to a refrigerator full of food and soft drinks. His father's attitude is apt to be tinged with a feeling of relief that he does not have to assume responsibility for controlling his son's behavior.

Such a boy does not easily find a male with whom to identify or on whom he can model behavior that will lead to a healthy masculine adjustment. The father's investment in the success of his son tends to be conceived as an extension of his own success. In all probability, unquestionably he is "quite a man," but he shows it more in business, at his club, than in his home. Where the boy's initiative is concerned, the father, urged by convention, restrains any tendency to challenge his son and thus to provoke oedipus guilt (51, p. 272). From his mother, the boy learns that he will be praised if he achieves; without her approval he is unhappy, anxious, fearful lest he lose her love. From both parents he learns that feelings of hostility, as well as their outward expression, are disapproved. He must not fight except in self-defense, and yet he must know *how* to defend himself.

In America, the small girl typically also learns that she must not be a "crybaby" or a "sissy." However, unlike the girl of several generations ago, she finds no clearly defined pattern to guide her between what is thought of as strictly "girl's behavior" and what is considered to be that of a tomboy.

In father-daughter relationships, the daughter tends to be indulged, undisciplined, though mothers may keep a watchful eye to see that she is not "spoiled." In general, the girl has a more favored position than the boy and emerges with a greater degree of self-confidence and certainty of her own identity. However, cross-sex hostilities, thus generated in the familial setting, are likely to persist into her adulthood. For she must be the self-made woman according to the standards of *her* era. She is therefore in competition with other girls who both set and are molded by new values. The girl's crisis will come when she becomes a mother and when the vicissitudes of child training will bring to the fore her infantile identification with, and dependence upon, her mother (51, p. 279).

Despite these confusing and, in some respects, unhealthy trends, many parents still are successfully bringing up their boys and girls to become good parents within an enduring union. Although family life in the United States is not disintegrating, the concepts of what is and what is not the right way to bring up children are without question in a state of confusion. The restrictions of an earlier generation seemed to obstruct the free and full development of personality potentials of both sexes. Values and customs at this point, however, do not reflect an integration of a new-found freedom into the biological and psychological foundations that give strength to the human family.

Financial Functions

The traditional division of labor, here as elsewhere, still holds the husband to be the titular head of the family. Legal requirements dictate that the husband support his wife and are stringent in placing responsibility for the support of dependent children. (Some few states require that the wife also support the husband.) Of the 40,205,000 families in the United States where both marital partners were present, 88.9 percent of the husbands and 30.5 percent of the wives were in the labor force (155, p. A-7). As noted previously, women still show a strong tendency to forego careers in favor of marriage, despite the fact that they are allowed increasingly greater freedom to participate in the business and professional world.

The important elements involved in conflicts between woman's occupational and domestic roles have already been noted. Likewise, the masculine role of provider is by no means devoid of strains. The basis of the family's position in the social structure is the occupational status of the husband and father (134, p. 368), acquired by virtue of his individual qualities, efforts, and achievement. To be sure, the prestige of accomplishment, responsibility, and authority carries great satisfactions. However, the many unrealistic pressures for success and the growing specialization in the professions, business, and industry make demands which, especially for the urban, middle-class husband, are increasing enormously. These factors tend largely to reduce the range of interests shared by husband and wife —one of the most common causes of strain and insecurity in today's marriage relationships. On the one hand is the overwhelming importance of the husband's occupational status to the family, and hence to the wife; yet on the other hand the marital relationship is relatively difficult to maintain on a level of human companionship. Typical social relationship patterns pursued outside marriage by the male whose interests are absorbed in his work are apt to be either: (1) a lack of personal intimacy and friendship with other women, particularly in mixed company, inhibited by fear of apparent infidelity; or (2) an interest in other women confined to the physical aspects of sex, and dissociated from those personal considerations significant to companionship or friendship, to say nothing of marriage (134, p. 372).

Thus, in filling his role as provider, the male must meet a social expectation which not only is essential to the maintenance of marriage but has a potential for causing difficulty in marital adjustment. He must cope with his own powers of initiative, his prestige, his standing in the community, and meet his responsibility as the chief source of income for the family. With success measured in materialistic terms, even stable men may flounder. Those less well integrated and motivated may shy away from or avoid altogether fulfilling this traditional trust: they may forego marriage, they may engage in an illegal occupation, enter some protective institutionalized occupational sphere, rely upon the assistance of state or welfare agencies, or desert their families. The case loads of social agencies are replete with examples of all these types.

PSYCHOSOCIAL ASPECTS OF BEHAVIOR

Properly to assess failures or successes in family functioning, the social caseworker needs to understand not only the relevant cultural determinants but also the nature of the family's environment and the biological and psychological factors which enter into social functioning of its individual members. With this objective in mind, it is necessary to delineate what each person must learn during his formative years in order to be relatively assured of mental health and of becoming a responsible, adult member of society. The psychoanalytic interpretation of behavior and personality development is followed. This is based on Freud's third theory, designed to explain the psychic structure and the content of mental processes (16, 30, 83, and 133; other source material may be found in the Bibliography).

Rational behavior, learned by an arduous process, can be maintained only through constant struggle on the part of the individual. This struggle is one between the primitive, dynamic trend existing within the organism and external, social demands. Indeed, throughout life the processes of integration and adaptation between the forces of the biological organism, the psychic self, and the social group are continuous. But it is in the formative years that the fundamental qualities of character structure are determined. For this reason, the factors involved for the child and his family during the important phases of his biological and emotional growth are of primary importance not only to the child but also to the social functioning of the total group.

Fundamental Growth Processes

In a prescribed sequence, the processes of physical growth occur relatively independently of environmental factors. With certain variations, the main phases are rather uniformly predetermined by hereditary factors. This development of the life curve takes place in every individual at about the same age, in the same order, and cannot be changed by later influences.

The physical endowment with which the child starts his life has been predetermined in the prenatal period. He does not inherit the behavior patterns required for independent existence. Moreover, his innate emotional needs and urges do not possess any capacity for automatic self-preservation or adaptation to the environment. These only appear and develop under two conditions: (1) as the slow process of biological growth makes this possible; (2) with the stimulation of human contact and training.

As already indicated, the main phases of psychic growth rather uniformly are determined by, and depend upon, the main phases of physical growth. It is the child's emotional reaction and that of his family to these phases of biological growth which most closely interact to determine the child's character structure, thus shaping his social adjustment. The reactions of the child to his social environment and the reactions of those around him to his presence vary greatly. Nonetheless, certain characteristics and crucial developmental issues in each successive period are generally applicable for the purposes of family diagnosis.

Identification

The biological functioning of the newborn infant normally requires little attention or direction. He can react to outside stimuli of noise and cold or to inner distress caused by hunger, stomachache, and so on, but his capacity for conscious control is weak.

In terms of his psychological and social development, his first hurdle is to learn to distinguish the inner world (himself) from the outer world (his mother). However, the process of learning external perception cannot begin until he can see his environment. This occurs at the age of about two months, when his eyes focus properly. His mother's face is usually the first image that the infant comes to recognize (98).

When this occurs, the process of differentiation begins, precursor of the eventual capacity for considered judgment in social functioning. At first this type of learning is almost a conditioned reflex. Because of the child's basic cognitive potentialities, however, when he is able to see his mother, he associates the sight of her face with the disappearance of the displeasure of hunger.

This is a momentous step in the child's psychic organization. For prior to this recognition of the mother, the baby has not cared *who* would furnish his food, so long as it was forthcoming. If the baby does *not* fully achieve this step, his adult psychic organization may be such that he will care little *where* food comes from so long as it is provided; his interest in another human being will exist only on this basis. An adult manifestation of this conditioning in infancy includes the "oral optimists," who expect confidently that everything will be provided. Extreme examples are severe alcoholics and drug addicts.

Still others, the "oral pessimists," quarrelsome and aggressive in their demands, are certain that they will be denied. Such personalities have limited capacity for genuine emotional investment in other persons. They are preoccupied solely with perpetuating an environment of continuous and unconditional giving of which they themselves are the beneficiaries (98).

In psychoanalytic literature, these first distinctions between the self and the outer world are presumed to be made through two psychic processes—*introjection* and *projection.* The distinction between the two corresponds to that between the physical acts of swallowing and of spitting out. One of the child's first decisions pertains to what he puts in his mouth: that which tastes good he sucks on and swallows; that which tastes bad, he spits out.

Just so are unpleasant ideas expelled from the mind by placing them in the outer world; that is, by attributing their origin to another (projection). Blaming outside forces is a normal defense for the infant. If a sense of reality and self-identity do not develop early, through maternal care, this form of inner defense will be retained in the adult personality. If this defense predominates in adulthood, it takes the form of paranoid suspicion and withdrawal, often to the point of psychosis. Persistence of this childhood defense into adulthood may be shown by the existence of pathological envy, fear of being robbed, and assignment to others of one's own feelings. Projection thus becomes the most dangerous form of adult defense against anxiety, since it originates in infancy and has not yielded to the process of learning to perceive and to test realities.

Conversely, the psychic mechanism of introjection is modeled after the process of eating. Just as those things which taste good are retained, so are pleasant ideas and thoughts incorporated into the self. Introjection, although necessary to the infant's development, can also assume pathological proportions in the adult, expressed by excessive self-preoccupation and self-love. More usually, it appears as a normal pleasure in eating. It may also be demonstrated by attitudes toward people, experience, and knowledge. A less desirable manifestation is a preference for learning by "drinking in," by light reading, through pictures—in short, for that which can be "sucked" in with little effort rather than obtained by "hard chewing."

Self-confidence

The first sign that a baby is beginning to achieve a social personality appears when he can allow his mother out of his sight without undue anxiety or rage. Here is the first evidence of a rudimentary sense of ego identity, usually achieved at about eight months; an ability to delay immediate gratification of an impulse, to control behavior for a brief period.

This takes place *if* the baby has learned during the first two months of life to trust that someone will minister to his needs with constancy, continuity, and sameness. This gives him a sense of being "all right," of regularly meeting the expectations of others; it forms the basis for identifying and controlling himself in later social situations. The child can endure frustrations if each frustration leads to an ever-renewed experience of sameness, and a sense of being a part of an ever-widening total social scheme. As a result of this feeling of trust he begins to emerge as an individual personality.

If the developmental process proceeds successfully, the desires of infancy will be manifested in adult life in confident responsiveness to other persons and situations. The desire simply to acquire things for their own sake will be sublimated into the wish to learn and to absorb knowledge. Generosity and empathy will contribute warmth to the personality, a receptivity to new ideas. Socially acceptable but less mature forms of coping with these wishes to receive may find expression in unusual generosity, in charming others into giving, in exaggerated activity and independence.

Gradually, the baby learns that his world is not always as he would like it; that it can be "bad" as well as "good." During the rages caused by the pain of teething, baby and parent meet a crucial test of what to do with aggressive impulses. The infant's friends either prove incapable of alleviating his distress, or they object to the only action that gives him relief—biting. Thus, from this experience comes a primary sense of "badness," the original sense of "evil," or the fragments of a conscience. To guide these reactions in such a way that the baby will gain the feeling that this "evil" which cannot be helped must be endured, constitutes a critical test of the relationship between the baby's inner forces and those of the outer world—his mother.

Self-direction

As the infant develops more powerful muscular equipment the stage is set for experimentation in the second and third years. This is the time for active response to a sudden wish, for making his own choices, for appropriating demandingly and insisting stubbornly. The child alternately clings to possessions or discards them; snuggles up or pushes himself free. He feels the urge for self-determination but frequently overextends himself as he discovers what he can do unassisted.

As with all stages of biological growth, these new physical powers hold psychic potentialities for the development of both benign and hostile social attitudes. If the child has come to feel faith in himself he can experiment with his toys and explore his environment. By purposeful repetition he will gradually experience the autonomy of free choice. On the other hand, because he does not yet have the power of discretion, he may get into trouble. The parent must firmly protect the child against his untrained sense of discrimination. Meaningless and arbitrary restrictions lead to shame and doubt of his own worth. At the same time, controls on destructive behavior are necessary or the child will overmanipulate himself and dominate his family, assuming a self-autonomy he has not really gained.

Self-mastery

There normally comes the time, however, when the child discovers that unconditional fulfillment of these newly discovered capacities cannot be realized. There are people who interfere and cannot be eliminated. They call an energetic halt to his immature exercise of independent thought and action.

The ultimate goal of the child in this stage is to gain the exclusive love of the mother or father, an endeavor which usually comes to a climax sometime between the ages of four and six (oedipal period). The child's inevitable failure to achieve these aims brings results which will shape the subsequent course of his life.

It is at this point that the child must turn from his sole attachment to his own parents toward the slow process of preparing himself to become a parent. Ideally, the child gives up his wish for exclusive possession of his parents and develops, instead, his conscience (superego). In achieving this step, much of the energy which was concentrated on the earlier infantile strivings now will be devoted to the task of self-observation and self-guidance (self-punishment), a task for which the parents supply the internalized goals.

In this process, the parent can assist the child to gain some notion of what ultimately will be involved for him in becoming a parent, some idea about social institutions and their functions, and the role he will eventually play as a responsible, participating member of society. It is of greatest importance in this period for the child to come to recognize that some prerogatives of adults are forbidden to children. The child's failure to give up such goals, and to form in their place the basis for a healthy conscience, often leads to neuroses or other personality disorders.

Productiveness

If by late childhood (approximately ages six to ten) the child has been successfully guided through preceding stages, he will not now be so ready to overextend himself and to coerce others in the effort to get what he wants. He will know that he must go to school, that there are neighbors whose rights are to be respected. He will know that he is a male child, that he will find a wife and eventually be a father; or a female child who will find a husband and in due time bear children.

Psychologically, he will accept the idea that he will some day be a parent, and he will recognize that, as a prerequisite to assuming this social function, he must learn to be a worker. The child's mastery of muscular coordination, the emergence of his capacity for thought and action, provide him with the substratum for learning to provide for himself and others. Productiveness gradually supersedes the whims and fantasies of the previous period of self-determination and free choice.

School attendance assists in expanding the child's social horizons and also invites the application of given skills and the performance of certain tasks toward a utilitarian goal. Problems may result from the fact that parents have not prepared the child for school life, the initial break with home ties. Moreover, the school may not encourage and sustain the potentialities which he has evidenced earlier. In either event, if he abandons hope of taking his place among his schoolmates who are learning to use their natural talents and skills for an eventually utilitarian purpose, a feeling of unworthiness may result and lead him back to the rivalry of the oedipal period.

Social Identity

With the onset of adolescence there is, in part, a dramatic recapitulation of the conflicts and attachments of early childhood, but with one conspicuous difference. Use of intelligence has progressed, logical thinking has advanced, social understanding and altruistic love have made their appearance. Biological maturity has resulted in a physical stature more or less equal to that of the parent. Most importantly, the personality has acquired a synthesizing capacity (ego development) far more complex and infinitely more resourceful than existed during the formative years. At this critical stage the psychological problem becomes essentially one of integrating previously made gains, mainly acquiring control over emotional outpour.

The dangers to healthy personality development lie in two extremes: (1) uncontrolled instinctual gratification, in the attempt to sever the parental tie and thus attain an individual identity; or (2) undue repression of the sexual drives. These extremes, if unresolved, declare themselves in unsocial behavior and an incapacity for any genuine love relationship, or else the personality becomes, and generally remains throughout life, inflexible, rigidly controlled, emotionally impoverished, and unsusceptible to the compromises that a changing reality demands.

For the adolescent the changing reality is represented by sexual maturation, new social responsibilities and interests. Emotional and physical separation from the parent must finally come about. The parent is divested of the exaggerated power and idealization with which the child once endowed him and from which he derived so much of his self-esteem. The estrangement and void that this process induces often lead to transient adolescent identifications and attachments. These may persist until new relationships can be formed and talents for realistic achievement are developed. When this occurs, family standards and ideals are reinstated as part of the young adult's personality.

This state of affairs accounts for the emotional inconsistency and unreliability so often seen in the adolescent. Previously established, stable, uniform, reliable, and enduring relationships with the parents give way to the more highly ambivalent love which was characteristic of early childhood. The developmental processes are partly undone. Love and hate toward the same person once again exist side by side with renewed intensity. A new compromise has to be achieved.

Of particular importance are changes which are also taking place in the adolescent's capacities for self-criticism and self-blame, or the functioning capacity of his superego (22). The automatic control and inhibition of instinctual energies now lose their reliability. Thus, at the same time that the adolescent is attempting to sever parental ties, he also becomes involved in this personal struggle with his superego; a rebellious fight against being dominated by his conscience. The strong feelings thereby created stem from a desire both to hurt the parents and to be emancipated from the demands of conscience. In severe form, this conflict may appear as antisocial behavior and less seriously as a constant resistance to various parental rules.

To insure in adulthood adaptive patterns which are less rigid than those inherited from the latency period and less transient and radical than those arising with puberty, character synthesis must take place in a progressive movement toward maturity. This will be characterized by an increased mastery of feeling and thought with respect to social reality rather than a reconstruction of, or preoccupation with, experiences of the past. At this point the task of the adolescent is one of finding out who he is, in his own right. "Who am I?"; "What can I do?"; "I am free, but what am I free to do?" must first be discovered before he can experience true intimacy in personal relationships. This period calls for such guidance as will provide concomitantly, and in balance, a reliable parental relationship that will not only allow the adolescent emotional freedom and dependent security but will also provide needed stimulation in the development of skills and aptitudes, choice of career, control of his impulses, and an ego ideal that can be emulated. These will not be accomplished without conflicts. It is normal for adolescence to be a period of turbulence.

When the developmental tasks of adolescence have been successfully accomplished, the young adult will have a personality flexible enough to admit sexual wishes, and at the same time will have succeeded in renouncing the infantile tie to the parent. He will be able to tolerate partial or substitute sexual gratifications and, if necessary, to postpone full expression of his sexuality without renouncing it as a goal. He will have succeeded in channeling his aggressive energy into a socially useful form which will maintain his self-esteem at a level high enough to prevent retaliative, exploitive, and competitive aims from dominating his behavior (22).

One great danger is that of role diffusion. In attempting to find his own social identity, the adolescent may overidentify with a hero; may lose his individuality in the safety of cliques and crowds; or may fall in love, not in the true sexual sense but because the mores demand that he appear sexually adequate (20).

Delinquent and psychotic behavior is not uncommon if role diffusion is based on strong doubt of appropriate sex membership. Frequently at this age, if properly diagnosed, such behavior can be treated with good results (51). Fear of the loss of social identity also may lead to a sense of isolation and self-absorption, together with an avoidance of the more intimate aspects of interpersonal experiences (68).

Emotional Maturity

With attainment of emotional maturity, psychic energy is less needed to further personality development. Ideally speaking, when an individual reaches this point, he is an adult, ready for an adult's responsibilities and privileges.

Complete maturity results when each succeeding stage of personality development has been such as to produce predominant qualities of generosity, productiveness, and creativity. Those who most nearly meet this ideal will have learned to care for things and people; will have adapted to the triumphs and disappointments of creating things and ideas; will have learned to be certain of their own productive capacity; will have achieved a friendliness with their own past, and a tolerance for pursuits and interests different from their own.

There will also be manifested in the adult the dual capacity for general work productiveness and for love in a heterosexual relationship. There will be a primary interest in the creation and guidance of the next generation. Such a person will participate in the social and cultural institutions of the larger community as well.

Under the best of circumstances, complete emotional maturity and freedom from childhood conflicts are rarely achieved. Relative attainment varies enormously from individual to individual. But those who do not acquire a degree of personal integrity, self-confidence, self-direction, self-control, productivity, and identity with the culture will be particularly vulnerable to psychosocial disorders.

III. HEALTHY FAMILY FUNCTIONING

BY DEFINITION, a highly socialized person exemplifies in his actions the majority of his culture's values. This degree of socialization is rarely attained by any one personality. Some conflict not only is inevitable but is desirable for the development of constructive social innovations, intellectual and artistic creations. These signs of social progress will hardly originate with the oversocialized individual. Oversocialization and overconformity also tend to eliminate that spontaneity of response which is of great value in interpersonal relationships as well as a source of personal pleasure to the individual himself.

For these reasons, the ideals of harmonious family living proposed here must be considered relative concepts. They need to be viewed within a wide range of variables that are characteristic of all persons in our society. And finally, they are not conceived as being principles or rules of a consciously applied philosophy. Rather, they are presumed to be attitudes and behavior which stem from inner convictions of a well-integrated personality.

The attitudes and behavior patterns described are formulated in clinical rather than sociological terms. They are designed to lend perspective in understanding the concepts and framework for family casework diagnosis as well as the classifications of disordered family types. An additional purpose is to provide the social caseworker with certain guides by which he can more accurately identify and evaluate evidences of social dysfunctioning and thereby plan and implement the needed treatment program in the family's behalf.

FAMILY LEADERSHIP

The basic human qualities of the family as a group derive from the nature of its structure and composition; namely, the biological and psychological differences between its male and female heads and the gratification of their respective needs when they become parents. The ensuing family obligations are the natural responsibility of the husband and wife.

The well-adjusted family, therefore, usually selects the father to assume the major leadership role. Leadership, as herein conceived, does not imply despotism, autocracy, or control. Rather, it offers an acceptable opportunity for the gratification of masculine assertiveness in a socially constructive way.

For the wife, aggressivity on the part of her husband gives her an opportunity to fulfill, in a socially useful and emotionally satisfying manner, the feminine masochism which is a part of her natural emotional structure. Her responsibility for domestic and maternal affairs is one means through which she may express these qualities.

Another important aspect of the father's leadership role pertains to the resulting attitudes of the family as a group. This aspect relates to the degree of acceptance on the part of the family of the father's dominance. Such submissiveness is advantageous not only to the family but also to society and probably accounts for the fact that family goals usually are oriented to the idea that "father's work comes first," with the household organized to meet this objective. Daily routines—the evening meal, recreation, children's playtime, discussion of vital family issues, and the making of basic family decisions—are organized insofar as possible to complement rather than conflict with the husband's work hours.

FAMILY IDENTIFICATIONS

Just as the acquisition of self-identity is important to individual adjustment, so is the attainment of family identity an essential part of family functioning. Healthy forms of family identification develop from experiences and associations within the family whereby each member knows "who" his own family is, as differentiated from other families, and generally manifests genuine self-confidence in, and loyalty to, the other members of his own family. These qualities derive from a consolidation of familial identifications which *also* reflect the constructive and valuable patterns of society.

One of the most common family identifications is related to the father's masculinity and work status. Other family identifications may be connected with church activities, vacations, holiday traditions, birthday celebrations, and the like. Inevitably, many of these are concerned with maternal-oriented occasions involving the pleasures of eating together. Indeed, more than any other facet of family life, customs relating to the dinner table assume the quality of an essential family-identification symbol. Whatever the emphases, these identifications are a vital part of ordered family life.

CHILD REARING

Although every adult has lived through childhood, the feeling of relative smallness, the anxieties, the disillusions, and the triumphs of growing up may have been forgotten. Nonetheless, they imprint themselves ineradicably upon the minds of all children, extend into and influence their adult attitudes and behavior.

Thus, the well-adjusted parent will have acquired, or can be helped to achieve, some awareness of, and tolerance for, certain natural responses to parenthood. For such a father and mother, parenthood will reactivate almost forgotten childhood memories, both pleasurable and painful. This inevitable human tendency colors parental attitudes and behavior throughout the entire child-rearing period, but is particularly manifested in connection with the birth of the first child. At this point in life, neither parent has had any previous experience, except that he was once a child himself. Therefore, their response to the presence of the child, their concept of his physical care, of parental love, of rewards and punishments, emanate from the memory they retain of their own father's and mother's values in this regard.

Ordinarily, these earlier attitudes and values effectively serve the parents as they gradually orient themselves to meet the practical and emotional responsibilities of each child's developmental needs. However, certain childhood experiences in their own past may interfere with their functioning as successful parents. Among these are particularly traumatic separations, illnesses, loves, hates, fears. As a result, a psychological barrier may arise as a protective device to avoid facing, ever again, the same feelings of unhappiness with which the individual could not cope as a child. This can adversely influence a parent's handling of similar situations in the lives of his own children.

Another important predetermining factor that affects parenthood is the extent to which each partner has learned, out of his own life experience, to want to beget and rear children. The aims and motivations that stimulate in any given person the wish to have or not to have children are limitless. However, in the well-adjusted family there will be evidence that both the father and the mother regard procreation and child rearing as integral parts of family life.

It is essential that the caseworker be cognizant of the common emotions which may be evoked in parents, and of their etiology, in order that the practical and psychological sacrifices of parenthood may be more easily understood. A common desire to create a family usually acts as a positive predisposing influence, which makes easier the inevitable readjustments which follow the birth of children. When husband and wife do not share a desire for children, subsequent problems caused by the presence of children become more than normally diffuse.

One partner may wish very much to become a parent and be willing to make the necessary sacrifices while the other may be either openly or reticently resistant. When the resolution of these differences does not precede the birth of children the willing parent may find himself carrying more than his share of the burden, or he may be exploited or dominated by the other, who has no incentive to assume the responsibilities of parenthood. As a result, integrated family functioning either is impossible or can be only partially achieved.

An additional factor relates to the degree of realism with which parents plan for the advent of children. A healthy adjustment requires that parents regulate the procreative cycle, in terms of their own health, financial security, and religious beliefs, so that their children are assured, insofar as possible, protective family care during their dependent years.

Physical Care

Division of responsibility for specific aspects of child rearing is more or less biologically determined. Normally, the mother ministers day in, day out, to the physical health and nutritional needs of the children. The father also has an important role. He will be dedicated to supplying money to feed, clothe, and educate his offspring for approximately sixteen to twenty years and to assuring his wife's maintenance at least during the children's infancy and childhood. He also supports her emotionally by his love and companionship so that she may devote her energies to her special maternal tasks (27, pp. 13–183).

As the child grows and develops, the character of his bodily care and needs alters, and, for the average mother, they become in some respects less taxing. However, these changes also bring with them new tasks and adjustments for both mother and child, as the former initiates various habit-training measures.

The well-adjusted parent provides his child with opportunities to develop muscular coordination and motility, prerequisites for physical skills. He will not try to make the child into a human machine nor allow him to go his own way unassisted, but will encourage and guide the natural processes of growth according to the child's biological rhythm and age level. Accurate knowledge concerning the usual timetable of boys' and girls' physical development is a reassuring factor in anticipating and dealing with each phase of growth. He does not then become unduly anxious about the child's rate of physical maturation unless such concern is actually warranted.

The caseworker is in a particularly advantageous position to assist parents in the various aspects of their child-rearing responsibility. He can make certain that the parents know the facts and sequence of physical development. Only then can he ascertain the father's or mother's potential for learning new ways of coping with the problems of child rearing. If needless fears are dispelled by the possession of fundamental biological facts, and thus the parent is enabled better to handle the child's needs, there will be good reason to deduce that the parent can probably tackle child-rearing problems of a different nature. Then the social worker can also help the parent especially to see that his goal is not to be rid of all problems and anxieties, but rather to learn as much as he can of more effective ways of resolving each situation.

Development of Love Relationships

For the normal husband and wife, parenthood offers the opportunity for full realization of their emotional needs for creativity, affection, loving, and being loved. Through his children the parent also may enjoy vicariously the benefits, privileges, successes, and pleasures he himself did not have or failed to reap to advantage. Psychodynamically, the parent attains these satisfactions by identifying with his offspring—just as the child identified with the parent in achieving his own identity.

The parent's own self-regard is such that he feels pride and joy in his child's increasing skills, abilities, and powers, as they emerge at each stage of development. The parent who can feel this way has found a psychologically sound and socially constructive way of reconciling his egotistic and altruistic aims. By so identifying himself with his child, he may also find compensation for the diminution of his own personal capacities and, ultimately, may feel that he has insured his own immortality—a most powerful human wish.

Ideally, both parents assume their parental role with full awareness that some of their own satisfactions and ambitions must temporarily be foregone. In the normal course of events, they will become psychologically oriented to other compensations in life. When this important point has been reached, neither father nor mother will normally conceive of himself as the sole recipient of the love and care available from family members.

Frequently, this is a lesson that must be relearned by parents. Unconsciously, at least, it is a repetition of the painful awareness that they themselves could not receive the total love of their own parents, the full impact of which began to dawn when they were about five years of age. It was then that they began the psychological process of reconciling themselves to the necessity of renouncing their desires for the exclusive love of father or mother. Thus, disillusioned, they were compelled to seek compensations, including their ultimate roles as parents.

And yet, in even the most mature adult, the relinquishment of privileges and the interference with personal pleasures commonly give rise to frustrations. Where there is a healthy awareness of this situation, the parent expects some degree of ill-feeling to be mixed with his love for his children. These sentiments are not avoided by a mistaken attempt to deny their existence, nor indulged by unlicensed expression. Rather they are feelings of resentment to be coped with, and are countered by measures which may neutralize the situation.

Many annoyances and frustrations are explained by the differences between the points of view of children and adults. Thus, the constant presence of children inevitably becomes a source of irritation to parents. Similarly, the ill-regulated and impulsive energy of a healthy, growing child constitutes an ever-present menace to the comfort and tranquillity of adults.

The best-adjusted mother, even when blessed with abundant health, periodically feels resentment because she is not free to go and come as she pleases. In our culture, the emphasis placed on independence and personal achievement reinforces this conflict for some mothers. Therefore, a mixture of positive and negative maternal feelings is apt to be present. In certain middle-class families, this is particularly true of the mother who, like her husband, has been educated to express her own creativeness in pursuits other than parenthood. Paradoxically, our cultural pattern also subtly devalues the woman who seeks sublimation of her creative tendencies through personal achievement other than motherhood. Therefore, whether women do or do not become mothers, certain feelings of frustration, guilt, and anxiety often accompany their wish to achieve in other fields.

Ordinarily, the father is less directly affected by the around-the-clock presence of children than is the mother. Nevertheless, sooner or later parenthood will interfere with his personal pleasures and comforts. For one thing, the presence of a child will mean sharing the love and affection of his wife.

To a certain degree, the father will feel jealousy as well as resentment, due to the compromises which the presence of children may impose regarding his choice of work, the realization of his ambitions, and the production of steady income. These are countered, however, as previously described, by a positive identification with his child. For both father and mother a healthy sexual adjustment also serves to rechannel these energies and to lessen the frustrations.

Self-identity Development

Normally, the mother meets the baby's infantile needs for affection and dependency completely, and then gradually imposes restrictions upon their immediate and complete gratification, and continues to do so, with changing emphases, throughout the dependent years. As maturation proceeds, signs of the child's independence and physical capabilities will be supported with respect to self-feeding, dressing, washing, caring for his clothes, toys, and other possessions. Play equipment which stimulates imagination and provides opportunity to develop physical skills will be introduced as an essential part of the child's training. The mother most naturally carries these responsibilities for children under five; thereafter, fathers normally take over with the boys, and mothers continue with the girls.

However, parental demands for grown-up behavior and independence do not in themselves signify a healthy parent-child relationship, nor do they ensure the desired development in the child. For the mother and father two other factors, in particular, are involved: (1) recognition of what the child can be expected to do for himself and what normally he can expect his mother or father to do for him at each successive stage of his growth; (2) confidence and security on the part of the parent who initiates, implements, and follows through with his expectations of the child. The well-adjusted father and mother are generally perceptive in timing, consistent in defining, and firm in maintaining their requirements for self-sufficiency in the child, and indicate, as well, what he can expect others to do for him, within and outside the family.

The average growing child takes pleasure in discovering new capabilities which enable him to do things independently. He is eager to achieve greater self-mastery. However, parental restraints cause the child to feel not only frustrated but also angry at the person who imposes the restriction. Thus, hostilities and resentments inevitably present problems with which both parent and child must cope.

In dealing with the hostile reactions of his child and with his own demands for self-sufficiency, one important human tendency in particular—ambivalence—involves the parent. This well-known emotional phenomenon is a common element of all interpersonal relationships and operates, to some degree, throughout life.

The child, too, experiences feelings of ambivalence. In fact, the intensity of these feelings is usually greater in childhood and, again, in adolescence than at any other time of life. For this reason, quick changes of mood are commonplace. He may be loving and sweet at one moment, hostile and frustrated the next. This creates an emotional situation which for most parents is one of the most difficult, but one of the most important to understand, accept, and deal with. One of the primary reasons this poses a problem is the intensity of the ambivalent feeling that the child shows toward the parent. Parents, in turn, become upset because the same emotions are consciously or unconsciously stimulated in them.

By and large, the father and mother differentiate between hostile *feelings* and hostile *acts,* tolerating the former but prohibiting the latter. Parents with this orientation acknowledge as normal a degree of hostility in all people; thus they tolerate their children's healthy verbal expressions of hostility so that it may become neutralized. At the same time, the parents prohibit the child from *acting* upon these impulses in a destructive fashion.

The parent who has some knowledge about the tendency to ambivalence does not feel unduly anxious about its exaggerated manifestations in the young child or adolescent. He undoubtedly will become irritated on occasion, but this will not make him feel basically alarmed, unloved, or that the child is rejecting him altogether. Rather he counters by being firm and providing channels through which the child may express destructive impulses in socially useful ways.

Given this solution, the child will be more willing to restrain his hostile behavior without too much protest and without being made to feel excessively guilty or anxious. In other words, the well-adjusted parent is not fundamentally frightened by the changing moods and outbursts of temper with which his young child responds to the ordinary frustrations that must be imposed. The parent is aware that temper tantrums normally occur at specific age levels, as a natural part of the process of development.

It is particularly important for parents also to recognize the phenomenon of regressive behavior and the role it plays in the development of self-identity and self-mastery. In essence, such behavior is the inclination to return to infantile patterns no longer appropriate to the child's age level. The parent who does not feel guilty about the fact that he, like all adults, sometimes, under certain conditions, resorts to childishness will meet with greater equanimity regressive manifestations in his children. The tendency to regression, too, is more pronounced in the young child, by virtue of the developmental stage of his ego, and in the adolescent, because of the turbulence of the ego and the unreliability of the superego in the process of becoming stabilized. The problem can and does occur in the latency child, and in later life, but at this time it is not usually so pronounced. The relatively stable mother and father have little difficulty in accepting, temporarily tolerating but not condoning, such normal manifestations of regressive tendencies in their growing children as are appropriate to their age levels.

One of the situations which frequently stimulate a child seemingly to renounce the developmental gains he has won is the birth of a sibling. Depending upon age, sex, and various other factors, any number of reactions can ensue because of the jealousy invoked by the presence of the "intruder." Among the most common is regression in respect to eating habits. Wetting and soiling may return, or babyish behavior in general may occur. These symptoms may appear despite the fact that parents have "prepared" their children for the birth of a sibling. They are often perplexed when this device fails. Under these circumstances, the parent who recognizes the problem, and temporarily indulges the child in his renunciation of "grown-up" behavior patterns, subsequently avoids a prolongation of the regressive period and lessens the chances of stimulating undue anxiety, overdemandingness, temper outbursts, head banging, and other destructive behavior. However, acceptance of regressive behavior does not usually constitute the greatest problem. Rather, the greatest challenge lies in being firm and consistent in defining privileges and imposing limitations.

Socialization

The socialization aspects of child rearing involve the well-adjusted parents in an interpersonal family process the primary goal of which is to establish in their children a normal, functioning superego and social conscience. In the usual family situation, children more readily accept necessary restraints and more easily relinquish infantile goals when they are made to feel first that the mother's love and, later, the father's love are worth keeping. When the child learns to have a deep trust in his parents' love, normally he wants to retain it. Thus, the child's acceptance of his parents' denials is motivated first by his wish to please his parents and, second, by his fear of losing their love if he disobeys them. From the dynamic process which ensues, the child's superego eventually takes shape and at about age five or six emerges as a social conscience which continues to develop throughout latency, adolescence, and even in adulthood.

In the stable family, the parents act as "executors," so to speak, of the child's superego until it finally emerges as a conscience, incorporated in the character structure. The father and mother accept this kind of responsibility in steering the course of development of the child's superego and conscience. They are clear about the fundamental differences between the privileges and limitations that are normal for children in the family and those that always belong to its adult members.

The parent who recognizes the prerogatives enjoyed by children and those enjoyed by adults will also adapt to the changing privileges and limitations that grow out of, and belong to, each successive stage of their children's growth, from infancy to adolescence. Ideally, the father and mother do not fear the use of controlled aggression in administering discipline, are not handicapped by an overindoctrination in "tolerance," nor by the fact that in the nature of things they have to be "rejecting" parents in the eyes of their children.

The parents who feel this way about the disciplinary aspects of child rearing will not be wishy-washy in setting and invoking standards of social behavior; neither will they be worried about being unjustly criticized for overpunitiveness. From their own life experiences they will know that relatively few parents totally reject their children. The feeling of being rejected, if it exists, is in all probability a distortion of the unconscious infantile wish for complete indulgence and exclusive love which, by the nature of things, can never be fulfilled.

The essential areas of behavior, the rules the parents establish, and the measures they undertake for implementing them will reflect the fundamental soundness of this approach to disciplining children. Ideally, parents will follow the conviction that it usually is better for mothers to be arbitrators for the girls in the family and for fathers to discipline the boys, especially when the children are over five years of age. Prior to this time, the mother usually handles disciplinary problems. Paternal characteristics best fit the father for making constructive use of his masculinity by acting as arbitrator for the more aggressive manifestations of behavior in all the older children.

There is a definite advantage in the father's assuming responsibility for all discipline concerned with the child's aggressivity. Children find it easier to identify with the masculine assertiveness of their father than with this quality in their mother. Therefore, restrictions are more easily accepted if they come from him. This division of the child-rearing responsibility, in turn, tends to free the feminine role of wife and mother from some of its complexities.

The father and mother teach their children that certain kinds of behavior are strictly forbidden. Sexual relations with parents and siblings, fire setting, stealing, truancy, assault, destruction of property, drinking, and violation of hours set for coming home are among the most important prohibitions. If the child is to control his own behavior with respect to these forbidden acts, he must have a normally functioning conscience. To attain this he must resign himself to the fact that he cannot occupy an exclusive and favored position with the mother or the father. As a result, the basis for a healthy conscience is established.

The mother and father so regulate their own behavior toward their child that the latter's sexual and aggressive strivings are rechanneled to serve the furthering of ego and superego development. In so doing, the normal parents will take certain kinds of responsibilities. The mother generally makes clear to her son, by telling him *when the occasion arises*, that he can never take the place of the father in her affection, he can never marry her, and that in fact she does not *want* to marry him or give him this kind of love. The father makes this clear with his daughter, with respect to his relationship with the mother.

The parent who can do this with sensitiveness and conviction helps the child over a tremendous emotional hurdle. This enables the child to express the rage and frustration he feels at being forced to renounce and sublimate his infantile sexual and aggressive strivings. On the other hand, parents who enter into the child's fantasy by attitude, word, behavior, or avoidance of the issue give him unrealistic hope that this can occur. In so doing, they consolidate neurosis in the child, heavily endangering his achievement of a well-integrated personality.

Laxness with respect to the seemingly inconsequential everyday family activities of dressing, undressing, bathing, using the toilet, and so on, can create an overstimulated sexual atmosphere with which the child cannot cope. Contrary to common belief, disregard of the need for privacy does not enable the child to achieve a healthy adult sexual adjustment within our social structure. Rather, such conditions are clinically known to produce anxiety-ridden children who, in turn, are likely to become impulse-ridden adults, with poorly established sex identities. The parent also helps the child in this aspect of his emotional development, and hence helps him to sound superego formation, particularly from the age of three on-ward, when definite "house rules" concerning personal privacy are established.

To a great extent, the success of these house rules is a matter of parental attitude and discretion, irrespective of living conditions. Although crowded quarters make privacy much more difficult to achieve, well-balanced parents may make compromise arrange-ments, and at the same time convey to their children the desirability of privacy. Under such circumstances, if the basic attitude of the parents is healthy, the lack of personal privacy will have a less damaging effect than it otherwise would have.

Of recent years, the idea has become popular that parents should consider their children as "equals" with respect to their ability to participate in, or cope with, situations which actually require ma-ture judgment and experience. However, stable parents recognize that certain family decisions are adult responsibilities; for example, how the available income is spent. To act otherwise misleads chil-dren as to their authority and what they can expect from themselves. This occurs mainly because the growing child's ego does not possess adequate powers of discrimination, nor has he had the life experi-ences that lead to maturity of judgment. Therefore, to ask a child to take such responsibility can only make him guilt-ridden and in-hibit his normal fantasy life, which is an essential part of the growth that leads to creativity and a rich adult personality. Rather, from the time children reach latency, they should be taught the value of money by being given allowances. Eventually, the boy or girl earns his own spending money, and gradually provides for certain of his own basic needs.

Regulation of their children's comings and goings is always deter-mined, by normal parents, in accordance with the age level and the occasion. Once established, the rule is observed firmly although it can be modified if it proves to be unreasonable. However, the rule that there will be specific "hours" is never rescinded, and a parent does not feel that his firmness subjects him to criticism from out-side the family.

These rules and regulations inevitably cause feelings of frustration. The parent can help his children over this hurdle by accompanying his firmness with reasonable explanations for the restrictions. He lets the children know that their feelings and thoughts are respected, but that these cannot be the dominant consideration in establishing rules of behavior. The parent also is aware that the child, within himself, must recognize his role in the family as inferior to that of his parents. However, the parent helps his child to see that this inferiority is not something peculiar to him, but is a necessary condition of being a child.

If the parent can do this, he will appreciate the fact that he must, to a certain extent, be a "rejecting" parent and yet not feel guilty about it. Knowledge of a well-known principle of education will strengthen his conviction; namely, if a child feels that he is loved in spite of anything he does, he will never bother to learn anything. It is a fact of life that he feels unloved when he is weaned, when he is toilet-trained, and when he has to give up his infantile sexual attachment to his parents. These are normal events in the growing up of all children.

The whole process whereby the well-balanced parent teaches his children the rules of social behavior after they reach the age of five or six is enormously enhanced with respect to the larger community if the teaching includes some information about:
1. Social institutions, so that the child begins to gain insight into ways in which he will participate
2. The social role he may assume as worker, provider, parent
3. How to earn recognition by producing things
4. Responsibility for home tasks and care of younger children.

During this period, he is also encouraged and given opportunity to extend social contacts, make friends, anticipate the responsibilities of school attendance, and gradually separate from home ties.

MARITAL FUNCTIONING

The act of marriage symbolizes the establishment of a family and normally introduces husband and wife immediately into a new social and emotional setting. It requires undertaking not only many different kinds of responsibilities, but also some never before experienced by either partner. Sooner or later the spouses have to meet the challenge posed by all three of the defined family functions: marital, financial, and child rearing. The readjustment which normally follows marriage is greatly facilitated if the partners have anticipated certain practical issues.

Premarital Orientation and Planning

Evidence of premarital planning and significant indications of the partners' genuine interest and realistic intent to meet family responsibilities are seen when the following conditions exist:

1. Prior to, and at the time of, marriage, the male partner is employed, has a relatively well-assured income sufficient to provide for himself and his wife a place to live as an independent family unit and the minimum essentials for maintaining a household.

2. The female has some domestic capabilities.

3. Both partners have good physical and mental health.

Premarital planning itself cannot, of course, make a successful marriage, nor does the failure to plan necessarily equate with marital unhappiness. Many unforeseen social, political, and economic conditions may interfere with this preparation for marriage. Nonetheless, such practical realism is to be desired even though certain compromises may have to be made. Marriages contracted, for example, in the pious hope or with the false idea that the necessities of living somehow will be provided carry within themselves the seeds of disillusionment and often failure.

Ideally, the partners have also anticipated and are prepared to meet some of the challenges posed by their mutual desire to have a satisfactory relationship, one that will support rather than work at cross purposes with the other family functions. Generally, it can be said that the marital relationship, as *one* aspect of family functioning, is fundamentally sound and well-ordered when there is evidence that:

1. Husband and wife have common interests in their male and female roles as marital partners and are bound by these.

2. They do not dissociate these marital interests from, nor find them at odds with, the requirements of their work and the developmental needs of their children.

Love Relationship

In the fullest sense of the term, "marital love" denotes the emotional satisfaction derived from having a sexual partner of the opposite sex, being a protector of the partner, and receiving his tender love and affection. This kind of marital love will mean that the partners have in the main renounced their infantile attachments to their own parents and are reconciled to a role in life which assures them libidinal satisfactions from a marriage partner. In other words, the emotional ties to their own families of origin are firm but no longer characterized by attitudes that endanger the intimacy of the relationship between husband and wife.

It also implies that the male takes the initiative, showing his love for his wife, protecting her, and demonstrating his affection, and that the female willingly reciprocates his love. (Evidence that the partners' love relationship is not well motivated toward these aims will be seen, for example, in demands for "exclusive" love, in the use of the love object solely as a source of narcissistic gratification, or as someone to dominate.)

Well-adjusted marital partners feel secure enough in each other's love to make friendships and outside associations readily with persons of both sexes. Neither partner regards these friends or associates as rivals or intruders who threaten the marital relationship.

It is normal for husbands and wives, on occasion, to be attracted to other women or men without becoming emotionally involved to the point of unfaithfulness. In the well-adjusted individual, such a flirtation temporarily stimulates sexual fantasies, which is a sound form of defense against acting upon such impulses. More importantly, however, the pleasure derived from the emotional return to the really loved marital partner immeasurably enhances the intimacy of their basic relationship.

The one part of the love relationship that is exclusive to husband and wife is that of giving and receiving love in the sexual act. For the normal male partner, the psychological orientation toward the sexual act is one of active interest and a realized potential for the aggressive role, tempered with tender affection for the female partner and resulting in simultaneous orgasm. For the normal female partner, the psychological orientation is interest in sexual receptivity and the realized potential for this role in the sexual act with a normal male, accompanied by tender affection and resulting in simultaneous orgasm.

Such a husband and wife will conceive the other to be the primary love object through whom sexual gratification is achieved. Ideally, the sexual act not only permits direct fulfillment of sexual needs but also serves to keep under control hostile proclivities. This occurs primarily because participation in the sexual act requires the direct use of aggressive energy which, however, is fused with the libido, taking the form of tender affection. Rivalry and competition are therefore less apt to erupt into intense and destructive forms of behavior.

Maintenance of Self-identity

An important element in marital functioning, as well as in all aspects of family living, is the character of the self-identity patterns of the partners and the ways in which they find it necessary to maintain them. To the degree that each marital partner has a certainty of feeling that he is a male, or that she is a female, with each willing to tackle all the problems intrinsic in this sex identification, so will feelings of self-doubt be increased or decreased by the marital relationship itself.

The self-identity of both husband and wife is ideally maintained by an emotional reciprocity that is complementary in character rather than identical. The emotionally stable husband demonstrates his firm sense of self-identity when he assumes his role as leader of the family, protector, and provider, and so is not fearful of using controlled aggression in disciplining older children. The emotionally stable wife feels secure in her husband's use of aggression in these socially useful ways and derives satisfaction therefrom. This, in turn, leaves her free to assume those functions that are more biologically and psychologically natural to her; namely, domestic, maternal, and marital responsibilities.

In this context, natural differences between male and female are supported by the marriage partnership in a way that enhances rather than undermines the self-identity of each. That is to say, a wife is not depreciated, dominated, or otherwise exploited because she happens to be a female; conversely, the husband is not subject to "unequal" treatment on the basis of the family function he performs or for other reasons because he is a male.

Marriage provides a unique opportunity for men and for women to project, provoke, and displace on the partner the dissatisfactions they feel within themselves with respect to their *own* sex identity. Those who deal with problems of maladjustment in married couples readily recognize these symptoms. In our culture, those uncertain of their own sex membership are known to explain personal failure by resorting to deprecating comparisons of male and female qualities, sometimes excusing business failures, sexual impotence, or frigidity on this score.

In the stable marital relationship, the husband gains respect and status in the eyes of his spouse by virtue of his male attributes, and the wife by virtue of her femininity.

Socialization

Of particular importance is the approach to the solution of problems. In the stable marriage, each partner acts in accordance with the fact that all social living, and family living in particular, demands continuous readjustment, that problems are to be solved by judicious action rather than disposed of by evading responsibility for their solution.

Such marital partners will have learned from their own life experiences to tolerate frustrations and disappointments. The anxiety associated thereto, however, stimulates rather than paralyzes the effort to discover measures that will lead to an adequate solution of a problem.

Where the problem concerns the physical, emotional, or social stability of the spouse, the opposite partner normally secures the necessary help to assure physical recovery, reestablishment of emotional equilibrium, or stabilized social behavior. The partner who is well-adjusted will, whenever possible, support in the spouse self-guidance to preserve initiative. When the afflicted partner cannot retain initiative, his spouse normally takes measures to protect his welfare.

Unnecessarily long delays in initiating appropriate action, overlooking or avoiding the reality of the problem, destructively exploiting the partner because of a handicap or a disabled condition, are destructive attitudes, not typical of the normal marriage.

FINANCIAL FUNCTIONING
Income Production

Both husband and wife enter marriage with the belief that income production and management are responsibilities requisite to marriage and to the creation and maintenance of a family. Normally, the husband is the basic provider, and with the birth of children he will for a considerable period remain the chief breadwinner. He is willing to forego the indulgence of certain self-interests if they require spending money at the expense of his family's welfare.

Irrespective of occupational level or type of endeavor, the husband usually derives satisfaction from his productivity, is self-motivated, takes initiative in working with others.

Income Management

The capacity to live within the family income depends in part upon what each partner has learned prior to marriage about planning a budget, controlling expenditures, establishing priorities, and otherwise exercising good judgment in the use of money. However, it also depends upon interaction and mutual accommodation of the partners to sound economic values in relation to a common family goal. Ideally, husband and wife share the same values about expenditures and manage their income cooperatively, or with one assuming major responsibility so that basic essentials are obtained and paid for.

By and large, the problems which occur in this area are likely to accompany unhealthy marital relationship patterns. If the marriage is sound, the responsibilities of the financial function are apt to be well discharged by the family heads.

Part Two

INTRODUCTION

THE MAJOR findings of this research and their implications for social casework comprise Part II. Within the broad context of family
casework, there are three elements which may be considered new
to the field: a classification system of defined psychosocial disorders
useful diagnostically as well as at the community planning level;
a classification of disordered family types conceived in clinical
terms; a framework for family diagnosis suitable for the analysis
of psychosocial data about families. The major findings, in fact,
represent an integrated unit; each is made consistent with the other
by the concepts and definitions of the framework for family diagnosis.

The chapters dealing with psychosocial disorders and the framework for family diagnosis are comprehensive presentations both of
the findings and of the foundations on which they rest. By plan,
the chapters concerned with the clinical features of the four dis
ordered family types do not include an interpretation of the principles on which the classification system is based. This background
material is a part of Chapter I.

IV. A CLASSIFICATION OF PSYCHOSOCIAL DISORDERS

FOR THE purposes of this text, the term "psychosocial" denotes two factors which are implicit in the social functioning of individuals and families and thus in the disorders that they may develop: (1) the personality functioning of the individual which enhances handicaps or obstructs functional accommodation to the necessities of social living; (2) the realities in the environment, or the external requirements of the typical social situation, with which he must cope. Although this concept is professionally accepted, heretofore its application in the formulation of a systematic classification of psychosocial disorders has not been attempted.

In general terms, the psychosocial disorder classification delineates the behavior and conditions which society identifies and for which it makes some provision through various social and legal processes and designated institutions. These disorders represent a breakdown in some area of social functioning which has been identified by community social agencies. The identification may have come about from the family's or individual's having established contact with one of these agencies, voluntarily or involuntarily. They are grouped in this text into five major categories:

1. *Adult disorders* encompass individual physical, mental, emotional, and behavior problems in the adult members of the family.

2. *Child disorders* cover individual physical, mental, emotional, and behavior problems in child members of the family.

3. *Child-rearing disorders* identify a failure on the part of the

adults of the family in meeting the responsibilities of parenthood.

4. *Marital disorders* represent social dysfunctioning in the area of the marriage relationship.

5. *Financial disorders* represent some social functioning failure on the part of the adult heads of the family in producing and managing income for support of the family.

One of the distinguishing features of this classification lies in the fact that the five major categories of psychosocial disorders essentially encompass the same realms of individual and family functioning as do the basic areas of the proposed framework for family diagnosis presented in Chapter IX. Therefore, the specific psychosocial disorders which are classified by the caseworker may be meaningfully related to clinical data in the corresponding area of the diagnostic framework. True, the arrangement of major categories in the classification of psychosocial disorders varies from that of the corresponding area of the diagnostic framework. Different also are the basic referents from which the specific definitions derive in each instance. Nevertheless, the major categories and the basic areas for family diagnosis are, for all practical purposes, the same.

Another distinctive feature of the classification is the fact that the psychosocial disorders constitute social indices of social dysfunctioning rather than clinical descriptions of behavior and conditions of family members. The norm for determining what constitutes a psychosocial disorder stems from socially and legally defined concepts. In essence, it is based upon specific responsibilities which members of society are legally obligated to assume, or are expected to take, to conserve valued cultural patterns.

A discussion of the processes by which society identifies and deals with these disorders will help to clarify the concepts underlying this classification and its significance to family casework diagnosis.

PROCESSES OF SOCIAL DETERMINATION

The continued functioning of any society depends upon the regular and adequate performance of certain specific social acts by the majority of its members. To achieve these objectives, there are a host of social and legal sanctions, institutions, and other pressures which motivate and inspire the forms of compliance needed. Laws and court decisions, for example, may be regarded as the embodiment of the directions in which a society would like to lead its members, and the means adopted for so doing (111). Of concern here are the various processes by which society identifies, and in so doing defines, the preferred behavior of its members, and that which is deemed variant, maladapted, nonconformist, frankly deviant, unacceptable, and so on.

There are three basic means by which psychosocial disorders are defined and identified within our social structure. To a greater or lesser degree, all have social and legal aspects:

1. Laws which stipulate specific manifestations of unacceptable behavior or conditions are passed by representatives of the people. They are enforced by the police, the courts, and correctional machinery. This procedure applies to all activities that are prohibited, and to certain kinds, including divorce, that are allowed only under legally controlled restrictions.

2. Society vests in recognized governmental agencies responsibility, which has the force of law, for dealing with certain kinds of behavior and conditions. Laws generally describe the behavior or condition and delegate its specific interpretation to local administrative authorities. Most of these disorders require protective intervention and are dealt with in this manner. A ready example is the way in which the problem of dependency is dealt with. Public welfare departments are vested with the general authority to grant financial aid to persons who meet the eligibility requirements of the Federal Social Security Act and the laws of the several states. In most instances, the local administrative units have wide latitude in determining who is eligible for assistance. Control of the placement of children also is handled mainly in this manner. Laws govern the conditions and procedures for commitment of the mentally ill and mentally deficient. Administrative policies and practices, however, determine which of the available facilities should be used in any given case.

3. A wide range of public and voluntary agencies is now supported in most urban communities in the expectation that they will deal therapeutically with failure in social functioning. With the development of social work, casework services in public welfare de-

partments, in juvenile courts, in medical care agencies, in voluntary family and children's agencies and institutions, now apply available knowledge and professional skills with the intent of improving the social sufficiency of the individuals and families in their case loads.

When these services are provided through tax-supported agencies, the broad base of social support is obvious. Legal or administrative directives regarding the type of disorders to be dealt with therapeutically often may not be so explicit as those that establish the need for protective intervention. But the services themselves are authorized by laws passed by elected representatives and financed from taxes levied by them. Services so authorized and supported therefore depend upon general public approval.

The services of voluntary agencies, however, originate from a narrower social base. These services grew out of the interest and impetus of religious, social, and nonsectarian groups, typical in our culture. To a considerable degree the control and direction of these agencies are still in the hands of such groups. Nevertheless, during the past three decades effective fund-raising techniques have drawn them closer together, from a functional standpoint. Almost all private agencies that provide any substantial volume of service are now financed, at least in part, through community-wide campaigns, to which nearly as many people contribute as pay taxes. It is fair to say that the general community now sanctions these voluntary health and welfare activities and looks upon them as an integral expression of society's will.

The therapeutic efforts of many of these agencies are directed toward rehabilitating individuals and families whose behavior has been identified through the legal and official processes of prohibition, restriction, and protective intervention. Such efforts to identify and treat psychosocial disorders at an early stage are likely to receive increased public approval as and when there is demonstrated professional skill in effecting desired therapeutic results.

Thus, community-supported sociolegal processes define variant and deviant forms of behavior. The nature of the disorders so identified determines the needed controls (corrective, protective, preventive). The behavior or condition may be: (1) prohibited; (2) allowed but permitted only under controlled restrictions; (3) not preferred, but legitimate because forced by circumstances not wholly within the control of the individual, and therefore requiring protective intervention by society; (4) identified as requiring therapeutic exploration because of the likelihood of deteriorating into such a disorder.

Prohibited

Behavior which is prohibited by society is easily recognized and is regarded as unacceptable by any reasonable standard. Bigamy is illegal. Prostitution is forbidden. An employer cannot refuse to pay his workmen wages agreed upon and due; no one can refuse to pay his rent, his grocery bills, his taxes. And laws pertaining to the juvenile offender carry the implication that even a minor cannot overtly violate the rights of others. These and a whole vast network of specific acts are legally identified, governed, and controlled in the interest of maintaining an integrated and secure social structure.

Restricted

These disorders consist of behavior and conditions that are not legally prohibited but are not preferred insofar as the social ideal is concerned. Therefore, specified legal procedures are stipulated for dealing with them.

A good example is to be found in the preferred social pattern of marriage; namely, that of a single union, enduring until the death of one partner. However, divorce, accompanied by variously stipulated kinds of responsibility for support of children, payment of alimony, and so on, is a permissive or legitimate evasion of this social requirement. It is not particularly encouraged, however.

Another example is found in the rules and procedures that govern the placement of children. The vast majority of parents are self-sufficient, and can and do provide the physical care, affection, and training necessary to the well-rounded development of their offspring. When this is not the case, society makes provision for, and thereby permits placement of, children in foster homes, in institutions, or under other forms of substitute care. The agencies that provide such care in society's behalf are also required to meet certain standards, and are subject to inspection; in many instances, they must secure a court order giving them temporary guardianship of the child. Such action is presumed to be in the best interests of the child, the parent, and society. Therefore, substitute care is accepted as a necessary departure from the ideal of normal family responsibility. However, if the majority of children in any society required such care, the survival of that society would obviously be jeopardized.

An illustration may be taken from the field of education. This country properly places a high value on adequate education for all children of school age. Public facilities are provided to meet this ideal. The importance of education is also reflected in the laws governing school attendance; children are not permitted to quit school except under certain conditions and at a specified age. In many states, these conditions include issuance of a certified work permit for the minor child. Thus, early dropouts from the educational regime are not encouraged even though they are permitted, subject to appropriate regulations.

Protective Intervention

The unique characteristic of the social and legal processes which identify psychosocial disorders requiring protective intervention stems from the social concept that, although contrary to accepted social ideals, such problems are caused primarily by individually determined physical and mental conditions or economic and social forces not wholly within the ability of the individual to control. Thus, it is a failure of social responsibility which may be said to be forced upon the individual. The situation or condition is not the preferred one, from society's standpoint, but the individual is not held accountable in a legal or moral sense.

Many community social agencies are now organized to deal primarily with psychosocial disorders which are in effect "forced evasions," or failures in the social roles expected of individuals and families. The most common examples of the disorders so identified are mental deficiency, psychotic illness, physical disability, and financial dependency, with the latter a result of events such as the death of a wage earner, flood or fire, seasonal unemployment, inadequate wages, limited education, and other circumstantial factors.

If the majority of persons in a society were so affected, such failures would constitute a serious threat to the maintenance of that society. This was sharply illustrated when widespread unemployment turned 25 percent of this country's families into recipients of some form of governmental aid, in the depression of the 1930s.

Therapeutic Exploration

Behavior and conditions that represent psychosocial disorders requiring therapeutic exploration are not too well understood. This process is a part of the function of both tax-supported and voluntary agencies. The purpose is to identify behavior and conditions that have not yet been identified through the legal or official processes of prohibition, restriction, or protective intervention but which may possibly reach the stage where this will occur. Recognition of the significance of therapeutic exploration for the detection of such incipient disorders therefore seems a logical concomitant to the thesis of this work.

Many illustrations could be cited. Some legally prohibited acts are not and may never be detected by legal processes. However, the very fact that these acts are legally unidentified violations of the law also means that they may eventually evoke legal action. Repeated infractions of employment rules, withholding income from dependents, desertion, neglect of children, cruel abuse of others, drug addiction, and like activities not only are regarded as unsocial, but warrant diagnostic exploration and treatment, with the aim of preventing repetition and perhaps even more serious antisocial acts.

Similarly, tendencies toward alcoholism, psychologically cruel subjugation of a marital partner, intermittent and prolonged absences, "running home to mother," irrational and provocative behavior, and other evidences of marital incompatibility may be regarded as precursors to more serious forms of psychosocial disorders, leading to the official necessity for prohibition or restriction. At various levels, parental indifference, inadequate physical care, lax or overrestrictive disciplinary measures, and other failures in the care of children may also eventually lead to the application of restrictive measures.

There well may be disagreement about the need for therapeutic exploration. However, the composite of increasing social interdependence and knowledge of human behavior tends to confirm the necessity for identifying incipient psychosocial disorders that have a potential for being detected by established legal processes.

The identification and classification of the various types of social behavior and individual conditions are recognized aspects of the casework practitioner's professional responsibility to two groups: the clients served by community-supported health and welfare services; and the agency and community which provide the services. Therefore, it may be assumed that an informed approach to family casework diagnosis needs to include a systematic classification of psychosocial disorders such as is presented here.

For the social caseworker, the greatest value of the classification of psychosocial disorders lies in the fact that it enables the identification of general areas of social dysfunctioning in a context that is consistent with a family casework diagnostic scheme. The evaluation of the specific aspects and nature of the dysfunctioning, however, will be the practitioner's primary concern and ultimate goal. The classification will further this aspect of the diagnostic process by giving initial focus to the task of identifying the probable areas of trouble, as well as the nature, extent, and scope of needed diagnostic exploration.

A second and important purpose of the classification of psychosocial disorders relates to its significance to preventive social planning. Its use may open the way for the ultimate attainment of uniformity and comparability in the study of community-wide distribution, concentration, and other epidemiological characteristics of psychosocial disorders. Epidemiological studies of this sort are yet to be undertaken in any significant and comprehensive way. There have been sporadic collections of data about particular problems in which particular groups or agencies have a particular interest.

However, the findings of one group cannot be related to those of another. This can be done only through a generally accepted classified framework of psychosocial disorders, within which can be achieved at least minimum comparability.

The same applies to analyzing the etiological significance of such data. The intent usually has been to gain knowledge about the factors which have caused the psychosocial disorder. But this intent, if realized, rarely benefits from, or contributes to, other research with a similar purpose, since each problem or disorder is differently defined, within a research design that has no relationship to any other comprehensive framework, based on commonly understood and accepted concepts. The utility of a clearly classified and consistently defined list of psychosocial disorders was well illustrated in the early phases of this research already described. Because the definitions of each were a matter of public record, they could be consistently applied and compared, case by case. As a result of this experience, the development of the classification system has been guided by two principles:

1. The definitions here used derive from the organized community's own definition of behavior and conditions over which it exerts varying degrees of legal or social control.

All psychosocial disorders are identified and classified according to the five major categories already listed. Such disorders, however, are further conceived to be of two basic types, Level A and Level B. In selecting the psychosocial disorders at each level a socially defined rather than a clinically determined context has been used. In other words, they are presumed to identify behavior and conditions which most people would understand and recognize as socially undesirable or open to question. The lists of Level A disorder items are clearly of this sort. The specific items of the Level B disorder type are, of course, open to question. Short of conducting a systematically designed opinion poll, there is no way of testing this judgment. However, the authors believe that the listings of Level B disorders serve the general purposes for which they were designed.

By definition, the kinds of disorders specified as Level A and Level B are mutually exclusive. Diagnostically speaking, however, most persons or families whose behavior and conditions require legal or official intervention (Level A disorders) will more often than not also have psychosocial disorders of the Level B type.

CRA's three experiments were precisely focused on three major Level A disorders—dependency, disordered behavior, and indigent disability. In the three counties, 75 percent of all families served by all public and private welfare agencies were found to have one or more of the principal Level A disorders. The other 25 percent were accounted for chiefly by families whose members were receiving pre- or postnatal nursing care; immunization or other preventive public health services; subsidized medical care not occasioned by physical disability; and child welfare service not in conjunction with child placement, delinquency, or other legally identified disorders.

2. This classification is based on social indices, not clinical; it is, therefore, not presumed to have etiological significance. The specific types of behavior and conditions listed are identified and determined primarily by legal and social processes. All behavior and conditions so identified are in all probability indicative of more fundamental pathological processes underlying the social dysfunctioning of the individual or family. However, the significance of this relationship is a matter for interpretation, a responsibility of the social caseworker.

Intensive clinical study of the sample cases which were provided by the cooperating family service agencies clearly suggested that the specific nature and degree of pathology in a family tended to be directly associated with the presence of typical Level A and Level B disorders. The presence of a multiplicity of Level A disorders was indicative, in the main, of more serious psychosocial dysfunctioning than was shown by the presence of Level B disorders alone. This is in itself diagnostically useful knowledge. When a multiplicity of severe Level B disorders was present in a family, Level A disorders also were likely to be present or developed during the course of the case. Evidence of this is to be found in the diagnostic materials from which have been drawn the identification and description of the four disordered family types presented in later chapters. The fourth and most pathologically disordered family type—the unsocial—is distinguished by a multiplicity of Level A disorders of a highly serious nature. A multiplicity and intensity of Level B disorders also are present.

INDIVIDUAL PSYCHOSOCIAL DISORDERS

Psychosocial disorders related to family members as individuals are divided into two major categories: adult disorders and child disorders. Both Level A and Level B disorders are classified within these two groups. The age that divides "adult" from "child" in any particular community would be that at which the child's condition and behavior cease to be handled by the juvenile authorities and are taken over by those who have jurisdiction over the adult.

Adult Disorders

Level A	Level B
Major crimes	Socially incompatible behavior
Minor crimes and misdemeanors	Distorted reactions to responsibility
Admissions or commitment to mental hospitals or institutions	Mental illness or deficiency (non-institutionalized)
	Physical disability affecting social efficiency

Level A adult disorders consist of behavior which is prohibited, or behavior and individual conditions which require protective intervention. All crimes, of course, come within the areas of legally prohibited behavior. Individuals who suffer from mental illness and mental deficiency which result in an impaired capacity for adequate social functioning require protective intervention in their behalf as an accepted social necessity. Admission or commitment to mental hospitals or institutions financed by the government (usually the state) gives evidence of a legally determined official concern and responsibility. Generally speaking, such protective intervention occurs when the individual's condition has reached maximum severity.

The distinction between major and minor crimes essentially is a legal or administrative differentiation between what is believed to be the most dangerous behavior and what is the least dangerous from the standpoint of the protection of society. No such administrative classification can be expected to serve as a diagnostic or prognostic guide, except in a general way. From a clinical standpoint, all acts classified as major crimes represent "acting out" of hostile destructive impulses, aggressively directed toward society. This is true of some but by no means all of the offenses categorized as minor crimes and misdemeanors.

Data from the CRA experimental project in San Mateo, California, for the prevention and control of disordered behavior, showed that major and minor criminal incidents occurred at an annual rate of 10.4 per 1,000 families in the county. The vast bulk of these were minor crimes and misdemeanors. The individuals were for the most part penalized by detention in the local jails, fines, and probation. They accounted for 97 percent of all the criminal behavior dealt with exclusively by local agencies.

Level B adult disorders are, of course, not officially identified; therefore, they are not subject to the legal processes which prohibit, restrict, or provide protective intervention. On the other hand, the behavior and conditions identified as Level B types of disorders may be indicative of the presence of varying degrees of psychosocial pathology that may reach Level A status:

Socially incompatible behavior. Excessive drunkenness, promiscuity, cruel and sadistic abuse, and unmarried parenthood are examples. Such behavior might easily break over into the category of officially prohibited behavior. Although few adults are completely free of some form or degree of similar indulgences, excesses are socially undesirable. Beyond doubt, unmarried parenthood is generally considered to be indicative of socially incompatible behavior.

Distorted reactions to responsibility. Examples include lack of initiative and self-reliance, easy loss of interest, stubborn resistance to responsibility. Such traits also may manifest themselves in unwarranted fearful expectation of disease, accompanied by exaggerated preoccupation with sundry curative methods.

Other examples may be overconscientiousness, unduly strong convictions about right and wrong, adherence to rigid practices in relation to religion, sex, race, and so on. Social attitudes toward such behavior are determined by its particular form and degree.

Most people exhibit some of these traits in some way at some time.

Although certain segments of the population regard psychosis in a family member as a disgrace, mass educational efforts have brought increased acceptance of the fact that people so affected are sick. Community provision for out-patient diagnosis and treatment is steadily increasing, in part as a substitute for hospitalization under official auspices.

Physical disabilities that affect social efficiency. Although the social undesirability of such conditions is widely recognized, blame is not attached to the individual. Communities now provide a wide variety of medical and rehabilitative services that would not otherwise be available to low-income and other community groups.

Child Disorders

Level A	Level B
Delinquency	Defiance of authority
Truancy	Social maladjustment
Noneconomic school dropouts	School failures
Admission or commitment to mental hospitals or institutions	Mental illness or deficiency (non-institutionalized)
	Irrational fears
	Physical disability

Community awareness of the child's disorders usually occurs when he attends school, plays with other children; in other words, when he begins to live as a "social" personality. For that reason, all items in our classification are most readily observable after the child reaches school age and most of them after the age of six or seven.

Among the Level A disorders, truancy is usually the first manifestation of juvenile nonconformist behavior that requires official action. Unexcused absences from school are prohibited. Delinquent behavior, often preceded or accompanied by truancy, may become a matter for social action in the childhood years, but data from the CRA San Mateo project have shown it to be most highly concentrated within the ages from fifteen to seventeen. In 1956, in fact, 74 percent of all delinquencies in the county were committed by adolescents of these ages. Delinquency, the juvenile counterpart and often the antecedent of adult criminal behavior, must be prohibited also. Because of the high premium put upon education, premature discontinuance of school is generally disapproved, except when it is compelled by economic reasons. Nevertheless, it is permitted under controlled restrictions.

In regard to Level B disorders, however, specific items of behavior evoke an earlier interest and recognition on the part of persons professionally concerned with the detection and treatment of the child with a psychosocial disorder:

Defiance of authority. Examples include continued defiance of teachers and others in authority, hostile attacks on other children, disregard of the rights and property of others, and similar acting-out manifestations of nonconformist attitudes.

Such behavior is readily identified by school teachers and others. Various studies, including the Gluecks' *Unraveling Juvenile Delinquency* (70), point to the predictive value of such symptoms in relation to future delinquent behavior.

Social maladjustment. This type of disorder includes excessive shyness, withdrawal from social contacts, prudishness, personalities easily intimidated. Such children are apt to be objects of ridicule and teasing by their playmates. While behavior of this kind is not apt to command as much adult attention, or to be looked upon with such concern, as overtly aggressive behavior, it may be prophetic of later mental disorders.

School failure. Low grades and failure to pass constitute reasonably objective signs of inability to measure up to social standards. Such incapacity may be a prelude to Level A school dropouts.

Mental illness or deficiency (noninstitutionalized). There is no general agreement as to what constitutes childhood psychosis, or at what age a child can be considered to be mentally ill. However, symptoms of confusion, lack of interest in the world around him, precocity accompanied by extreme hostility when people interfere with his self-preoccupation, are possible danger signals that psychosis may develop in early adolescence.

Irrational fears. Obsessional fears of going to school, of animals, of getting hurt, of being dirty, and other expressions of anxiety may be prophetic, or indicative of an established neurosis.

Physical disability. Serious or disabling illness may arrest the sequence of normal physical maturation and personality development. Public health well-baby clinics give evidence of the communities' organized interest in preventing such occurrences.

FAMILY PSYCHOSOCIAL DISORDERS

Family psychosocial disorders are grouped under headings which reflect the three main functions which society expects the family to perform: financial functions; marital functions; child-rearing functions.

Financial Disorders

Level A	Level B
Dependency	Lack of personal incentive
Indigent disability	Poor work record
	Open conflict with employer
	Frequent dismissal from jobs
	Unofficial nonsupport
	Nonamortized debts due to:
	impulsive spending
	purchase of luxury items

With respect to Level A financial disorders, the Social Security Act of 1935, with subsequent amendments, clearly stipulates that dependency is a condition that requires protective intervention. Families whose income is inadequate to meet officially defined needs for food, clothing, and shelter are eligible for governmental assistance to achieve this minimum. This condition is now accepted as one caused by personal impairments or economic circumstances. The degree to which, during a period of full employment, dependency is due to intrinsic impairments beyond the individual's control is well documented in CRA's three experimental projects. In 96 percent of the dependent families in these counties, either there was no potential wage earner or he was over sixty-five, chronically ill, mentally ill, retarded, or otherwise handicapped in a competitive labor market.

Indigent disability was first identified as a Level A psychosocial disorder in connection with CRA's project in Washington County, Maryland. It is defined as "the necessity for financial assistance, medical care, or health service from community subsidized sources, in a family in which at least one member suffers a physical illness or handicap of three months or more duration, this condition having been severe enough to result in limitation of ability to engage in usual activity." Thus, indigent disability is a Level A financial disorder of any person or family who is the recipient of subsidized medical care.

In Washington County, families with this problem constituted about 15 percent of all families in the community with disabled members. In the three project counties they represented about one half of all families receiving subsidized health service for any reason and absorbed about two thirds of the community's total expenditures for health purposes.

Level B financial disorders consist of behavior easily recognized by caseworker, personnel officers, union leaders, neighbors, and friends.

Poor work records, lack of incentive, quarrels and conflicts with the employer, repeated dismissals, are major factors in labor turnover, absenteeism, and other problems that create difficulties for management no less than for the wage earner's family and friends. Debts are of common occurrence in a culture which leans heavily on installment buying. But when they are due to impulsive, ill-considered spending, and are not amortized by responsible payments, they are looked upon with disfavor. "Unofficial" nonsupport usually means that the wage-earning member of the family spends the contents of his pay envelope on himself rather than on his family—a practice not generally condoned. In urban communities, such symptoms as these bulk heavily in the case loads of many community service agencies.

Marital Disorders

Level A	Level B
Divorce	Lack of, or distorted patterns of:
Separation (official)	affection
Desertion (official)	self-esteem
	social activities
	Lack of helpful concern in:
	wage earning
	homemaking
	physical or mental illness

Level A marital disorders are clear-cut. Marriage is of concern to all societies; it may be dissolved other than by death, but only by and within certain legal procedures, designed to preserve the durability of the socially accepted marriage structure. The three principal methods by which a marriage may be terminated in this country—divorce, legal separation, desertion—reflect varying forms of legally sanctioned marital dissolution. In volume, divorce far outdistances the others.

In San Mateo County, during 1956, divorce, legal separation, or desertion occurred at the rate of 9.8 per 1,000 families. This accounted for 33.6 percent of the incidence of all types of Level A disordered behavior identified (33).

Level B marital disorders reflect the main areas in which husband and wife normally expect reciprocity and helpfulness. The items, however, are not difficult to recognize.

When two partners belittle each other, show meager signs of affection, do not share social activities, this overt evidence signifies a lack of satisfying emotional give-and-take. When the wife has no interest in her husband's occupation other than in his pay envelope and the husband thoroughly discounts her domestic role, little mutual helpfulness can be expected. While marriages that exhibit such symptomatology may not break up, they either are prone to do so or are vulnerable to the stresses of marital living. Such cases too bulk large in the case loads of family service, child guidance, and other community agencies.

Child-rearing Disorders

Level A	Level B
Child neglect	Inadequate physical care
Child separation (placement)	Distorted affectional reactions
	Distorted direction and guidance
	Incompetent socialization practices

Of all the family's functions, that of begetting and rearing children is most highly valued by society. Firm cultural standards applicable to bringing up and educating the child within the family circle are not easily defined and identified. Today, especially among the middle class, there is considerable interest in the growing literature on "how to bring up your children," material which stems from both qualified and unqualified sources, "experts" in human relations.

This general state of confusion is illustrated by great variations in the manner in which community concern about children is administratively expressed and applied throughout the country. In the CRA study of San Mateo County, for example, all the public and private services organized for therapeutic purposes were found to be focused upon problems either of child-rearing or child disorders; none, primarily, upon other evidences of adult, marital, or financial disorders.

At the same time, there is little uniformity in definition of "child neglect." Decision as to whether or not this condition shall be determined officially by court procedure, or unofficially by some community agency, often depends, not upon the nature of the situation itself, but upon whether or not the probable use of tax money for subsequent care makes it necessary for an agency to bring the case to court. Similarly, policies and practices determining *why* and *when* a child should be separated from his own home and, if so, where he should be placed, vary not only from community to community, but from agency to agency.

Level A child-rearing disorders consist of child neglect, which is prohibited, and the separation of children from their own homes for placement, which is permitted but restricted. Very often the child is removed from his own home, not only as a result of officially determined child neglect, but also because of other factors which make the separation seem necessary both to the parent and to the community agency. Yet both reasons for removal of the child represent some impaired capacity on the part of parents, for whatever reason, to provide their children with the protection, affection, and training which are deemed essential to their attainment of successful emotional and physical maturity.

In 1956, children from 435 San Mateo families were under care away from their own homes, a rate of 3.5 "separated" children out of every 1,000 families in the county. The cost of their care amounted to $337,539 annually, 18 percent of the money spent on all categories of disordered behavior, exclusive of hospitalization for the mentally ill or retarded.

Level B child-rearing disorders consist of behavior that denotes laxness and distorted or deviant attitudes on the part of parents toward the developmental needs of children. The following have been found to be significant to the development of disorders which, if not modified through treatment of parents and/or child, may well lead the child to develop adult behavior ill-suited to his social responsibilities:

Inadequate physical care. This includes not only neglect of the child's health, but also overexactness and regimentation. The former is evidenced by irregular meals; negligible or limited assistance in teaching control of bodily functions; and heavy reliance on relatives or others in both respects. The latter is seen in overemphasis on perfection in home tasks, rigid adherence to eating the "right" foods, little flexibility in training, "overblame" for childhood accidents.

Distorted affection. Patterns of distortion are almost innumerable. Extremes of overdevotion, spoiling, babying, "giving in," may be contrasted with equally undesirable sadistic treatment, subjugation, hate or dislike, assertions that the child was never wanted. In another form, the parent gives affection and protection only when the child demonstrates his own love. This is easily seen among parents who ask a child's advice rather than providing guidance so that he may develop judgment. Especially when a mother is separated from her child by hospitalization or death, or when she is preoccupied with or prefers another child, or when she is herself psychotic, or other personal reasons have prior claim, inconstancy or diminution of parental love is apt to result.

Unhealthy relations of a sexually stimulating nature are not so readily observable by an outsider. However, overfondling, sleeping with the child, lack of privacy between adult and child, may be so regarded; in their most extreme form such relationships may include exposure to adult sexual activities and, in some instances, to incestuous acts.

Distorted direction and guidance. Especially in our American culture, a high premium is placed upon the normal development of initiative and self-reliance. One ill-conceived way to foster this quality is by insistence on perfectionism in school achievement, overdirection in choice of school subjects, hobbies, playmates, occupational interest. Overprotection of the child from the normal vicissitudes of life manifests itself in unfounded fears that the child will get hurt, fall into bad company, become sexually delinquent.

Other practices which destroy the development of self-confidence include depreciating the child as a boy or girl, making unfavorable comparisons between children, failing to allow for normal expression of hostile feelings, and discounting the advantages of knowledge and learning as means of self-realization.

Incompetent socialization practices. Practices which are known to result in faulty or defective social judgment and behavior include: (1) indecisiveness in inculcating the importance of school attendance, respect for the law, advantages of work; (2) overrestriction in defining privileges, but irresponsibility in dealing with misbehavior, excusing or blaming others for the activity; (3) extreme forms of punishment, and so on.

V. THE PERFECTIONISTIC FAMILY

FAMILIES CLASSED as "perfectionistic" place undue emphasis upon being without fault and upon avoiding open friction. "Perfectionism" has both a moralistic and a narcissistic connotation, the latter referring to the individual's awareness of his innate worth and self-respect. Excessive self-reproach and anxiety, caused by real or imagined failures, characteristically result in both parent and child from the recurrent feeling that they can never quite measure up, whether to the standards set for them by others or to those that are self-imposed.

By placing exaggerated importance on the individual's responsibility for self-criticism, personal initiative, achievement, and a "good social adjustment," the parents emotionally overtax themselves and their children. The extreme ill-effects of this pattern upon the family usually are mitigated by the fact that one partner is likely to show a greater degree of stability and flexibility than the other. It is the aggregate of these differences, the degree of stability of the partners, and the overemphasis on perfectionism that sets the emotional tone of this family class and distinguishes it from the others.

The social caseworker will find that the perfectionistic family's psychosocial disorders belong primarily to Level B rather than to Level A. The crisis that most frequently prompts the adults to seek outside guidance will concern dysfunctions classifiable as marital, child, child-rearing or adult psychosocial disorders. In essence, this immediate pressure will constitute one aspect of the problem which the adult considers troublesome or threatening to his welfare or that of other family members. By and large, this precipitant will be an external event or stress which mobilizes apprehension and uncertainty within the adult family member. He may or may not accurately perceive its significance and relationship to the total constellation of factors that contribute to the basic diagnosed problem. These psychosocial disorders have the following characteristics, as identified by the social caseworker:

CHILD-REARING DISORDERS

In the perfectionistic family these disorders may center around parental concern about habit-training practices, affectional responses to a particular child, and judgment in guiding development of self-reliance and socialized behavior.

CHILD DISORDERS

These disorders are typified by anxiety and guilt-ridden behavior that interfere with the child's normal adjustment. Anxiety may be manifest in phobias, hyperactivity, aggressive conduct, stubbornness, and so on, which have retarded the child's development of socially useful adaptive skills.

MARITAL DISORDERS

Marital disorders reflect dissatisfactions in the emotional give-and-take of the husband-wife affectional relationship, including the sexual act, and in the preservation of mutual self-esteem. At least one partner will show signs of being inhibited or evasive in personal relationships, unable to give fully of himself.

FINANCIAL DISORDERS

Disorders that involve inadequate income or failure to support are not apt to be found in this family. Whatever differences may arise in this area are manifested as an aspect of marital dissatisfactions.

ADULT DISORDERS

Individual disorders of the adult partners are reflected in anxiety-dominated behavior patterns that distort realistic handling of life situations but do not interfere materially with "good" social conduct. Physical disabilities, likely to be present in the adult, may impair ordinary activity, although they do not typically do so.

CHILD-REARING FUNCTIONS
Parental Functioning

Although the partners of the perfectionistic family wish to create a family and are generally aware of what parenthood involves, the initial attainment of this status is unplanned. This is true despite the fact that the importance of planning is a basic tenet of both the husband's and the wife's philosophy of personal, social, and family living. As a rule, the couple intend to realize certain objectives before the birth of children. These objectives reflect both personal ambitions and concepts of family living, such as the husband's discharge from military service and his career firmly launched; ownership of a home, certain household equipment, a car, and so on. Worthy though the goals may be in themselves, plans for their attainment nonetheless often go awry. This customarily is occasioned by the birth of the couple's first child, who was conceived at a time convenient for the gratification of the parents' biological urges but is born at a time inconvenient for the achievement of these other vital goals. Under such circumstances, the inevitable frustrations become associated with the attainment of parenthood. Subsequent parental responses to the first-born and the personal sacrifices required are colored by this basic unwillingness to have had him in the first place.

Irritations and disappointment in having his plans upset are voiced by the prospective father. The mother, although "unprepared," becomes less and less bothered once she knows she actually is going to have a child. When he is born, the baby is "accepted," "liked," and his upbringing is conscientiously undertaken. Nonetheless, out of the emotions of the situation, this child, among all children born into this family, assumes particular significance for both parents. He is usually the one who develops recognizable emotional disorders in early childhood, and definitely by latency, which become a matter of concern to the parents. Children not associated with such events tend to be less vulnerable to developmental disorders and problems of social adjustment.

Both father and mother have acquired, through identification with their own parents, preconceived ideas of what a "good" parent should be. Mothers, in the majority of instances, will have had the maternal domestic role overemphasized as the ideal by their own mothers. Stress on independence, working for what one receives, and looking after others also leads these mothers to have similar expectations from their own children. Often there is a strong competitive tendency to be a "better" mother than was an own mother. In these instances children come to represent living proof of success or failure. As a secondary compensation, such a mother may also hope to attain perfection for herself through the child. Tendencies which are present in the fathers are an emphasis upon thrift and on "getting ahead." These parental goals are marked as defensive by the overemphasis on, and perfectionism expected in, individual responsibility, self-criticism, personal initiative, scholastic achievement, and conformance to socially accepted standards of behavior. Hence they constitute evidence of pathological dysfunctioning.

Similar is another parental idea that is evidence of dysfunctioning; namely, that the best interests of child and family are served if familial friction is avoided. Stress on perfectionism combined with the overconstricted feeling that logically ensues when friction must be avoided tends to force too early repression of sexual and aggressive impulses in some of the children and premature acceleration of self-reliance. Children actively or passively protest this kind of denial of the opportunity to become persons in their own right. Perplexities and frustrations are experienced by both parents; they are baffled by their children, unable to understand why they do not behave according to the "book" and fail to follow the standards held up for them.

There is also present in at least one parent a predisposition to self-criticism and excessive concern over his parental failure. Hostilities felt toward the child, which are engendered by this state of affairs, stimulate guilt and anxiety and the avowed wish to do something about it. Frightened by this hostility, the parent is prompted to seek help from a social agency. Also significant to correct diagnosis of this family class is the positive counterinfluence exerted by the more stable parent upon the behavior of the less stable. The success of this depends in large measure upon the sex of the parent and child in question.

PHYSICAL MATURATION

Parents of the perfectionistic family feel a reasonable satisfaction in providing for the physical development of their children. Fundamentally, both share the same views and nearly always concur on the division of responsibility and the quality of care that is given.

The mother usually expects and takes primary responsibility for personal care, nutritional needs, and training. Although the father is interested in the child's welfare, he does not participate actively during the child's early years. However, certain of the mother's educational emphases in child training are not consistently approved by the father. He tends toward greater leniency and periodically intervenes to reduce the effect of the mother's overexacting expectations. Opposing views, although a subject of controversy, do not typically become highly charged and exploited as ends in themselves. At the same time, the dominant leniency of the father and the overrigidity of the mother do not blend sufficiently in practice to balance the ill-effects which both extremes produce upon the children.

Although she may initiate training at the appropriate time, the mother's fault lies in being perfectionistic in her methods. She expects too much maturity of the child for his age. Bowel training is established but is more than normally upsetting to the mother, and thus undue significance is given to this procedure by the child. Insufficient allowance is made for "accidents" or for the usual childish failures. With respect to food, overemphasis is placed on eating everything on the plate, dawdling is always punishable by sending the child from the table, table manners are severely criticized, and so on.

Through frequent criticism, the child is made to feel unnecessarily guilty and anxious over his failures. Excessively punitive, cruel restraining measures, however, are not characteristic of this family class.

LOVE RELATIONSHIPS

Although at least one parent in these families feels considerable warmth for the children, the constancy of this affection is temporarily interrupted by the anxiety which is induced by certain aspects of the child's personality development. A key factor, this results in an alternation of acceptance and rejection of the child, although not in rejection of him as a total personality. It may be rationalized, for example, by the fear of "spoiling."

In general, this means that the psychic reaction of these parents may be something like this: "I love my child, but there are certain things he does that make me anxious. I try but I cannot love *this* part of him. To do so brings up unpleasant memories of my own. I must correct these through my child both for myself and 'for his own good.' "

The specific aspects of personality development to which most parents in the perfectionistic family will be sensitive are reflected in the following typical reactions:

Oversensitivity to normal self-assertive behavior appears as temporary withdrawal of love from the child, manifested in provocative battles and in squelching normal expressions of aggressivity in play. "Good" is construed to mean quiet, clean, and so on.

Oversensitivity to a boy's emerging masculine strivings takes the form of temporary withdrawal of love, mainly by the mother, manifested by singling out the boy child for criticism. Pitched battles of wills between parent and child are stimulated by the fact that the child is male.

Occasional oversensitivity to a girl's independent strivings appears as temporary withdrawal of love, primarily by the mother, as the daughter shows signs of a normal transfer of emotional interests to others, outside the family orbit. This condition is manifested by the parent's periodic protestations of feeling unloved, lost, or abandoned by the child, of which she is made aware.

SELF-IDENTITY

Independence and judgment in making choices and dealing with the normal trials of social intercourse at play and at school are qualities emphasized by these parents and desired in their children. However, teaching the principle of independence is replaced by overdirecting activities and "overteaching." Present in at least one parent, and usually in both, are perfectionistic ideals of behavior, always just beyond the child's capacity for comfortable mastery, in terms of his age and maturity. Although self-reliance and judgment are expected and independence of choice approved, the gradual development of these capacities attuned to the child's innate pleasure in self-autonomy is not stimulated by this approach. The result, mostly unrecognized by the parent, is the dominance of the parent's choice rather than the child's. Although the child develops a certain degree of self-reliance, his real self-identity is partly submerged.

The specific point of overemphasis varies with the individual parent. Examples that occur most frequently in the sample are indicated by the following symptoms:

Overemphasis of social adjustment takes the form of parental acceptance of the child's behavior as long as he has many social contacts, achieves recognition, "gets along" with everybody. Social "success" is equated with being nonhostile but, at the same time, "sticking up" for one's own rights, an impossible and unrealistic thesis based on emotional nonacceptance of the presence of aggressive impulses.

Distorted application of child-rearing concepts found in "psychology books" is shown by the inordinate amounts of time given to playing with children, helping with schoolwork, trying to answer all sex questions in full, irrespective of the child's age. There are criticisms that the child is not cooperating at "maximum capacity." Hobbies, school courses, and so forth, are chosen in accordance with the parents' interests rather than to inculcate the principle of independence and guide the child's decisions. (The parent is apt to think that he does follow these principles.)

Exploitation of sexual differences is present occasionally when the mother prefers girls. She tends to overidentify with the girl child, and thus overexacting standards are demanded of the boy. Home chores are a bone of contention; the mother wishes he would act "much more grown up," punishes him for trivialities, but is easily upset by outside criticism of the boy.

SOCIALIZATION

Parents of the perfectionistic family take active responsibility for teaching their children the advantages of becoming a worker, of extending social contacts, of respecting the property and rights of others, and, in anticipation of gradual separation from home ties, the importance of school attendance. Certain antisocial acts are strictly forbidden. Although the parents are well-intentioned and responsible, coercion characterized by "overshaping" is the principal means they use to develop the child's capacity for self-observation, self-criticism, self-punishment, and restitution. Thus, the child learns to control his hostilities and other nonacceptable impulses. However, this is accomplished through the demands of an overrigid superego, frequently manifested in provocative behavior and in self-depreciating symptoms.

Child-rearing practices concerned with socialization may vary. Fear of outside criticism leads these parents to exact strict obedience, although the rigidity of one parent may be balanced to some extent by the less exacting demands of the other. Too much is expected of the child in the way of anticipating the consequence of his own acts; punishment takes the form of denying social privileges, sending him from the room, and so on. Exasperation from failure to control the child's behavior may result in slapping and spanking him. This, in time, causes excessive guilt on the part of the parent, because of his own intensity of feeling rather than because any physical harm has been inflicted on the child. Overpunitive, sadistically cruel measures are not typical of parents in this class.

Child Development
EVENTS AND CIRCUMSTANCES

The child of the perfectionistic family is apt to live with his own parents through his early formative years and into adolescence. If separation occurs, the usual reasons are the death of one parent, divorce, or, occasionally, hospitalization of a parent. The remaining parent characteristically continues daily care and contact with the children.

Substitute arrangements when necessary are made with relatives, who are early replaced by a stepmother or stepfather. Seldom are breaches in parent-child contact due to sporadic separations of husband and wife, criminality, abandonment, or leaving the child solely to the care of relatives or social agencies.

Significant events of emotional significance to the parent, however, do influence and affect child development. The most common of these are absence of the father because of military service, physical illness, or mental illness—essentially, circumstances beyond his personal control. The characteristic attitude of the mother to such situations is veiled resentment toward the father, due to the added family responsibilities she must bear alone. Either a particular child becomes negatively identified with the circumstances of the father's absence, or all the children are so involved. In either instance, the mother's feelings of resentment are displaced to the children. Typically, however, the mother is aware that this is occurring, and although she is incapable of altering her feelings she possesses some ability to exert conscious control over her actions as well as to use supportive help in tempering the ill-effects upon the children.

EARLY CHILDHOOD

Any child under six who has a basic trust in the ever-renewed sameness of his mother's feeling for him can more easily postpone gratification of his wishes and modify his behavior according to social needs. The behavior of the majority of young children in the perfectionistic family gives evidence that this developmental task is not easily or fully mastered. The perfectionistic but vacillating conviction that guides the mother's prohibitions and permissions accounts for this. Such standards face a severe test, particularly in the three-, four- and five-year-old's reaction to them.

LOVE RELATIONSHIPS

The interesting thing about the children through five years of age in the perfectionistic family is their general responsiveness to contacts with both adults and children, coexisting with symptoms that denote insecurities in their love relationships with their own mothers. When a child in this age group is either the oldest child of the family or an only child he is the one the parents center upon as a problem, because of his aggression or because he is the first-born. A second or third child tends to be outgoing with others but overcompliant to the mother, in order to retain her love. This strongly reflects the distinctive parental pattern of alternation of acceptance and rejection of the child, on the basis of changing aspects of his personality development.

The following symptoms and their common precipitants are characteristic of the love relationship with the parent:

Responsiveness coupled with stubbornness and anxiety occurs mainly in the first-born or oldest of the children under six in the family. Insecurity in the mother's love is manifested by "testing" her to the nth degree through various devices known to be provoking: overmanipulation of himself and others by temper outbursts; easy irritation at having to share with siblings; rebellion against routines important to the mother. Neurotic symptoms that frequently accompany these protests are wakefulness, excessive fear of wetting the bed, night wandering to the parents' bedroom, and so on.

The mother frequently and markedly disapproves of the child's behavior although she encourages him to stand on his own feet—all of which increases the child's sense of being small and his doubts about his own worth. The parents give in to the child, let him sleep in their bedroom, and so on.

Responsiveness with anxiety is apparent in younger children in this age group who are attached to their mothers but retain her love by overcompliance. They do what she says without question, for which they receive her praise. While they can be separated from her for reasonable periods of time without too much worry, essentially they are fearful of being left. Anxiety symptoms that denote the source of these fears may be observed in their play activity.

Such behavior is commonly precipitated when the mother's love is conditioned on perfectionism, with the child sometimes interpreting obedience more literally than the parent intended.

SELF-IDENTITY

In these families the self-identity development of the child through his fifth year follows a typical pattern. Acceptance of self-feeding, self-dressing, independence in toilet habits, and verbal communication with the parents characteristically are achieved by the child at the time appropriate to his maturative level. However, feeding problems and rejection of sleeping schedules often occur in the four- and five-year-old as symptoms of regression.

Regression due to the birth of a sibling, exacerbated by the mother's recognition of this phenomenon of regression but non-acceptance of these slipbacks, accounts for most of the problems pertaining to self-reliance.

SOCIALIZATION

The children give evidence that they have some measure of security with their mother despite the fact that they are beset by anxiety. Their defenses against the discomfort of this insecurity take the form of early developed neurotic symptoms that interfere with their adjustment at home more than with their adjustment to playmates. If the condition is not corrected while the child is still small, the symptoms increasingly absorb his psychic energies, making concentration at school age difficult. There are characteristic symptoms:

Toilet training, correctly initiated and timed by the mother, results in few delays in establishment of good habits. Once these habits are ingrained, the children do not tend to regress except as indicated under "self-identity"; rather, they acquire character traits that lay the groundwork for compulsion neuroses expressed in obsessive tendencies.

Playmates of the child's own age are sought and are usually enjoyed. Occasionally, a child may prefer to play by himself and appears to be either bored by, or timid with, other children.

Play interests display imagination combined with realism, for the most part. Certain of the more passive, overanxious children are made fearful by play or stories which stimulate fantasies of behavior forbidden by the parent. For example, a three-year-old child who has been made to feel excessively guilty if she has an "accident" (wetting) cannot bear to listen to the song "I'm a little teapot." The association of word sound requires no comment. It frightens her. Another, who feels she is "bad," because of meaningless and frequent spanking by her mother, expresses her self-doubts and relieves guilt in compulsive play by repeatedly spanking her dolls, admonishing them in the fashion of her mother.

LATENCY AND ADOLESCENCE

In latency and adolescence, as in early childhood, a particular boy or girl in the perfectionistic family may display symptoms that denote developmental problems of greater intensity than those of the average child. This is usually the child who is not wholly accepted by his mother because of her strong tendency to associate him with the deprivations she suffered during her husband's absence in military service, or when they were just establishing their home. In the sample studied, the children so identified were mostly boys. However, in the majority of latency children of this family type, the boys gave evidence of identifying with the father's interests and the girls with their mother's dominant traits. In adolescence, however, this is less true of girl children, who are apt to form a highly ambivalent tie to the mother and a positive one to the father.

The diagnostic and prognostic implications of behavior symptoms of all children in the perfectionistic family must always be interpreted in the light of a distinctive parental response; namely, the parents' acknowledged concern and the steps undertaken to modify the situation for the child. Although the majority of parents probably seek outside guidance at the suggestion of someone else, they feel that they should be able to handle the problem alone, they have some idea as to the cause, and will assume personal responsibility.

LOVE RELATIONSHIPS

The parental qualities emulated by the latency child and the adolescent will be indicative of a meaningful emotional tie with one or both parents, albeit one based on guilt and anxiety. The most characteristic pattern is a reciprocal identification of boy with father and of girl with mother—with a conflicted emotional tie to the second parent. The particular source of anxiety varies with the individual child and the parent. As manifested in attitude and behavior, the following symptoms are common:

Meaningful identification with one parent and provocative aggression to the other are characteristic. With boys in the latency and adolescent group, provocative behavior is usually directed toward the mother. They try to start arguments; are "sassy"; retaliate with purposive "accidents" in response to punishment—kick out the screen door, pretend not to hear her directions, and so on.

Generally, there is a passive rapport between father and son. Occasionally, however, there is a mixture of provocative behavior and positive identification. For example, a twelve-year-old boy glories in aggravating his father by being overly good in his presence, superficially polite, always saying "yes, ma'am" and "yes, sir"; whines, "I can't do it without your help"; definitely wants to be a policeman like his father. Annoying and incomprehensible to the parents is the fact that many of these boys can do things adequately alone but protest parental direction or act only if an authoritative approach is taken by the father.

Identification with the mother's self-assertive traits is most typical of the girl child in latency who emulates her mother's more volatile emotional expressions. For this behavior she may get temporary disapproval but not rejection. The girl child, typically, speaks her own mind; expresses anger, frustration, and gladness; watches her mother, then acts as she does. Commonly mixed with this reaction is an exaggerated need to be with the mother. In both instances, the maternal response denotes a certain pleasure in her daughter's spunkiness, as well as interest in being near her. The clinging pattern is related primarily to sibling rivalry, particularly if the girl is the oldest child in the family.

In adolescence, the girl is apt to continue the first part of the identification pattern but to transfer her allegiance to the father, standing up for him against the mother.

Sibling rivalry in the perfectionistic family assumes more than average intensity, due to the particular emotional structure of the family. As contrasted with those of the unsocial family class, for example, parents of the perfectionistic family are upset by the rivalries and competition among children, as well as by their own inability to handle the state of affairs thus created. As a result, they provide the children with an emotional situation which invites further provocation. The following points of conflict in sibling rivalry are typical, resulting mostly from the child's earlier feelings of having been displaced in the affections of the parent at the birth of a brother or sister.

Boys persistently tease their younger sisters, quarrel over choice of television programs and the right to use playthings, consider girls a nuisance, and so on, while girls take a similar attitude toward younger brothers.

What constitutes the problem in the perfectionistic family is the fact that the children use sibling rivalry to control their parents. The extremes of sadistic, cruel behavior, physical battles, and total depreciation of siblings are not characteristic of these children. However, the persistence into latency of sibling jealousies characteristic of the two- and three-year-old, and the focus on the status of boys *vs.* girls, if not corrected, will reinforce unhealthy forms of male-female competition that will carry over into adulthood.

SELF-IDENTITY

Behavior indicative of the latency and adolescent child's self-assertiveness, his development of native talents, his use of socially adaptive skills, based on a belief in his own integrity, are more firmly established for the girls than for the boys in the perfectionistic family. Independence in caring for personal needs, helping with assigned home tasks, managing an allowance, and so on, are the rule for both, with periodic stubbornness induced by parental perfectionistic standards.

This is accomplished in most instances as a result of the exaggerated premium placed by parents on perfection in adaptive skills and the quality of self-reliance expected. The child's surface adjustment is thus overcompensatory, rather than firm, because it covers a basic deficiency in self-esteem. Psychodynamically, the perfectionism of the parents' ideal for independence, achievement, and self-reliance amounts to the unattainable for the child. Thus he experiences repeated "failures," regardless of how well he achieves realistic goals. In this sense, success is unrewarding because it is never enough or quite right. Self-depreciation and self-doubt ensue because the child has been made to feel unduly guilty over his inadequacies. Underneath, however, such a child is angered by meaningless parental demands which, in effect, render him helpless. What to do with his hostility becomes the problem. If he expresses it directly, he runs the risk of further parental rejection for showing his hostility, which his conscience tells him is dangerous. His provocative behavior is the defense he uses to protect his self-integrity. Such behavior also meets the anxiety and unhappiness induced by the dictates of his harsh and cruel conscience; that is, making his parents angry at him temporarily resolves his guilt and gives him justification for showing his displeasure toward them— "kicking out the screen." For these children, the defenses are mainly against the superego, as well as against provocative elements in the environment.

Both boys and girls are, as a rule, in their appropriate grade placement and derive pleasure from their studies. Among boys, academic problems are apt to be centered in particular subjects, such as reading. Girls are less likely to have difficulties with their schoolwork.

School attendance is readily accepted. Misbehavior occurs mainly outside the classroom; for example, the child may cause a disturbance on the school bus. Truancy and other forms of uncooperativeness with school personnel are not typical. If persistent misbehavior occurs in the classroom it consists of talking out of turn or protective lying to cover up mistakes.

SOCIALIZATION

These children show an interest in seeking and keeping friends of their own age, of both sexes, and in participating in social activities. However, it is difficult for some of the older children in the perfectionistic family to share in competitive games and other forms of social exchange.

The girls adapt to most aspects of social life more readily than do the boys. Diagnostically and prognostically, there is the wish to have friends, but prestige conflicts often hamper them. Their behavior usually is in approximate conformance to the rules of social behavior of the larger community.

Social adjustment is commonly evidenced in characteristic ways:

Actively seeking and keeping friends in their own age group is typical of the girl children. They try to get along with others; are cooperative rather than dominating in games and social affairs; are relatively at ease with both sexes and in rapport with adults.

Prestige conflicts, which occur mainly in boy children, arise from having to win in competitive games, or they "won't play." They may show preference for friends from broken families.

For the boys, these prestige conflicts directly reflect the parents' perfectionistic expectations. They are *not* disliked, but they become unhappy because they conclude that they must be disliked by their friends if they are not at the top or in control in all competitive activities. Their selection of friends from broken homes, or of a different nationality, causes their parents some concern. For the boys, this is an attempt to create a social situation in which they can feel less personal pressure for perfection. At the same time, they express resentment toward the parents by doing what they know will bother them. This is a reversal, of a sort, of the parental standards. However, the results are socially benign in that the friends selected ordinarily do not get the boys into too much difficulty in the community.

MARITAL FUNCTIONS

For the husband and wife of the perfectionistic family, the marriage relationship also must meet preconceived ideas of "perfection." They must succeed in making a "go of it," "stick it out" if at all possible. The partners believe they are trying to work things out on the principle of "equality," "sharing," "compromise," and consideration. However, "sharing" for them means "informing" the other, not exchanging ideas with him. In essence, there is intellectual rather than emotional appreciation of what is really involved in learning to live with a spouse according to the principles of reciprocity and mutual readjustment. This is characteristic of at least one partner and sometimes of both. Although a marriage based on mutuality is the conscious ideal, seldom does either partner feel that these goals are satisfactorily fulfilled, nor, in fact, is there evidence that they have been.

The perfectionistic goals themselves are the cause of the marital dysfunctioning and reflect intrinsic sensitivities in the partners' own personalities. This degree of perfectionism is actually a defense deriving from excessive fear of criticism should failure result. Thus disillusionment is inescapable for both marital partners. This is difficult to bear, and pride demands that the reasons be accounted for. At least one of these particular partners readily offers some personal inadequacies as an explanation for marital failure. Because the more adult part of their personalities rejects (makes them feel guilty over) these essentially infantile attempts to receive love without giving love (perfect dependency), they take the opposite stand (reaction formation) of expecting perfection from themselves and from their partner. The emphasis on perfection rather than on some other quality grows out of the particular attitude of their own parents, as detailed in the family of origin history.

Although masochistic character traits are present, these partners rarely revel in self-flagellation. Another distinctive feature is that the character neuroses are usually more incapacitating in one partner than in the other. Thus the more adaptable partner is better able to keep the marital relationship in relative balance.

Reciprocal Love Relationships
OUTSIDE THE SEXUAL ACT

The tenderness, consideration, and affection reciprocated between the marital partners of the perfectionistic family are conditioned by specific predilections contained in their personalities. In the wife there is: (1) oversensitivity to criticism as a wife and mother; and/ or (2) acceptance of her own adequacy, with the wish to instill in her spouse greater self-confidence. In the husband, there is: (1) oversensitivity to making mistakes or being impeachable; and/or (2) acceptance of, and high regard for, his wife's ability to do things better than he can.

The precise emotional tenor of the love relationship is dependent upon which traits predominate or are fused in the respective partners. In general, there is present, in at least one partner, ungrudging consideration, affection, and interest in alternation, with a response that reduces genuine intimacy. In the other, this pattern will be more distorted. Responses upsetting to the love relationship in greater or lesser degree are apt to stem from the following aims, as expressed in attitude and behavior:

Opportunistic aims take the form of giving love and consideration so long as the relationship offers the chance for narcissistic identification with the spouse on the basis of his work achievement, or attributing to him idealized qualities which the partner himself would like to possess. Typical is a "pushing" for acceleration in achieving success. Narcissistic identification does not include emphasis upon accumulation of material possessions per se, nor vicarious gratification in the other's overaggressive behavior, sexual aberration, and so forth.

Retentive withholding aims take the form of allocating to, and receiving love and consideration from, the spouse in whatever order and at whatever time best suits the partner concerned. Absent are cruel, restraining, stubborn patterns of minute control.

Competitive jealousy is expressed in oversensitivity to real or imagined intruders upon the love relationship—children, mother-in-law, other men or women. Accompanying this jealousy are also feelings of self-criticism and responsibility based on the wish to hold the love of the partner. Usually absent are greatly distorted projections and delusional paranoic reactions.

The marital relationship can become highly charged, with recriminations for both husband and wife. The husband may respond with affection if the wife shows appreciation of him, which "she should do." He hates to feel but does feel, obligated and under constant pressure never to be at fault. If he concedes that she can do things better than he, then she should not need reassurance of his interest. The wife also emphasizes the husband's lack of appreciation, her unmet need for shared emotional bolstering, and, even if she is the more capable, is irritated because he is not more aggressive.

After an emotional crisis deriving from these dynamics there is usually a swing to the other side: "We're both unhappy and don't like this lack of intimacy"; "She's all right if she'd appreciate me a little more and consent to intercourse"; "He's good except for this angry episode"; "I'm partially responsible," and so on.

WITHIN THE SEXUAL ACT

There is usually present in the male partner an orientation to genital sexuality wherein the object (female) is normal and the fundamental nature of the striving is basically undisturbed. In the female, both the nature of the sexual striving and the object (male) are essentially normal. Various forms of foreplay may be a part of the sexual act but, generally speaking, are not the main objectives constituting ends in themselves.

Tendencies that interfere with the male's full achievement of sexual gratification are related to guilt and anxiety in the performance of the sexual act itself. The specific inhibiting factors may stem from a variety of factors. Diagnostically, it is significant that sexual energies not directly expressed due to inhibitions characteristically achieve an outlet in some form of creative activity. Frequently, there is a sufficiently strong incentive for increased satisfaction in the sexual act to cause the male to seek insight into the emotionally inhibiting factors which prevent this. A great deal depends upon the female partner's orientation to sexuality as to how successfully these problems can be modified without the use of intensive psychiatric treatment.

The male partner is frequently shy in performance of the sexual act, with varying degrees of impotency and dissatisfaction resulting. He is often described by the female partner as being considerate and interested, usually taking the initiative. Typically, the husband acknowledges that his wife is not too responsive, but he does not mind so long as she permits intercourse. In general, the male partner is less conflicted and able to attain a greater degree of freedom and sexual maturity than the female.

The factor which interferes with the female partner's full attainment of sexual satisfaction is the feeling that somehow sex is "bad" and therefore cannot be enjoyed. From childhood she retains exaggerated fears of supposed dangers adherent to sexual intercourse with orgasm. The point of conflict rests in her inability to reconcile the desire to derive pleasure therefrom with her guilt feelings which ensue if the wish is acknowledged and achieved. On the one hand, the female acts strangely victimized by, but fascinated with, the sexual role although it is unacceptable because of the anxiety that acceptance creates. The source and content of the anxiety can stem from many factors, depending upon the particular individual. Most frequent are neurotic fears that can be traced to the feeling that her mother would disapprove. In other cases, the female fears that somehow she will herself be harmed; in still others, to take responsibility for full participation in the sexual act means to relinquish the right to be dependent and taken care of.

In the female partner, attitudes and practices frequently include: submission to the sexual act because of duty, thus avoiding admission of sexual urges; experience of orgasm although intercourse is a forbidden pleasure; the inclination to postpone or refuse sexual intercourse although it is enjoyed; reluctant admission that "on occasion" intercourse is a pleasant but necessary marital responsibility; confusion about her inability to enjoy sexual relations, based upon the unfounded idea that her mother felt the same way.

Self-identity

As a rule, the perfectionistic couple's marriage partnership is not used as a vehicle for sustaining grossly distorted concepts of self-identity. At least one partner places value on the spouse's male or female identity, the particular family function for which he is responsible, with realistic confidence in his performance, but this usually alternates with attitudes that also induce in the other partner feelings of self-depreciation. This alternation of respect and depreciation creates problems in the marriage partnership and is characteristically manifested by one or more of the following:

Emotional withdrawal of confidence takes the form of preoccupation with work, business associates, household tasks, and community activities and is accompanied by unverbalized feelings of being unappreciated or unworthy (mild depression).

Personal devaluation by the female is expressed by nagging about the insufficient help given her in necessary home tasks and her spouse's selfish interest in business or outside associates. The male's criticisms of his wife are that she does not "give enough" in the sexual act or that she is not as competent a housekeeper as his standards demand.

If there is personal devaluation of the partner's sex identity or if there is criticism of the way in which he carries his particular responsibility, competitive jealousy symptoms in love relationships as well as opportunistic narcissistic aims are nearly always present.

Socialization

There are present in at least one partner attitudes that encourage good health practices and recuperation if either one is physically disabled; foster recovery of emotional equilibrium if there is mental illness; support reestablishment of self-control if behavior is over-aggressive or self-destructive. Such concern is frequently typical of both partners.

Similarly, in measures undertaken for his own and the partner's welfare at least one partner assumes actual responsibility. Although frustration and anxiety may be moderately high, retaliatory competitive and obstructionist tactics do not predominate. It may be necessary for one partner to overadapt to the inadequacies of the other if the necessary treatment is to be obtained for the ailing spouse. This does not ordinarily result in indefinite delays to the detriment of the affected partner or family. In the process, however, overanxiety may ensue as a symptom of unacknowledged resentment over the "defect" and momentarily may cloud realistic evaluation of the facts.

PROBLEM-SOLVING

The decisions made and actions taken pertaining to work, the marriage, and child rearing are conceived by at least one partner to be matters of compromise. However, individual conflicts in both partners are likely to interfere with judicious decisions in the resolution of problems of child rearing and the marital relationship. Essentially, the partners are inhibited or overconstricted in facing issues in this regard.

In behavior, inhibition and overconstriction are most commonly manifested in deliberate suppression of discussion and/or in overstriving and conscientiousness in coping independently with problems. The purpose in "solving" the problem by not discussing it is to avoid friction. There is no actual refusal or protest against discussion but rather avoidance of an unpleasant situation (usually by the male). Mutual concurrence is not possible when these symptoms exist.

Overstriving takes the form of continuously trying to solve and to take responsibility for problems in order to dispel the anxiety of self-doubt and tendencies toward self-depreciation. The solution of the difficulty is felt to be beyond the individual's capacity, and periodically the anxiety thus created (usually in the female) interferes with judgment in taking action.

Problems of the marriage partnership as they relate to feeling loved and appreciated as a male or as a female are of particular concern to these partners. The incentive to work out differences that engender insecurity, hostility, frustration, is sufficiently strong in at least one partner that it usually leads to some modification of the situation for the better. In other words, the perfectionism does not prevent the majority of partners from seeking help but encourages it for three reasons. Lack of success or the threat of failure crumples the controlling perfectionistic defense. When this occurs, a sense of helplessness ensues and is recognized for what it is. Fear of loss of control thus leads to doing something to restore the balance. Although feelings in the marriage relationship may be highly charged, the response to casework and/or psychotherapy is generally positive, if we may judge by results in the sample studied.

FINANCIAL FUNCTIONS

The perfectionistic family maintains its economic self-sufficiency and manages its financial affairs satisfactorily. The marriage partners share a belief that income production and management are requisite to the creation and maintenance of their family.

Income Production

Division of labor for providing income is nearly always planned; conflicting views on this score rarely occur. When both parents agree to assume joint responsibility for support of the family it is usually to supplement the husband's inadequate earnings and is not ordinarily related to the wife's avoidance of parental responsibilities or her competition with the husband. Occasionally, her employment threatens the husband's work status and thus appears as a symptom of dysfunctioning in the marital relationship.

The male wage earner in this family type derives a relatively high degree of satisfaction from being a productive person. He works cooperatively with others or as a leader, as the case may be. An ordinary amount of appreciation and encouragement is needed from the spouse or employer, but in the main, interest is self-sustained. Although successful in their work, certain of these wage earners are apt to feel overanxious about being productive in their own right, continuing to strive but depreciating their essential abilities. The wife usually supplies the realistic encouragement needed to keep her husband's self-esteem and work performance intact. However, this may become a point of conflict which represents a displacement of problems that rightfully belong in the affectional and sexual area of the marital relationship.

The male's behavior in his job situation is generally reliable. Changes of occupation, if any, are made because of better opportunities; the type of work selected is regular; reprimand or dismissal for inefficiency or cause is not typical. The occupational choice may vary considerably from semiskilled labor to self-employment to a profession. This wage earner is reasonably well-qualified for his chosen work.

Income Management

Male heads of these families learn from their own families of origin to place value on providing the physical necessities of food, clothing, shelter, and medical needs for themselves and others. Their intention is to be the main providers, and requisite living standards are usually realistically conceived. Judgment is exercised in anticipating and meeting the actual needs of the family.

The provider uses the money available to him for the maintenance of the family. In the main this is given ungrudgingly. Debts may be incurred, but these generally are amortized within the allotted time and by ordinarily accepted means.

Planning of expenditures is of great importance to at least one partner. Usually, actual spending of income is delegated to a single partner, mutually agreed upon. Here again, the concept of sharing is accepted, but often this consists of "informing" rather than discussing the issues. This does not result in ill-advised expenditures or unrealistic management but becomes a source of resentment. The more passive partner, who does not protest the arrangement, often interprets lack of sharing as a sign that his spouse considers his ideas worthless.

There also is apt to be concern about overspending, rigid avoidance of debts, and adherence to budgeting. When this is not characteristic of both, it is generally a trait of the husband, who then tries to "teach" his wife better habits, frequently worsening her feelings rather than improving her practices. However, actual management is satisfactory, with these overexacting tendencies becoming one aspect of the more basic problems of marital unhappiness.

ADULT CHARACTERISTICS
Physical Condition and Intelligence

Physical disability, when present in the male adult, is apt to be some cardiac involvement known to be associated with tension and anxiety. For all practical purposes, such disabilities are not incapacitating to everyday functioning. Physical illness is managed well, so far as following medical directions is concerned, particularly on the part of the male partner.

Impairments of intelligence are not characteristic of the marital partners of the perfectionistic family. In view of the particular social and emotional strivings of these partners, it is improbable that a "defective" mate would be selected.

Ego Defenses

Starting with the perfectionistic family and proceeding through the unsocial family, a progressive range of degrees of regression or fixation [1] in the adult marital partners might correspond with increasing degrees of severity in individual psychopathology. Manifested evidence in the dominant partner, or both, of the breakdown from the normal more nearly corresponds to what takes place in obsessive compulsive character types. As compared with those of the partners in the other family groups, the ego defenses of the perfectionistic family partners are of a better and higher order (75).

In many males in this family type, aggressivity has been channeled primarily through sublimation, displacement, and reaction formation, in work, constructing things, physical activity. Sexual energies are sublimated or inhibited when they are not directly expressed.

Denial is also used as a defense against unpleasant external stimuli. The defense prominently used to ward off anxiety or inner tension is inhibition and reaction formation against impulses of aggressivity. Use of projection and acting-out behavior as a neurotic defense is not typical.

The intensity of emotional need which cannot delay immediate gratification is low; rather, there is some motivation, in most instances, to undertake the solution of a problem. Ego-alien impulses are not expressed in acts of an antisocial nature. Ego defenses of the males are more flexible and their use less exaggerated than in the other three family classes.

The female partner of the perfectionistic family adopts one or more of the following defense mechanisms in support of repression: overcompensation; or restitution in provocative behavior, denial, and inhibition. In some instances, psychosomatic complaints are a part of the clinical picture.

By overcompensation in maternal activities and looking after others, the mother covers up guilt feelings and keeps her hostility repressed. She also replaces nonacceptable sexual feelings with shyness and denial of deriving any gratification therefrom. In provoca-

[1] Pertains to psychological development (psychosexual and ego).

tive behavior, she expresses her own hostile feelings by inducing another to attack first. Thus, her own aggressive behavior appears as self-defense, for which she cannot be criticized. Accompanying these various defenses are periodic anxiety reactions. Anxiety per se, however, is not a mechanism of defense. It appears when other defenses do not effectively repress the nonacceptable impulses.

Although repression is a universal mechanism and has an outstanding significance in all psychopathology, its use in blocking out large tracts of feeling is not characteristic of the majority of females of this family class. In general, tolerance for anxiety is greater here than in female partners of other classes, stimulating action for solution of problems rather than immobilization. Use of pathological forms of projection, extreme repression, evasion of responsibility, overoptimism, and acting out as neurotic defenses are not prominent.

Emotional Stability

As in all family classes, psychotic breaks may occur. To a greater degree than in the other classes, the remaining spouse tempers the bad effects of this condition on the children, usually taking a responsible attitude for securing treatment for the afflicted partner. It is not the presence or absence of psychotic illness that distinguishes the familial pattern, but the way in which the heads of the family respond to this particular stress. This emphasis on the significance of the characteristic emotional and behavior responses of the spouses to such crises differentiates family diagnosis from individual diagnosis. In the perfectionistic family, at least one partner acts or can act responsibly with some guidance.

The chances of severe mental disturbance affecting the male or the female partners are about equal. However, a serious psychotic illness is likely to occur in only one partner. Most often occurring in the sample studied were the psychotic disorders generally classified as "affective reactions." These psychoses are marked by severe disorders of mood, with resultant disturbance of thought and behavior in consonance with the affect. The type most frequently found was manic-depressive reaction, depressed type (a borderline psychosis diagnosed as severe phobic neurosis); anxiety was also present. Schizophrenic and paranoid reactions were not present and are not thought to be characteristic of the partners of this family class. Other diagnosed emotional disorders fell mainly in the classifications of personality trait disturbance with character neurosis, mostly compulsive personality with anxiety and obsessive reactions (75).

CHILD CHARACTERISTICS
Physical Condition and Intelligence

Physical, intellectual, and emotional processes are factors known to be associated with capacity for social functioning. Physical and intellectual impairments are rarely present in the children of the perfectionistic family; thus their problems of adaptation are predominantly traceable to disturbances in emotional development.

Intelligence tends to be well within the normal range and is sometimes superior. Sitting, walking, talking, and the development of cognitive powers are characteristically normal. The children's physical health is good, and they are not subject to chronic or acute illnesses.

In the sample studied only an occasional child suffered from a physical disability. In large measure, these instances were handled realistically by the parent without increasing the secondary gain element. If a child should contract a disease, recovery is usually uneventful. However, one could predict that should a child develop chronic illness or should he be mentally deficient, these parents might be overanxious and feel guilty. At the same time, there is also the strong likelihood that at least one parent would be able to view the problem with some objectivity and act in behalf of the child's best interests, either independently or with outside guidance.

Attention paid to health and nutritional needs by the parents probably accounts for the children's well-being, as well as the fact that illness is not given undue importance as a means for resolving emotional conflicts. The exception might be in the case of a psychotic parent whose illness has psychosomatic features.

Psychic Disturbance

The psychic disturbances in the latency children of the perfectionistic family suggest that they possess better integrative capacities for adjustment than do many children in the other family classes. Only when a symptom remains fixed in spite of its interfering with social adaptation are emotional conditions considered pathological in childhood. In two thirds of the perfectionistic families studied, with children in their sixth year and through the twelfth year, one child or more per family suffered from a psychic disturbance. Present in a single child were two or more of the following types of disorders: infantile phenomena; motor disorders; conduct disorders; common neuroses. From clinical observation it is known that these several types of emotional disturbance never occur in isolation. If one is present there will always be a second, even a third, and so on. The two most prominent constellations in the child of the perfectionistic family are conduct disorders and neuroses, with motor disorders as a third factor in a substantial number. Psychoses and vegetative disorders were not present, and infantile phenomena very rarely occurred.

The type of conduct disorder that occurs most frequently is provocative behavior in response to the environment. This interferes chiefly with the child's social living at home, but in some instances in the community as well. The behavior is mainly in reaction to one of the parents, with alternating defiance and submission, frequently accompanied by a motor disorder and lack of concentration as an aspect of neurotic traits or neuroses. Such disorders as aggressive, destructive, self-punishing behavior, sadistic cruelties, sexual delinquency, and avoidance of close relationships are unusual.

The adolescent child of the perfectionistic family is apt to suffer from two main types of disturbances: (1) sudden withdrawal of emotional ties from one or both parents; and (2) lack of any outward evidence of adolescent inner unrest.

In the instance of sudden transfer of emotional attachment from the parent to someone outside the family, the adolescent is prone to identify with contemporaries, forming emotional attachments to friends of both sexes. These friends usually are not "undesirable" nor are they apt to be delinquent. Consequently, the adolescent's new allegiances do not get him into trouble insofar as antisocial behavior is concerned. This adolescent generally remains in the home as an "inconsiderate boarder," so to speak. Indifference characterizes the behavior toward the mother; for example, one girl did not speak to her mother but remained quiet and withdrawn or was highly critical of her mother when punished. This sudden breaking of the tie to the parent of the same sex is pathological and affords the girl little emotional support in handling her sexual impulses through identification with her mother during this important period.

The male adolescent may follow the same pattern, but in the cases studied he was more inclined to continue to be the "good" child of latency, wrapped up in family relationships rather than making a thrust toward independence. The exaggeration of this reluctance to grow up is not extensive but does represent an over-strict conscience which acts as a barrier against the normal maturative process. Typical are consideration of the mother, unusual in the normal adolescent boy, and submissiveness to the father. An example is a seventeen-year-old boy who was interested in going to college and whose plans were encouraged by his father. He never caused any trouble—but at this age he was still having reading difficulties that required a tutor. Clinical studies (Klein 99, 1949) show that reading problems are four times more common among boys than among girls. They are often associated with a strong oral dependent attachment of the boy to the mother, coupled with fear of a stern father or with passive homosexual feelings for a nonassertive father.

In the sample the latter constellation was typical. The psychodynamics in the cases in question are explained by the fact that reading difficulties are frequently accompanied by an intrinsic and persistent curiosity that requires participation of an adult for its satisfaction. That is to say, an adult must *tell* the child about the subject matter; it is not emotionally "safe" for him to read or find things out for himself. This was the case in the adolescents of the sample studied. In this type of father-son relationship, the strong passive wishes of the adolescent toward the father make him shrink from finding things out for himself. For, in essence, to find things out for one's self denotes for such an adolescent not only independence but also curiosity; the curiosity about learning thus becomes unconsciously equated with sexuality, a forbidden interest.

The repressive attitude and moralistic values given to sexual interests by the parents of the perfectionistic family account for this arrestment in the psychosocial development which is a particular manifestation in certain adolescents. Not only are difficulties in reading an expression of this inherent repressive attitude toward normal sexual interests, but also the reading difficulty itself is a form of rebellion against assuming a more grown-up attitude of finding out things for oneself.

More severe forms of psychic disturbances are not as common in this as in other family classes.

MALE PARTNER'S FAMILY OF ORIGIN

Characteristically, the structure of the family of origin of the male partner of the perfectionistic family is remarkably stable and does not of itself account for his problems of adjustment as husband and father. His own father and mother are likely to have been present during the male partner's formative years and through his adolescence. Breach of this contact, if it occurred, seldom came before his adolescence, and was usually caused by divorce. Atypical are traumas of separation associated with death of a parent, desertion, absence due to criminality, mental illness, physical illness, or abandonment. Rarely if ever were substitute child care arrangements experienced. In such an event, the remaining own parent characteristically assumed responsibility with the temporary aid of relatives until remarriage. The male partner also tends to sustain continuous contact with his own children by his physical presence in the home.

Adequacy of Financial Support

The fathers, in the perfectionistic male partners' families of origin, usually were the main providers for the family and assumed this function responsibly and adequately except during conditions of economic depression. These fathers placed emphasis on work, thrift, paying debts. Their sons were expected to earn as soon as they were able; if necessary, they often contributed to the support of the family. A moral aspect colors these parental expectations.

Work was something to be done with no questions asked and no differences of opinion with the parent voiced.

The male may recall that when he was a boy "there was no escape from my parents' wishes"; "My father expected obedience without having to explain the 'whys and wherefores'"; "My mother was more understanding."

There is little indication that in childhood these males were cruelly punished or sadistically treated as an end in itself. Although not feeling close to their fathers, many will reveal their identification with both the positive and negative aspects of the paternal personality. There may be the unwelcome realization: "I am treating my family the same way my father treated me—expecting them to be unimpeachable and faultless"; "I respect him although he never understood my feelings"; "As an active, energetic man I can appreciate the defeatist attitude he took after his paralytic stroke."

To feel adequate in their occupations is important to these men as heads of their own families. Real pleasure in a job well done is experienced by those males in whom the self-reproach pattern is not extreme and inflexible. Many others, however, admittedly or not, will be beset by self-doubts which their actual ability and efficiency do not warrant. Job pressures, intensified by the cultural premium placed on success, weigh heavily upon their guilt-ridden shoulders. For these particular men the moral connotation given to an imperfect performance is expressed in the following symptoms: inordinate amounts of overtime or homework; distrust of their own ideas but also a feeling of guilt because "I hesitate to make them known, feeling the boss will think they aren't any good"; "I feel I am a success but some of my friends are better; I should be too"; "I dare not take my off hours at the clinic. Should something go wrong I won't be there but I'll be blamed."

Love Relationships

The feature most prominent in the perfectionistic male's family of origin is the absence of overtly manifested and verbally expressed feelings of affection communicated from parent to child, particularly from father to son. The father tended to be undemonstrative, accepting the son's behavior as the latter submitted to correction and direction, irrespective of his need for spontaneous behavior. Although not seductive with their sons, mothers commonly encouraged a close emotional tie. In the sample studied, all males happened to be the eldest or youngest sons in their families of origin; their mothers often had only a moderate liking for their son's wife, feeling that she was not "good enough." Although they did not actively oppose the marriage, in a sense they sought to perpetuate the mother-son tie.

The factor that interferes most with the male's adult love relationships derives from two sources: (1) the moralistic connotation given by his parents to the sexual act; (2) the aggressive or independent action, outside the prescribed parental standard, which was considered reprehensible.

Nevertheless, there is evidence that some parent must have paid attention to these males when they were children and that they were cared for, although not wholly in the way they would have liked. It must have been worth their while to conform, with some hoped-for recompense influencing their wish to please, because in adulthood they are able to relate to others. They can be considerate of their families and also possess the wish, if not the fully developed capacity, to have a mutually satisfying sexual relationship with a female.

However, in reviewing the family of origin pattern it will be seen that sex was rarely discussed freely between father and son. Therefore, little recognition was given at adolescence to the presence of sexual urges in the male child. Thus the male partner came to feel that sexual feelings were something he should not readily acknowledge. As a result, he entered marriage with an inhibited attitude but not an essentially feminine orientation.

Self-identity

In his family of origin, the perfectionistic family male partner probably will have learned two basic ways in which to handle his aggressive impulses: (1) to withdraw from controversial situations; (2) to turn such impulses inward, blaming himself. There is frequently a fusing of these two. This derives from a familial atmosphere in which parental exactness and sternness equated the child's questioning and disagreement with weakness, defect, and imperfection. This could result only in self-criticism, should the impulse to protest parental standards come to mind. Therefore, if the male partner as a child were to avoid feeling unvalued, mediocre, and hurt, and if he were to placate the pricks of conscience, excessive self-control became necessary. Because bitterness of feeling over this state of affairs does not vanish into thin air, the male, in adulthood, has come to feel "I never can do anything right; there must be something wrong with me. But I must keep trying to pass muster. I can't be second, third, or fourth-rate."

Common symptoms of such childhood conflicts, manifested in the adult male of the perfectionistic family, are as follows:

In the work situation, aspects of these character traits stand them in good stead but at tremendous emotional cost: "I haven't blown my top on the job for fifteen years"; "If your intentions are good you don't make a mistake."

Within the intimacy of child rearing these sensitive points are not so easily avoided: "I can't make a mistake in front of my children"; "I have a chronic dislike of arguments," meaning that "problems will go away if we don't talk about them." As growing children manifest signs of aggressivity, these problems do not go away by avoidance. In spite of himself, the male is provoked to anger and becomes upset on two scores—because of showing his own hostility and because of feeling second-rate as a father.

In the marital relationship the wish to avoid personality conflicts makes the resolution of differences and the mending of hurt feelings a difficult job. This is compounded by the male's need to deny resentment of the one closest to him who has a right to make emotional demands. "Hurt" is the term often used to express this resentment, denoting his sensitivity to acknowledging hostile feelings, as well as his damaged pride.

Ordinarily, the main source of unhappiness in the love relationship, both in and apart from the sexual act, leads to temporary estrangement and an impoverishment of the marriage relationship. In most instances, there is an avowed affection for the marital partner. In child rearing also, there will be evident some positive identification with the children.

Socialization

Standards of social behavior, personal responsibility for self-criticism, and consideration of others were defined and established by the parents in the male's family of origin according to an over-strict interpretation of ethics and moral principles. Either the parental demands required overacquiescence, or the male as a child responded with a greater submission than the parent intended.

Careful supervision of social contacts was common, particularly as these involved boy-girl relationships and the chance of sexual involvement. Often the male child deferred to the parent up to middle adolescence, then broke away by asserting himself in finding his own social interests, type of work, pleasure, and so forth. As a rule, identification with the original family unit is not totally denied. Personal contact may or may not be sustained, but a throwing over of all connections is unusual.

Because of the positive elements in the parental ties, these males have a relatively good social conscience, albeit one that is over-rigid and acts as a constricting influence in certain aspects of social adaptation. They are not susceptible to antisocial behavioral acts, but the nature of their defenses against such impulses can, under certain circumstances, lead to the development of these tendencies in their own children.

FEMALE PARTNER'S FAMILY OF ORIGIN

Two differing types of family structure in the female partner's family of origin tend to produce in her a proneness to feel deficient as wife and mother. The same parental attitudes toward girl children are characteristic of each structure. First is a family background in which the female partner acquired a stepmother when she was three to five years of age, while her own father was restrictive with respect to heterosexual interests. This very situation heightened and complicated the female child's resolution of competitive strivings for the father's interest. Second is a family background in which the female partner's own mother emphasized a career and/or home-maker role, underplaying the pleasures of sexuality, with similar values reinforced by the father. Among female partners of the per-fectionistic family who suffered from psychosis, the degree of pa-thology found in the families of origin was greater than among those not so afflicted, but the dynamic constellation of factors in their family of origin history that produced the psychopathological syn-drome was essentially the same.

In the female partner's family of origin, one or both own parents ordinarily assumed personal responsibility for care of the children. The majority of females had the continuous presence of both own parents, from infancy through adolescence. A smaller but impor-tant group experienced separation from an own mother by reason of her death; or from an own father, usually as a result of the par-ents' divorce. Almost without exception, this breach in contact oc-curred when the female was between three and five years of age, the developmental period when oedipal loves and conflicts are nor-mally very active. Thus this group of female partners showed prob-lems of adult adjustment as wife and mother, reflecting the early oedipal conflicts which surrounded their losing battle for the favored position with their fathers. The resolution of the oedipal attachment was made more difficult by the presence of a stepmother. The pres-ence of a stepfather, in contrast, threatened the dependent relation-ship with the mother.

Substitute parents, in most instances, temporarily or permanently supplemented an own mother or father, with the "normal" family structure eventually reconstituted and maintained. Most of these mothers remarried after a divorce or the death of the spouse. Fol-lowing a mother's death, the father typically remarried, but in the interval did not take the need for a maternal substitute lightly. He remained with his children, relying upon an older daughter or his own mother until the advent of the stepmother. If divorced, he kept contact with the daughter. Thus, stepmothers and stepfathers appeared as the main parental substitute, distinguishing this aspect of the female's family of origin history from that of other classes.

The interval between the loss of an own father and the acquisition of a stepfather was apt to be greater than between the death of an own mother and the father's remarriage. However, these families of origin notably dealt with such events in ways that tended to lessen rather than to heighten the possible damaging effects of separation of a child from an own parent. Use of foster homes, institutional placement, or reliance on community agencies were not part of the family picture. The simple fact of breach of contact in childhood, under these circumstances, and the remaining parent's attitude do not in themselves explain the female partner's feeling about her role as wife and mother. Her age at the time of the loss and her particular reaction to it must be taken into account in finding the clue to her emotional vulnerabilities in adulthood. Also it should be noted that the family structural histories of the psychotic female partners in this class show a different pattern.

Adequacy of Financial Support

The economic picture in the female partner's family of origin was a stable one, irrespective of variations in family structure. Reasonable financial security was the rule, with parents expecting to take this responsibility and apparently capable of so doing. Fathers were adequate producers of income and providers for their families, supporting mother and children even in the event of divorce. If both parents worked, mothers usually assisted fathers in their business. The occupational range, for example, included farmer, salesman, army officer, comptroller, professional singer, and proprietor of own business. Reliance upon community agencies or relatives for financial assistance was not typical—nor were illegal activities or erratic work records.

Thus the female partner as a child and adolescent experienced no marked material deprivation. Her basic physical wants were met without worry, although in some instances too much stress was laid on scrimping and saving.

Administration of domestic affairs was efficiently handled by the mother or stepmother, even if she were employed. In this respect the female was exposed to a maternal pattern which included woman's responsibility for the home. Nevertheless, the female partner's feelings of inadequacy in this area, even though she is a capable adult, have been colored by the conditions under which parental love was given.

Love Relationships

The same essential social and moral views prevailed in the homes of the female partners who had stepmothers as in those where both parents were present. As in the male partner's family of origin, perfectionism was the parental condition of acceptance, with "defects" given a moralistic connotation. In essence, it was acceptable for a daughter to become a wife and mother, or to become a schoolteacher or a secretary, or to enter some other profession. It was not acceptable in the eyes of the parents for the girl child to be interested in becoming a physically attractive female, or to conceive of the sexual act as a pleasurable experience. Childbirth and menstruation were to be "endured" as a woman's lot rather than being interpreted as aspects of femininity which would give the female her sex identity at maturity.

For the female partner who had a stepmother, the conditions under which parental love was given were difficult to identify with certainty. Retrospective material always contains an element of distortion. In view of the circumstances surrounding these partners' early life, recall is even more likely to be inaccurate because an own mother lost by death is apt to be overidealized. Therefore, deservedly or undeservedly, the stepmothers who replaced the mothers of these female partners commonly received the full force of the growing girls' competitive feelings. That which stood out in all such instances was the female partner's recalled "feeling" that her father showed greater solicitousness and indulgence of the stepmother than of her. At the same time, he is remembered as having kept a tight rein on her heterosexual contacts and interests. Stepmothers are remembered as controlling and firm although not "mean" or obdurate; father and stepmother were felt to have excluded her. Although the resulting adult adjustment does not altogether bear this out, there is indication that insufficient help, or the wrong kind, was given the female in developing a sense of her own intrinsic worth. As an adult, she makes independent choices but she does not trust her own judgment. She continues to be plagued by these earlier fears of displeasing the parent.

Typical childhood memories are: "My stepmother always 'babied' my father"; "She was mean to me"; "I couldn't stand up to my stepmother; she even selected my wedding dress and trousseau without consulting me"; "My stepmother forced me to eat everything on my plate—if I didn't, I got the same food at the next meal"; "I never want to be like her"; "Everyone in the family was more capable than I was."

For those females who have their own mothers, the following are common recollections: "There were no shades of gray, everything was black or white with my mother"; "She was always bustling around directing everybody"; "Children were to be seen and not heard; attempts were made to please mother, but everything was always wrong"; "She still tries to tell me how to run my own house."

There is an ever-recurring feeling of personal deficiency, of being taken to task, and of censure. If the mother emphasized domesticity, the female child's interest and performance in this area were felt to have received sparing praise—"It is too little or not enough." If a career or intellectual achievement were highly prized, failure to fulfill these goals according to the parent's own choices and standards called forth the inevitable, "This will never do." Examples of mother-daughter reactions are: "My mother encouraged me to become a professional singer as she was. She is both disappointed and disapproving of me because I did not combine a career and homemaking"; "When I didn't make all A's my mother refused to attend my graduation. I feel as if I let her down"; "Value is placed on money earned, which means success to her."

Sexuality was a subject similarly treated by the parents in all perfectionistic females' families of origin, irrespective of the presence of stepmothers or of own mothers and fathers. Parental attitudes either instilled in the girl child a fear of physical harm or exaggerated guilt in anticipation of the sexual act. Female sexual functions were interpreted as being an inappreciable but necessary part of marriage. Sexual feelings were not to be fully acknowledged, nor could their gratification be enjoyed. Before marriage, ordinary sexual interests of the adolescent were frowned upon. Following are examples of the female partners' recalled parental interpretations of female sexuality:

Among fathers, excessive supervision or restriction of the daughter's contacts with boys was coupled with ambitions for her future along lines the father selected—schoolteaching, excelling in sports, and so on, depending upon his particular bent. More often than not, the father disapproved of but did not actually prevent the girl's marriage.

Mothers also limited the girl's heterosexual interests. The subject of sex in all its aspects was taboo and thus rarely explained. Communicated was the "feeling" that the sexual act was dangerous or dirty, but the harm to come was not specifically identified.

This female partner is apt to remember that as an adolescent she liked her father, had a strong wish to please him, retired in favor of his wishes and ambitions for her. He was, however, not openly seductive, was often referred to as "nice but not too warm": "I admired him but he hardly spoke"; "I did whatever I thought would please him."

The tie to the mother becomes more openly ambivalent the older the female becomes. Essentially, she has identified with her mother's attitudes toward sexuality, but still drives herself to meet her mother's expectations in other areas.

Therefore, as a wife and mother the female partner of the perfectionistic family can never quite let herself enjoy these experiences to the fullest, nor does she feel it is really acceptable to make herself attractive in appearance. For example, among the individuals in the cases studied, one wife came to feel, as a result of casework treatment, that gratification of her sexual impulses was less reprehensible. Subsequently, she found the sexual relationship with her husband greatly improved. However, the reproaching parental voice still haunted her. Her husband reported that the following morning she commented to him: "Now I pay for my fun—I am menstruating"— in other words, retribution for acceptance of the female role.

The fact that many of these women can learn through a relationship with a female caseworker to feel less self-accusing when submitting to the pleasures of the sexual act indicates that the relationship with their own mothers had certain positive aspects. At the same time, own mothers were probably also competitive with their daughters. This is evident from their continued need to outvie them in domestic and career roles. The daughters' solution under these circumstances, because of hurt pride and feelings of guilt, characteristically has been to withdraw or to "retire in favor of someone else"—but with continued self-reproach.

For her, as with her husband, there is always a moral as well as a narcissistic problem at issue. However, she does not give up altogether because the sexual act, homemaking, and motherhood, from which she tends to withdraw, still retain positive values for her.

Self-identity

Other life experiences that tend to increase the female partner's doubt and want of confidence, as a mother and as a wife, concern identifications and rivalries with sisters, aunts, and brothers. These probably represent displacements from own parents but illustrate further the etiological significance of her adult behavior. Commonly found are feelings that a younger sister was more preferred; that older sisters usurped the maternal role and were too "bossy"; that girl cousins were always more popular; and feelings of shame over her own "unattractive" figure.

Illness or death of a female relative or a mother which had been ascribed to the birth process or to some aspect of sexuality occasionally acted as further cause for fear of attaining the full female role. Hushed talk, with moralistic implications of retribution and sin, was communicated to the female child or the adolescent but the real facts were rarely known.

It thus becomes clear why the female partner tends to feel that she is in an "uncertain position" with her husband; to believe that she is "not as efficient as other women"; to consider her mother-in-law "more adequate"—and thus a thorn in her side—with her confidence undermined by her husband's persistent nagging, but finding it necessary to "keep her feelings bottled up." For others it is logical that they emphasize the intellectual—"good English is important"; place their husbands' interests first; are unable to "bear seeing his imperfections"; and are afraid that any show of affection "inevitably leads to the sexual act."

Socialization

Identification with the social values held important in the culture is typical of the parents or parent substitutes of the female partner's family of origin. Level A psychosocial disorders, including antisocial acts, did not appear as problems. Overstrictness on the part of the father in regard to the female's having boy friends, a factor already mentioned, as well as overclose supervision of social contacts were characteristic.

In adulthood, the female partner displays a stern social conscience that rarely is corruptible or results in antisocial behavior. Overcompliance to the mores and a striving for a "good" social adjustment are more usual. Many are active in community affairs and church work.

VI. THE INADEQUATE FAMILY

THE "INADEQUATE FAMILY" has second place in the disordered family types' continuum of increasingly poor resistance to ordinary stresses of familial living. Social functioning is characterized by a too-ready reliance upon others for encouragement, continued support, guidance, and help in resolving problems which the average family would be able to resolve for itself. The aggregate effect, and one which distinguishes this family type, is that this mixture of character traits dominates both partners, a fact which sets the emotional tone of the inadequate family.

As diagnosed by the social caseworker, the disordered symptom picture is apt to consist of both Level A and Level B types of psychosocial disorders. Level A disorders are found in three main areas: (1) child rearing; (2) child; and (3) financial. Level B disorders cover the entire range: (1) child rearing; (2) child; (3) marital; (4) financial; and (5) adult. The distinguishing aspects of each type of disorder derive from the particular nature of the dysfunctioning typical of this family.

CHILD-REARING DISORDERS

Level A child-rearing disorders consist mainly of complaints of parental neglect filed with a children's or family court. Child placement is not too common because responsibility for the affairs of the inadequate family are generally assumed by the family of origin. This close parental tie sometimes works to the advantage but frequently to the detriment of the family's total functioning.

Level B child-rearing disorders are typified by haphazard physical care, questionable habit-training practices, immature affectional responses, limited assistance in guiding development of self-reliance, and poorly implemented rules of social behavior. These parents are not themselves prone to be spontaneously concerned about such lacks in their child-rearing practices. Rather, they will feel helpless, perplexed, and overwhelmed by the situation as family demands increase.

The real significance of the relationship between these child-rearing disorders and resulting disorders in the children is not fully recognized. Mothers tend either to want to dump the matter in the lap of the social caseworker or to verbalize their relief when told what to do. Fathers dislike having to meet such situations at all. They avoid action unless ordered to participate in solving their problems. Sometimes, however, it may be the father who is more ready to accept guidance.

CHILD DISORDERS

The most common Level A psychosocial disorder in the latency child is truancy from school, often with parental permission to stay home "to help." Overtly nonconformist behavior and open defiance are not usual. Delinquency is characteristic mainly of the mentally defective child or of the female adolescent who may become pregnant out of wedlock. In the sample studied, delinquency was confined chiefly to these two types of children. However, the possibility of delinquency in the male child should not be overlooked, particularly since these children, although tending to conform, are also subject to exploitation by others, and their behavior depends upon their particular social milieu. Commitments of a child because of his mental illness are not typical, although school or institutional placement of a mental defective does occur.

The behavior of the school-aged children of the inadequate family is not necessarily viewed as socially undesirable by family, friends, neighbors, teachers. By and large, these children are neither antagonistic to, nor disliked by, their peers; they are likely to be inactive, or overcompliant and ingratiating to adults and those in authority.

MARITAL DISORDERS

Level A marital disorders in the sample studied consisted mainly of separations and desertions. Divorce does not occur with as much regularity as in the egocentric and unsocial family types, although previous marriages may have been so dissolved.

Level B marital disorders arise mainly from dissatisfactions in the emotional give-and-take of the husband-wife relationship. The result in marital functioning is discouragement, frustration, postponement of decisions to resolve problems, or a childlike faith that everything will come out all right as if by "magic." This "magic" orientation on the part of the female partner is associated with Level A separation and desertion as well as with child neglect and dependency.

FINANCIAL DISORDERS

The inadequate family is prone to any kind of financial disorder. At some point in its history the receipt of financial help from relatives is highly probable, as is Level A dependency on total or partial financial assistance from public or private welfare agencies for maintenance or medical care. If the family of origin is financially secure, a financial disorder resulting in Level A dependency will not develop. The basic symptom, however, is no different. Nonsupport at either Level A or B also may appear sporadically.

ADULT DISORDERS

Adult disorders are not apt to be manifested in Level A type of delinquent conduct that becomes punishable by law. Thus, divergent behavior that constitutes a major or minor crime is not typical. Regression into psychotic illness requiring hospitalization is a possibility. However, the incidence of adult psychosis in the sample studied was low in comparison to its occurrence in the other functionally disordered family types.

Level B disorders that reflect the personality functioning of the inadequate family heads generally may be classified by the social caseworker as "immature reactions to responsibility." The main social manifestation will be noted by the partner's need to be prodded, a softness in effort with weak accomplishment, the tendency to turn to another to make decisions, do his thinking, and direct his activities. Physical impairments of a nondisabling nature are fairly common to some female partners; the male partner, however, is generally healthy.

CHILD-REARING FUNCTIONS
Parental Functioning

In most instances, the partners of the inadequate family marry early, expect to have children, establish a home, and raise their progeny within it. More often than not, in the early part of the marriage, there will be on the part of at least one partner, and usually of both, a seeming obsession with the idea of producing children. However, parental goals are founded upon hope rather than on genuine anticipation of what will be involved when they actually have children.

EVENTS AND CIRCUMSTANCES

A seemingly contradictory element—an unwillingness to be burdened with the responsibilities of child care—negates somewhat the genuineness of the partners' desire for parenthood. Typical are the frequent desertions by fathers prior to, and at the time of, a child's birth, although always they return within a short time. Much later, when the fourth, fifth, or sixth child has been born, both parents will acknowledge this unwillingness. At this point, the mother and/or father complain that "they have too many," and resentment is expressed over the burden along with the wish to have no more children.

Characteristic of the mother's reaction are such remarks as: "I know we have too many children, but they are so cute and lovable"; "I shouldn't get pregnant so often, but it just happens. I know my health is being affected"; "Four were enough, but I guess one more won't make any difference." In the sample, religious affiliation seemed to bear no significant relationship to these attitudes. However, this might not always be true.

From her own life experience, the mother acts as though she considered sexual intercourse permissible only if the goal is procreation. Her many pregnancies offer to the outside world incontestable evidence of sexual activity and constitute for the mother her main justification for engaging in it. Also, the initiative for controlling her own behavior equates with responsibility for her acts and a decreasing dependence on others, a responsibility which, in this as in other aspects of living, these mothers tend to avoid. The father's response to parenthood is conditioned by two factors: (1) the passive expectation that he will receive satisfaction from others rather than find it for himself; (2) a pseudo independence—"I'll only look after myself"—assumed because of the minimal amount of love and consideration which he has received in his own life. The procreation of numerous children is for many fathers an attempt to assure themselves that they are "whole men" and an expression of their hope to receive from offspring the love they missed in their own childhood.

Thus, in these partners, reactions to parenthood are colored by a strong need to receive love and protection *from* a child, rather than to bestow these as parents *upon* a child. Both mothers and fathers, although differently motivated in essential details, have strong incentives to produce children. The husbands, desirous of becoming fathers, often cannot accept the fact that for medical reasons their wives should not have more children. Miscarriages, the birth of a handicapped child, the death of a child or children, a family constituted of all boys and no girls, or vice versa, often stimulate these parents to enlarge their families. Despite the fact that the developmental needs of children may be neglected, the emotional constellations which have been described unconsciously take precedence, even though the consequences do not bring the hoped-for satisfactions.

PHYSICAL MATURATION

Lack of planfulness and failure to make an acknowledged division of responsibility for the physical care of their children are distinctive features of child rearing in the inadequate family. The mother usually accepts primary responsibility but finds it burdensome and overwhelming. Haphazard practices in caring for the family are characteristic, with little or no adherence to the scheduled household management which is designed to meet the health, nutritional, and maturational needs of children. There are unmistakable symptoms of this problem:

Haphazard physical care is common. Preschool children may prepare their own meals, feed and supervise their siblings. Babies are given food and personal care, but their nutritional needs often are unrecognized. Irregularity of mealtime schedules, the serving of "snack" foods, and the child's complete freedom to select his food are general.

Neglect, a Level A disorder, is apt to appear in these families as a result of their poor judgment. As a matter of fact, poor judgment about what children can and should decide and do for themselves rather than calculated denial of physical care is the core of the difficulty.

The average person often interprets the emotional responses of parent to child in this family type as expressions of easy warmth and affection. Overlooked or unknown are the inadequate supervision and physical protection offered to the child in his dependent years.

LOVE RELATIONSHIPS

For at least one parent, and usually for both, the main element in the emotional tie to the child is the fact that the parent receives love from the child. Thus, these parents do not teach him how to love others through first making it possible for him to want to love his parents. This particular response, typical in the inadequate family, may present itself in various and sometimes disguised forms:

Parental preference for a helpless child is common. A helpless baby or a young, defective, or handicapped child has particular appeal to mother and/or father. Their identification with such a child is that of a child with a child. The attention paid to him is not primarily for the purpose of guiding his development. On the contrary, it is given because through him the parent achieves vicarious satisfaction of the longed-for-dependency status experienced, or denied, in his own childhood.

Parental love may be conditioned on the child's taking care of the parent. This is primarily a response to the child who is no longer "little." The older a son or daughter, the less acceptable he becomes to the parent unless he can take responsibility for the other children as well as meet the parent's practical and emotional demands for love and protection. However, the older child, in turn, expects the same thing from the parent. Neither is able to fulfill these needs in the other. Unable to meet this parental expectation, the latency and adolescent child often indiscriminately seeks numerous superficial relationships outside the home. Teachers and other adults often find such children appealing because of their seeking, compliant, dependent attitude.

The emotional response of the parents to any one of their many children may take any of several forms: ignoring the child's presence; acting as if the child were a plaything; showing frustration and infantile anger when the child, left too much to his own devices, clings to his parents; or relying upon the child for advice rather than giving him parental guidance.

SELF-IDENTITY

The fathers (and, in some instances, the mothers) of these families are pleased with the size of their family but display limited interest in the children as developing personalities with their own identities. "They are all loved alike," with "no favorites" or real individualization, except perhaps that an older son or daughter is designated as "a big help." Little or no differentiation is made between childhood and adult status, with the parents taking the attitude that a child requires no teaching or guidance in order to become self-reliant and independent.

Sometimes the neglectful mother acknowledges that perhaps she should pay more attention to the children, but she finds it "too much trouble." She scolds and nags and punishes the children when they annoy her, or lets them "sort of raise themselves; I never have to tell them what to do."

In other instances, the mother's failure to initiate procedures may be based on an ultramodern child-rearing principle; namely, if left alone, children will teach themselves and keep busy at what they like to do. Thus, children are allowed complete freedom of choice in eating habits and play—"I can't keep at them all the time and I do not want to"; "They are good kids, largely in charge of themselves"—praised when they do well, but not punished when they fail to do so.

Academic achievement and school attendance are neither greatly valued nor disvalued; rather there is no particular importance placed on formal education as one source that can help build the child's sense of independence.

These parents (except in the case of psychotics) do not use their children as objects upon which to vent directly their destructive impulses. When the mother yells and screams, it is because the child's normal demands for her protection threaten her own dependency status and, most importantly, because her capacity for giving is far less than that of the ordinary mother. She reacts in the only way she knows. It is not uncommon, for example, for the mother in the inadequate family to require a school-aged child to stay home from school and help her, although such help is poorly directed or supervised. The children, however, often interpret these parental responses as indications of rejection, which in fact may be the case.

SOCIALIZATION

In one sense, this family could be described as the "inadequately socialized family" since their actual behavior cannot be considered to be motivated by aggressively antisocial aims. At the same time, the social conscience possessed by these parents does not adequately equip them for actively teaching the rules of social behavior in a convincing way to their children. They remain as spectators, so to speak. So long as someone else makes the rules, they can follow them, provided they are also allowed a dependent relationship— albeit at the price of real self-autonomy.

Most of these parents, when they were children, were either: (1) encouraged to turn to an own parent for all decisions, in return for which they gained dependent love and approval; or (2) were expected prematurely to be self-reliant. These two backgrounds account for the adult behavior symptom noted. Both in the case of the male and of the female partners, their families of origin will have given importance to established rules of social behavior. Therefore, these partners are not prone to antisocial acts. However, they are highly vulnerable to getting into trouble by default, are easily frustrated under stress of responsibility, and are sometimes subject to exploitation or influence by any new "authority." In this sense, their superegos are weak, rendering them incapable of standing up for their own convictions.

As parents they are indecisive with their own children in establishing privileges and limitations for social behavior at home and in the larger community. Parental procedures are apt not only to be ill-conceived but also ineffectively implemented.

As reflected in child rearing, parental indecisiveness in defining privileges and limitations reflects this parental orientation. A frequent maternal reaction is: "They need somebody besides me to tell them what to do." There is freedom to roam the neighborhood at will: "Except for household chores, they're pretty free to do what they want"; "My children get to know the neighbors before anyone else." Fathers, described as gentle, and soft-spoken, find it difficult to be firm—"When I make a restriction, I pass out popsicles." There is little follow-up to determine that limitations are respected.

As noted previously, the parents of the inadequate family may have no objection to others outside the family assuming the responsibility of teaching their children what social behavior can and cannot be condoned. Relatives are apt to try to fill the breach. Social agencies, the school, and sometimes the court may also take on this function. Occasionally, such intervention and criticism are protested by these parents; in the main, however, the help is accepted and, in many instances, even welcomed and followed—if support is continuously forthcoming. Initial reluctance on the part of these families to accept guidance is frequently construed by the caseworker to mean that they are "hard-to-reach" families. The reverse is actually the case, provided their tendency to rely on the encouragement of others in making decisions is recognized. Often the fear that their children will be "taken away" accounts for the parents' initial resistance. However, it is not too difficult to dispel this surface manifestation, once the underlying dynamics are recognized and substantiated from family of origin history.

Child Development
EVENTS AND CIRCUMSTANCES

The majority of children in the inadequate family will have had the continuous presence of both parents from birth through adolescence. A smaller but still typical group will have experienced a temporary separation, in most instances from the father.

The reason for nearly all breaks in contact between parent and child is sporadic separation of parents. The father may leave home briefly or even desert, usually when a child is born. Under these circumstances the mother usually keeps the children with her. In some instances she and the children may go to the home of her own mother. Although she is not apt to abandon the children, she may threaten them with this possibility. The father, upon his return to the fold, often reinforces their fear of abandonment by telling the children that the mother also may desert them.

Divorce, as a reason for separation of parent and child, is unlikely, due to the symbiotic attachment of husband and wife. Hospitalization for mental illness occasionally accounts for breach in parental contact.

Substitute arrangements for joint parental care usually consist of an own mother alone or an own mother who is assisted by relatives. Typically, a grandmother or an aunt turns up to fill the gap on a temporary basis. Relatives, in preference to professional foster homes or institutions, are used for child care and, for better or for worse, are in the familial picture on a more or less continuous basis.

Although the inadequate family is not apt to be disrupted by divorce, the unpredictable goings and comings of the father equate in the mind of the young child with personal desertion, particularly when the mother threatens to abandon him as well. In the mind of the older child, reunion of the parents after sporadic separations makes little sense, confuses him with respect to parental loyalties, and causes him to question to whom he really belongs. However, the fact that these parents, particularly the mother, are rarely altogether out of the situation makes for a kind of continuity in the life of the children. Unreliable though it may be, this degree of parental contact at least is worth the child's keeping.

EARLY CHILDHOOD

The factors in the inadequate family, as well as in other family types, that lend distinction to the behavior of the young child are the precipitants in the environment which give rise to the behavior. In general, these young children have simple fears and cling to their mothers, a symptom which denotes early indulgence in the love relationship with the mother, later followed by precipitous breaking of this tie. Also present will be marked delays in the gradual development of self-reliance and toilet training; backwardness in learning to talk, or inhibited speech; shyness in social contacts with contemporaries; and constricted play interests.

LOVE RELATIONSHIPS

The reactions of most young children of the inadequate family indicative of a lack of trust in the parents' love are revealed in two typical patterns which usually are fused. Simple fears and babyish behavior take the form of insomnia, fear of the dark, and, most prominently, fears of people in general, as seen in babyish behavior, clinging to the mother, and inability to let her out of sight. Occasionally, this uncertainty is shown in aggressive, protesting behavior, manifested in persistent temper outbursts and food fads combined with babyish behavior.

The behavior symptoms that denote anxiety about the mother's love arise from two main sources peculiar to the inadequate family's environment: (1) the parent's leaving the child too much to his own devices; actual or threatened temporary separations of parent from child, usually with three-, four- and five-year-olds; and (2) the mother's spoiling and trying to keep the child under two years of age as an infant.

Paying attention to him only when he is annoying, leaving him to himself for long periods of time, following irregular schedules for feeding, sleeping, and so on, leave the young child of the inadequate family defenseless and fearful. A sense of trust in himself and in others does not readily develop within this setting and emotional atmosphere.

SELF-IDENTITY AND SOCIALIZATION

The inadequate family children who suffer from simple fears manifest their delayed developmental progress in socialization by soiling, wetting, and smearing beyond their third year. Those children who react with babyish behavior, or overaggressive protesting behavior, often express their problems of self-identity development by inhibited speech, refusal to talk to the mother, or stammering. The precipitants in both groups are the mother's failure to train them, based on her feeling that the children will learn for themselves as they grow older.

Socialization problems may also appear in learning habits of general self-care. Improperly solved conflicts in this phase of early childhood become prototypes for neurotic and behavior problems in a subsequent period. For example, the latency child of the inadequate family has poorly developed standards of behavior which he accepts as his own, and he has not gradually increased his mental and physical skills to the degree that he should. Those who were offered no parental incentive for control of their excretory functions are in latency apt to be inhibited in developing interests and pleasures in play activities, in learning, and in exploring new fields.

In making friends the young child of the inadequate family tends to be shy, fearful, and nonassertive. Play interests are constricted, with normal curiosity inhibited. Later, these children are apt to be imitative rather than creative. While such a child tends to conform outwardly to demands made upon him by his environment, his own superego is not sufficiently developed that it gives him confidence in making independent judgments. Therefore, his social conscience, in many ways, will be a reflection of that of others in his social milieu.

Common precipitants of this child's problems are the mother's encouragement of a dependent tie when the child is very young, helpless, sickly, or mentally retarded. This support is withdrawn from the healthy or nonhandicapped child when he reaches the age of three years or so, leaving him to his own devices. In some instances, the mother may be a depressive who forms a close symbiotic tie with her very young child and draws him into her own world, so to speak, thus laying the groundwork for a variety of difficulties which will interfere with his social living at home and in the larger world of school and neighborhood.

LATENCY AND ADOLESCENCE

LOVE RELATIONSHIPS

The young child in the inadequate family who displays anxiety and fears in the love relationship with his mother because he is left too much to his devices seems to carry forward into later years aspects of this basically weak emotional tie to his parents. In latency and adolescence, these children do not develop with any regularity a meaningful identification with the significant parent that results in their capacity to form object relationships in which they can give as well as receive. The quality and depth of the parental tie are most clearly reflected in the way the child maintains his social relationships, the self-reliance he attains (ego development), and his approximate conformance to realistic sociolegal restrictions of the larger community (superego development).

Emotional ties of limited depth characterize attachment between parent and older child. Frequently, there is the capacity in the older child to identify with a group of his peers or with siblings. Lacking, however, is a strong relationship with individual friends or adults. Others persist in attaching themselves in a parasitic way to the parent or, more often, to a parent representative outside the family. In a few instances, overaggressive, striking-out behavior toward the parent may be stimulated at adolescence.

Thus the nature of the inadequate family child's parental tie becomes more obvious and assumes greater significance when he reaches school age. Relationships with persons other than the parents are then forced upon him, and, as a result, he is faced with the necessity of having to cope with human relationships outside the family orbit.

SELF-IDENTITY

With respect to developing a sense of self-identity and self-reliance, there are two main courses open to the older child in the inadequate family: to fend for himself, by necessity, still plagued by underlying neurotic fears; or to continue a parasitic attachment to his parent.

In relation to independence from the parent, the latency or adolescent child typically either acquires a pseudo independence or lacks self-sufficiency because of overreliance upon a parent. The child who acquires the pattern of pseudo independence does not rely on the parent for anything, roams freely, but actually knows little of how to care for himself in a manner that gives him real self-confidence. This results not from a strong dependent tie arising out of his mother's doing too much, but rather from her expecting of him too much self-teaching. If the child does not know how to take care of himself, or how to do home tasks, he does not act. He must rely upon the parent to look after him, whether or not this is adequately done.

By and large, these children accept school attendance although there is a tendency to be indifferent—again reflecting their parents' values, by which school is neither wholeheartedly approved nor disregarded. Scholarship is apt to be average, but there is a tendency toward poor, below average, or failing grades. Learning difficulties are related to reading problems, trouble in concentration, or lackadaisical habits of homework.

In general, he conforms in his school behavior, but persistent misbehavior, when it does occur, is quite severe. Such a child is apt to be an out-of-wedlock child or mentally retarded. Behavior syndromes for girls of this group are truancy, lying, defying or striking the teacher, and incorrigibility which ends with expulsion; for the boys, persistent scrapes, stealing from schoolmates, "accidentally" hitting girls with stones. Truancy on the part of the nondefective child can also be a factor disassociated from these or other forms of misbehavior. In such cases, unexcused absence from school will be with the parents' tacit permission. In many cases, official action does not immediately or necessarily follow.

Although many children are born into these families, a repressive attitude toward sexuality itself is maintained in the home. It is repressive in the sense that sex is not frankly discussed nor acknowledged as a part of life, although the children obviously are aware of its existence. The child's preoccupation with sex play, should it occur, stems primarily from unsatisfied curiosity, not from parental attitudes or behavior which acts seductively upon the child.

SOCIALIZATION

The latency and adolescent children of the inadequate family are typically passive insofar as social contacts with peers and adults of both sexes are concerned. They do not actively seek or try to keep friends. Neither are they antagonistic and disliked, nor do they undertake to compete too actively with other children. With the defective child there is always the likelihood of unsocial aggressive behavior, destructiveness, and cruel acts toward other children.

The older children behave in approximate conformance to the sociolegal restrictions of school and community, but with a tendency toward overcompliance. There is less freedom of thought and expression than is desirable for the fullest use of adaptive skills, nor are these children consciously aware of these lacks in themselves.

Exposure to delinquent behavior by association with friends will depend upon the particular community in which the family lives. When delinquency is present, behavior tends to be of a striking-out nature rather than a shrewd, skillful attempt to avoid being caught. This occurs mainly in the mentally defective or brain-damaged child.

Delinquency in the sample studied was found mainly among adolescent girls, manifested in sexual promiscuity and out-of-wedlock pregnancy. These affairs were with males who had glaring personality defects. Consequently, the heterosexual adjustment could not be considered truly adult. The adolescent girl generally released her illegitimate child easily to the care of others.

Antisocial proclivities seemingly are not so frequent among the boys of inadequate families, unless they are children from a previous union or are mentally defective or illegitimate.

MARITAL FUNCTIONS
Reciprocal Love Relationships

In general, the marital partners in the inadequate family are drawn to one another on the common ground of wanting a mutually exclusive, giving-and-receiving love relationship. In the courtship period and at the beginning of the marriage there usually develops a self-centered, shared intimacy and interdependence. This kind of love relationship assumes pathological proportions in social adaptation mainly if children result from the union. When the partners are capable of begetting children, parenthood is, in most instances, a certainty. If children are not born, the marital relationship may keep a balance over a considerable period. A moralistic connotation is ascribed to sexual interests. In both male and female partners this has a direct bearing on their conception of, and behavior in, the sexual act.

OUTSIDE THE SEXUAL ACT

The distinctive quality of the marital love relationship of the inadequate family partners shows itself most frequently in any one of several forms. Very likely to occur in both partners is a self-centered parasitic interest in each other; intimacy is encouraged, but the closeness tends to exclude other family members. It is this exclusion of others that makes the love relationship pathological. Despite the rapport that may exist and the satisfactions felt between husband and wife, it is a morbid dependence because of its interference with other family functions.

Next in frequency, but less typical of the love relationship of the marital partners in the inadequate family, is the male partner who desires to be the sole recipient of all consideration from a wife who actually desires a mutual giving and receiving. In this instance, it will be evident that the wife has mistakenly interpreted as a sign of devotion her husband's wish to receive all her affection. However, she will learn that his love is conditioned on his being the only recipient and that he does not wish a mutual relationship.

If such a husband is nonbelligerent, he will remain with his wife although he feels disillusioned and dissatisfied. If, however, the wife is nondemanding due to depressive symptoms, or to self-absorption with her own emotions, and has a minimum of interest not only in her husband but in all object relationships, aggressively inconsiderate behavior or desertion on the part of the male partner may ensue.

For the aggressively inconsiderate partner, the denial of the kind of love he wants from his mate constitutes a rejection, regardless of extenuating circumstances. He interprets the denial as a threat to their relationship. This is something his ego cannot tolerate. In the inadequate family, this particular marital interaction is responsible for the separations and desertions which occur. On the other hand, desertion or separation rarely results when aggressively inconsiderate responses do not also characterize the male who wants to be the sole recipient of all love.

WITHIN THE SEXUAL ACT

In both male and female of the inadequate family, the object of sexual interest is normal: an adult partner of the opposite sex. The fundamental nature of the sexual striving is undisturbed in the sense that there are no gross deviations from the main objectives of genital sexuality. However, in sexual functioning these partners manifest symptoms which denote a particular kind of arrestment in psychosexual development.

That which stands out in the adult male's love relationship, both within and outside the sexual act, is his predisposition toward finding satisfaction in receiving from others, not in providing it for himself and for others. This is clearly seen in his inability to reconcile his sexual needs to timing and planning births, his work responsibilities, and so forth. His expectations within, and orientation to, the sexual act bear the same hallmark.

Orientation to, and performance in, the sexual act itself takes on the qualities of other aspects of object relationships formed by the male partner. All are highly colored by dependent receptive demands, with the expectation or hope that the female will be all-giving in this area as in others. He is interested in the sexual act and is the aggressor in that he is the one who requests sexual intercourse consistently and frequently. Within the act itself he is nonassertive, and although he obviously achieves ejaculation, he typically complains that the sexual relationship with his wife is not too satisfying. She does not succeed in "arousing" him; there is a lack of "cuddled closeness"; he does not feel like being affectionate but wants her to be. He wants sex more often, is resentful when refused. At such times he feels rejected, may seek other women, but that is not satisfying either. If mutual satisfaction is attained, it is usually without anticipation of the possibility of the female's becoming pregnant. These attitudes are a result of the husband's personal, as distinct from religious, objections to the wife's use of contraceptives.

In adulthood, the inadequate female's rejection of sexual intercourse as a pleasurable act in itself is based on two different but related aspects of her psychosexual developmental history. Symptomatically, she is apt to feel that the sex act itself is "wrong" but is a duty, permissible only as the goal is procreation. Her emotional rejection of adult sexuality in its fullest dynamic sense will probably be based on these constellations of factors:

1 Her fear that if she behaves as a grown woman, of which the sex act is a part, she will forfeit her dependency status, an orientation deriving from her own mother's attitude

2 Her feeling that to take the initiative in intercourse or in the prevention of pregnancy means that she is a responsible adult, something she tends to avoid in other aspects of living as well

3 Her fear of becoming pregnant, an aspect of point 2, which intensifies her conflicts with respect to the sexual act

4 The size of her own family of origin, and her ordinal position in the family.

As with the male, the female's passive-dependent receptive tendencies are reflected in her attitude toward, and participation in, the sexual act. Despite the bearing of many children, the female partner in the inadequate family is sexually inhibited, with the act itself seen as a duty, not enjoyed, and of minimal frequency. Typical is her avoidance of discussing the subject altogether. However, several diagnostically significant symptoms of her behavior stand out in relation to the sex act. There is refusal of sexual intercourse, based on the realistic fear of becoming pregnant; but she takes no precautions to prevent conception and thus relieve her anxiety on this score. She will report, for example, that she "never seeks sexual intercourse and would gladly go without it" and that she "has no idea as to whether or not she has orgasm."

Self-identity

The husband and wife of the inadequate family maintain their self-identity through the marriage partnership in one or two characteristic ways: (1) overidealization, a pathological form of indiscriminate faith in the other partner as a male or female and in his adequacy as a family man or woman; (2) devaluation of the partner, based on disillusionment over his failure to measure up to unrealistic ideals for unconditional giving.

Overidealization is manifest when the partner's confidence in his spouse reflects a kind of optimism not usually substantiated by the facts. In the face of obvious deficiencies, for example, there may be such expressions as, "He is a good man who does the best he can"; "I'm lucky to have such a good wife." The husband looks to his wife with confidence, relying on her strength, knowledge, and dependability, or there is an extraordinary wish to please the partner, accompanied by protectiveness, maternal and nondemanding qualities.

These expressions of confidence, with little foundation in fact, constitute false reassurances, in a manner of speaking, as differentiated from a normal idealization of the partner—the realistically placed trust and encouragement which are given to, and required by, the ordinary person. In certain respects, it is this mutual support that keeps these partners going. However, these characteristics are evidence of pathological dysfunctioning between these marital partners because more often than not such attitudes do not result in realistic clarification of issues of family living, nor do they lead to greater adequacy in the family's social functioning.

Personal devaluation and disillusionment on the part of the wife are noticeable in disappointment that her "husband has no outstanding achievement." The male wants to be a "good husband" but does not know how: "When my wife is upset I am confused and uncertain." The wife wishes that her husband would take more responsibility with the children; "outside of that, he's just what I want." The husband says that his wife is wonderful, "but the house is really messy."

The hostility vested in devaluating the partner is neither intense nor charged with highly prejudicial attitudes, nor is a major conflict engendered by the particular ego defenses employed by either partner in maintaining this kind of emotional tie. Rather, each entertains the wish that the other would be "more giving." However, the fear of not having even this degree of dependence upon another makes the relationship, for these partners, worth keeping.

Socialization

In the inadequate family, the practical measures taken in behalf of a partner when physical disability or mental illness occurs, or in problems of social behavior, are accomplished by overadapting to the other's needs. Each has an awareness of the problems facing the other, and a kind of protective concern for him which, however, usually is not judiciously evaluated or adequately sustained. Overadjusting to a spouse's undesirable attitudes toward an illness, toward getting needed medical care, or to his reluctance to seek psychiatric treatment, are a few examples. The composite result is that each partner's considered action in the other's behalf frequently is delayed rather than actually thwarted. By and large, protective intervention under such conditions must be undertaken by others in behalf of the afflicted partner.

PROBLEM-SOLVING

In practically all instances, therefore, distinctive to the inadequate family, one or both partners either rely on the judgment of someone else in making decisions or behave as though problems would be recognized, evaluated, and solved by some magic formula. There will always be present some combination of these two problem-solving orientations in the marital partners.

Overreliance in problem-solving is evident when both husband and wife expect the opposite partner to provide continuous support, guidance, help, and reassurance in making decisions. Each is unable independently to scrutinize, evaluate, and take considered action without this kind of bolstering. If such be forthcoming, it is quite likely that the partner will take over the other's values and act accordingly. When both partners have these same tendencies in about the same degree, mutual concurrence and compromise are not possible; there is discouragement and frustration, and decisions are postponed or avoided.

Thus reliance on another's judgment is prominent in both partners and is almost always the male partner's orientation to problem-solving. If the wife does not also rely on encouragement, she will resort to dependence on the so-called "magic formula."

The "magic formula" is called upon mainly by the female partner. There is an awareness that something is wrong, but always there is the expectation that someone else will take the initiative in solving the difficulty. A childlike faith characterizes the response that "everything will come out all right," as though by magic. In some instances, the female partner may be emotionally withdrawn, anxiously preoccupied with her own fantasies or psychosomatic complaints, symptoms indicative of a more severe mental disorder.

Although overreliance and the "magic formula" have similar elements symptomatically, there is a clinical and psychodynamic distinction. As herein defined, reliance on encouragement denotes the wish to be more aggressive and independent if given "permission" by somone held in esteem. Those who entertain the pious hope that all will be well, as if by magic, deny this responsibility. Those who rely on another's encouragement or approval recognize problems, but they cannot independently evaluate their significance and exercise the judgment needed for appropriate action without more than an ordinary amount of outside guidance. In contrast, the "magic formula" person is unable to see, evaluate, or act upon problems. Of significance in the inadequate family is the almost inevitable association of the "magic formula" problem-solving orientation, in the female, with the presence of all instances of child neglect, dependency, separation, and desertion, Level A. It thus becomes understandable why these parents perceive and meet inadequately their problems of child rearing, and that neglect often results. Occasionally, this pattern may be characteristic of both partners.

FINANCIAL FUNCTIONS

As in other matters of family life, most fathers in the inadequate family have good intentions with respect to providing the physical necessities for their wives and children. They typically avow this intention and see themselves as wage earners and providers. However, these socially valued goals are not usually fulfilled. In general, this failure can be ascribed to poor judgment in anticipating the endless needs of a growing family and what is involved in meeting them.

Income Production

The husband, to all intents and purposes, carries the provider role. The wife's employment, if any, is on a more or less hit-or-miss basis, irregular, or part-time, to supplement the husband's income. When the husband fails completely, or provides inadequately for his family, the wife rarely assumes full responsibility for income production. More often than not she will accept her husband's low standards, agree that he should borrow through company credit unions, obtain help from relatives or, in some instances, from community agencies.

The male wage earner is seldom strongly motivated to achieve as a person in his own right. Although he may like his work, he does not experience too much personal satisfaction from it; neither is he particularly dissatisfied. A minimum wage or a mediocre job with no chance of promotion may be quite acceptable. If the male happens to come from a family of origin with considerable money, he will depend upon income from that source and be content to do incidental bits of work. In such instances, the male's motivation as a provider and a productive person remains the same, although the income available to his own family will be adequate.

On the job itself the male partner is apt to be steady and to get along with his fellow workers, but generally he is nonassertive. He will probably rely heavily upon approval and support from his employer. In the sample studied, the preferred type of employment included such occupations as truck driver, shoemaker, welder, key cutter, roofer, stockroom clerk, maintenance man, and so forth. Although in most instances his education amounts to eighth-grade schooling or less, this fact probably bears no significant relationship to the male's intention to provide for the family or to the strength of his incentive to be a productive person. In the sample studied, weak motivation toward productivity but good intentions to provide characterized the male wage earner, irrespective of his skills and educational level.

Income Management

The obligation to support the family is usually undertaken, but the money earned is inadequate according to ordinary living standards. The immediate circumstances but not the etiological reasons for failure to support the family adequately will probably consist of one of two constellations of factors: (1) low standards of living, with basic needs unrecognized and thus unmet; (2) extravagant standards of living, with luxury items purchased at the sacrifice of essentials. This second syndrome results in most of the unamortized debts and the borrowing of the inadequate family.

Debts per se assume little diagnostic significance from family class to family class unless viewed in the context of the total financial functions syndrome. For the inadequate family, the motives which prompt debt contraction, as well as the partner's habits of borrowing, are of a particular nature. Money is rarely obtained from banks or from loan companies. In all instances an element of "being given to" which has greater appeal to many of these family heads than does the obligation of repayment that is always attached to legal borrowing. Even in the instance of borrowing from company unions, less responsibility and risk are entailed than in credit buying from a retail store.

A latent possibility in all inadequate families is that available money will not be used for support of the family. This is accounted for by the male wage earner's low tolerance for the self-discipline necessary to forego personal indulgences. Certain environmental conditions will exacerbate this weakness. If his wife, for example, suffers from psychosis or circumscribed psychosis, this circumstance may be sufficient to lower the tolerance level and to precipitate his failure to provide. Level A dependency then may result. In other instances, the precipitant leading to nonsupport may not be entirely obvious. Personal frustration created by the inability to meet overoptimistic goals may result in the male provider's periodic desertions. Whatever the symptoms of financial disorders in the inadequate family, they will reflect the wage earner's unrealistically founded intention to provide, and his weakly motivated drive with respect to work achievement.

Reliance on relatives to supplement the wage earner's income usually means turning to a mother or father in a family of origin who regularly provides all the clothing for the children or subsidizes the male head's earnings. Impulsive, unjustified spending of an already insufficient income will be for the purchase of inappropriate clothes for the children, television sets, refrigerators, automobiles, a vacation in a large city hotel, and so on. Ill-advised expenditures are made chiefly in behalf of the family rather than for the personal indulgence of a single individual. Debts thereby created are financed through credit unions. More importantly, there will be no cash on hand for payment of rent, purchase of necessary clothing, groceries, and other essentials.

In the inadequate families that accept low living standards, there is, on the part of both husband and wife, an unawareness of actual family needs. Thus, by default, others come to the rescue—agencies, relatives, and so on. In these instances, debts are not apt to accumulate, although Level A type dependency may occur.

ADULT CHARACTERISTICS
Physical Condition and Intelligence

Among the adult heads of the inadequate family, an impaired capacity to adapt to family life is determined less by physical and intellectual disabilities than by arrestments in emotional development. The physical well-being of the male adults tends to be normal; in fact, they are inordinately healthy. Occasionally, there are nondisabling physical handicaps, such as speech defects or cataracts. For all practical purposes, however, these do not interfere with the male's everyday functioning. Emotional attitudes toward a physical disability may but typically do not become exaggerated for purposes of secondary gain.

There is a slightly higher tendency in the female heads toward disabling illnesses which interfere to some degree with their running the household. The most severe ailments, among cases found in the sample studied, were pituitary tumor, psychosis, and kidney disease. Nondisabling illnesses are apt to be present in about the same proportion as in other family classes. The nature of the illnesses, however, assumes significance when compared with the physical ailments of the females in other family classes. The most typical examples are malfunctioning of the gall bladder, kidney, and thyroid, and neurodermatitis.

Ego Defenses

Of the main psychological mechanisms, repression is used to a considerable extent by the adult male of the inadequate family. This is a tendency to deny or forget, beyond power of conscious recall, unpleasant external events or nonacceptable internal impulses. This represents a fundamentally weak ego in that repression is the main defense the undeveloped personality of the child is able to employ. This means, as it affects adult adjustment, that sexual and aggressive energies are not available and thus have not been diverted as a source of strength in the service of the ego or in social adaptation. Thus object relationships are impoverished, and reality-testing ability is impaired.

Some aggressive, hostile acting-out behavior may appear as a neurotic symptom but not to a degree of intensity which would result in antisocial acts. Nor is projection a common defense. Overoptimism, flight, and evasion of responsibility loom high. These ego defenses represent a stage in ego development rather than a neurotic psychological process.

The symptoms seen in social functioning which are most characteristic of these ego defenses are: meager achievement; failure in one task resulting in permanent disinclination to repeat the act (low motivation) unless given continuous reassurance; willingness to be a spectator; avoidance of unpleasant relationships or situations by physically removing oneself (running home to mother, for example). This passive orientation can have its antisocial effect when the external situation demands action, as in family living. In this circumstance there is for the male a constant recreating of unpleasant situations which he wishes to avoid. In such instances, quarrelsome, provocative, belligerent, and irritable behavior may be a corollary.

Repression, as a secondary defense, is also characteristic of the adult female. Repression both of hostilities and of sexual impulses operates prominently. This means that object relationships, although clinging, are not great in depth. Unless the female happens to have a husband who wishes to take care of a helpless "depreciated" person, accepting her as a child rather than as an adult, sexual woman, the very fact of marriage, in some instances, produces guilt reactions in reference to sexuality. Under these circumstances, resorting to psychosomatic symptoms is not an uncommon manifestation of the problem. In supporting the defense of repression, denial is used, designed to abolish unpleasant situations which threaten from the environment.

Although certain neurotic processes overlie a fundamental character structure weakness, the female partner's trouble is primarily one of disturbance in ego development. Thus, her tolerance of anxiety is low, and her awareness of danger from the environment, and capacity to evaluate inner and outer problems for judicious solution, is limited.

The majority of females in the inadequate family adopt an overoptimistic attitude under ordinary conditions of family stress. They entertain the expectation that everything will be provided and feel sure that this will happen, in defiance of facts to the contrary. Some few not only are overoptimistic but further evade responsibility for doing the necessary practical things by a ready exchange of one environment, relationship, or activity for another, to avoid the unpleasantness which problems create.

The female does not resort to acting-out behavior or extensive use of pathological forms of projection, nor does she conceive of the world as an object for manipulation and exploitation. There is present a weak, inconsistent inner authority (superego) which is subject to influence and replacement by a new standard but is accompanied by a highly rigid superego (unconscious guilt) in regard to sexuality.

Emotional Stability

The partners of the inadequate family are more difficult to identify in the sequence of increasing degrees of severity in psychopathology of the disordered family types. Nevertheless, there is clinically visible from the case materials a preponderance of passive dependent characteristics with severe neurotic conflicts. There are tendencies toward depressive symptoms (not psychotic depression), evidenced by types of apathy, giving up easily, absence of impulse-driven characteristics, and an inability to make use of energies (75).

The passivity characteristic of these individual marital partners might arise from several sources: (1) a fear of aggression; (2) a depressive manifestation (not psychosis) in which there is a loss of vitality and interest; (3) the possibility of constitutional limitations or defects (75).

CHILD CHARACTERISTICS
Physical Condition and Intelligence

Children in the inadequate families are apt to be susceptible to particular physical impairments and developmental delays, many of which are chronic, irreversible, or of congenital origin. Noncongenital physical disorders are severe and handicapping to the social development of the child. They may include, for example, rheumatoid arthritis, defective eyes, ears, or teeth. Less handicapping are acute disabilities such as pneumonia and nutritional deficiencies.

Mental retardation, organic brain damage, aphasia, and hydrocephalus are among the irreversible and congenital impairments found. Delayed speech is often associated with these disorders. The histories of mothers of the children so affected reveal many miscarriages and premature births. Stammering and inability to talk plainly or to pronounce certain words—speech difficulties without known organic factors—are present in a significant number of both younger and older children, and usually occur in several children within a single family. Other disabilities are usually characteristic of only one child in a family. However, in one third of the families in this class at least one child per family suffered from some such impairment.

Psychic Disturbance

A substantial majority of the inadequate families with children between the ages of six and twelve are likely to have one or more children with symptoms that denote an emotional disturbance. In an individual child, the main constellation will be conduct disorders, motor disorders, and neurosis.

Conduct disorders are not particularly distinctive. As with the children in the perfectionistic family, provocative behavior in response to parental attitudes is present. By contrast, however, avoidance of close relationships is as likely to occur, but not to the same extent as with the children in the egocentric and unsocial family. Aggressive unsocial conduct or destructive behavior with avoidance of punishment occur mainly in the latency child who also has organic brain damage or is mentally retarded.

Motor disorders are apt to be frequent in the latency child and are manifested in stammering. Hyperactivity rather than inhibited bodily movements or rhythmic head rolling is also typical.

Infantile phenomena, such as soiling and enuresis, may be part of the clinical picture of the latency child but are less common than in the children of the egocentric and unsocial families. They are also less typical within the inadequate family type than the occurrence of conduct disorders, motor disorders, and neuroses.

Almost any kind of disturbance can be found among adolescents in the inadequate family. This fact can probably be explained by the coexistence of adolescents with normal intelligence and the relatively high incidence of mental retardation, associated with, or exclusive of, organic defects in children.

Sudden withdrawal of emotional ties to the parent is the most frequent symptom of adolescent pathology. What differentiates this from that type found in other family classes is that the thrust is made toward emotional separation from the parent, but the effort is soon abandoned, and there is a return to a kind of conformance normal for the eight-, nine-, and ten-year-old of latency. Superficial social contacts with friends outside the family may appear to be good, but relationships are not permitted to become too close nor is independence achieved. There are guilt and anxiety toward the normal maturative process.

The adolescent girl of this group will sometimes form a transient sexual relationship with an older male, resulting in illegitimate pregnancy. The child will be released for adoption, and the girl will resume her relationships in the home, more or less on the same basis as previously; namely, she will remain the "little girl." Such symptoms may be accompanied by periodic sullen withdrawn reactions, anger outbursts, or a variety of psychosomatic symptoms.

Regression is familiar in psychotic illness. This psychic disturbance occurs mainly in girls, particularly if there is also present in the family an older sibling who is retarded or defective. Under these circumstances, a normal child will receive little sustained emotional support from the parent. Allegiances to other persons do not represent an outflow of feeling but a superficial, meaningless tie. Surprising changes in attitudes and outward behavior, characteristic of this illness, are to be found. In one adolescent, the symptoms included: falling in love at age fifteen, with plans to marry an unstable twenty-two-year-old youth incarcerated for robbery; wildly championing the cause of social justice; posturing; sitting on the classroom floor; wearing an arm splint to school; and so on.

There were limited data on the male adolescent of the inadequate family, but there is a suggestion that the pattern typical of the latency boy may hold true for the adolescent boy. Whether this is so will be determined to a large extent by the aspects of the social milieu to which the boy is exposed.

MALE PARTNER'S FAMILY OF ORIGIN

There is slightly less than a fifty-fifty chance that the male partner of the inadequate family will have had the continuing presence of both his own parents from birth to the age of sixteen. Mothers, in most cases, consistently were present during this period of the male partner's life. Occasionally, however, a mother's death had occurred before the male was sixteen years old. Fathers were apt to be a negative factor in that their absence inevitably adversely affected the normal course of the male partner's emotional growth. The usual reason for his separation from the child, was death; rarely if ever was there parental separation, divorce, or desertion.

Mothers, when widowed, did not remarry; fathers were apt to do so. However, substitute arrangements afforded the male, as a child, typically did not include acquisition of a stepparent or placement in foster homes or institutions. The characteristic pattern was for a relative to assume responsibility, if the need arose.

In the vast majority of cases, the age of the male partner at the time he lost his father through death was from thirteen to fifteen— the period when the search for self-identity is once more reactivated. This developmental problem was made extraordinarily difficult for these partners who had no substitute male figure with whom to identify.

Adequacy of Financial Support

The major portion of fathers in the male partner's family of origin were adequate providers. However, a number were marginally so, and a few failed altogether. The outstanding feature of this latter group of fathers is that their work patterns showed limited satisfaction gained from achievement. They were, for example, unambitious, never seemed to get ahead, or did not work steadily. Although this is not characteristic of all families of origin, the work pattern of the father was likely to be less favorable than is ordinarily true of most families.

Of particular significance was the mother's reaction when the father failed to give support. Unlike the mothers in male families of origin of most other family classes, these women relied upon their sons to replace the fathers as a source of financial support. Few, if any, mothers assumed the wage-earning responsibility in the absence of the father. The male was viewed as a meal ticket, his productivity unvalued for itself.

Achievement of Love Relationships

For the most part, these males grew up in one of two basic settings. In one, the overpatient mother discouraged her son's independent strivings, and encouraged his reliance upon her as a substitute for self-autonomy and development of adult masculine sexual strivings. The father, on the other hand, translated his overstrict religious beliefs into demands upon his son for immediate obedience and repression of aggressive impulses. In the other, the mother, preoccupied with her own goals and satisfactions, expected her son to pursue and find his own goals independently. In some instances, although he was expected to provide for his own physical needs and contribute to the family, the son was pushed out as soon as possible. The father was similar in his response to the son, or was overstrict. In this particular setting, it is not only the quality but the minimal amount of love for the boy that is of significance.

Psychodynamically, the effect of such upbringing upon the male's adult love relationships is clear. In the first instance, if the son accepts adult sexuality on any basis other than a passive relationship, relying upon the female to take the initiative, he feels that he forfeits the right to be taken care of. In other words, he has inappropriately applied to marriage an original condition of maternal love; therefore, it is safer to remain a "little boy." At the same time, to be aggressive in the sexual act, as well as in other aspects of living, carries the threat of punishment such as was formerly administered by his father.

In the family of origin history the pseudo independence necessitated by familial attitudes, together with the minimal amount of love given by the mother and father, results in an adult male who is overdemanding in the sexual act, seeking love he has not had but in the end acquiring only a general feeling of dissatisfaction. His overdemanding behavior is an attempt both to supplement his already existing feeling of being loved deficiently and to assure himself that he is a whole man.

Self-identity and Socialization

The male partners of the inadequate family group reflect the influence of two prevailing characteristics of their familial background with respect to self-identity and socialization: maternal overindulgence of the son; and emotional neglect by both father and mother, sometimes including overpunitiveness on the part of the father.

As adult family heads they refuse, or are unwilling, to make any decisions or choices without turning to another for confirmation or approval—usually to a woman, who may be the wife or the male's own mother. There is little overt protest over giving up this right of self-determination. Hostilities, for the most part, are deeply repressed, with impairment in social functioning marked. This degree of nonassertiveness leaves these males unprotected, unable to defend their beliefs, and open to possible exploitation under conditions of stress in social and family living.

Others will assume the responsibility for decisions but exercise poor judgment because of a mistrust of others. Reliance on others and cooperative human relationships, therefore, are consciously avoided. Although the conscious attitude is one of independence, these males' unsuccessful attempts to run their own lives frequently result in the need for relatives or the community to take the responsibility. This behavior reflects the fact that when these males were growing up no one ever helped or cared to help them in this respect. Therefore, they feel concerned only with their own self-interests.

Laxness in ethical and moral standards was not typical of the males' family of origin in the families studied, nor were instances of sexual promiscuity on the part of mother or father. Unduly repressive parental attitudes in regard to verbal expression of hostilities were outstanding and often reflected a strict religious background. The caseworker frequently recorded that these families of origin were stable, closely knit groups. However, this cohesiveness was an inhibiting and overconstricting factor. Although it did reinforce tendencies toward self-control with respect to antisocial acts, this was at the expense of self-reliance and at a sacrifice of self-identity.

FEMALE PARTNER'S FAMILY OF ORIGIN

In contrast to the situation found in families of origin of male partners of the inadequate family, of significance to the female partners were the numbers and kinds of events that altered the composition of their natural familial unit, as well as the substitute group. Conspicuous in their histories are the losses they suffered in infancy, early childhood, and early adolescence through death of an own father, mother, and/or foster parents or grandmothers serving as parents. In the majority of instances, an own parent or parental surrogate died before the female partner was fourteen years of age; in a number of cases, both the natural mother as well as the person who took her place died before the girl was thirteen years old.

The traumas indigenous to the early or repeated physical separations of a child from parental or maternal contact, as they affect ego development and formation of a sense of self-trust, are well known. In the vast majority of cases, this female partner, as a child, had been exposed to an inconstancy of love between herself and a mother, a father, or both, by reason of their absence. The relationship with substitute parents was tenuous and unreliable for similar reasons. In a smaller number of cases, separation of the female child from father or mother by reason of desertion or disinterest also was a striking feature. The interesting part about such desertions of the child or failures to take parental responsibility is that, to all intents and purposes, the female partner as a child was "given away," but her father or mother continued to drift in and out of her life at various intervals. In such cases, great conflict was created in her mind, accompanied by fantasies of real or imaginary reasons for this situation: To whom did she really belong? Who was she? Why was she not taken care of by her own parents? As an adult, consequently, she has a weak personal identity. Whether she is hostile to or idealizes the absent parent depends upon the attitude taken by the remaining parent or parent substitute.

It therefore becomes not only the fact of separation that is of importance here but also the number of separations, the ages of the female children at the time, the reasons (death or disinterest) and the remaining parent's or parent substitute's failure to minimize the damage to the child's already weak ego. This means that, as adults, these females have a confused image in their unconscious minds of mothers and fathers to whom their earliest love (libidinal) strivings are, or might have been, attached.

In families where both father and mother are present, relatives do not play a significant role. Over half of the females in the sample came from families of four to twenty children; about one fourth, from one-child families.

Adequacy of Financial Support

There is an equal likelihood that fathers will be adequate or inadequate providers. As compared with the situation in families of origin in the other family classes, default in financial responsibility looms much greater, due to the high incidence of deaths of fathers. However, in these families, even when the father was still living there was a more consistent pattern to support inadequately, to default completely, or to rely on community agencies than was true of families of origin in other classes. There also seemed to be a tendency to turn to agencies rather than to relatives, not only for financial assistance but also to place the children. Another tendency seemed to be toward acceptance of a minimum income or meager standard of living, suggesting low motivation to derive satisfaction in productive work. This kind of adjustment has strong rescmblances to the history of the unsocial family of origin. At the same time, there were a number of families in which achievement and self-sufficiency were maintained, but without the degree of emphasis and stress which characterizes the families of origin of the female partners in other family classes.

Love Relationships

Three main trends stand out with respect to conditions which influenced the amount and quality of love available to female partners of the inadequate family in their families of origin: (1) overindulgence; (2) emotional neglect on the part of one or both own parents; and (3) in a smaller number of cases, physical and emotional neglect by both own parents.

Overindulgence was prominent exclusively in mothers or mother substitutes. In all instances, the female was an only or the youngest child, having experienced loss of an own father or mother by death. As a child, the female clung to the parent, made no choices for herself, and found satisfactions in receiving from others rather than in discovering them for herself or for others.

Thus a one-child family favored a close tie between mother and daughter, or between maternal substitute and daughter. In the absence of the father, a heavy emotional investment of each in the other impaired the daughter's chances for becoming self-reliant, for relinquishing the dependent tie to the mother, and for forming healthy heterosexual relationships. In the mind of a child, the physical separation of the father by death may be conceived as "desertion." Psychodynamically speaking, emotional neglect also becomes a factor, since the absent parent was not replaced with an adequate substitute. These particular females, as contrasted with others, show little protest to the forfeit of their rights of self-expression; one possible explanation is the fact that, actually, they were well taken care of.

Emotional neglect consisted of emotional neglect along with overstrictness toward the female child's heterosexual and social interests. In the main, both father and mother were present. Interestingly enough, the female child was not expected to work or to help support the family, even though income might have been minimal. There was little emphasis or value placed on self-sufficiency in this respect. However, great value was placed on foregoing the ordinary pleasures of dating, dressing like other adolescents, and engaging in social activities.

The emotional neglect manifested itself in ways that gave the female a feeling of personal unworthiness, although she was adequately cared for and protected. Possibly contributing to this feeling were mothers who were unwilling to have this child in the first place; fathers who wanted a boy instead of a girl; mothers who were too busy pursuing their own interests; and fathers who remarried and relinquished contact because of a stepmother's rejecting attitude toward the daughter.

Physical and emotional neglect can best be described by citing specific cases: an alcoholic widow who demanded that her children look after her but find their own means for emotional satisfactions; an alcoholic father, periodically deserting, who was consistently in the family picture but inconstant and seductive in his emotional attitude toward the female child; and a mother who condoned such behavior and at the same time allowed the children to stay in the home as long as they brought in money.

As an only child, a youngest child, or one among numerous children, the female partner of the inadequate family has been predisposed and sensitized either to being indulged (and thus is unwilling to share in any relationship) or to being displaced by younger brothers and sisters and having to share with them. Thus the combination of parental attitudes, size of family, and her ordinal position in the family are the distinctive sources of her orientation to adult sexuality. Her impaired capacity to enjoy a pleasurable sexual relationship with a male is made manifest symptomatically, on the one hand, by her use of the fear of pregnancy as a rationalization to avoid sexual intercourse; and, on the other, by her many pregnancies, which she does not really want, as her only justification for engaging in the act. In her feelings, the situation is irreconcilable.

Self-identity

Any one of the three predominant kinds of family of origin histories typical of the inadequate family group predisposes the female partner to poor judgment or helpless floundering under stress. She is not strongly activated toward self-reliance, and her love for another is apt to resemble greatly that of a dependent child for its mother.

Her capacity in adulthood for self-directive activity in making choices or decisions related to the responsibilities of family life takes two particular forms. In far the largest number of instances, she refuses to make decisions, relying wholly upon others to do so for her or turning to others for confirmation of a stand. Psychodynamically, she probably feels that if she makes known her wishes or ideas she will forfeit a previously held and cherished position of complete dependence upon another. However, this gain is purchased at the sacrifice of her own self-identity and of being an individual in her own right.

There is little conscious protest to this submergence of her personality. Hostile reactions, normally felt and expressed, sublimated or displaced, are deeply repressed in these female partners, in return for which they expect to be taken care of. Self-directive activity is thus at a minimum.

Some few will assume pseudo independence because, in the course of their growing up, no one ever helped them to test their own judgment but left them to find their way unassisted (emotional and physical neglect). This independent activity, however, is fraught with lack of perceptiveness and injudiciousness. More frequently than not, independence of this sort eventually brings to the fore the intervention of relatives or community.

Socialization

Desertion by the fathers and neglect that necessitates state guardianship are always possibilities in the female's family of origin. Psychosis requiring commitment of parents and divorce were not common in the group studied.

However, it is possible that other forms of disordered behavior, Level A, were present but not documented as such. For example, in the cases studied one mother was alcoholic; two fathers were alcoholic and sexually promiscuous, flaunting such activities rather than attempting to hide them from family members. In one fourth of the families of origin, some form of disordered behavior exclusive of mental commitments and divorce was present in a parent. In the remaining 75 percent, the tendency was toward overstrictness, particularly as this related to the female's opportunities for social contacts with boys and girls of her own age, and to overrepressive attitudes toward normal manifestations of sexual strivings.

VII. THE EGOCENTRIC FAMILY

THIS FAMILY class holds third position in the continuum of rising susceptibility to family malfunctioning among the disordered family types. It is designated the "egocentric family" with reference to the ego-dominated and self-seeking intentions that markedly color the social conduct of these family members. In at least one of the adult partners in this family, and usually in both, compensatory behavior manifested in an excess of self-interest and an overstress on the importance of some form of social status or personal prestige extends through the realm of all interpersonal relationships.

These predominating character traits of self-centeredness, overbearing manner, and opinionated attitudes in the marriage partners exacerbate and are exacerbated by the problems of child rearing and the opportunistic aims of the marriage partnership. Although, in manifest behavior, this particular syndrome of egocentricity differs between male and female, the basic problems underlying this adjustment almost always derive from the same kinds of defects in psychosocial and ego development in both partners. It is the aggregate effect of these narcissistic needs, directly or vicariously expressed in social behavior, that establishes the distinctive emotional tone of this family.

The psychosocial disorder picture presented by the egocentric family is likely to consist of Level A disorders in child development and marital functioning, occasionally in child rearing. Level B disorders will cover the entire range: child-rearing, child, marital, financial, and adult disorders. The symptomatology of each is distinctive and greatly colored by self-seeking, controlling tendencies.

CHILD-REARING DISORDERS

Level A disorders occur under two conditions: (1) at the mother's instigation the child is placed, following the breakup of a previous marriage, to rejoin her after her remarriage; (2) at the instigation of a community agency or professional person a child is placed in a foster home or institution as a therapeutic measure. Because the child has both negative and narcissistic value for the parents, they ordinarily do not relinquish custody or supervision. Placement is likely for the reasons named only in the egocentric family, as distinct from other disordered family types. If neglect is a legal charge, to enable placement, the charge will be for emotional rather than physical neglect. Except as noted, the child-rearing practices of the egocentric family do not miscarry in a fashion that leads to legal intervention.

Level B child-rearing disorders are glaringly present in all egocentric families, both those with minor children and those with children over twenty-one years of age. In all likelihood, these child-rearing disorders will be of long standing. The mother will generally give a lucid description of her own current and past parental behavior and frequently will offer plausible explanations for it; she may be alarmed and fearful that the child's behavior eventually will threaten her remarried status, or that an older child is "getting out of control." The father's response is apt to be one of pseudo frankness. He is direct and often brief, but he also implies "hands off."

Both partners avoid facing their own emotional involvement as parents and minimize the seriousness of the child's difficulty—"He's just an average high-strung boy." Each one blames the problem on the other, because of involvement in the antagonisms of the marital relationship. In other words, counseling or casework is utilized not to discover what parental practices are jeopardizing the child's development, but to depreciate the marriage partner.

CHILD DISORDERS

Level A child disorders may develop in certain latency and adolescent children of the egocentric family. They are apt to be of three kinds: delinquency; truancy; and hospitalization for mental illness.

Level B child disorders will be present in at least one child in the egocentric family whether he is of preschool age, school age, or older. The greatest handicap to the social adjustment of these children is an impaired capacity to form meaningful personal relationships.

MARITAL DISORDERS

Level A marital disorders manifested in divorce in the egocentric family are differentiated from those of other family classes by the fact that both partners are apt to have had a previous marriage dissolved by divorce. Although there is a high proclivity in these partners to dissolve the marriage, there is a correspondingly high tendency to remarry. Desertions and separations are not the rule.

Level B marital disorders symptomatic of marital dysfunctioning are extensive and severe. More often than not they have existed since the beginning of the marriage. Interest in the spouse will be dominated by definite opportunistic considerations. Taking into consideration all disordered family types, the marital disorders of the egocentric family most vividly reveal the basic pathology that permeates the total family dysfunctioning.

FINANCIAL DISORDERS

Level A financial disorders are rare in the egocentric family—dependency, nonsupport, and legal involvement in debts are not typical. Death or divorce may dissolve the marriage, thus creating a temporary financial need. However, the tendency to remarry minimizes dependency as a continuing problem.

Level B financial disorders are replete and an aspect of the marital difficulties. Egocentricities in regard to money and its use characterize these disorders. Quarrels as to who gets the greatest benefit from the family income, should have the most possessions, is the better organizer, can more adequately budget, most often fails to observe rules of household management, and so on, are commonly big points of controversy. Often the husband or wife is completely beholden to the spouse because he controls all money.

ADULT DISORDERS

Level A adult disorders do not develop with any distinctive regularity. Psychotic breaks that require hospitalization occur with about the same frequency as in the perfectionistic family; more often than in the inadequate family; less often than in the unsocial family. Disorders of an antisocial nature, such as major and minor crimes, misdemeanors, and so on, are not typical, nor is mental deficiency that requires hospitalization.

Level B adult disorders, however, readily identifiable in the adults of the egocentric family, could under certain circumstances move into the Level A disorder category. This is mainly because sexually deviative behavior such as voyeurism, exhibitionism, fetishism, incest, and so on may become concerns of the larger community. If this happens, it increases the risk of apprehension and legal involvement. However, alcoholism, sexual promiscuity, and dishonest tendencies are usually contained within a personally controlled social setting.

CHILD-REARING FUNCTIONS
Parental Functioning

Among the purposes entering into the egocentric family's marriage partnership, the attitude toward parenthood has particular significance. Rarely are the begetting and rearing of children acknowledged reasons for the marriage of these two partners. Thus, rejection of parenthood constitutes the key to a particular dynamic constellation of factors which influence this family's child-rearing practices.

EVENTS AND CIRCUMSTANCES

The bearing of children, or the ability to do so, is the source of the central emotional conflict of these mothers, oversensitizing them to the emotional implications of parenthood and markedly affecting their subsequent child-rearing practices. Among the fathers, conflicts arise for one of three reasons: (1) complete rejection of the idea of fatherhood; (2) passive acceptance of it, with little active interest; (3) selfish desires of any nature. All three reactions denote rejection of parenthood in the fullest social sense.

The mothers, highly ambivalent about their ability to bear children, commonly react to the actual birth of a child in one of two ways: either the child is welcomed as proof of fertility ("I had a child to prove I could"); or it is *not* welcomed because of preconceived notions that impregnation was not possible ("I never thought I could have a child"). In both instances, these reactions denote poorly established sex identity. Severe nausea and nervousness during the prenatal period often afflict those mothers who doubted they could have children. They characteristically attribute such symptoms to the husband's inconsiderateness or to other forms of his neglect during the pregnancy. Both types of mothers often consider the birth process traumatic, recalling experiences of difficult instrument delivery, laceration, and so on. Such mothers have been observed to be unable to cooperate in bearing down during childbirth, holding on to the child, so to speak, and thus making delivery more complicated.

The father who rejects parenthood outright is apt to be inconsiderate or cruel to his wife during the prenatal period. After birth he feels justified in punishing the child severely. If the child is a girl, he may also be seductive. The father who passively accepts parenthood continues the same attitude, "leaving everything up to the mother." Such fathers, in this family type, are mainly those who suffer from psychotic illness. The selfishly motivated male responds to fatherhood with boastful behavior, has limited awareness of his parental responsibility or of his child as an individual.

The mother's attachment to the child is colored by one of two factors: (1) the narcissistic value the child affords; or (2) the child's identification with a person who has had negative and anxiety-provoking value for her. She may, for example, identify a son with her depreciated, divorced husband, the father of the child, which elicits her fears that his tendencies will emerge in the boy. Or she may identify the child with an unloved or feared brother or father, which evokes anxiety that the child may become like them. Or she may attempt to reverse a maternal pattern of neglect on the part of her own mother by treating her child with the strictness she thought she craved when she was young. Thus the child serves neurotic purposes which make his presence necessary to the mothers. For these reasons, the mothers in the egocentric family do not easily relinquish their maternal rights because they are highly ambivalent about having children in the first place.

Distinctive to this class, but logical in the light of the foregoing emotional attitudes toward parenthood, is the fifty-fifty chance that parenthood will be attained in one of two ways: (1) by the birth of a single child or by a single adoption; (2) the composite result of adoption, acquisition of a stepchild, and the birth of own children. This is partly explained by the high proclivity toward divorce, with a correspondingly high tendency toward both remarriage and the adoption of children. It is rare, however, for both parents to bring children of a former marriage to the new union.

In the normal family, adoption is not motivated by parental aims which subsequently handicap the adopted child's development. However, the constellations of emotional forces which prompt adoptions in the egocentric family are such that these parents make unfavorable comparisons of the adopted child with an own child, or have unrealistic expectations of the adopted child, conceiving of him as an extension of themselves.

PHYSICAL MATURATION

Physical care of children in the egocentric family is given by the mother, who compulsively maintains adequate standards, in some instances to the point of regimentation. The father provides the wherewithal by which basic needs can be met but shows little personal interest in the children.

Differences do not arise between parents over the methods and quality of the physical care given their children. Rather their conflicts center upon the father's conviction that he suffers personal deprivation as a result of his wife's preoccupation with the children.

Such differences are understandably stimulated by the nature of things; namely (1) the mother's compulsive overprotection of the children and encouragement of their dependence upon her, which automatically excludes the father; (2) the father's infantile competitiveness, jealousy, and dependence, which are thereby provoked and accelerated to the detriment of all concerned. Therefore, when he protests his wife's child-rearing methods it is in anger over being left out, or as an excuse for depreciating her capacities as a female. Although such criticisms contain elements of validity, they are not motivated by concern for the child. Rather they represent his efforts to compensate for, and to mask feelings of, his own inadequacies as a male.

The mother's orientation to the physical needs of her children takes the form of an overstress on health and cleanliness. Mixtures of strong pride and resentment are manifested by her detailing every step taken to guard her children's physical well-being, with stress on all *she* does for them, smothering them with more than adequate physical care, subjecting them to frequent, unnecessary physical examinations, overregimentation, and rigidity in following doctor's directions.

This maternal overconcern does, in fact, have some justification. Children in this family type suffer from a variety of physical disabilities with known psychogenic components, such as allergic diseases, including bronchial asthma, eczema, neurodermatitis, constipation, ulcerative colitis. These disabilities place upon any mother-child relationship special demands which are not always easy for her to meet, and result in a certain degree of frustration for both. However, in the egocentric family the mother's efforts to meet these needs are characterized as follows:

Overprotection, combined with overrigid demands, fosters persistence of these particular disabilities in the child rather than allays the symptoms. This clinical picture of maternal-child relationship is strikingly similar to that reported by others in studies of the asthmatic child and his mother.

Eating is overemphasized. Preparation of large meals and special foods of her preference, is often accompanied by unreasonable restrictions on the child's choice—with such rationalizations as "eating such food makes the child so messy."

Toilet training is initiated early and is often forced. The mother may brag that she started the training when the child was a year old; that at two years and nine months he was "dry" 50 percent of the time, with bowel control established. In personal care, expectations are high, and the mother hammers on cleanliness.

LOVE RELATIONSHIPS

The predominant maternal reaction is a mixture of sexually tinged seductive attitudes and behavior with overrestrictiveness. Paternal reactions consist of either: (1) overtly hostile, harsh, and competitive behavior toward the child as an individual; or (2) an inconstancy of feeling that emotionally separates him from the child as a total personality. Occasionally, seduction and overrestrictiveness are present in both parents, but rarely in the father alone, in this particular family.

In most instances, mothers have an excessive emotional investment in boy children, and fathers, when seductive, are attracted to girl children. In either event, excessive restrictiveness in other aspects of child development is always a counterpart of the seductive parental response. On the one hand he is treated as an adult, and on the other, as a baby.

Through attitude, behavior, or both, the parent overstimulates the child's sexual impulses at the same time that he overrestricts the child's expression of normal aggressivity and hostility toward the seductive parent. This becomes an impossible psychological situation for the child. He is kept continuously dependent upon, and guilty toward, the parent, not only because of the seductiveness but also because of the restrictions upon aggressive behavior. There is no recourse for him but to remain a "child" and to develop neurotic symptoms as he gets older, these superimposed upon an essentially infantile character.

The egocentric family, composed of father and mother with a single child, an adopted child, or with combinations of own children and stepchildren, provides a particular opportunity for the parents to act out their conflicts through their children. Specific symptoms are typical of child-parent love relationship syndromes.

The child is valued as a "possession." In social feelings and behavior the mother expresses pride but little warmth for her children, often referring to the "boy," the "baby," the "girl," rather than by name or relationship. Persistent defensiveness, insisting that her children get along well, is typical: "They are *my* children, so of course I love them." If difficulties are pointed out by others, she blames the father or outside forces. (This is characteristic of the mother who has borne a child to prove her ability to do so.)

Fathers who love their children as possessions, seeing them as concrete evidence of their potency, characteristically play with them when they feel like it, enjoy roughhousing, but become impatient and irritated when children become sleepy or fussy, and often resort to spanking to stop their crying.

The child is an object of eroticized aggressivity. This parental response occurs mainly among fathers who may be subtly sadistic or overtly hostile, with an active dislike of the child, both tinged with sexual overtones: "I firmly believe in strapping until he jumps up and down." This kind of father is apt to lecture, nag, and criticize his adolescent daughters, but also to have a morbid preoccupation with the girls' sexual maturation. With some boys, the father's anxiety and fascination with sexuality result in suspicions of masturbation, followed by angry accusations, founded or unfounded, and deprecation of the boy.

The child is a substitute for adult love. The maternal reaction fluctuates between sexually stimulating and overprotective attitudes and behavior toward a boy child: overfondling, kissing, cuddling, allowing the child to rub her body, watch her bathe, and so on. When the child reaches the ages of eight, nine, and ten, the mother usually complains that he is a "baby," nags and criticizes but feels she must "give" more to him because of the father's dislike of the child. In a sense, she attempts to counterbalance destructive attitudes in the other parent, but her concept of how to do this is highly distorted.

When fathers use the child as a substitute for adult love, either the mothers also do so, with little conflict, or the father's seduction is directed toward a stepdaughter or an adopted child. In the first instance, although under strict supervision of the mother, the child's attachment to the father is encouraged. Under such circumstances, his relationship takes on a maternal quality which extends to the seductive; for example, he may spend several hours in bed soothing a seven- or eight-year-old girl to sleep. Incestuous acts with a stepdaughter are usually met by the mother with blame of the child, and disbelief followed by momentary anger at the husband. Temporary but ineffective measures are taken for the daughter's protection. She possesses minimal insight and concern as to the effect of the experience on the child.

Attachment based on marked identifications can exist on the part of either the mother or father but is mainly a maternal reaction. Toward daughters there is an identification with one's self: "I wish to spare my daughter all the pain I experienced"; "I always felt so close to Betty; there is a great void with her away"; "I am easily sympathetic because I know how I felt as a girl"; "I try to teach her to be a 'good' girl." At the same time, the mother's own behavior may be contradictory to what she teaches; for example, there may be extramarital sexual affairs, or an extramarital pregnancy obvious to the adolescent daughter but unacknowledged by the mother as a means of "protection."

With boy children, the identifications tend toward negative feelings, such as recoiling from the son who is a reminder in appearance and actions of the first husband; or fear that there is a predisposition in a particular child to psychosis because of its presence in two other relatives. With an adopted child there is pride if he behaves; disappointment, not anger, when he does not measure up: "He isn't like our first boy."

Thus, the particular predispositions within both parents reinforce each other, with a combined result which develops in their children unhealthy aims in the formation of object relationships. To a great extent, these mothers achieve vicarious gratification of their own infantile sexual strivings by loving the child who unconsciously represents themselves. Fathers are similarly motivated, but they also achieve a greater degree of vicarious gratification of ego-alien aggressive impulses through restraining patterns of minute control.

The development of self-identity, self-reliance, and a social conscience is well known to be closely tied to the love relationship between parent and child. The parental practices in the egocentric family markedly curtail this process in the child, due to the following tendencies: (1) overprotection from the normal vicissitudes of life, mainly by the mother; (2) overrepression of hostilities or normal outlets for expression of aggression by both parents.

Parents accept the behavior of the child and make love available to him as long as he acquiesces in being protected from exposure to the problems of ordinary social intercourse. Although the mother teaches the child that there are problems in life, she neither lets him experience them nor does she guide him in developing a sense of discrimination and judgment so that he can in future apply these principles himself. Opportunities for acquiring self-reliance are correspondingly restricted, depending upon the mother's particular anxiety.

Mothers of the egocentric family teach the young child in typical ways to become self-reliant. Forced and too early independence and self-sufficiency in personal habits and control of bodily functions result in socially useful activity prematurely acquired. There is limited chance for independent exploration and discovery. Operating simultaneously is the emotional indulgence of other dependency needs and the gratification of infantile sexual strivings. Restrictions in social contacts and protection from responsibility for personal behavior comprise the key handicapping factor of this constellation.

By the time the child has reached latency and adolescence, the maternal overprotection is more extensive and becomes superimposed upon the earlier pattern. Social activity with children of his own age is restricted. The parent intervenes in the child's behalf to solve his social problems for him; or continued parental anxiety about health may result in overrestrictive measures, arising from the fear that the child will get hurt, get into bad company, be sexually attacked, or from lack of confidence in his essential honesty, and so on.

Although both parents have a low tolerance for accepting their children's feelings of hostility toward them, they openly fight with each other and are hostile to the child and to other people. It is again a seductive situation, for by parental example the child is given permission to exploit others in personal relationships. The dishonesty of "Do as I say but not as I do" becomes a source of conflict and deep resentment in adult life.

Perfectionism in regard to school achievement and getting routines "just right," heavily weighted with a compulsive quality, typifies some families, a carry-over from the perfectionism of too-early training in control of bodily functions.

SOCIALIZATION

In teaching rules of social behavior, the egocentric family's approach is characterized by contradictory processes. Rigid standards are overcoercively imposed for home consumption, but eyes are closed to the implications of misbehavior elsewhere, depending upon who is affected. As in the development of self-identity, a significant part of this pattern is the parents' indulgence in transgressions which presumably they do not permit the child. The effects of this lip service upon the development of a normally functioning conscience become more evident as the child reaches school age and achieves greater physical adequacy.

Outstanding tendencies in socialization which have been noted among these parents include the unconscious support of faulty conscience. The parent upholds standards of social behavior but at the same time lies, disregards principles of honesty and the need to consider the rights of others. Collusion among family members, mainly mother and child, is manifested, for example, in sneaking money for the child behind the father's back. Parents scream, lecture, and demand immediate obedience at home but are casual about behavior outside, readily excusing the child by blaming the teacher's failure, a neighbor child, and so on. Irresponsible tendencies in the child are thus condoned, faulty superego development is encouraged, and the social conscience that emerges may be susceptible to easy corruption.

Child Development

Social behavior of the children in the egocentric family reflects the marked narcissistic value they have for the parent. A secondary influence determined by, and resulting from, the first relates to breaks in contact between a child and his own parent and the reasons for them.

EVENTS AND CIRCUMSTANCES

Breaks in the child's contact with an own parent and the meanings attached to these occurrences by the parents assume particular significance in egocentric families, and are causally associated with the subsequent syndromes of child behavior. In the main, breaches in contact are more apt to occur between father and child than between mother and child, unless the child is adopted. Of the families studied in the sample, those in which at least one child was separated from an own father but remained with his own mother numerically equaled those in which a single child was living with both parents.

The most frequent reasons for separation of children from an own parent are the divorce of own parents or an own parent's giving the child in adoption. Typically, children of marital unions dissolved by divorce become part of newly formed family units. In the main, this follows when mothers remarry. Thus, by this second union, the child acquires a stepfather and stepsiblings. It is the meaning which own parents, or step- or adoptive parents, attach to these situations as the child becomes associated with them, that is of greatest significance.

Occasionally, a child is separated at the mother's instigation, immediately following the breakup of her marriage. However, substitute arrangements, if made, usually are temporary, and the child is soon reunited with the mother. If this reunion does not occur shortly after the placement, the child is apt to remain in an institution or foster home until he is twelve, thirteen, or fourteen years old, and then to be returned to his own mother because the substitute arrangement is no longer available.

LOVE RELATIONSHIPS

Persistent symptoms of insecurity in the child under six of the egocentric family are indicative of anxiety about the conditions under which he can receive and maintain maternal love. Tenseness and nervousness in the very young child are manifested in well-developed phobias. In the four-year-old, tenseness occurs simultaneously with overaggressive behavior. In the one- and two-year-old, this tenseness is evidenced by constipation, food fads, and lack of interest in adults other than the mother. These features combine with increasingly frequent temper outbursts over minor restrictions. In the three- or four-year-old, the clinical picture is one of wakefulness, fear of animals, doctors, masks, nurses, combined with uncontrollable temper outbursts at restrictions, particularly bodily restraint.

These symptoms derive from a mother who is overrigid in training the child to control his bodily functions and who also is seductive in her behavior. The latter is evidenced in her giving in to the child's infantile wishes for emotional indulgence by overfondling, sleeping with him, and, by the time the child is three or four, continuing to be careless about exposing herself in the nude, allowing an "open-bathroom-door policy." Fathers are severe, punitive, spank because of crying, and so forth.

SELF-IDENTITY

Self-reliance, muscular skills, the ability and incentive to talk, to accept self-feeding, sleeping schedules, and the like are best acquired by the average child through gradual and kind encouragement from the parent. As this process lessens the young child's helplessness, it lessens also his susceptibility to anxiety. Conversely, anxiety is stimulated when he is compelled to rely too heavily upon himself.

Precociousness in achieving self-reliance is not unusual in the young child of this family type, but such independence does not indicate a true sense of security. The symptom picture again is a mixture.

Mothers may refer to the child as "the baby" when he is no longer an infant. At the same time, by reason of overaccelerated development, at age two the child may say the alphabet, tell his age by holding up one finger; by age three, feed, dress himself, and handle toilet habits independently. By age three and one-half he may be able to get his own breakfast. These particular skills of self-reliance pertain mostly to self-control and to mastery of bodily care and excretory functions, achieved through overcompliance with parental demands and conditions of love.

In this family type, the forced acceleration of self-reliance in early childhood also is combined with seduction by the mother. By age four or five, the overcompliance of the earlier period may be reversed, in protest against the overrestrictive, compulsive mother. As physical maturity becomes more advanced, behavior often becomes destructive. Asthma, enuresis, and constipation are among typical symptoms developed in this period. They are one evidence of anxieties as well as of arrestments in character development.

The combined overrestrictive and seductive elements in the behavior of the parent greatly deter or complicate the solution of this child's emotional problems at the oedipal period; namely, the time he must begin to renounce his infantile attachments to the parent. The groundwork for a faulty superego is thus laid and, with the onset of latency, learning inhibitions may be introduced and socialization become most difficult.

SOCIALIZATION

Control of bodily functions, expanding interests in toys, playmates, and so on, are aspects of the developmental stages for all children through five. Although quite adequate in looking after his body, the young child in the egocentric family has limited capacity to form social relationships. By the age of three or four, when he should be interested in both adults and children, he is either overactive with other children, thus alienating them, or overshy. Spontaneous interest in independent exploration of how toys work is apt to be inhibited. At the same time that his aggressive impulses are channeled prematurely into socially useful activities, his emotional dependency needs are being met by sexually stimulating behavior. This places him in a position of overcompliance to retain his parents' love. However, the strong natural urge to defend his own integrity continues.

When he is five or six years old, destructive behavior may appear. The child is then more mature physically and thus more capable of acting upon his impulses. He also learns that he can thereby control his parents. He may feel that in doing so he is taking a last stand in defense of his own identity. He often regresses as well to infantile symptoms, such as enuresis, thumb-sucking, masturbation, and so on.

LATENCY AND ADOLESCENCE

Symptoms which characterize the young child in the egocentric family seemingly are carried forward into latency and adolescence, at which time additional symptoms are superimposed. Compared to that in early childhood, his physical adequacy at six or seven and thereafter gives him increasing command over his environment. At the same time, new problems of emotional growth are introduced. These problems take on a particular character definitely related to the kind of emotional maturity achieved up to this point.

The character structure that these children carry over into latency and adolescence indicates marked fixations or regression to the anal and oedipal period. The former encompasses the training period of holding on and letting go, rivalries and ambivalence. The latter includes the sexual period of infantile dependent attachment to the parent of the opposite sex. The character traits and social behavior of these children are not materially altered at latency and adolescence, but assume greater proportions and more serious implications.

The development of latency and adolescent children in the egocentric family is continually influenced by the personality predilections of the parents which are seductive in nature; in most instances, mothers with boy children and fathers with adolescent daughters, although occasionally a mother will overidentify with a daughter. The child has been led to feel that he possesses or can gain the exclusive love of the parent. At the same time that he is not permitted overt expression of his aggressive impulses, they are being stimulated nonetheless by the parents' own transgressions. The parent unconsciously gives permission or is seductive on this score also.

LOVE RELATIONSHIPS

The older child's capacity for object relationships or meaningful emotional ties, as expressed toward the parent in the egocentric family, takes two general forms: (1) transient and superficial emotional ties; (2) some relationship capacity, but one which is heavily weighted with neurotic anxiety coupled with provocative or overdefiant, submissive responses to the parent.

By the time he reaches the latency or adolescent period the child of the egocentric family recognizes that the parent is really "dishonest." He identifies with this aspect of the parent's personality and sees no reason why he also should not be dishonest. He thus becomes like the parents, seducing and exploiting them as well as others.

Behavior symptoms most typical of children at the age of latency in the egocentric family denote the specific nature of their tie to the parent:

Exploitation of the parent is coexistent with mistrust. Although the child displays a variety of reaction formations, there is at this age level a high sensitivity to the emotional weaknesses of the parents, which can be provoked and thus exploited. Whether by combinations of aggressive behavior, withdrawal, physical symptoms, or other means, the emotional tie to the parent is sustained on this basis. Although intense, it does not always denote a relationship of depth and security but it is rarely broken.

Unemotional, sullen, or surly responses to both parents are coupled with other symptoms of a more aggressive nature. These may or may not be points of sensitivity for the parents and thus a source of exploitation. Outstanding examples are demandingness or "pickyness" about food, overeating, deliberate embarrassment of parents in public by boisterous behavior, defecating on a neighbor's floor, running away in a rainstorm. Accompanying these patterns and usually following in their wake are other forms of exploiting parents: pitting the mother against the father in his own infantile interest; acknowledgment of being "naughty" but then continuing the same transgressions or regressing to babyish behavior; accusations that the mother does "not love me."

Distrust of the parent is coexistent with sexual attachment. The father condones a boy's highly eroticized attachment to the mother; child and mother play "sweetie"—"You love me more than you do daddy, don't you?" When not indulged in every whim, the child screams, throws furniture, and so on. The girl child daydreams, clings to her mother, but fears the "bad thoughts" she has about her mother; at the same time, she contrives ways to get her stepfather's attention, by feigning illness, for example, so that he will rub her leg.

In the main, boy children have an intense but highly conflicted attachment to the mother. It is still eroticized, whether or not the symptoms are as gross as the foregoing. The sexual element is always present, with unusual curiosity about the mother's body, a turning to the mother rather than to the father for a confidant. At the same time, there is an active distrust of her and fear of the father, or, if there is a stepfather, there is actual searching to locate the own father.

Occurring in latency, where "good" behavior is more apt to be the rule, the symptoms of these children take on added significance in terms of their capacity eventually to form meaningful adult object relationships. For both girls and boys the central core of their problem is practically identical.

Certain behavior symptoms most typical of adolescent children in the egocentric family denote development of love relationship to parents. The boy adolescent has a weak tie to the father; a feminine, hostile tie to the mother. Again the provocative element, with underlying distrust, characterizes the boy's emotional tie to his mother. He wants to please and so becomes like her by acquiring a passive feminine orientation, always accompanied by resentment and arguments, calculated to annoy her. The father is in the background by the time this particular boy reaches adolescence—"My father is not interested in me; we never talk together"; "I like him only when he gives me generous gifts"; "I complained to the Juvenile Court because my father makes me work and doesn't supply my clothes."

A sudden breaking of the emotional tie is the most typical response of adolescent girls toward the mother. There is either deliberate flaunting of contempt for her, or indifference shown by shrugging off any reference to the parent—"I just smile and do as I please." Or there may be a hasty marriage in rebellion against a close tie maintained by the mother despite a feeling of detachment on the part of the girl. Occasionally, such a girl is susceptible to the seduction of a stepfather. Her response following such an episode is, "I thought mother didn't love daddy any more." Here again is a dependent but superficial tie to the mother which the girl attempts to break by turning to anyone who will show affection for her. This is not evidence of true adult sexuality but an unsuccessful thrust toward it.

SELF-IDENTITY

The accelerated independence acquired by many of the egocentric family's children in early childhood is retained by a few in latency and adolescence. However, the majority evade continued growth and maintain their dependence on the parent by controlling him, and in many instances they actually regress.

Those who retain some of the tendencies toward accelerated independence fluctuate between overdefiance and submission. Male children are apt to develop passive tendencies (still overcompliant to the parent).

Children in latency and adolescence who evade self-reliance by control of the parent, because a parent submits to their demands, take a reverse stand toward maintaining personal cleanliness from that displayed in earlier childhood. The adolescent may range from outright sloppiness to sheer enjoyment of being dirty. The child in latency may soil at home and sometimes at school, urinate on the floor when angry, and so on. Other exaggerated behavior apt to be characteristic of both age groups is slowness in dressing, waiting for the mother to nag or take over, demanding that meals be served on a tray in the living room, utterly disregarding stipulated hours for bedtime and rising, refusing to do home tasks of which they are capable.

Scholarship is typically average to excellent. A few children may fail. Those in latency who still remain overcompliant at home are nuisances at school, causing the teacher much trouble in such annoying ways as pushing in line, talking out of turn, and so on. Those who have rebelled at home frequently are cooperative at school, are well liked by teachers despite disturbances they may cause. By and large, however, adolescents who are rebellious at home are truants from school.

It happens that for certain children of the egocentric family, development of self-identity is furthered in the school experience. They can apply themselves academically and are strongly compulsive in this respect as well as in other forms of behavior. The group who were "overtaught" by the parent have a tendency toward precociousness. They find some narcissistic pleasure in abstract learning but maintain poor social relationships. However, their acquired knowledge is usually used to exploit others. These bright children perplex the average person because it is difficult to reconcile their ability to apply themselves in school, to be smart, with the pathological social behavior observed in their interpersonal relationships.

The egocentric family child's scholastic ability as contrasted with his inability to make friends strongly suggests that his central conflict is focused on specific parental figures in the family itself. In social adjustment these conflicts are displaced to children outside the family and to siblings. Sibling rivalry within the egocentric family is highly charged, with hostility of unusual intensity. Persistent quarrels, physical battles, excessive bossiness, and sometimes cruelty to younger siblings are frequent. When stepbrothers and sisters are acquired, displacement from the position of only child presents a greater than average problem for these children, due to parental attitudes and identifications.

The sexual impulses and curiosity of the average child between six and twelve years of age are not inactive but to a great extent are rechanneled into the task of learning physical skills and acquiring intellectual acumen. Stimulated by school attendance, at this age socialization becomes necessary and results in new friendships and the desire to please and keep such friends. A temporary equilibrium is reached in personality development in these years, as compared with the years through five, and is a prelude to the onset of adolescence.

In the majority of egocentric families, the latency child continues to be preoccupied with sexuality, either directly or through neurotic symptoms indicative of unresolved sexual problems of earlier periods. He also experiences prestige conflicts or is unsocial and aggressive in his relationships with peers. In a smaller number of families the children are overinhibited in sexual interests. They are passive rather than antagonistic and generally avoid close social relationships.

In seven-, eight-, nine-, and ten-year-old boys of the egocentric family the specific symptoms of sexual preoccupation are compulsive masturbation, fire-setting, bed-wetting as a substitute for masturbation, a compulsive wish to feel the mother and watch her bathe. The girl child rocks and pounds herself in bed (childhood schizophrenia).

Adolescent children of these families fall into two groups with respect to sexual adjustment: boys who act out sexually and girls who are overinhibited. This age period, when sexual impulses are intensified and the move toward the heterosexuality of adulthood is in process, poses a problem for any adolescent. Both sudden and too early gratification, through the sexual act, and total rejection of sexuality are dangers. Both extremes threaten eventual attainment of adult sexuality.

Specific examples of abnormal adjustment among adolescents of the egocentric family class include boys who tend to become involved in homosexual gangs or who molest girls sexually, with cruel mistreatment. Other forms of delinquency, such as larceny and disorderly conduct, usually accompany this behavior and come to the attention of juvenile authorities. Adolescent girls are generally fearful of boys, avoid them, show little interest. Delinquent activity may also be present, such as car theft, stealing, and so on.

The material suggests that the sexual adjustment of both boy and girl adolescents denotes a resistance to growing up, in the sense that normal socializing with the opposite sex holds for them many fears. Either it is avoided or it assumes distorted forms, or else delinquency, perversions, and so forth, are substituted.

SOCIALIZATION

Regardless of emotional ties to the parent or of self-identity achieved, at least one child of latency age or an adolescent in the egocentric family will be impaired in his capacities to form personal relationships with his peers or with adults. This is an outstanding and key factor since many of these are one-child families.

Children of these families are excluded by playmates and friends of their own age because of prestige conflicts, avoidance of relationships, or unsocial aggressive behavior. Listed in the order of frequency of occurrence are examples of each:

Prestige conflicts are evident when, because of his behavior and attitude, the child does not make friends. He feels unfairly treated when he loses a game, has difficulty in adhering to rules of the playground, responds with fear or temper when frustrated, prefers children older or younger than he, is a spoilsport when he does not win, tries to purchase friendships.

Avoidance of friendships is common. The child will not play with other children, preferring to have his mother read to him. He is overquiet and reticent, choosing to play by himself; never leaves his own yard, wanders off, or disappears. In adolescence, friendships are short-lived; girls are apt to have a boy as an only friend but no girl friends—with fear of dating in general. Sexual promiscuity is not characteristic.

Unsocial aggressive behavior toward peers occasionally occurs. Striking out, impulsive physical attack, whether provoked or unprovoked, punching, fighting, bullying, result in his being disliked and shunned except perhaps for one or two roughneck friends.

By and large, the older children of the egocentric family either conform to the rules of social behavior in the community and at school by overcompliance or are shrewd and exploiting in breaking rules. In the latter instance they cannily sense what can be done without getting caught. Exposure to delinquent behavior is not generally typical in these families. If there *is* exposure, it is by reason of association with a delinquent older brother or sister, rather than as a result of living in an undesirable neighborhood or with parents who have committed antisocial acts.

MARITAL FUNCTIONS

Rarely does husband or wife of the egocentric family cite "love" as one of the reasons for the marriage. Rather, the marriage partner achieves value and importance in the eyes of the other only insofar as he serves as the object through whom specific emotional needs can be gratified, directly or vicariously. Although these considerations normally influence the selection of all loved persons, they are predominant and extensive among the partners of this family type.

Reciprocal Love Relationships
OUTSIDE THE SEXUAL ACT

The quality of love which each partner in the egocentric family bestows upon the other is dominated by a strong ego that functions without the help of a sufficiently normal functioning superego so as to involve genuine consideration and affection. Thus the intimate interpersonal aspects of heterosexual living, as between husband and wife, cause one of the greatest difficulties in the egocentric family, endangering not only the purposes of the marriage but those of child rearing as well.

A strong ego in this case does not imply a well-integrated personality. Rather it means that these character traits overcompensate for lack of a firm sense of sex identity. This accounts for and explains seeming contradictions in their adaptation to particular family functions. One usually finds, for example, that the partners are capable managers, self-sufficient in planning and executing practical matters. Personal achievement is an accomplished surface reality. This evidence of social success coexisting with a wide departure from a desired optimal balance in the marriage love relationship is the typical marital syndrome for this family type.

"Opportunistic consideration" and "retentive withholding of consideration" are the terms used to indicate the emotional quality of the love and affection each spouse most likely expects to give to, or to receive from, the other. Either one or both of these patterns will be present in some form in one partner in the egocentric family, and most frequently in both husband and wife. The most probable exception is an inconsiderate husband, withholding and controlling, married to a wife who wishes a dependent, mutually giving and receiving kind of love relationship but who also exerts a subtle kind of control in her self-depreciating submission.

Syndromes characteristic of love relationships in this marriage therefore are to be noted. Opportunistic consideration is reciprocated insofar as the partner offers the opportunity for self-glorification and self-preservation. Thus, through another person, vicariously or directly, a perpetual flow of love is directed toward the self.

The female's expressed interest in the husband is based on prestige: "I like him because of his education and work"; "He is a man with a future." She emphasizes his status as a provider. Her personal interest in him is casual, but she is cooperative so long as material possessions are forthcoming. She may be disappointed that he is not more romantic, but "he's wonderful" as a provider.

In most instances in the sample studied, this female orientation formed a constellation with a husband who was not only opportunistic but also overcontrolling and withholding, by means of cruel restraints and minute control. In all instances, he saw his role as provider only. In return, he was to be admired and considered superior to his wife. Coupled with these expectations he demanded conformance and perfectionism in looking after his physical needs. Emotionally, he took no responsibility and made no decisions; all details of daily living were managed by the wife: "Her place is to keep house and entertain my business friends"; "I want a good housekeeper, that's all."

Other forms of opportunistic consideration are often based on vicarious gratification of nonacceptable sexual and/or aggressive impulses through the partner. One male, for example, demanded that his wife prove that she was a virgin before marriage; his wife complied, attracted by his unconventionality and his "adoration" of her.

WITHIN THE SEXUAL ACT

The male partner in the egocentric family experiences serious conflicts in maintaining an active sexual role with a female partner. With the great majority, the nature and/or the object of the striving are apt to be disturbed to such an extent that for all practical purposes intercourse is rejected as a primary source of direct sexual gratification.

Disturbances in the nature of sexual striving take the following forms: sadistic tendencies, with inflicting of pain a great part of the sexual act; voyeurism; primary gratification in retelling the partner of sexual activities with another female or hearing of those she has with another man; encouraging the wife to have extramarital affairs.

Replacement of the normal object by an unnatural one is likely to include pedophilia and homosexuality. Strong but not fully accepted preference for persons of the same sex is evinced in lack of interest in, and little need for, sexual activity with a female adult, accompanied usually by sexually stimulating behavior toward the child in the family. Coexistent with this attitude, in some instances, is a condoning of the child's acts of aggression, excusing him by blaming others or "pretending not to see."

In the sample studied, abnormalities in the object of sexual interest as well as in the nature of the sexual striving were present only in the male (77) and evidenced by morbid fascination with the wife's underclothing, shoes, and so on (fetishism). In certain instances, the male was excessively concerned with the size of his penis, fearing it to be too small, a symptom symbolically characteristic of the castration fear (7).

The female partner's capacity for sexual relationship with a normal male is minimal. Both the nature and the object of the sexual strivings are disturbed to a considerable degree.

Disturbances are apparent in two general ways: (1) Sexual intercourse with the marriage partner is a matter of form, with no particular interest in the act and little pleasure derived therefrom. (2) Fascination and pleasure are vicariously derived from identifying with the husband's deviant sexual tendencies. Sex, as such, may or may not be a point of conscious conflict between the husband

and wife. This is explained, in part, by the fact that neither one has a firm sex identification of his own, and since the sexual act itself is not important to either one, each is acceptable to the other. In addition, the wife does not ordinarily express within the sexual act itself her hostile feelings toward men in general.

The female partner's disinterest in achieving sexual gratification with a normal male is almost always accompanied by: (1) sexually stimulating behavior toward her boy children, who are substitute objects for her sexual needs; (2) overrestriction in regard to the sexual behavior of her girl children, although she may encourage them to defy the dictates of society in other areas.

These partners, fascinated with deviant forms of male-female sexuality, are apt to indulge in sexually stimulating practices in the children's presence, apparently deriving certain satisfactions from the exhibitionism. Appearance in the nude as a regular practice and the wife's capitulation to the husband's demands for sexual activity irrespective of the situation in the home are other possible symptoms.

Self-identity

In the egocentric family the opposite partner is consciously valued primarily as he contributes or does not contribute to the maintenance of the individual husband's or wife's own narcissistically oriented goals. A kind of negative reciprocity is apt to exist.

One partner respects and has confidence in the other only if he is or becomes the person the spouse wants him to be. In most instances, this way of sustaining self-esteem is acceptable to the recipient because of the nature of his own particular narcissistic needs and to the giver because of his identification with these strivings.

The conscious values supported in this type of relationship have certain characteristics. As a rule, in the beginning of the marriage the wife inflates her husband's unfounded sense of self-esteem with respect to his status as a male. For example, she praises his physical prowess, his big muscles; asserts that except for his "odd" sexual behavior or impotence he is her ideal; recognizes his family's greater social status.

The pathology of the wife's mechanism for sustaining her own and her husband's self-identity will also be characterized by a series of criticisms of a particular nature; namely, that "he will not listen to my problems, pay attention and try to understand my ideas"; "His conversations bore me"; "He is untrustworthy and weak." She complains of his laxity, contrasted to her own good management. Although the wife may also express marked feelings of self-depreciation as a woman—"What do other women have that I don't?"; "Why is my marriage a failure?"; "Why must I pay for everything I get?" —these are often rhetorical questions. Although she feels insecure or "dumb," she also knows how to control her husband with threats, pouting, tears, and so on.

The husband shows his limited respect for his wife as a person in any number of ways which are all unconsciously calculated to make him feel "superior." He deprecates her intellectual capacities as compared with his. He relegates her to the important but devalued role of keeping his house, running his errands, laying out his clothes. He is then unduly critical, denies warranted commendation, does not talk about his work because she would not "understand." He says that her discussion of problems is a sign of weakness.

Thus, to a great extent this aspect of the marriage partnership is tinged with sado-masochistic feelings and behavior. The wife becomes the object of the husband's aggressions, and his devaluation of her not only exploits but also increases the wife's already weak sense of feminine identity. Nonetheless, to a great extent she is equal to this: in turn, she exploits her husband by accepting this role so that she may have material possessions and the opportunity to control him.

Socialization

The marriage partnership in the egocentric family rarely fosters realistic appraisal of, and considered judgment in, dealing with a spouse's physical illness, emotional disturbance, or delinquent conduct. Nor do these partners view marriage as a process of continuous readjustment for each, with problems to be solved, not "gotten rid of."

HELPFUL CONCERN

In this family type, certain behavior and attitudes characterize the concern displayed by a spouse for a handicapped partner. In the event of mental illness or conduct bordering on the delinquent, both partners tend to close their eyes to the real implications of the symptoms. By so doing, they actually condone such behavior. This is not an unawareness of the fact that the spouse lacks adequate personal resources for control of his behavior. Rather its continuance has a secondary gain value, through providing an opportunity for one spouse to manipulate the other. Protective intervention in behalf of the afflicted partner usually occurs at the insistence of an outside source, or as a result of an incident that invokes legal action.

In the event of the wife's physical illness, the husband offers little emotional support to assure her recovery, although he provides needed medical care. When he himself is ill, he is unduly concerned, especially if his disablement impairs his occupational pursuits, which he needs to sustain his weak sex identity.

Thus, the emotional support and the practical help given the partner within the marriage relationship do not encourage the most constructive management of these individual impairments. However, one of the partners is quite likely to seek expert guidance in regard to marital problems of which these particular impairments may well be a part. Such action probably will be undertaken for narcissistic reasons, not in order to initiate salutary measures in behalf of the spouse. The stronger inclination in these partners is to deny that anything is wrong, particularly when an outside source makes a suggestion to this effect.

PROBLEM-SOLVING

The orientation of both partners with respect to solving problems is likely to reflect uncompromising and absolute values. Each expects the other to make continuous readjustments to his autocratically determined standards.

For these partners, feelings rather than judgment determine and dominate a point of view. In other words, there is limited capacity to evaluate the way in which emotion interferes with judicious action in the resolution of differences. Closely allied to this orientation is the projection of blame; problems are "resolved" by assigning to others responsibility for their existence. This approach is usually typical of both partners. Occasionally, the male partner will rely on his wife's encouragement or initiative in solving problems, in which case she carries this responsibility in an autocratic and un-compromising way.

FINANCIAL FUNCTIONS
Income Production and Management

In the egocentric family, assumption of the provider role by the husband is the rule. He may be the only wage earner, or both husband and wife may be employed. There is generally no disagreement or conflict about this division of labor. Earnings are pooled if they have agreed that the wife should continue in full-time employment. Rarely if ever is she the main family breadwinner.

The husband's attitude toward his work, in many instances, shows an inflated self-conception of his own worth, but for all practical purposes he is successful and self-motivated. There is a strong tendency to overcompensate for unacknowledged feelings of inadequacy as a male, based on a poorly established sex identification. This husband is apt to overemphasize to his wife his success, his status, prestige, promotions, resourcefulness. Bragging about his own importance is characteristic: "I make friends easily"; "I'm a pushover in getting along"; "I feel I have more than ordinary ability." These are usually valid self-appraisals, but the overstress marks them as defensive concealments of nonacceptable tendencies in himself. As part of this particular clinical picture, an inordinate amount of overtime may be spent at work, in learning new skills, taking specialized courses, and so on.

Some few husbands in this class are not strongly motivated to achieve, feeling that they are not "good enough." Nonetheless, they can take direction and are steady on the job.

The employed wives in these families have similar tendencies. They are apt to have ability and to be successful. Many have worked prior to marriage and possess some skill. When both partners work, their rivalry does not seem to be so great as when the husband alone is the main wage earner. Under this circumstance the husband's inclination toward braggadocio is much more in evidence.

The husband's occupation is varied, but it is likely to have certain prestige values or precision requirements. For example, he may be an engineer, research assistant, biology teacher, certified public accountant. Or, the job may provide exhibitionistic opportunities such as are found in advertising, real estate selling, sales promotion, merchandising. Often the wife has been a schoolteacher, registered nurse, dietitian's aid, bookkeeper, or telephone operator. In the main, both husband and wife possess a variety of occupational skills.

Although husbands expect to earn a living and to support their families, they are likely to have a marked propensity to save scrupulously, to allocate allowances on a tight basis, to provide only the essentials for the family but withhold the surplus for personal indulgences and luxuries. At the same time, there is a fifty-fifty chance in this family type that the income will be managed well, either by the wife or by the husband, with a low incidence of impulsive spending. Nonamortized debts, nonsupport by desertion, and/or financial assistance from a community agency are not typical in either instance.

Thus, in financial functioning, the pattern revealed by the egocentric family includes the ability to look after others. Their family of origin histories substantiate an identification with either their mother or father, on this score.

ADULT CHARACTERISTICS
Physical Condition and Intelligence

The parents in the egocentric family are in relatively good health and free from disabling illness. Numerically, nondisabling illnesses are essentially no different from those of the other three family types. Distinctions lie in the character of the illness.

The males of the egocentric family, by and large, are apt to be healthy. Illnesses may include hernia, ulcer, and aftereffects of poliomyelitis. The female is more prone to physical ailments than is the male, with menstrual and gynecological disorders most frequent and arthritis, high blood pressure, and hernia next.

Ego Defenses

Ego defenses most typically used by the male of the egocentric family are exaggerated forms of reaction formation, or substitution of a socially valued attitude for an ego-alien impulse. Second in prominence is the frequent use of projection in relation to a loved object. Acting out of infantile sexual impulses is prominent.

The female, too, frequently resorts to a pathological use of projection as a main defense. Her capacity for self-criticism is thus impaired, suggesting interruption in superego development. The derivation of this mechanism is explained to a great extent by her family of origin history, where overpunitive and overcoercive attitudes played a large part. Reaction formation in an exaggerated form also appears as her defense mechanism in handling destructive aggressive impulses. This is manifested in so-called "socially valued" attitudes toward self-sufficiency, such as overconcern about her children. Reaction formation, used interchangeably with verbal self-blame, is the defense pattern the female partner employs in handling anxieties created by the marital relationship. As with the male, acting out of infantile sexual wishes is apt to be a defense.

Other defenses tend toward extreme irritability or exploitation. There is not much difference between the male and female on this score.

Emotional Stability

The clinical material with respect to both partners of the egocentric family seems to show a predominance of the kinds of problems clinically observed in character types with excessive narcissistic needs and a considerable oral-level influence. In narcissistic characters of this type, male and female identity may often not be well established. Compensatory behavior manifested in sexual experimentation and, frequently, in sexual deviations is the unconscious attempt to handle this problem of poorly established sex identity.

Failure may be reflected in repeated divorces and remarriages (75).

That which differentiates this narcissistic character group from the hysteric is that hysteria in itself is not associated with acting out. The acting-out defense of the narcissistic character as compared with the other forms of acting out is characterized by the predominance of the previously noted oral-level elements; namely, extreme sensory excesses of an oral nature, including various sexual deviations, use of drugs, alcohol, and other forms of addiction. Because of the oral component, this type of character is difficult to deal with, therapeutically speaking (75). As compared with the unsocial family partners, however, the egocentric partners have relatively better integrated egos and superegos, and their acting out is of a more sexual nature.

The presence of psychotic illness in the mother or father is no more frequent in the egocentric family than in any of the other three family types. In females, the diagnosed psychoses present in the sample were schizophrenic reaction, paranoid type; schizophrenic reaction, catatonic type (arm paralysis); and psychotic depressive reaction. In the males, diagnoses included schizophrenic reaction, paranoid type; and schizophrenic reaction, paranoid type, with pathological behavior of fetishism. Typically, the psychotic breaks occurred during the course of a case. Either they resulted in hospitalization or the patient remained at home, continuing to show recognizable residual disturbances.

CHILD CHARACTERISTICS
Physical Condition and Intelligence

Unique to the children of the egocentric family in the sample studied were acute and chronic physical complaints of a particular nature. Disabilities, such as broken bones, that are not permanently impairing resulted from accidents. Chronic ailments were of two general sorts, both known to have psychogenic components. First in frequency were allergies and bronchial asthma, sinus trouble, nosebleed, and so on. Second in occurrence were disturbances of the lower intestinal tract, severe constipation, ulcers, or stricture of the rectum.

These ailments were present in children of the egocentric family in just over a quarter of the sample studied. It is generally accepted in medicine that when an allergy exists there must be some constitutional predisposition to a particular allergen. Usually, a typical syndrome of mother-child relationship exacerbates the physical problem. Our materials substantiate this clinical picture. For example, in the general population, adolescence is the usual time for children to develop asthma, although pediatric clinics do record cases at earlier ages. However, in the egocentric family, all children so afflicted had developed their allergic and intestinal disabilities before the age of seven.

Congenital conditions can exist in any family, but by comparison with other family types there were few occurrences in the egocentric family—and those were some type of mental retardation.

Psychic Disturbance of Latency

In practically all families classified as egocentric in the sample, if a latency child were present, he suffered from psychic disturbances. In no instance was there only a single psychic disorder. The constellation of conduct disorders and neuroses predominated in a very large majority of children of egocentric families; this constellation plus infantile phenomena and/or motor disorders appeared in slightly over half of the families. Diagnosed psychoses, although negligible numerically, are nonetheless significant with respect to this family type.

Conduct disorders take two forms in the latency child of the egocentric family: (1) withdrawn behavior, which means avoidance of close relationships with adults and children; (2) aggression shrewdly calculated to avoid punishment, and sadistic acts to younger children and animals. Within these two constellations of conduct disorders, infantile phenomena appeared as thumb-sucking, compulsive masturbation, nocturnal and diurnal enuresis, soiling. Urinating and defecating, in most instances, represented a hostile striking-out gesture toward parents or those in authority. Within the context of this family type, such symptoms serve as a spiteful and hostile protest against an overrigid but seductive mother and a punitive, harsh father. Motor disorders, if a part of the clinical picture, consisted of purposeless movements, hyperactivity, head rolling, or body rocking.

The predominance of infantile phenomena in the latency child is noteworthy as compared with that in children of the other family types, with the exception of the unsocial. In the eight-, nine-, and ten-year-old child, such symptoms indicate a fixation in, or regression to, earlier stages of the three- or four-year-old's personality development. Thus in the latency child of the egocentric family the use of excretory functions as a means for expressing aggressions denotes a severe degree of pathology. Similarly, wetting and excessive masturbation, mainly by boys, are probably indications of castration fear stimulated by an overpunitive father and a seductive mother.

The multifactored aspects of these psychic disturbances make up the usual picture. Although symptoms rarely occur in isolation, the preponderance of infantile phenomena in children from seven to ten, coupled with the nature of the conduct disorders, points to severe impairments in psychic development of these children, a foreboding of greater difficulties to come if they are not treated.

Psychic Disturbance of Adolescence

When psychic disturbances are present in the adolescent of the egocentric family they probably signify one of two conditions: (1) severe pathology bordering on psychotic illness; or (2) reluctance to grow up. Occasionally, there will be a sudden withdrawal of emotional ties, with new attachments to gangs of delinquent adolescents.

Reversal of affect occurs when the adolescent's dependence upon the parent is turned to revolt. As a result, there is no room for independent growth, and compulsive opposition proves as crippling as obedience. Under such circumstances, the acting out is apt to occur only within the family. The danger to the personality of the adolescent, however, lies in the projective defenses that may develop. Extreme forms noted were paranoid behavior, depression, and self-abasement.

Withdrawal of affect, characteristic of the initial stages of psychotic illness, occurred in certain adolescents in the egocentric family. Typical were fantasies of saving the world.

Repression manifested by a state of confusion, with negligible distinction between the external and the internal world, also occurred in some adolescents of this group.

Reluctance to grow up is typical of the "good" latency child and is apt to be characteristic of the adolescent boy in the egocentric family. He remains attached to his mother, is considerate of her, and submissive to his father. Psychosomatic symptoms and disinclination to form friendships outside the home are among other possibilities.

Sudden withdrawal of emotional ties is common for adolescent boys and girls in the egocentric family. At home, the boys may ignore parental entreaties and away from home continue to disregard rules of social behavior. Girls may marry suddenly and leave home, but remain tied as securely as before in an emotional relationship with their mother.

MALE PARTNER'S FAMILY OF ORIGIN

During childhood, male partners of the egocentric family usually had the consistent presence of their own mothers from infancy through the twelfth year; in most instances, even longer. In the great majority of cases, own fathers were present from the male's birth until he reached the age of sixteen. Separation occurred primarily as a result of the father's death, usually when the male reached adolescence.

Although some of these mothers were widowed, they did not remarry. Substitute parents were not a part of the childhood picture, and there was no instance of placement with relatives, in foster homes, or in institutions. There is no indication of maternal rejection in the sense that the mother relinquished responsibility for her son by reason of divorce, desertion, or lack of affection.

As a point of differential diagnosis, the presence or absence of an own father, variations in family structure, use of substitute parents, and reason for separation from an own parent are markedly similar for the egocentric family male and for the male in the perfectionistic family. The real distinction lies in other factors.

Adequacy of Financial Support

Own fathers of the male partner were adequate providers, their chosen occupations varying from farmer to sales manager to teacher. Mothers worked to support the family after the father's death. In some families, both parents were regularly employed.

Love Relationships

The mother dominated the male partner's family of origin. Fathers were primarily guilty of emotional neglect, failing to recognize or to accept responsibility for their son's developmental needs. Either they were preoccupied with business and social interests or they ignored the son outright. As a result, the mother assumed the primary responsibility for his upbringing.

All own mothers were aggressive, adequate women who accepted their sons if they submitted to arbitrary correction and direction of their activities, irrespective of their need for spontaneous self-direction. The mother's rationalization was probably to the effect that she loved the boy so much that he must be molded in the image of what she thought he should be. The aspect of childhood development which was upsetting to these mothers was the emergence of their son's masculine and aggressive strivings. Thus, to retain the mother's love the son had to submerge these strivings and/or become like her. In cases where the father was dead, the mother placed the male child in the latter's role. Seductive, smothering, excessive emotional investment in sons was typical in all families where the father was not present.

Outstandingly absent or insignificant were conditions of love and acceptance based on parental ideals which the son was expected to meet even though he was unable to do so. Nor did these parents submit completely to the immature and unreasonable demands of the child, without regard for their own rights.

Self-identity

The families of origin of the males of the egocentric family set a pattern for identification with a father figure who valued accomplishment in his chosen occupation and in taking care of others. This was reinforced by the mothers, who also derived satisfaction and status from work achievement. Obviously, these influences are seen in the fact that males of the egocentric family usually emphasize the importance of recognition and economic advancement. They assume responsibility as providers for wife and child, in accordance with cultural standards. The psychodynamics of this accomplishment are further explained by the conditions under which love was given to the male as a child by his own father and mother. It explains, as well, the quality of love given to him by his parents and its influence upon the kind of object relationship he is capable of forming as an adult. This is accounted for in overdirection and seductiveness on the part of an own mother, coupled with the father's lack of emotional investment in his son. Both contribute to and increase his adult personality problems and the self-identity he has acquired. Identification with both father and mother with respect to achievement is evident.

However, the males of the egocentric family brought to adulthood severe conflicts regarding their right to a masculine identity in the fullest sexual sense. The explanation for this rests with the mothers' emotional investment in the sons and the fathers' remoteness toward them. The self-confidence and the sense of ego identity which they have attained are reflected in their decisions pertaining to family life, and are expressed in various ways.

Resistance by passive obstructionistic tactics is linked with the expectation, and frequently the demand, that the wife assume responsibility for deciding issues. At the same time, hostile, spiteful responses, blame, and criticism ensue when she does this.

The psychic reaction underlying the husband's behavior is probably the feeling that no matter what is done it will probably not be right, and he can never please anyway. To avoid repetition of earlier unpleasant experiences, he resists, leaving himself open to criticism. In so doing, his resentments pile up and finally come out in these controlling, obstructionistic techniques.

Oversubmissiveness in making choices is expressed by allowing his wife to make them. There is a ready giving-in, accompanied, however, by the attitude that in so doing he will be exploited, cheated, or punished. Hostile outbursts in protest, projection, or blame punctuate this submission, often evoking punishment.

The psychic reaction to making choices is the feeling that no matter what he decides, he will be punished. But, here again, there are hostile outbursts and projections, the latter to ease unconscious guilt over such impulses.

In current functioning, the male partner's conflict over sexual identity usually assumes one of two forms: infantile sexual strivings *directly* expressed in sexual perversions; or, more characteristically, in strong but *unconscious* homosexual tendencies. Underlying both of these reaction formations are intense hostile feelings toward women.

SOCIALIZATION

Overstrictness in training and arbitrary decisions as to right and wrong characterized the emotional atmosphere of the egocentric family male's home. Antisocial behavior, as defined under Level A psychosocial disorders, was not identified in members of his family of origin. In current functioning this also is true of the male partner's adjustment except as indicated under typical psychosocial disorders.

FEMALE PARTNER'S FAMILY OF ORIGIN

The life history of the female partner in the egocentric family also shows that own mothers were present during infancy, and through age sixteen in the vast majority of cases. If and when separation occurred, it was likely to be when the child was under three years of age, in most instances. However, fathers were apt not to be present. Occasionally, neither mother nor father was present. The reasons for the father's absence were death or desertion. When both parents were absent, the usual reason was the mother's death, followed by desertion of the father, who was never heard from again.

Two striking factors stand out with respect to continuity of contact between own parents and child and also serve to explain substitute arrangements: (1) Both father and mother were frequently separated from the female at an early age as compared to the female partner's history in the other classes. Substitute arrangements, necessitated by the absence of both parents, included foster homes, older sisters, grandmothers, or institutions. (2) The mother relied on older children to supplement her own maternal role in the absence of the father. These variations created a family atmosphere that differed from the normal. Interestingly, these mothers did not desert the female partner in childhood, but tended to leave her in the care of someone else. In general, the mothers invested little genuine emotion in this child, leaving the maternal tasks of childrearing or education to older children or to grandmothers.

Adequacy of Financial Support

In general, the female partner's family of origin was self-supporting; instances of financial assistance were noted. In the majority, the father was the chief provider, his earnings often supplemented by the mother's employment. In a lesser number, the female partner's older brothers, sisters, or maternal grandmother assumed this responsibility in the absence of the father. If the mother had no husband she relied upon older children as a source of revenue or upon income from her maternal grandmother. There seems to be no indication that as a child the female partner worked for the support of the family. Rather she was taken care of, and thus subject to control, by a brother or sister, but her own mother was always present.

Love Relationships

Two factors, either singly or in combination, distinguish the kind of "love" the mother and father or parental substitutes bestowed upon the female partner of the egocentric family in her childhood:

(1) emotional neglect, denoting that the child was expected to pursue her own goals and find her own satisfactions unassisted; (2) overpunitive or coercive measures, using the child as a target for hostile, aggressive impulses.

The mother's neglect of the female partner as a child had a dual aspect. Although she did not use her as an object of hostility, the mother actively permitted the daughter to receive the full impact of the father's, older brothers', or older sisters' dominating, indulgent, or seductive behavior. In other words, the mother did not ignore completely; she failed to protect the child from the coercive, punitive behavior of others, thus condoning it by default or by not "seeing" it.

Among own fathers of the female partner, neglect of her in childhood was primarily in the legal sense, through desertion, separation, or "whereabouts unknown." When both father and mother were emotionally neglectful, although physically present, they also allowed others (grandmothers, sisters) to be coercive, overpunitive, or oversubmissive with the female child. The sexual attraction of father to daughter or brother to sister was expressed in hostile provocative behavior toward the girl as her feminine strivings began to emerge at adolescence.

Self-identity

Most female partners in the egocentric family make some attempt to defend their self-identity. Raised in a family atmosphere in which overpunitive measures were used, in adulthood this female has a mixed reaction toward self-directive activity. She entertains a feeling that she will be punished no matter what she does, so she is oversubmissive to her husband, letting him dictate what shall be done. Once having submitted, however, she protests this state of affairs from time to time in retaliatory behavior.

The second most typical self-concept, arising from this background, is very much like that of the male partner's; that is, the conscious attitude that someone else (usually the spouse) should take responsibility. Although she may accept responsibility, she constantly provokes the husband by obstructionist techniques, with a periodic passive refusal to do anything. Her self-identity is tinged with self-doubt, and although she is not impulsive, her decisions and self-direction are impaired insofar as her relationship with her husband and children are concerned.

Socialization

Antisocial behavior and laxity with respect to law and order were not characteristic of either parent of the female partner in the egocentric family, nor were there overstrict religious attitudes. Neglect of children was related to desertion and divorce. In one sense, there was cohesiveness among family members in that almost all mothers tended to keep the family together despite absence of the father. Children were expected to look after one another, with the maternal grandmother exerting extraordinary influence as a dominating figure, even when both parents were present. This latter factor is almost unique to the family of origin of the female partner of the egocentric family.

VIII. THE UNSOCIAL FAMILY

THE MEMBERS of this family type are the least emotionally equipped of the four disordered family classes to experience the pleasures and meet the frustrations of their psychosocial responsibilities. The class has been designated "unsocial" to denote the family's lack of social rapport with other people and with their environment. The emotional tone and characteristic behavior of the unsocial family are conditioned by one or more tendencies that are always present in both partners and usually in their children: (1) a paucity of ideals in the resolution of ordinary problems, with social demands and reality given secondary consideration; (2) deviant social conduct that constitutes a major or minor offense against the culture; (3) thought processes and powers of concentration so twisted that the individual often is unable to care for himself, may endanger his own welfare or another's, or is a victim of designing persons.

In other words, more than one family member is personally and socially maladjusted to an extent that entails serious consequences, either social or legal. These pervading handicaps adversely affect male-female relationships in the marriage partnership, the parent-child relationships, work habits, child development, and relationships with the community at large.

Strong inclinations in the adult toward acting-out behavior, delinquent conduct, and/or regression into psychosis, and the fact that one or more of these adaptive responses always is present in both partners, distinguish the unsocial family from other family types. However, only when taken in the aggregate do these particular admixtures of traits in the adults produce social behavior characteristic of the unsocial family type. Income level and social status are not the primary factors that determine this family class.

The nature of the psychosocial disorders in the unsocial family mirrors the handicaps to social adjustment present in the adult heads. Consequently, there is a strong possibility that several of these will be Level A disorders or will become so.

CHILD-REARING DISORDERS

Child-rearing disorders are serious, multiple, and persistent in all unsocial families. Level A child-rearing disorders are likely to be identified as child neglect or child dependency. Both may result in child placement for the following typical reasons: divorce; separation; a parent's hospitalization for mental illness; criminality; relinquishment of parental responsibility associated with not wanting the child; the child's illegitimacy, delinquency or mental illness that requires detention or treatment away from home.

Disrespect for social authority inevitably is communicated by the parent to the child, whether directly or in devious ways. The presence of a psychotic parent and/or a parent who has himself committed antisocial acts increases the severity of these child-rearing practices.

CHILD DISORDERS

Level A child disorders are very likely to be present. Those most frequent are: delinquency; truancy; psychotic illness or severe personality disorders that require, or eventually may demand, detention, probationary supervision, incarceration, or hospitalization of the child. It should not be assumed that all school-aged and adolescent children of the unsocial family become delinquent or are hospitalized for mental illness. Whether or not child disorders become Level A type will be determined largely by the social prestige and income the family has at its disposal for providing legal protection and treatment of the child.

The outstanding feature underpinning Level B child disorders in the older child of the unsocial family is his tendency to identify with one parent and to hold the other in low regard. A secondary but prominent aspect of these parental ties is the high intensity of jealousies that exist among the children.

MARITAL DISORDERS

As in other aspects of living, the marital disorders in the unsocial family are distinguished by a multiplicity of symptoms and rapidly changing attitudes. Level A marital disorders occur because the partners prefer to solve such problems by legal measures. Therefore, the services of family or domestic relations courts, complaints to the local police, and, in many instances, divorce courts are used by the partners and indicate Level A disorders. If divorce ensues it is not uncommon for the partners to remarry one another; in extreme cases, a divorce occurs so that a new marriage of convenience can take place. Bigamy is always a possibility as is a marital alliance without benefit of legal process.

FINANCIAL DISORDERS

Level A financial disorders are more common to the unsocial family than to the ordinary family. As previously indicated, dependency, with either total or partial financial assistance for maintenance and sometimes for child placement, is very possible. Nonamortized debts and court orders for nonsupport may form another constellation of Level A financial disorders.

Level B financial disorders reflect the fact that money is of pressing and signal importance to this family type. Two general conditions precipitate financial crises: (1) money not earned or, if earned, not used for basic family requirements; and (2) available income procured by illegal means.

ADULT DISORDERS

The high occurrence of psychopathological conditions handicapping to social adjustment and mental health leads to a variety of serious adult disorders in both partners of the unsocial family.

Level A adult disorders are common, including: hospitalization for mental illness; major or minor crimes, such as embezzlement, forgery, disorderly conduct, drug addiction; and sexual deviance, including incest.

In the male partner, Level B adult disorders are indicative of the dominance of receptive demands and/or passive feminine tendencies. Social indices of receptive demands may be noted in such immature reactions to responsibility as alcoholism, drug addiction, helplessness in taking command of even a minor situation, strong attachment to an own mother, requiring her presence, or excesses in emotional outbursts when unappreciated. Passive feminine tendencies may be expressed by a series of extramarital affairs, pathological lying, and forgery.

In the female partner, adult disorders will probably be characterized by unrestrained freedom in directing hostilities toward the male and, in general, toward any form of authority. Her hostility and exploitation of the male may also be demonstrated in promiscuity, relegation of the husband to a position of nonentity by ignoring and depreciating him, or consciously or unconsciously aiding and abetting his pursuance of antisocial acts, aberrant behavior, and so forth.

CHILD-REARING FUNCTIONS
Parental Functioning
EVENTS AND CIRCUMSTANCES

In general, the status of parenthood is acquired in the unsocial family as a result of impulsive action, without reflection or anticipation and many times without genuine interest in fulfilling the emotional and social responsibilities of child rearing. Certain parental reactions are possible, both prior to and after the birth of their children.

Outright rejection of parenthood may occur. The mother's acknowledgment that she never wanted any children, when accompanied by a like paternal reaction, usually results in the mother's yielding to the father's demands to "sell the baby," "to place it at birth," "give it away" to a relative, and so on. Usually, these children are not adopted but are returned ultimately to their own mothers at the insistence of placement agencies. This takes place as adolescence approaches, or at a time when the parent thinks the child can be a source of revenue.

Parenthood can be a provocative element in marriage. There are many facets to this reaction. By and large, fathers do not want children. This is displayed in various ways—demanding abortion; deserting before the baby comes; taking drugs as a protest during the wife's pregnancy; regressing to illness throughout the prenatal period; blaming the wife for having conceived.

Mothers never want the child when they are first pregnant but later are delighted—"I just want to watch my children grow up." Although she does not invest genuine emotion in the child himself, for the mother each birth has provocative value in relation to the husband. Having children against his will keeps things stirred up, denies him the sole attention he craves. In some instances, the mother derives pleasure from a pregnancy or birth because it is always associated with a separation from her husband. Children thus give her the feeling that "I have something of my own."

Illegitimately conceived children and extramarital pregnancies, when used as a means of forcing marriage, may thereafter be used to manipulate or provoke the father.

An egocentric value in parenthood exists since parents of the unsocial family want children solely for some reason of self-interest. The mother has a high preference for boy children, with parenthood acceptable only on this basis. The father is pleased by his wife's pregnancy, since this allays his fears of her being out with other men; or, with the birth of a child, the father can assume the maternal role to the exclusion of appropriate masculine activity.

Emotional investment in the husband to the exclusion of the child is common. Some mothers are primarily concerned with sustaining the marriage partnership, with minimum concern for the child's developmental needs. Stepfathers consistently dislike stepchildren, often to the point of cruelty and denial of physical care. Mothers typically reject, as a threat to their marriage security, an own child who has been brought to a second or third union.

PHYSICAL MATURATION

A variety of persons may take primary responsibility for the physical care of children in the unsocial family: mother, father, relatives, older children, substitute parents, foster home parents, or institutions. Distinctive in these families is not only the tendency to leave the total care of their children to others, mainly to community agencies, but also the relative frequency with which certain fathers prefer to assume the maternal function of ministering to the needs of the children. This arrangement, in most instances, does not supplement the mother's care but constitutes a replacement of her functions, a reversal of the usual male-female role as a way of life.

The quality and consistency of physical care given to children in these families are seen in typical situations and practices:

Adequate physical care is given to children who are placed by community agencies or with relatives. Occasionally, a mother will provide protection, attend to nutrition, health, hygiene, and so on. Often, however, this attention is accompanied by overregimentation and rigid practices. Training in control of bodily functions may be both forced and too early. At the other extreme, there may be a denial of any problem—"They are all so good"—or trouble in enforcing bedtime schedules. Occasionally, a father will attempt to supplement his wife's inadequacies, but in doing so will be overstrict and inflexible.

Haphazard care is too frequent. No adherence to schedules, irregularity of household management, limited assistance in teaching the child self-care, are likely patterns on the part of both parents. Mothers of this sort are ineffectual, may see what is needed but be unable to follow through in providing it.

Other haphazard practices include dependence upon canned foods to meet nutritional needs, laxity about physical checkups, failure to supply or give prescribed medication, and so on. In such instances the fathers, having similar standards, shift responsibility whenever possible, or consider that by providing the funds they have fulfilled society's demands, irrespective of the standard of care actually given. In merged families, the mother's children by former marriages are likely to receive haphazard care as a result of the stepfather's outright refusal to provide for any children but those of the current union, which dictum the mother accepts.

Fathers sometimes prefer the maternal role. In this type of case, mothers elect to be the wage earners and fathers provide physical care and protection for the children. Pathological interest in caring for an infant is not uncommon, with absorption in the child to the complete denial of an active masculine role. A psychotic father, for example, may give full care to five- and six-year-old sons who, the mother knows, are fearful of him. Nevertheless, she continues her employment.

Inadequate housing is not necessarily typical of the unsocial family but occurs more frequently in this class than in the others. If living arrangements are undesirable, with lack of privacy for sleeping, use of bathroom facilities, and so on, the parents are usually indifferent to the situation; they feel that "any place is all right."

LOVE RELATIONSHIPS

The affectional tie of parent to child in the unsocial family is highly colored by the parents' own insatiable dependent cravings, as well as by their exploiting orientation toward the world in general. Three reactions provide the key: (1) inconstancy of feeling for the child as a total person, resulting in emotional separation of parent from child; (2) hostility, with avowed dislike of the child, using him as an object for direct expression of destructive impulses; and (3) overdevotion, with encouragement of dependence upon a single parent to the exclusion of all other attachments.

The following constellations of maternal and paternal affectional responses are those most typical of the unsocial family type:

Maternal inconstancy of love, coupled with hostile aggressive paternal reaction, is associated with the child's illegitimacy or the mother's psychotic illness. Because of his illegitimacy, and immediate placement, the child may be ignored for many years, and later unwillingly accepted into the family of a new marriage. As a result of tendencies toward depressive reactions bordering on psychosis, these mothers generally are characterized by remoteness and by rejection of all close personal relationships. Frequently, this is accompanied by promiscuous sexual behavior and the birth of children conceived extramaritally. Concern over such behavior may be expressed as, "I must not see my boy friend," but rarely is this resolve acted upon.

Fathers in this constellation are extremely hostile toward the child or children. For example, they may resort to cruel treatment, begrudge material necessities and restrict the mother from providing them. On the one hand, such a father may scream at girl children, and on the other hand be seductive with them. He may upbraid the boy child, questioning his legitimacy: "You're no son of mine."

The high occurrence of the parental response of inconstancy of love is accounted for in three general ways: (1) abnormalcy of the parent, due to psychotic illness, with all object relationships severely impaired; (2) physical separation of the child from the parent, in such ways as leaving him to the care of others, desertion, or divorce; (3) emotional separation of parent from child, growing out of the child's illegitimacy, the parent's preoccupation with the marriage relationship with his own emotions (nonpsychotic). Of significance is the fact that withdrawal of interest or lack of genuine emotional investment in a child on the part of one parent is not counterbalanced by positive attitudes on the part of the second parent.

Maternal overdevotion, coupled with hostile or inconstant paternal reaction, takes varied forms. The mother encourages a flow of love from the children toward herself but at the same time insists upon their disrespect of the father. This may be expressed openly, by keeping the children isolated from him in separate parts of the home, or indirectly through encouragement of overdependence upon her. This is accompanied by the mother's failure to protect the children from the father's mistreatment. Often, she provokes the children to hostility toward the father, both as a retaliatory gesture and in order to enjoy vicariously her own antagonisms toward him and, in fact, toward the children. Thus her overdevotion and her "satisfaction in producing children" are deeply tinged with hostility. One common attitude is that the children are possessions: "At least I have something of my own"; "They are *my* children."

The hostile father in this constellation may display several highly contrasting attitudes. For example, on the one hand, he demands demonstrative affection from a small child, with bursts of anger when it is not forthcoming, and on the other hand, weeps when he cannot see his children. Or he takes pleasure in playing with the child, as would another child, but then in anger throws away all the youngster's toys. Or he desires a family consisting entirely of boys, resents and mistreats girl children.

The inconstancy of the father's love, or his remoteness from his child, is often interspersed with hostility or periodic desertion, with return to his own mother's home. He alternately ignores his children and expresses marked dislike on the grounds that "they are too expensive."

Overdevoted fathers are attached to babies or very young children. In the cases studied, in each instance these fathers were suffering from a psychotic illness, while the mothers evidenced little interest in assuming the maternal function. This may or may not always be true, however.

The emotional remoteness typical of the father's inconstancy of love and the controlling overdevotion characteristic of maternal reactions in this constellation produce a particularly vicious combination when the father's responses also are actively hostile. Occasionally, with both parents of the unsocial family the main element of the emotional tie to their children is extremely hostile and destructive. For example, one mother washed her twelve-year-old enuretic daughter's face in urine, and the father required her to stand on one foot for an hour as additional punishment. In another instance, a mother thought it was all right for the father to beat the children as hard as he liked with a strap, so long as he was not drunk.

More usually in the unsocial family, however, hostile fathers are physically cruel and mothers vent their hostility under the guise of overindulgence. These two parental responses not only keep the child dependent upon the mother but also free him to express his hatred toward the father.

SELF-IDENTITY

The nature of the parent-child love relationship makes the achievement of self-esteem and appropriate sex identity difficult for the children of the unsocial family. As indicated earlier, the presence of out-of-wedlock children and/or prolonged separation from own parents dating from early childhood will further complicate the situation.

Relegation of the child to an inferior status often occurs when he returns to the home after placement. The mother, with little awareness of him as an individual and with limited interest in assuming parental responsibility, has trouble imposing limitations on social behavior, threatens to send the child away again ("I can't stand this behavior"), consigns him to the position of chore boy or "little manager," and so on. Girl children, interestingly enough, often form a strong masochistic but highly ambivalent attachment to the mother, despite their depreciated position in the family: "I'll be good if I can only stay with my mother."

The stepfather, under these circumstances, openly disparages or even mistreats both boy and girl children, comparing them unfavorably with his own, and shows a marked tendency to demand that boy children perform "girls'" tasks. He openly taunts the children with their illegitimate status and with his refusal to adopt them.

When the child has not been separated from his own parents, the mother openly belittles the father and demands that the children do so also, inconsistently protecting them from, and then exposing them to, his cruelties. Depending upon whether she wishes to oppose her husband by isolation tactics or by active aggression, this mother encourages their children to be hostile to him or keeps them from him.

Restriction of ordinary social contacts may occur. The mother may be overcontrolling, highly critical of the children's friends unless she herself likes them. She may confine a child's play to his own yard.

Belittling the child's capacities, either by direct criticism—"She doesn't have what it takes"—or by preferring to do everything herself, or both, the mother degrades her children as individuals. She denies them the opportunity to learn to do things independently and thus acquire a sense of worth: "I can't be bothered"; "I'd rather do the dishes myself than see to it that they do their chores"; "I can't get them up in the morning, so why try?"

Exploitation of sexual differences by the father is common. The father primarily makes the child feel inferior when he openly favors a child of the opposite sex. The mother condones this in various ways, offering no real protection from such criticisms. Marked preferences for boys result in "picking on" girls, or a father's calling a girl child "his boy," thus confusing her sex identification.

The frequent reversal of parental roles and the frequent depreciation of fathers by mothers constitute two powerful parental tendencies that interfere with the development of self-identity in the children. This behavior, coupled with the mother's overprotection of the children, not only confuses self-identity patterns but also reinforces a hostile clinging dependence upon the mother. For the girls, heterosexual relationships are apt to be tenuous and often sexually promiscuous. The boys have an unworthy male figure, a punitive one, or no father at all, with whom to identify. Mixed sex identifications are inevitable for them.

Interest in academic achievement is rarely displayed by either parent of this family class. Occasionally, a parent may want a child to outstrip all the neighborhood children at school and may gain pleasure from his doing so. This pleasure, however, derives from seeing the child get something the parent has not had rather than from parental interest in the development of the child's native capacities.

SOCIALIZATION

In this aspect of child rearing, the unsocial family presents a kaleidoscopic picture. Rarely do parental practices denote a single consistent attitude or socially effective method of teaching children the value of school attendance, instilling respect for the rights of others, and stimulating a wish for approximate conformance to the sociolegal mores.

There are two constellations of key parental practices in the unsocial family with respect to socialization of the child:

Disrespect for social authority is the most frequent and most distinctive. Parental disregard for rules of social behavior is its chief feature, with indecisive, overpunitive, coercive attitudes and behavior and/or laxity in sexual behavior also coloring the clinical picture. Disrespect for authority may be communicated to the child in a variety of ways and often is demonstrated by the parents' own antisocial acts. At least one parent is likely to convey this attitude of disregard, which is detrimental to the development of a normal functioning conscience in the children and thus to their socialization.

Indecisiveness in one parent and overpunitiveness in the other constitute the next most distinctive constellation of socialization practices. In the first instance, one parent takes no firm stand one way or the other, while the second parent uses severe punishment as a primary means for teaching rules of social behavior. These particular child-rearing practices assume pathological proportions as a result of the fact that one parent or the other is usually psychotic or has been apprehended for antisocial activities.

These two particular syndromes of child-rearing practices may take any or all of the following forms in an unsocial family:

Sabotage of sociolegal intervention is common. In general, it is the mothers who outrightly encourage the children to defy society's dictates of behavior in the larger community. When sexual delinquencies of daughters occur, the mothers fight the juvenile authorities who take corrective measures. There is permission for truancy, and attempts to have a decision invalidated when the child is brought into court. There may be instances of a mother's bribing the children to do her bidding, with questionable promises of rewards; disbelief and denial of a son's obvious guilt when he is apprehended for homosexual activities; encouragement of a boy's defiance of authorities when he has been caught stealing, while at the same time the mother herself maneuvers to get money surreptitiously in order to indulge her whims of the moment.

The behavior reactions of fathers in this constellation vary. These men are most likely to be indecisive and ineffectual, as a result of psychotic illness. Occasionally, they may have stolen money. The mothers are the dominating influences, ruling with an iron hand, but according to their own standards.

"Overlooking" sociolegal rules of behavior is typical. This practice is carried out by fathers and by mothers in two distinct ways, both of which denote marked defects in superego development. For these reasons there is a negative kind of complementarity between the two partners which reinforces the regressive and unhealthy aspects of their respective personalities.

The mother's reaction is an awareness that things are not as they should be, but she closes her eyes to its implications: "I know Jean is bad in school, but I can't do anything about it"; "I tell Richard, 'Don't do this,' but he keeps on begging money so what can I do?"; "If we're going to stay together we'll all just forget about your father's molesting you." Sexual promiscuity is marked in this group of mothers, sometimes resulting in the birth of illegitimate children. The mother may admonish herself, but her compulsive need for erotic satisfaction is not balanced by an active conscience which would lead her to control her own behavior. Other defections are compulsive lying and spending children's social security benefits on their stepfather.

The fathers' reaction is likely to be affected by their apprehension and prosecution for a variety of antisocial acts, such as grand larceny, welfare fraud, forgery, embezzlement, narcotic addiction, assault, incest. By their example, they thus demonstrate that the world in general is an object for exploitation. Fear of mental illness, a strong feminine orientation, or alcoholic psychosis may also be among the complicating factors. In any instance, they offer to the boy child a poor model for identification and hardly stimulate the wish to conform to society's expectations. To the girl child, the defective conscience of her mother or father is communicated in attitude and behavior which to all intents and purposes give her permission to behave similarly.

Child Development

The unsocial family is apt to consist of three to five children; rarely is it a one-child family. Adult children and those in late adolescence tend to remain attached to the family group as single persons; if married, they return home sporadically or leave children (illegitimate or legitimate) in the care of the mother.

It is difficult to learn much about their children from the parents in the unsocial families for two general reasons:

1. The psychosocial disorders present require immediate and practical attention. Such pressure makes difficult the full diagnostic work-up that would give a complete picture of each child's adjustment.

2. Each parent is markedly preoccupied with his own emotions or with his relationship to his marital partner. He is willing to talk about his children only when community action or other external circumstances force him to give attention to them, or as discussion serves to gratify further his own needs of the moment. Of equal importance is the strong tendency of these parents to act out their emotional conflicts or to regress to psychoses. These two psychological conditions do not mobilize anxiety in a form that results in considered action in behalf of their children.

For these reasons, the social caseworker needs to exert more than ordinary initiative to secure adequate data. Even without specific information about a child's adjustment, however, the caseworker can often make reliable tentative judgments. An example of such a situation would be the case of a mother suffering from psychotic illness, depressive reaction, who had drifted in and out of three marriages. She had three extramarital pregnancies as well as two children by her former husband, who was cruel and sadistic. With no substitute parent, the developmental progress of the children in this family obviously was seriously endangered.

EVENTS AND CIRCUMSTANCES

Continuity of contact between the children and their own parents is very likely to be interrupted for at least one child in the unsocial family and sometimes for several children. The varied and multitudinous reasons for the separations are peculiar to this family class.

Reasons for separation of child from an own parent that occur almost exclusively in the unsocial family class are the parents' and/or child's hospitalization for mental illness, criminality, or the illegitimacy of the child. Other reasons of equal frequency are sporadic separation of the parents, divorce, and leaving the child to the care of others. The fact that more than one child in a family usually has experienced a separation from the parent is partly accounted for by the high incidence both of hospitalization for mental illness and of penal incarceration of a parent, with all the children affected thereby. The same situation holds true as a result of divorce and, to a lesser extent, when children were born out of wedlock or were "given" to relatives or into the care of others.

Substitute arrangements also are varied and may be multiple. Remarriage of a mother is common, with the children thereby acquiring a stepfather. However, the same children often have had previous substitute arrangements, such as foster parents or institutional placement. Relatives play a particular role. They do not supplement the own parent because of a temporary emergency, as is characteristic of the inadequate family, nor do they acquire legal custody of the children by adoption. Rather, the children are "given" to a sister or a mother, who for all practical purposes acts *in loco parentis* but never legally assumes that status.

The reasons for the child's separation from an own parent, the many factors intervening before they are reunited, and the intrinsic emotional conditions of the parents are of such a nature that the child does not experience enduring emotional attachments vital to the formation of meaningful object relationships nor does he acquire a normally functioning conscience.

EARLY CHILDHOOD

Behavior symptoms of the children of this age group in the unsocial family warn of more serious dysfunction in later years, unless the circumstances are corrected by changes in parental handling.

LOVE RELATIONSHIPS

The young child's response to the mother or mother substitute is persistently dominated by fears and anxiety. A second reaction to the mother, often accompanying the first, is hostile protesting behavior. Certain typical symptoms are found in the unsocial family child under six years of age.

Anxieties in the love relationship with the mother are manifested in sleep disturbances, a symptom common to many two-and-one-half, three-, and four-year-old children in this family. These include night terrors, screaming upon awakening, wakefulness, fighting sleep, and night wandering. To overcome the awareness of anxiety and the discomfort created by his lack of security in his mother, the child also resorts to hostile, aggressive behavior symptoms, such as persistent temper outbursts at frustrations, violent denunciations of the mother, defiance, stubbornness, feeding difficulties, or overeating. Regressive tendencies to thumb-sucking may appear in a four-year-old.

Common precipitants of anxiety and hostile aggression are related to one or more parental practices, in each of two groupings. In one, the child witnesses sexual intercourse of the parents because he sleeps in the parents' bedroom. In the second, the child also sees adult genital exposure as a result of parental laxness in maintaining privacy in bathing. Both situations act seductively upon the child.

A third group of factors consists of neglect, when the mother leaves the child alone for hours, as well as severe physical punishment or threats of bodily harm by the mother and/or father. There may be free disciplinary use of a strap; resort to red pepper to break the thumb-sucking habit; overstrictness to impose quiet as a condition of love; marked and frequent disapproval, with the father wanting to "sell" the child and the mother saying that she never wanted him.

Another constellation typical of the young child in this family class contains elements of the first—anxiety and hostile protests—combined with a third factor, babyish behavior inappropriate to the child's maturative level. This takes the form of clinging to the mother and inability to let her out of sight without becoming upset. There is an anxious fearfulness in wanting to be near the mother, shyness and inhibition toward other people, repeated need for reassurance that mother is not "mad," and so on.

A common precipitant is the mother's infantilization of the child.

She draws him close to her and away from the father, considering the child hers alone; or communicates to him her preoccupation with her bodily processes and physical symptoms. The emotional tie of mother and child is sustained by this common bond. Adaptive habits are not encouraged, and thus the motherliness has a defective quality.

Fathers in this constellation tend to be overstrict and competitive with young children, unable to tolerate their misbehavior.

These maternal and paternal responses are typical aspects of the unsocial family in which the marital relationship is characterized by tenuous emotional ties. Divorce may be imminent, quarrels take place in front of the children, and the father is absent from home sporadically.

Many of the symptoms characteristic of the young child of the unsocial family, if seen in the average child of this age, would be considered mild, transitory in nature, and normal aspects of development. For the child in the unsocial family, however, both the persistence of the symptoms and the associated precipitants in the environment forewarn of future difficulties. Thumb-sucking, for example, previously so offensive to most parents, has gained respectability in many quarters. Nonetheless, it is remiss, under any circumstances, not to search for the dissatisfactions in the life of a four-year-old—no longer an infant—that makes him seek solace in thumb-sucking as a main source of pleasure in his waking life.

Other symptoms seen in these young children indicate that anxieties threatening their very identity arise from insecure love relationships and fears of bodily injury. Resorting to various autistic pleasures, developing sleep disturbances, and indulging in over-aggressive striking-out behavior represent their attempts to allay these fears, in the only way available to them. The wariness of human relationships exhibited by these children can lead to more and more withdrawn autistic behavior if they are not treated. Feelings of unworthiness and fears of bodily injury in the three-, four-, or five-year-old child are the roots of serious problems of masculine or feminine identification which develop later.

When fear of "genital harm" [1] is excessive, as it is in certain of

---

[1] This term refers to castration fears that actually or symbolically stem from the fear of danger to, or loss of, the genital organs, usually as punishment for

these children, due to parental attitudes and forms of punishment, the child in the unsocial family handles that fear with exaggerated aggressiveness, a warning of destructive behavior problems to come. In the case of more babyish children, attempts to overcome the fear of genital harm may take the opposite form. Boys, as they grow older, become passive, shy, afraid of all aggressive activities, preferring the feminine role. Girls, in order to ward off feelings of personal inadequacy and unworthiness of the mother's love, may be unable to form meaningful object relationships and refuse to accept their feminine status, either through avoidance of heterosexual contact or excessive aggressiveness and competitive hostility with men.

Sleep disturbances are rarely isolated symptoms. Insomnia in the adult, as in childhood, is indicative of anxiety and has its beginnings in the anxious insecurities of these early years. For the children in the unsocial family, anxiety arises because they must be on guard against an environment which has been made frightening by a neglectful, cruel, or rejecting parent. The fear that misbehavior (nonacceptable impulses not yet under the child's control) can break through in sleep creates wakefulness and a clinging to parents as a guard against terrifying dreams of injury or punishment. In the three- and four-year-old children of this family such anxiety is excessive.

SELF-IDENTITY

Provided the relationship with the mother is a pleasurable one, children will solve easily the conflict between free self-expression and their dependent wishes for the mother's love, modifying their activity according to her demands. For example, to please the mother, they will want to urinate in the toilet and not on the floor, tie their own shoes rather than expect someone else to do it for them, go to the toilet independently, curb their desires to destroy things or to appropriate toys selfishly. In the unsocial family, however, both the choice of substitute outlets and the acquisition of adaptive skills are made more difficult because these children do not feel the heightened pleasure that results from the mother's loving approval of their actions.

---

forbidden sexual desires. It is also used figuratively to denote a state of impotence, powerlessness, helplessness, defeat (11).

Usually, the child under six in the unsocial family achieves accelerated or premature physiological control. Toilet training may be established in every child of such a family at ages as early as eighteen months, twelve months, or even nine months. Premature control of excretory functions is accomplished by the child's overcompliance with the too early and forced training of an overrigid, compulsive mother who is also either emotionally remote, physically punishing, or, sometimes, psychotic.

Although this child has muscular control of his excretory functions, he does not acquire habits of self-reliance and socially useful adaptive skills of self-care. Delayed self-reliance is apparent in such symptoms as lack of independence in toilet habits (going to the toilet alone), refusal to accept sleep schedules, unwillingness to talk, overquietness, stuttering.

As a result of the mother's lack of interest or her remoteness, the emotionally disturbed or alcoholic father assumes the maternal role, doing everything for the child, but inconsistently. The mother's mixed responses of hostility and overprotectiveness keep the child dependent upon her, but at the same time increase his problems of adaptation.

Psychodynamically speaking, the parental practices of the unsocial family inhibit the child's impulsive behavior through his fear of punishment, but *before* he has been able to develop self-reliant skills. The child then tries to maintain his self-identity by negativism, stubbornness, and defiance, at each point of frustration, ambivalently hating the parent or turning toward himself to find autistic security in pleasures such as thumb-sucking and compulsive masturbation.

SOCIALIZATION

The young child of the unsocial family is overshy in asserting himself with other children, fearful and hesitant in initiating contacts with playmates. By age four or five, some of these children wander away from home, appeal to passersby for money, or resort to other forms of begging. These tendencies stem from two main precipitating sources—intimidation of the child by oversevere parental discipline and/or fear of others, engendered by the parent's overprotecting the child from the normal give-and-take of social contact.

LATENCY AND ADOLESCENCE

The outstanding feature of latency and adolescent children in the unsocial family is their tendency to identify with one parent against the other, with a high polarity of feeling differentiating the identifications. A secondary but prominent aspect of this pattern is the high intensity of sibling rivalries and jealousies which exists among the children. These are promoted and sustained by the parents' open avowals of favoritism toward, or rejection of, specific children. The frequent acquisition of stepsiblings accounts in part for this problem. In a large measure, parental acceptance or rejection of a child is based on his sex identity, a fact which contributes to persisting sibling rivalries.

LOVE RELATIONSHIPS

In the unsocial family, the love relationships which develop between latency and adolescent children and their parents assume three dominant forms. In order of most frequent occurrence they are: (1) parasitic dependent tie of children to the parent, mainly to the mother; (2) overaggressive, self-centered demands from both parents; and (3) protective withdrawal from, or avoidance of, close relationships with either parent.

Parasitic dependence is evident when either boys or girls attach themselves to the mother with great tenacity, characterized by clinging, ingratiating qualities, which, as the child grows older, becomes exploitation. In all instances, the father either is actively hated, because depreciated by the mother, or is avoided from fear of his punishment.

In latency children this is seen in one or more of the following ways: securing the mother's attention and care by identifying with her on a hypochondriacal basis; crying if not within earshot of her; running to her for protection whenever the father appears. The father is feared because of his bizarre, psychotic behavior or because he inflicts punishment. Although the mother soothes and caresses the child when encounters with the father occur, she provides no consistent protection from him.

In adolescents, the pattern is the same, but the symptomatic behavior and the identifications differ according to sex. Adolescent girls are submissive to and maintain a close tie to their mothers, frequently turn over all their earnings, bring their illegitimate children home for the mother to take care of. They ignore their father's presence, except to make known to him their contempt.

Adolescent boys identify with their mothers. For example, they turn to her for fulfillment of all their needs, express their fondness, but use her to secure material possessions, or use illness (as does the mother) as an escape from responsibility. Under such circumstances, fathers are threatened by this attachment. Their emotional security is further undermined if the mother and son request that he leave the home.

Among adolescent girls of the unsocial family a parasitic dependent tie to the mother results in the formation of tenuous and superficial emotional ties with adults and peers. These girls are promiscuous and exploiting with men. Boys have noticeably feminine orientation and, although not openly aggressive and hostile to their mothers, act upon these impulses outside the family, often in antisocial behavior, deviant sexual practices, and so on.

Overaggressive self-centeredness in both boy and girl adolescents reveals itself in impulsive, striking-out, disturbed behavior toward the parent. Sometimes this alternates with masochistic submission to the parent. In superficial behavior these responses are similar to those of the overdefiant, submissive child of the perfectionistic family, who both acts disturbed and is unhappy. The main differentiating factor is that the self-centered adolescent of the unsocial family acts more uninhibited than unhappy, having no effective defenses for self-control. In the majority of instances, this also will be typical of the adolescent girl.

The pre-adolescent or adolescent girls and their mothers engage in mutually provoked battles, each degrading the other, often with physical encounters. There frequently follows the girl's promise to be "good" if she is not sent away. Intervention to defend the mother from the father's abuse may be followed by temporary masochistic submission to the general depreciation meted out by the parents. Fathers are despised and often dreaded because of their cruelties.

These overaggressive, self-centered reactions will be based in the adolescent's own needs and feelings of deprivation. In the unsocial family, these feelings are realistically founded, since from early childhood the adolescent will have experienced no enduring emotional tie to a parent person. This may be due to one or more causes: long periods of separation from the parents in a foster home or institution; illegitimacy, resulting in rejection or in being included in a merged family with a cruel stepfather. As a result, the capacities for repression of impulses and the defenses that should have developed for control of his aggressions are defective. In other words, there has been no meaningful parental attachment as an incentive to develop these traits.

Protective withdrawal which results in avoidance of close personal relationships with parents and others occurs most frequently in the adolescent child of the unsocial family and of the egocentric family. There is a marked preoccupation with the self, with the child's own fantasy life, and with food. The child's intellectual interests are apt to be abstract and used for his own amusement. Such adolescents may be actually or potentially psychotic.

SELF-IDENTITY

The behavior of the vast majority of latency and adolescent children of the unsocial family indicates that they are not developing a firm sense of ego identity and a capacity for self-directive activity. Neither in their independent habits nor in socially adaptive skills do they show an increasing wish for self-control, a pleasure in striving for realistic goals, or an understanding of the effects of their own behavior on other people. Such degree of self-reliance, control, and adaptive skill as they do acquire indicates disturbances in ego growth and lack of confidence in their own integrity.

Those latency and adolescent children whose love relationship to the mother is of a parastic, clinging nature and to the father, one of disregard, show definite symptoms. The specific area of adjustment affected will vary with the particular child.

Overreliance on the parent in the latency child may be expressed in overcompliance with the parent's wish to assist him in dressing, to accompany him to the bathroom and to administer other aspects of his personal care. Although of infrequent occurrence, it is always possible that this particular overreliance of a girl child upon her father may lead to an incestuous relationship.

The adolescent child knows through previous experience that the mother will prefer to do things for him—as an overmotherly gesture—rather than to value his doing things for himself and others. The resulting lack of incentive and of pleasure in self-mastery is usually evident in a number of areas, almost always characterized by his awareness that he is "getting by with something." For example, the mere fact that a child dislikes chores results in his not having to do them; he may pretend that his earnings are greater or less than they actually are, depending upon whether he is reporting to the mother or the father; he may feign illness to avoid a variety of self-reliant tasks.

Latency and adolescent children in the unsocial family whose love relationship with the parents is aggressive and self-centered reveal their arrested ego development, and lack of belief in their own integrity, through specific attitudes and behavior. Pseudo-independence, alternating with evasion by control, is characteristic. Children will fend for themselves, independently of the parent, but their self-reliant interests are primarily self-oriented, without consideration of father, mother, siblings. Alternating with this pattern is provocative, spiteful, often destructive, defiant behavior to avoid home tasks, personal hygiene, or whatever is a particular point of conflict. A typical episode is an adolescent girl's screaming so that the "neighbors will think they are killing her," then conforming momentarily by doing household chores, only to revert to the same defiance. Lack of self-esteem and a hostile protest against the parent are frequently expressed in slovenly habits of dress, failure to wash, wearing dirty, offensively odorous clothes, and so on. Occasionally, a twelve-year-old boy or girl will be enuretic.

This group of hostile and self-centered latency and adolescent children have all experienced either early placement or separation from a single parent, the father. Neither those who are overreliant on the parents nor those who have a pseudo independence from them have received sufficient help from parental persons during their beginning years to make them want to give up dependency goals. Incentives toward self-mastery in order to keep the love of the parent, intensified by the wish to avoid his displeasure, are wholly lacking in their lives.

A kind of necessity for self-sufficiency has been invoked by insufficient parental guidance and support during childhood, the time when the ego capacities of these adolescents were too weak to master anxiety and suffering. To overcome the pain of the insecurity thus engendered, these particular children turn back to themselves for comfort, and also resort to hostile, aggressive behavior. Unable to handle these anxieties alone, the adolescents in the unsocial family resort to these unsatisfactory attempts to maintain what self-identity they do possess. For them, physical maturity proceeds but emotional growth is retarded, the ego retaining weak characteristics normal in a developing child but abnormal at this age. Society inevitably makes greater demands for mature behavior than these children can approximate. As a result, self-esteem and identity are correspondingly and increasingly threatened, particularly at adolescence when earlier infantile wishes are renewed and the ego is in the process of becoming consolidated.

Latency and adolescent children who are withdrawn in their emotional ties to the parent may exhibit pseudo-independent patterns of self-sufficiency or overreliance as they develop their sense of self-identity. These children automatically carry responsibility for their personal needs and home tasks, often eliciting the maternal response, "I don't have to scold, he is such a good boy," although at the same time, at eight years of age, such a child may have become enuretic. In other instances, there is total reliance upon the mother's direction, planning, guidance, instruction, and overprotective assistance in managing personal care. In extreme cases, some of these children may be borderline psychotics, with a potentiality for psychotic illness as adolescence progresses.

The achievement and interest in schooling which the latency and adolescent child in the unsocial family may display do not provide diagnostic criteria of any significance to identification of the family class. There may be marked dislike of school, disinterest, or acceptance. The same is true of actual academic achievement. Some few will be good students; others may be average, below average, failing, or even below their normal grade placement according to the standards of the particular school. By comparison with children of other family types, those of the unsocial family have the highest incidence of academic failure, retardation, and tendency to quit school out of disinterest. Although diagnostically, prognostically, and therapeutically, school achievement is significant in the study of any individual child, it is not a primary key factor in identifying and evaluating the child of the unsocial family.

SOCIALIZATION

At latency and adolescence, children of the unsocial family meet trouble with the larger society. It is in the areas of social relationships with individuals and society in general, as represented by police, school, and others in an authoritative protective role, that defects in their superego development show up. The socially adaptive skills of these children are of such a nature that they are likely to be exploited and depreciated by others, or they themselves may become unsocial aggressors, pugnaciously attacking or shrewdly exploiting others.

Behavior indicative of defective superego development, limited capacity for object relations, and confused or mixed masculine-feminine identifications, is clearly recognized in their relationship with friends, in their sex behavior, and in their approximate conformance to sociolegal mores.

Latency children with a parasitic, clinging love relationship to the mother, depending too much upon her rather than learning self-reliance, present a socialization behavior that contrasts with that of adolescents who have the same parental love relationship patterns.

Passive, nonantagonistic behavior in relationships with children of the same age is characteristic of the latency child. Although not disliked by his peers, he prefers to play alone or with siblings; often, he does not venture outside the home yard. Sexual interests are overinhibited, and there is a generally overcompliant attitude of conformance to rules of social behavior at school and in the wider community.

In contrast, the adolescent of this group reveals a different picture, due to his greater physical maturity and the resurgence of sexual and aggressive impulses at this period.

Prestige conflicts are common in adolescence. Typically, a girl will have no friends of her own sex but will chose an older boy member of a gang of which she is also a member. Girls may say they are uncomfortable with friends of their own age and sex.

The sexual behavior of this group of adolescent girls is delinquent in nature with a series of illegitimate pregnancies resulting from promiscuity. This girl usually selects a sexual partner with glaring personality defects, is strongly compelled to be used sexually but experiences no pleasure from the act. There is easy release of her child to another's care, in this instance her own mother. Shrewd and exploiting, she sees the world as fair game.

The adolescent boys are likely also to associate with a gang but have little rapport with any individual. Prestige conflicts are evident, for example, when a boy has a single friend of another race or engages in overt homosexual acts. Heterosexual relationships are avoided or are minimal.

Sex identification for this group of adolescent boys is feminine-oriented. There are repeated bouts with those in authority—the law, school, police—striking out aggressively at others, never learning by experience. When apprehended for antisocial acts, such as stealing cars, truancy, physical attack, and so on, the boy feels victimized, although he is the aggressor.

In socialization, latency and adolescent children of the unsocial family who are overaggressive and self-centered in response to their parents present the following picture of personal relationships with those of their own age and in relation to the standards of behavior for the larger community:

As unsocial aggressors, latency and adolescent girls of this group are not generally liked by peers, alienating themselves by hostile, destructive attacks on other children, threats, remarks calculated to "turn their stomachs," and so on. Prestige conflicts are also indicated by preference for younger children or for a boy friend of a different racial background. The fourteen-, fifteen-, and sixteen-year-old adolescent early becomes involved in promiscuous sexual affairs with pick-up dates, and typically may plan to marry a youth five or ten years her senior.

Lack of conformance to the rules of social behavior is characterized in latency by striking out aggressively; in the adolescent, by antisocial acts. When this is directed against the parents, it takes the form of stealing from them and forging checks with their names.

Passive, nonantagonistic latency or adolescent boys of this group have a tendency to avoid outside social relationships with adults, peers, and children, concentrating their hostilities within the family. Antisocial acts are not characteristic, but lack of appropriate sex identification is evident. If these children do engage in delinquent activities they are apt to be shrewd about it, stealing articles of particular interest to them. If they are caught, they pretend innocence and bewilderment.

Latency and adolescent children in the unsocial family who have withdrawn their emotional ties from their parents present certain characteristics in socialization. Unsuccessful participation in social contacts with any age group reveals an inability to form object relationships of any depth and is typified by fearfulness in the presence of people in general, particularly peers, or by alienation of friends because of bizarre, unpredictable behavior. Examples are an adolescent girl who fights whenever she has the "feeling" that others are making unfavorable remarks about her; a twelve-year-old boy who dresses up in girls' clothing and plays "mother"; an adolescent who repeatedly wears a heavy wool sweater in ninety-degree heat. The withdrawal from human contact occurs in varying degrees in these children, but there is always the possibility that these symptoms denote or portend psychotic illness.

MARITAL FUNCTIONS

For the average person, basic attitudes toward a marital partner are blended in such a fashion that there is, in general, a recognizable and prevailing response. However, in the unsocial family, a multiplicity of highly intense feelings, diffuse and subject to rapid change, characterize the chief elements of the emotional ties that bind this husband and wife.

Reciprocal Love Relationships
OUTSIDE THE SEXUAL ACT

Two major aims dominate the love relationship of the partners in the unsocial family: (1) the wish to be the sole recipient of all loving care from the spouse; (2) the wish to deny such care by being aggressively inconsiderate to the spouse. These responses may appear in a single partner, as cardinal types or as mixtures. A secondary aim, supplementing these two, usually appears as one aspect of the more basic pattern. This is of an opportunistic nature; namely, to gain vicarious pleasure in the spouse's destructive social behavior or to use him as an object of exploitation.

The wish to be the sole recipient manifests itself in the unsocial family partner through demands that the spouse make this partner the object of all loving care and consideration. Encroachments, real or imagined, often are regarded as threats to the marital relationship, and result in jealousy, envy, and suspiciousness. Extraordinary attention may be paid to the smallest indication of the spouse's interest in another. Unable to regard anything indifferently, such a partner magnifies ordinary incidents; in the extreme, this becomes delusional jealousy. Psychodynamically speaking, the partner to whom this jealous spouse owes faith is charged with, and blamed for, suspected inclinations in order to absolve the spouse's own impulse toward infidelity (projected jealousy).

The partner does not expect to reciprocate these feelings and behavior. Instead of seeking love by giving love, his demand for love is childlike. Hoping to be admired not for his achievements but for his own sake, he appeals for sympathy, as if to a mother, or employs childish devices of self-aggrandizement, depreciation of others, and the like. Such demands are impractical, because the environment does not grant to an adult these childhood prerogatives. Frustration is inevitable for such a spouse, since he seeks in the marriage partnership an infantile satisfaction that is not available to him as an adult.

The aggressive inconsideration of this marital partner takes the form of deliberate abuse, denial of care and affection through overtly cruel acts (not necessarily physical attack), with feelings of love and hate markedly diffuse. The degree of polarity or ambivalence is high, with the loved person an object of direct expressions of hostile aggression.

Opportunistic aims are markedly colored by the wish to be the sole recipient of love, and to be aggressively inconsiderate. Therefore, specific manifestations in behavior and attitude have a destructive influence on the unsocial family partner which differs from that exerted on the partner of the egocentric family, where opportunistic aims also are prominent.

In attitude and behavior, two constellations characterize the marital love relationships in the unsocial family.

The self-centered hostile male and the opportunistic female comprise the most common constellation. The male's selection of a mate and maintenance of the relationship are based on any one of the following: his preference for "ugly" women ("Then I will not need to be jealous of other men"); his desire to be indulged by his mate although he belittles her importance; "remaking" or protection of a depreciated woman; appreciation of his mate's breezy, humorous manner—and her money in the bank—but making no demands for sexuality; the wish for a "mother"; reliance upon his wife, and encouraging her sexual promiscuity; bragging about having taken his wife away from a friend in the service ("I am attractive to women").

The female partner's interest in her husband has a particular opportunistic theme that to a certain extent complements that of the male partner. Oft repeated are such comments as: "I feel like a mother to him"; "He has his weaknesses, but he depends upon me"; "It's like having another child; he acts like such a baby but wants to be boss." Invariably coupled with this is her need to have the status of a married woman in the community. This wife will accept the role of wage earner for the family; praise and indulge her husband on the one hand; manipulate, control, and try to remake him on the other. In brief, protecting, mothering, and manipulating are the primary tendencies which comprise the emotional tie of this partner's love relationship.

The sole recipient syndrome (aggressively inconsiderate male and opportunistic hostile female) is expressed by the male partner in accusing the wife of trying to ruin his life; demanding that she be responsible for "controlling" his behavior; stamping away when the spouse refuses to allow him to "help" on his own terms; oscillating from a feeling he could "conquer worlds" if his wife "cared" to demanding that she be "like a mother," anticipate his needs, and show appreciation of him; wanting to be the undisputed head of the family yet ignoring and abusing his wife.

The female partner's reaction is one of disregard of the husband. She manipulates him and sets her own standards. She knows she has failed as a wife but is undaunted, or projects failures on her emotionally deprived childhood, or expects her spouse to focus on her but considers him weak ("Who do you think you are?"). Shortly after marriage she may have imposed sexual abstinence upon him, telling him that she is not impressed by his masculinity.

The interaction of the aims characteristic of these two constellations of love relationships, in the unsocial family partners, is apt to have certain results. Although mothering and protection are what the husband says he wants, the dependence encouraged by the wife renders him even more helpless and floundering: "She's robbed me of being a man"; "I try to provoke her to leave me." The wife often remains exasperatingly serene in the face of his anger and infantilism: "I know I am right"; "I may be a failure in my marriage but I am adequate in everything else!"; "I've been good to stay with him, he needs my protection"; "I always let him stay on when he begs me—suppose he wouldn't come back?"; "I am an independent cuss; I want to manage"; "I like the status of being married."

Other variations are "marriages of convenience," so to speak, in which the wife wants a husband who is a sexual partner only and who also is willing to be seduced, manipulated, and submissive; or the male wishes to avoid the sexual act and assume the maternal role, a situation which is accepted by the wife, who may or may not seek sexual satisfaction extramaritally.

WITHIN THE SEXUAL ACT

The male partner experiences problems in all main areas, such as reconciliation of orgasm and extragenital sexual needs, reconciliation of love and sexuality, reconciliation of sexual needs to procreation and work. Two main patterns stand out: (1) lack of interest in masculine sexual activity, wherein extreme passivity or orientation to the feminine-receptive sexual role is outstanding and the sex act with a female is primarily a matter of form; and (2) in a smaller number of cases, cruel, sadistic, exploiting tendencies, carried over to the sexual act, repeat in the sexual role the orientation of this partner toward life in general.

Reconciliation of love and sexuality and reconciliation of their sexual needs to child rearing appear to be the main problem areas for the females. Two groups stand out.

Well over half are not interested in the sexual act itself, and, although they have had children, sexual intercourse with a male is for them only an automatic performance. The significant, diagnostic factors, substantiated in family of origin data, are the attitude and behavior which accompany this denial of femininity or appropriate sex membership. Toward the adult male partner there is a hostile, depreciating attitude which is expressed either verbally or by ignoring him, thus reducing his stature in the family to that of a nonentity.

Coexisting with this pattern is the feminine partner's heavy emotional investment in the children. A lack of tender affection, of common interests, and of consideration toward the male partner round out this picture.

The remainder of these females are sexually impulsive, exchanging one male sexual object for another. This is apparent in their promiscuous extramarital affairs, which indicate insatiable dependency cravings and an infantile orientation to adult sexuality.

Thus, the capacities of these female partners for participation in a normal sexual relationship are minimal or lacking. Nonsexual feelings for the spouse are heavily weighted with hostilities and destructive impulses, which in a sense substitute for the sexual act itself. Or the orientation to adult sexuality is impulsive acting out, in an indiscriminate fashion, with no genuine emotion attached to the act or the object.

Self-identity

The nature of love relationships, outside and within the sexual act, forecasts the kind of reciprocity which will exist between husband and wife of the unsocial family in maintaining their individual self-identities. These partners endeavor to maintain their self-esteem in the marriage partnership by the use of one or both of two devices: (1) appeals to the spouse or to others for sympathy and pity; (2) self-aggrandizement through depreciation of the partner. The following constellations are examples of identical behavior patterns of husband and wife:

Personal devaluation—criticisms and depreciation of the partner—may be leveled mutually on the basis of sex identity: "I treat him like one of our little girls"; "I let him cash his own check occasionally to boost his morale"; "She's a beast; an old battle axe"; "Women are supposed to submit to men"; "She's nothing; she has to wear 'falsies.'" Racial differences and intellectual capacities are also subjects of disparagement: "dumb Polack"; "stupid nitwit," and so on.

In this constellation of identical patterns the overtness of the mutual attack is the chief characteristic, obviously designed by each partner to bolster his own shaky sense of self-esteem by belittling and striking out at others. Extramarital affairs and excessive drinking are typical of the male partner.

Examples of contrasting behavior patterns of husband and wife are personal devaluation and appeals for sympathy. Numerous methods are utilized by this group of partners to maintain self-esteem through the marriage partnership.

The male partner attempts to maintain his self-esteem and position by open depreciation of his spouse as a wife and sex partner on the one hand, and by appeals for her sympathy and pity on the other. He may publicly criticize his wife's physical appearance, not talk to her because he considers her intellectually inferior, but say, as if to make everything all right, "I offered her a divorce but she won't take it," or beg her to take him back.

The female partner in this constellation maintains her own self-identity through the husband by a combination of devices which results in his being devalued as an individual in his own right. Too, she exerts strong control: "I'm determined to make him over"; "I want to be married and supported so I'm staying whether he likes it or not"; "He'll go to the A.A. group *I* select; I know I am right." On the other hand, she also appeals for sympathy to him and to others: "I'm faithful and try to keep things nice"; "I have to push you all the time; maybe you're afraid of reality"; "It's a strain, wondering what you're doing every minute."

Both the identical and the contrasting patterns for maintaining self-esteem through the marriage reflect immature self-concepts on the part of both spouses. For this reason, the self-identity of each partner is incapable of being supported within any adult relationship. Just as impossible of gratification as their demands for unconditional love and attention are their demands for respect. Even among those who receive the mothering they want, frustration is still inevitable because their needs are insatiable. Others are frustrated because a further threat to their already damaged self-esteem and self-identity is involved. Thus, overprotestations of adequacy, demands for respect, and depreciation of others are defenses against recognizing in themselves these unpleasant truths.

The use of these defenses does not always imply that these partners possess an active sense of guilt, arising from an unconscious feeling that the thing the individual wants and cannot have is bad. More often than not in the unsocial family the partners are inevitably doomed to disillusionment since society does not grant the fulfillment of such infantile wishes to any adult although a more mature person may experience disappointments. The adult portion of his personality will reject such infantile strivings in himself and he will have conscious guilt about having these wishes. Such an active sense of guilt is not as apt to be experienced by the unsocial family marriage partners. Their interpersonal relationships are always fraught with frustration, because through them they attempt to perpetuate an infantile self.

Socialization

The marital partners in the unsocial family rarely support each other in a fashion that fosters self-observation, self-criticism, personal responsibility for living within the law, concern for the welfare of others, and so forth. Therefore, in the event of physical disability, mental illness, irrational or antisocial behavior on the part of one or both, there is little realistic appraisal of the seriousness of problems which may result in correctional measures or necessary protective intervention.

HELPFUL CONCERN

Three responses characterize the personal responsibility assumed by the unsocial family partners for the health and welfare of each other. They may appear in various combinations.

There may be *harsh criticism* of the partner's lack of initiative, the fact of his physical illness, lack of emotional control, or antisocial behavior: "I am not in the least impressed by his suicidal attempts."

Disregard, by overlooking or refusal to take cognizance of the partner's lack of, or inadequate powers of, initiative is common. Intervention in the partner's behalf only occurs at the insistence of an outside source. The secondary gain which one of these partners achieves by stimulating the other to act out, in antisocial behavior, his own conflicts is an example of this disregard, and exerts a powerful influence in perpetuating an unhealthy situation.

Obstructionist tactics may also be used to protect the partner from the consequences of breaking the law, or to thwart medical or psychiatric treatment. Those wives who mother the husband to his detriment delay undertaking any realistic corrective measures. For example, in the case of drug addiction, the failure to intervene is frequently rationalized as a concern for the partner's welfare and the need to "protect" him.

PROBLEM-SOLVING

In the unsocial family, married life is not viewed as a process of continuous readjustment for each partner, with problems to be scrutinized, evaluated, and solved by considered action, or through mutual concurrence. Distinctive to these partners is an approach to the solution of problems by undisciplined exploitation. This may appear as an identical pattern in both partners or, with equal frequency, as one side of a contrasting pattern.

When both husband and wife indulge in undisciplined exploitation, each partner, together with the rest of the world, is considered to exist for the sole purpose of expediting a solution to a problem, according to the individual's whim of the moment. Evaluation of personal feelings, and of the interpersonal aspects of the marital relationship which have contributed to a difficulty, may take place, but usually not for the purpose of finding a judicious solution for all concerned. The goal is to manipulate the situation and/or the spouse so that differences are resolved according to the partner's own self-interests.

Projection of blame may be a secondary factor. In this case one marital partner sees the other partner as being responsible for all their disagreements and difficulties. These are resolved by assigning the cause to someone outside the self—the husband or wife.

When only one partner—usually the male—resorts to undisciplined exploitation, the female partner relies on a kind of magic formula thinking in meeting problems. She maintains an unfounded but actively expressed faith that the partner will take necessary action. There is ordinarily awareness that things are amiss, but belief that everything will come out all right.

Withdrawal of interest, an alternate reaction of the female, is characteristic of the psychotic or near psychotic person who is only remotely aware of others. In the marital relationship, there is a passive expectation that the partner will handle problems if there are any. An anxious preoccupation with her own emotional life fantasies, psychosomatic complaints, and bodily functions rather than with external factors renders her incapable of scrutinizing, evaluating, or taking action with respect to the solution of problems.

These identical and contrasting patterns may have one or more of the following results with respect to solving problems: impulsive action without forethought; calculated action based on ill-considered judgment; lack of action resulting from indiscriminate faith in another's capacities and abilities.

FINANCIAL FUNCTIONS
Income Production

The provider role in the unsocial family may be assumed by husband or wife alone, by both partners, or by community-supported financial assistance agencies. Characteristically, the partners are in general agreement as to the division of labor regardless of their actual consistency or adequacy in giving financial support. They prefer an arrangement whereby either or both partners assume this responsibility, or the wife alone does so.

The female partner becomes the sole provider when the usual male-female roles are reversed by agreement. The wife elects to work and the husband to remain in the home, performing domestic and child-rearing duties. This pattern of division of labor denotes certain problems in sex identification and, in many instances, psychotic illness.

In job performance two patterns stand out with respect to the male partner of the unsocial family: poor work records and/or resort to illegal means of obtaining money.

The male partner's work adjustment is typified by frequent changes in jobs; unwillingness to exert effort; resentment toward supervisor or person in authority; feeling of being "picked on" and unappreciated; expectations of unwarranted praise followed by hostile outbursts when this is not forthcoming; tendency to blame the job situation for failure, dismissal for cause, and so on. Occasionally, the husband is a steady employee and likes his work, but his ambition is limited.

Typical of this male's antisocial methods of securing money are forgery, larceny, and stealing from his employer, all of which denote tendencies to get something at the expense of others.

The male partner's occupation can run the gamut from laborer to salesman to schoolteacher. The distribution is apt to be weighted more heavily, however, with skilled and unskilled laborers, such as the steelworker, a mixer of cement, cook, bartender, railroad watchman, with truck driver prominent on the list. Eighth-grade schooling or less is not uncommon. However, the same kinds of difficulties in job performance are experienced, and with equal frequency, by the males of this type who have more education.

The female partner is apt to be an efficient and steady worker. By and large, if she is employed it is on a full-time basis. Her job records show a concentration on clerical or service occupations: secretarial work, bookkeeping, waiting on table, dressmaking, and clerking.

As with other aspects of his life, the attitudes and behavior of the male partner of the unsocial family toward work achievement both mask and directly express his lack of personal incentive to become a productive adult in his own right. The pervasiveness and the multifactored aspects of his infantile character traits have been identified in his job adjustment. Unfortunately, the ego defenses utilized by these male partners are likely to be nearly if not outright antisocial. Thus, overcompensatory defenses leading to satisfactions in work are not the rule. Rather, a hostile demand for special privileges, as a means of keeping the ego intact, or an easy loss of confidence as expressed in aggressive behavior, becomes the characteristic pattern.

A typical example is that of a young husband who was "forced" to marry, due to his wife's pregnancy. He acknowledged the wish not to have children but did nothing to meet this problem. His standards of giving and receiving as a family provider were set according to his wishes for spending money on himself. At the same time, he always expected to rely upon his wife, his father, and his mother to bail him out of trouble as it suited his own needs. The stress caused by his wife's mental illness obviously increased the frustrations of this young man, whose ability to tolerate emotional or environmental distress was limited in any event. His reactions to his wife's illness were resentment, disregard, and hostility.

In another instance, a young man thirty-one years of age who had always experienced difficulties in interpersonal relationships was dishonorably discharged from the Navy for stealing. In his subsequent work experience, after marriage, he consistently made demands for special consideration, was belligerent with coworkers, provoked quarrels with his supervisor when his unjustified demands were not met. Upon being fired from his job, he expected his father to straighten things out or get him another job. As a husband, he displayed the same attitude and behavior; he expected to exploit his wife, as he tried to exploit the world in general. He had twice been prosecuted for embezzlement.

Income Management

To be the sole provider for his family's financial needs is rarely an acknowledged intention of the male partner in the unsocial family. Although he may make attempts to hold a job, and may earn money, this bears little relationship to his willingness to support his family. Evasion of this responsibility usually appears not in a single problem factor but in the following constellation: non-amortized debts; court orders for nonsupport; withholding of income for personal indulgences at the expense of family needs; and, rarely, ill-advised luxury expenditures that benefit the total family. In some instances, apprehension for illegal activities is part of the symptomatic picture.

It is the families showing this syndrome of financial disorders, coupled with poor work records of the male and/or female partners, that either constitute the group of unsocial families which have a history of Level A dependency on community-supported agencies or will join this group. When dependency is not present, it is prevented by an employed female partner who is adequate in job performance, by the willingness of relatives to support the family, or by the male partner's successfully eluding arrest for illegal pursuits.

Under any circumstances, management of income in the unsocial family is typically unplanned or the funds are poorly budgeted by both husband and wife. If the female partner has some capacity in this regard, she is seldom inclined to sustain control over her husband's erratic spending habits. The more usual pattern is impulsive, ill-advised expenditures according to the female partner's own standards, especially if she is the main source of income. Earnings of children who reach employment age are often turned over to, and managed by, the mother.

ADULT CHARACTERISTICS
Physical Condition and Intelligence

The adults of the unsocial family are no more prone to physical illness than are the marital partners of the other family classes. Physical disease or illness is not often of a disabling nature, vocationally, unless it appears as an aspect of, or in itself constitutes an emotional disturbance. More often than not, physical illness is part of the symptomatic picture of psychotic illness, and occasionally of a psychophysiological reaction denoting a mental disorder.

The female's physical ailments tend to center in the diagnostic groupings of skin disorders and genitourinary infections. This woman tends to be preoccupied with her ailments; skin moles, for example, will be a subject of worry and interest. Medical help may be sought constantly, but in a day or two the physician's prescription is apt to be thrown away.

The male partner has few physical symptoms. When present in the sample they usually were associated diagnostically with an emotional disturbance: headaches with depressive reaction and phobias; ear disorders with schizophrenic reaction, undifferentiated type; acute gastrointestinal difficulties, drug addiction, and so on, with personality disorder.

The male and female partners generally have average intelligence. However, mental deficiency in one partner is more likely to be a factor in this family class than in any of the others. The functional impairment is apt to be moderate; that is, the intelligence quotient is in the upper limits of the 50–70 range. This degree of defect is considered to require special training and/or guidance, vocationally speaking. A secondary diagnosis of psychotic illness or severe personality disorder will not be uncommon. An intelligence quotient below 50, requiring custodial care or protective care, was not present in the sample.

Ego Defenses

The predominance of psychosis and tendencies toward delinquent conduct in one or both partners of the unsocial family fits into the end of the scale of family types with respect to degrees of regression or fixation at early levels of personality development. In either case, these two—psychosis and delinquent conduct characteristics—indicate strong superego defects, the grosser ego defects, or both, irrespective of etiology (75).

Psychosis represents the greater failure of the ego's defensive operation or its regression into a psychotic state. When speaking of "regression" into psychosis, reference is being made to the regression of the *ego* (not to etiology), with the accompanying loss of normal ego functioning and reality testing. Psychotic disorders can appear in the male and female partner of the unsocial family with equal frequency.

The characteristics of the delinquent conduct with acting out as a prominent defense are somewhat different in the male and female partners. Acting out in itself may not only indicate a superego defect in these partners but may also be a defense against psychosis. For example, it has been observed that some individuals when denied the opportunity to express or act out their delinquent tendencies regress into psychosis. In psychosis the superego may also become ineffective, which is to a certain extent the same type of personality defect characteristic of the delinquent (75).

Thus, these two patterns prominent in the partners of the unsocial family indicate severe ego and superego defects, irrespective of etiology. The etiology could be toxic, constitutional, or failure to have attained sufficient ego maturity for a variety of reasons, such as unhealthy family background.

Predominant character traits in the male partner are apt to denote dependent passive-receptive tendencies in the personality. "Dependency," as here used, refers to the wish to be taken care of, fed, and looked after like a little child; "passivity" refers to feminine-receptive strivings. Both may be aggressively acted out or non-aggressively expressed in social behavior; for example, through passive obstructionist tactics; helplessness in taking command of a situation; disregard of work rules; quarrels with coworkers and those in authority; rages; antisocial acts of disorderly conduct, embezzlement, forgery, desertion, nonsupport.

The female partner has character traits similar to those of the male partner and resorts to many of the same mechanisms of defense. In some families a strong component of masochism is apparent with excessive self-criticism, a pretense that the conscience is better than it is.

Acting out, when used as a defense by the female partner, does not result in the same kinds of antisocial acts as those carried out by the male but does have antisocial implications. Nonlegalized marital unions, out-of-wedlock children, thwarting the rules of the court, are some examples that involve the larger community. Within the family she gets what she wants for herself but is not afraid of her own hostile impulses. She can rationalize and readily project blame upon others, upon society, and so on; they are wrong—not she. Other defenses that are prominent in both partners include: denial, a primitive defense directed against painful experiences stimulated by external events, which are met by denial in word and act; fantasy, a form of denial, consisting mainly of morbid preoccupation with the subject's own thoughts and thus socially useless; and projection, or the assigning of the individual's own feelings to another, used by these particular partners as a defense against aggressivity or other alien wishes which are too painful to admit but which cannot be repressed.

Emotional Stability

Psychotic illness in the partners of the unsocial family is of such a nature that it more frequently results in hospitalization, through protective intervention of some community agency, than is true of other families. The partner who is not afflicted by psychotic illness in all likelihood will have a character structure denoting some form of personality disorder, either personality trait disturbance or pattern disturbance. Consequently, the partner who has a psychotic illness is apt to remain in the family home, avoiding hospitalization for a longer period of time than is advisable either for himself or for others. His spouse neither assesses his symptoms soon enough nor does so in a fashion that leads to obtaining needed treatment.

Psychotic disorders appear in the male or female partner with equal frequency. The diagnosed psychotic illness is apt to be schizophrenic reaction, a group of psychotic reactions characterized by fundamental disturbances in reality relationships and concept formations, with affective, behavioral, and intellectual disturbance in varying degrees and mixtures.

Schizophrenic reaction, paranoid type, is characterized by autistic unrealistic thinking. Mental content is chiefly comprised of delusions of persecution and/or grandeur and ideas of superiority. Unpredictable behavior and attitudes of hostility and aggression are fairly constant. Systematized paranoid hypochondriacal states are included in this group. Schizophrenic reactions accompanied by obsessive compulsive defenses or by alcoholism are among other possibilities.

Often for those who are not hospitalized, a psychiatric diagnosis will indicate schizophrenic reaction, undifferentiated type, or so-called "latent," "incipient," "prepsychotic" states in which the patient exhibits mixed symptoms of a chronic schizophrenic reaction. Typical also are diagnosed schizophrenic reactions, residual type, occurring after a definite psychotic episode. The patient has improved sufficiently to get along in the community but continues to show recognizable disturbances of thinking, affect, and/or behavior.

Occasionally, the female partner of the unsocial family will have manic depressive reactions, depressive type. This group of affective reactions is not as typical to this family class, however, as are the schizophrenic reactions.

Schizophrenic reaction, residual type, is fairly common in that many of the partners of the unsocial family will have had psychotic episodes, either with or without hospitalization, but will not have had treatment over a sufficiently long enough period to assure recovery. Psychiatrically, they are capable of adjusting to life outside an institution. Psychosocially speaking, their emotional disturbance continues to be demonstrated in behavior and attitudes often ill-suited to the demands and responsibilities of parenthood, the marriage relationship, or providing for the financial needs of the family.

CHILD CHARACTERISTICS
Physical Condition and Intelligence

Children of the unsocial family are not characteristically afflicted with physical disabilities. When such are present, the disability in a single child is apt to be severe and may fall into any one or more of the entire range of diagnostic groupings: respiratory—colds, pneumonia; eyes and ears—mastoid; nervous system—grand mal epilepsy, *spina bifida;* musculoskeletal—hernia, poliomyelitis; digestive tract —constipation, ruptured appendix. Children with such chronic physical disabilities as residual poliomyelitis and grand mal epilepsy derive a secondary gain of a controlling nature from their illness: "Don't make me nervous or I will have a spell."

Of particular interest, in the sample studied, was the need for surgery, as compared with the conditions among children in other family types. Examples were: mastoidectomy; appendectomy due to ruptured appendix; herniadectomy; and removal of spleen. Communicable diseases for which immunization can be secured also were more common in this than in other family classes.

The intelligence of children in the unsocial family is generally within the normal range, according to accepted psychological tests and school performance standards. Mental deficiency, though not found in the great majority of cases, may be an intrinsic characteristic of some few children. This condition is further exaggerated by parental attitudes already discussed in connection with child rearing as well as by additional disabilities in the child that are almost always associated with mental deficiency. Among these complicating factors are psychotic reactions or conduct disorders, coupled with a physical disability such as epilepsy.

The degree of mental deficiency will probably denote moderate functional impairment, with an intelligence quotient in the upper limits of the 50–70 range. For the school-aged child, this means special grade placement, academic training and guidance. For the adolescent, vocational guidance will be indicated as well.

It should *not* be inferred that mental deficiency might not occur in any family type. However, when this condition is present in the child of the unsocial family the parental reactions and the behavior of the child will differ in the ways indicated from those of other family types. In the inadequate family, the behavior of the mentally deficient child is likely to be similar to that of such a child in the unsocial family. However, parental behavior in response to the child's condition will not be the same in the two family types.

Psychic Disturbance of Latency

In the unsocial family sample, at least one of the children between the ages of six and twelve years on whom there were data had a psychic disturbance consisting of all or several of the following disorders: infantile phenomena; motor disorders; conduct problems; common neuroses and psychoses.

Infantile phenomena found in the male child of the unsocial family at latency were a proneness to enuresis with conduct disorders, motor disorders, and neurotic traits as part of the total configuration of symptoms.

With or without infantile phenomena, the particular type of conduct disorder most frequent was either an avoidance of close relationships with adults and children or destructive aggressive behavior, followed by self-punishing behavior with a tendency to get caught. As contrasted to the latency child of the egocentric family, who is more shrewd and calculating, the child of this age in the unsocial family has developed a greater degree of masochism and self-punishing techniques. These latter character traits and defenses may lead more easily to regression into psychosis than do those of the child who experiences fewer active guilt feelings.

Although sexual delinquency, a form of conduct disorder, is uncommon for most latency children it may appear in the child within this age range in the unsocial family. It probably will involve paternal seduction of a girl child, resulting in an incestuous relationship which is maintained over a period of time before being "discovered" by the other parent. In the strictest sense, this cannot be considered sexual delinquency on the part of the child, because of her age and because of parental initiative and participation. However, her greater vulnerability to such seduction grows out of a lack of mutual trust between mother and daughter. Only after an elapse of considerable time, in one such case, was it possible for the girl to confide to the mother the nature of her relationship with the father.

Motor disorders in the latency child of the unsocial family consist of a lack of concentrated effort with some tendency toward excessive purposeless activity. Psychotic illness can occur in the latency child of ten to twelve years of age, but he is usually responsive to treatment if removed from the home to a psychotherapeutic setting.

Psychotic Disturbance of Adolescence

It is normal for any adolescent to behave in an inconsistent and unpredictable manner for a considerable length of time—to fight his impulses and to accept them; to love his parents and to hate them; to revolt against, and to be dependent upon, them; to thrive on imitation while searching for his own self-identity; to be idealistic and unselfish but also to be self-centered, egoistic, calculating. Such fluctuations between extreme opposites of feeling and behavior are deemed highly abnormal at any other time of life. At this period they may signify nothing more than the fact that the adult personality takes a long time to emerge, and the individual adolescent is in no rush to close the door to all the varying possibilities.

Pathological development results when such fluctuations become one-sided—leaning toward suppression, revolt, flight, withdrawal, regression, or asceticism. The defensive methods employed by adolescent youths against their impulses and/or against infantile-parental ties produce pathological results when they are overused, overstressed, or used in isolation. Each abnormal type of adolescent development also represents a potentially useful way of regaining emotional equilibrium, if it is combined with other defenses of moderate intensity. In the majority of adolescents in the unsocial family, their adolescent reactions represent deep-rooted personality trait disorders rather than transient expressions of emancipatory strivings and oscillations.

The psychic disturbances of the adolescent in the unsocial family have been classified according to the defenses the boy or girl uses in breaking the infantile emotional tie to the parent. These disturbances usually may be identified by a sudden withdrawal of the emotional tie and its transfer to someone outside the family.

Typical new attachments made by the adolescent of the unsocial family are apt to be found in homosexual or heterosexual friendships and gangs. The adolescent boy or girl may leave home altogether; or may remain there, assuming the attitude of an inconsiderate boarder and displaying indifference, callousness, and hostility insofar as all family members are concerned. It does not matter which occurs, because the essential qualities of the infantile attachment to the parent remain unchanged.

The girl adolescent selects rough crowds of delinquent boys, usually allying herself with a single male who is older or of a different race. Prostitution and out-of-wedlock children, sexual intercourse indiscriminately engaged in, followed by early marriage, are some of the ultimate results.

Adolescent boys in their early teens also are apt to ally themselves with a gang of delinquents, be away from home for days, but always return. The seventeen-, eighteen-, or nineteen-year-old may join the army but make a poor adjustment and come back home, where he then embarks on more serious antisocial activities.

It is not uncommon for the older male adolescent to attempt to break the parental tie by engaging in overt homosexual activities, as well as car stealing, robbing. A psychiatric diagnosis of personality disturbance, sexual deviation, or deviant sexuality, symptomatic of more extensive syndromes such as schizophrenia, is possible.

Psychodynamically speaking, just what occurs in this type of transfer of emotional ties is that the adolescent's aggressive and sexual impulses cease to threaten him because the parent who represents his infantile attachments is merely stripped of his importance. Consequently guilt and anxiety (superego) decrease, the ego becomes more tolerant of, and can therefore act upon, the sexual and aggressive impulses when they arise. The adolescent of the unsocial family only imagines himself free of infantile parental ties and actually remains as securely tied as before. The contrast in the new attachments selected, or the overemphasis on new allegiances, and the suddenness or the onesidedness of the change mark this behavior as defensive and abnormal.

Some few adolescents in the unsocial family attempt to sever infantile parental ties by the defense of reaction formation; that is, reversal of affect. Certain symptoms in the adolescent boy or girl indicate a reversal of love to hate or disrespect. The adolescent turns upon the self the hostility felt toward the parent. Tendencies toward self-abasement, self-injury, projection and suspiciousness are evident; but acting out, if any, will be within the family. Interpersonal relationships are not formed outside the family.

Those adolescents who are impaired by mental deficiency will present a confusing diagnostic picture in their attempts to cast off the infantile parental tie. Behavior at home will be hostile and aggressive, appearing as reversal of affect. At the same time, the adolescent may ally himself with a sexual partner and be disliked, troublesome, and unpredictable in school, with peers, and so forth. However, a diagnosis of mental deficiency, with subsequent correction of school program and removal to a social setting appropriate to the boy or girl's capacities, usually results in the subsidence of acting-out symptoms in the larger community. Nevertheless, the parental relationship and the damage done to the personality remain unchanged.

MALE PARTNER'S FAMILY OF ORIGIN

The majority of male partners of the unsocial family had continuous contact with both parents from the time of their birth through the age of sixteen. The few male partners who had been separated from both parents or from the father were either under two years of age or adolescent at the time. Although the instances of separation were few, they were greater in number for these male partners than for those in any other family class.

Thus, the specific pathology in adult social adjustment of the majority of these male partners is not attributable to shifts in family structure. Rather, the mother-son relationship looms as an important etiological factor, since in the major portion of the cases the mother's presence in the family was apt to be continuous. For the smaller number who experienced separation from an own parent, the age, the traumatic nature of the circumstances precipitating the breach in contact, the impersonal character of the substitute arrangements, and the extensiveness of the duration provide distinctive keys to the source and nature of the emotional vulnerabilities of their adult personalities.

However, irrespective of whether or not the male partners experienced separation from an own parent, their adult adjustment reveals some form of psychotic illness, antisocial behavior, or alcoholism. Therefore, factors other than separation of parent from child must always be considered diagnostically in determining the etiology of behavior in the male partners in this family type.

Adequacy of Financial Support

By and large, when the fathers of the male partners were present, they supported their families adequately. Only occasionally did the mother work. Various occupations were pursued by the fathers. Carpenter, salesman, repairman, insurance worker, factory worker and proprietor of a business were among the most frequent. These families of origin relied more readily upon some form of public assistance, either directly or by use of child placement facilities, than did the families of origin of the male partners in other classes. Therefore, a background of failure to support, with resulting dependency, is one factor to be considered diagnostically in this male partner's history.

Of far greater diagnostic importance, however, is the fact that self-sufficiency and self-reliance were rarely stressed by either of the male partner's parents in a fashion that motivated him toward acquisition of good work habits, confidence in his own ability, pleasure in achievement and independence. Although in many instances the father himself was a steady and successful worker, because of his limited interest in, or dislike of, his son there was no basis for the male partner's identification with him on this score. The situation was further complicated by the mother's predilections toward indulging certain of her son's needs, depriving him of normal gratification of other needs, and relegating the father to a minor role.

Identification of the boy with the father, under these circumstances, was also at the risk of rejection by the mother, a chance a young child cannot take because of his emotionally dependent status.

Male partners who were raised in orphanages or institutions had the physical protection that such group living affords, but either they were unable to learn habits of work because of an already mal-developed ego, or they were never provided with an incentive toward self-reliance, or both.

Thus, in general, these male partners, with either an own family or institutional background history, were not provided with an incentive to assume the provider role, to become self-reliant, and to have confidence in themselves as heads of families.

Love Relationships

Distinctive to the family of origin of the male partners in the un-social family are parental submissiveness and overindulgence in relation to adult capacity for mature love relationships. In far the greatest number of instances, the mothers or mother substitutes of the male partners submitted to their sons' most infantile dependent cravings and did not restrict their behavior or expect them to exercise self-restraint in acquiring a full masculine identification. In essence, the male partner, in childhood, was made to feel that he could control his parents at will.

This overindulgence by his mother was usually accompanied by a coerciveness which reflected her lack of esteem for the father and for males in general. In other words, she welcomed a flow of love from the son, who was accepted by her only upon the condition that he also reject the father, whom she presented as a depreciated figure. In this parental setting, fathers tended to be overstrict and cold, showing no affection, or were extremely passive in maintaining their status as males, capitulating to their wives' belittling attitudes and domination.

To meet such childhood conditions of parental love, the behavior of the male partner in the unsocial family indicates that he may have attempted any of several solutions. As a child, he may have feared his father, never feeling close to him. As a youth, such a boy was uninformed of the "facts of life." He thus would attach himself to his mother, trying to please her by taking over household responsibility and giving her money. As an adult, this marital partner has uncontrollable and violent temper outbursts over the least frustration, particularly when his wife does not appreciate his housework. He has tenuous love relationships and engages in a series of extra-marital affairs.

In other instances, the male has been indulged with material possessions in childhood by his mother, who gave in to his wishes, contrary to the father's will. At the same time, she relegated her son to a passive feminine role as housekeeper, making him wait on her. He accepted the role and gained pleasure in so doing.

As an adult marital partner, his emotional ties are tenuous; he remains attached to, and requires the presence of, his mother, feels disgust for his passive father. Under the stresses of family living, he resorts to alcoholism to satisfy his dependency cravings, to extra-marital affairs to overcompensate for his passivity, to pathological lying and forgery to bolster his self-esteem by exploiting others.

The basic adult problem which stems from the family backgrounds of the male partners in the unsocial family is their strong tendency to identify with their own mothers. They have incorporated aspects of her passive feminine and aggressive qualities. For example, their preference for household, feminine, and maternal activities is a defense against their frustrated masculine strivings. Alcoholism, drug addiction, and fleeing back to mother under stress are defenses against their dependent receptive strivings.

This adult picture may be reversed, insofar as surface behavior is concerned, and be characterized by much resentment, aggressive behavior, and accusation leveled at the father and/or mother in the family of origin. In either case, the adult behavior of the unsocial family male indicates a dominance of receptive demands and passive feminine tendencies. The diagnostic picture based on personal histories of these male partners suggests the presence of quantities of unneutralized aggressive impulses as well as thwarted sexual strivings within their personalities. The low incidence of overt problems of sexual acting out does not imply that sexual problems do not exist. Rather they appear in various unhealthy substitute forms, as noted.

Parental neglect occurs when the male has been a subject of child placement. This is evidenced when his parents fail to keep in touch with him thereafter or a brother takes over the father's role, with little consideration of the feelings of others—a situation condoned by the mother. For those separated from a single parent the chances are that the remaining parent, usually the mother, is apt to be sexually promiscuous or alcoholic, but to keep the son with her.

Among these male partners, some of the reasons for separation from parents in childhood included: "accidental" death of a mother at the hands of a father while he cleaned a shotgun, followed by the father's desertion of the family; sexual promiscuity of a mother who was deemed an unfit parent and divorced by her husband who was uninterested in his son; the death of a father prior to the male's birth, followed two years later by his mother's death from grief and refusal of food. In adolescence, the main reasons for separation of the male from his father were separation, divorce, suicide.

The substitute arrangements provided by the parents did little to counterbalance these events. For the most part, children's homes constituted the substitute family, usually for a period of from five to ten years. Sometimes an aunt or grandmother would care for the boy, or an industrial school placement occurred at adolescence.

Self-identity

The male partners of the unsocial family will have had little opportunity in their own or in substitute family settings to develop a firm sense of self-identity, to test their own capacities for making considered judgments, and to withstand frustrations. Psychodynamically, these personal lacks or the maldevelopment of these capacities were accounted for either by (1) the traumatic circumstances attendant upon separation from his own parent or parents during his childhood; or by (2) the mother's indulgence and effeminization of her son, coupled with a passive father's disinterest in him or an overstrict father's emasculating attitudes toward him.

In the familial background of the first group, the absence of enduring emotional ties to parent persons, following the separation of parent from child, accounts for these lacks. In the second, masculine competition was discouraged and often forbidden by both parents, a situation which resulted in maldevelopment of related capacities. Both situations gave birth to problems in achieving an appropriate sex identification. Hence, all aspects of the male partner's adult social adjustment are adversely affected: his marriage partnership, child rearing, work achievement, and general social behavior. Judgments are formed and decisions are made impulsively and oriented to the desires of the moment. Frequently, this pattern alternates with a complete refusal to accept responsibility for making decisions.

Socialization

In the majority of cases the mothers or fathers in the male partner's family of origin did not commit antisocial acts in the legal sense. This is interesting, in view of the fact that many of these parents have produced sons who get into this kind of trouble in adult years. Nonetheless, there is much to support the thesis that although these parents suffered from severe personality disturbances, antisocial acts did not ordinarily ensue. The most extreme instances suggesting personality defects or disintegration were sexual promiscuity of mothers, psychotic illness and alcoholism of mother and/or father. In a small number of cases, laxness in the parents' own sexual behavior and in teaching the rules of social conformance to their children presents a family of origin for the male partner in the unsocial family contrasting with that of the other family types.

The significant and key factor rests in the parent's failure to teach the male child to forego certain immediate pleasures for the sake of the longer time gain. The acquisition of personal independence, first to please the parent and later the individual himself, normally makes it worth the child's while to conform willingly. This, however, did not occur in the case of most males in this family type.

The defective superego of those male partners who were not separated from an own parent derives from the particular quality and intensity of the mother-son relationship, and the mother's relationship to the male partner's father. In this particular setting, the mothers encouraged the sons' infantile attachment to them. Therefore, the major developmental step of incorporating into the personality a normal functioning conscience was rarely accomplished in these male partners.

FEMALE PARTNER'S FAMILY OF ORIGIN

Like the male partner in the unsocial family, the majority of female partners had the continuous presence of both own parents, up to and beyond adolescence. When this female partner lost her mother, it usually occurred in her preadolescent or adolescent period and was due to the mother's death; no separations from the mother occurred in early childhood. When this partner lost her father, however, it was either through his death or because he divorced her mother, during her early childhood or just as she was entering latency.

The general pattern of substitute arrangements is both interesting and significant when compared to similar situations in the male partner's history. In contrast to males' family of origin, the female partner's family rarely relied on outside community resources for substitute care. Although death was the main reason for separation of parent from child, the remaining parent of the female partner did not remarry; thus there were no stepmothers or stepfathers. In the main, the substitute parents were relatives who supplemented an own mother or father, as in the egocentric female's family of origin.

When mothers were left with primary responsibility for the family, they worked and relied on a female relative to care for their children. Fathers, when left with parental responsibility, showed a marked tendency to maintain the home, relying upon older children to assume the maternal function. Occasionally, a paternal grandmother or aunt would "look in." However, contrary to the practice of the mothers of the female partners in the egocentric family, it was not typical for either parent to turn to an own mother to assume or to supplement the parental role.

Thus, female partners of the unsocial family who lost their mothers through death in preadolescence or adolescence were apt to be raised by an own father and siblings, but with no firm mother substitute. Parental supervision under these circumstances tended to be overpermissive. A sexually stimulating home atmosphere commonly pervaded this female child's entrance into adolescence, created by seductive attitudes on the part of a father or brother.

Adequacy of Financial Support

There was a consistent pattern of economic self-reliance among the families of origin of the unsocial family female partners. The father assumed this function when he was present; when the father was absent the mother took over this responsibility. Income was generally adequate; if it was insufficient, usually because of the father's death, mothers, older children, or relatives supplemented the family resources.

These facts, and the part played by other children of the family or by female relatives when there was a loss of one parent, suggest a family cohesiveness and reliability in the area of financial support. However, the quality of this cohesiveness is such that it also supports deviant forms of behavior in other areas of social functioning, as has been observed in the female partner's adult adjustment.

Love Relationships

A predisposition toward unrestrained freedom in directing hostilities toward men and toward authority in general was acquired from their families of origin by the largest group of female partners of the unsocial family. A countertendency also was acquired—the repression of sexual impulses in the full meaning of adult sexuality, except as these impulses highly color their hostility. The source of this pattern in the family of origin is found in a combination of factors.

Maternal overindulgence is common. In childhood the female partner's mother tended to all of her dependent needs, in return for which she virtually forfeited the privilege of achieving a feminine sexual identity in her own right. However, equally important was an atmosphere which allowed the free expression of hostility toward men and depreciation of them as males. Thus the female partner maintained a dependent tie to her mother, substituting this for a mature sexual relationship with an adult male.

Fathers were overpunitive, using the female partner as an object for direct expression of hostilities.

Psychodynamically speaking, when individuality is forfeited in order to maintain dependency, the hostility engendered by this loss must find an outlet somewhere. In this instance, the female partner was given an outlet by her mother's encouragement to express directly, or to project onto another, her hostile destructive impulses. By this device the mother also escaped the hostility her daughter would otherwise have expressed toward her. In this particular family setting, the father's cruelties also gave the female partner justification and an added excuse for exploiting men in one form or another. In adult behavior, the female pattern of exploitation may take the form of promiscuity, relegating the husband to the position of a nonentity by ignoring or depreciating him or consciously or unconsciously aiding and abetting his pursuance of antisocial acts.

The female partners in the unsocial family who had no mothers, and whose fathers were alternately rigid and seductive, became sexually frigid adults, but also fostered their male partners' regressive tendencies either by overprotecting them from, or encouraging them in, such activities as defiance of the law. These tendencies of the female partners complement the male's basic personality problems in a highly destructive and negative way.

Self-identity

By and large, the female partners of the unsocial family do not resist or refuse to make decisions or choices, but make them impulsively, dictated solely by the whim of the moment and without judicious consideration and thought. As in object relationships, the intensity of the motivating impulses which dictate a particular decision is usually high; thus, a strong stand may be taken to defend a poor decision. These women probably conceive of themselves as having a certain omnipotence and power, which they exercise irrespective of the rights of others or of another's claim to a self-identity of his own.

There is a smaller group of female partners who are oversubmissive in making choices, allowing others to take this responsibility. However, once this is done, they are readily suspicious or entertain the idea that they are exploited.

Socialization

As in the male's family of origin, instances of such antisocial behavior as sexual promiscuity and dishonesty were not usually present in the female partner's parents. Nonetheless, in a high proportion of cases, either one or both of her parents were defective in terms of social and moral standards affecting her personality development.

By and large, this flaw was found to lie in the parents' hostile attitudes toward people in general, unconsciously communicated to their children. Overrestrictiveness stemming from religious beliefs inappropriately interpreted and applied, rather than from laxness, was the rule. The content of this overstrictness was such that it prevented the female from acquiring a firmly based sexual orientation toward a normal male, but permitted her unlicensed expression of hostile impulses toward men. Laxness on the part of the father was likely to be expressed in seductive behavior toward the daughter after the mother's death.

Thus, antisocial behavior in the family of origin, lack of respect for law and order, dependency, and exploitation of the community were not significant factors in producing the superego and ego-capacity characteristic of the majority of female partners of the unsocial family. The answer is to be found, rather, in the intensity of particular qualities in the mother-daughter relationship, as combined with the particular traits typical of the father.

IX. FRAMEWORK FOR FAMILY DIAGNOSIS

THE DYNAMIC interaction between family members and the decisive influence of this interaction upon the life-adaptive patterns of the individual have been so clearly observed by students of human behavior that their importance need only be reaffirmed. Such evidence is abundant in the literature, particularly that which deals with the diagnosis and treatment of persons who have problems in psychosocial adaptation. Diagnostically and therapeutically, the family and social aspects of behavior increasingly are taken into account by the practitioner, not only as they impinge upon the normal character development and social functioning of the individual, but also as they encroach upon his pathology (86, pp. xii, xiii; 131, pp. 112–13). Thus, it is not only plausible but also fundamental that the family be selected as the main psychosocial referent in constructing the framework for the diagnosis of psychosocial ills.

Although social casework has its special method for investigating the psychosocial components of individual and family adjustment, it does not have at its disposal scientific instruments to assist in this process. Unlike the doctor who depends upon a variety of technically accurate devices, and the lawyer who relies upon existing laws and court decisions, the social caseworker must use language symbols as his technical instruments. Thus semantics, definitions, and concepts and their referents take on particular significance in this field.

This chapter proposes a framework for family diagnosis which is designed to serve as a tool of social casework investigation. Its accuracy and usefulness depend on the underlying concepts and the extent to which these are commonly understood and accepted.

In the ensuing discussion, therefore, we endeavor to identify, define, and interpret the principal elements of the framework, as well as the concepts that integrate each within the total structure. It is the third in the series of clinical findings from this research.[1]

By intention, the framework for family diagnosis is comprehensive in scope. It is also inescapably complex. To minimize this problem we have endeavored to simplify the presentation by introducing the framework from the following focal points: (1) a structural outline which delineates the basic areas, major factors, and subfactors; (2) the five basic areas, with emphasis on definitions, the relationship each bears to the other, and the concepts which determine their diagnostic significance within the framework; (3) the major factors of family social functioning, with particular attention to clarification of the concepts that underly these factors.

In social casework, the ultimate purpose of any diagnostic study is the scientific planning of a rehabilitative program. Specifically, it is to discover why a given family and its members present their own particular kind of social dysfunctioning. The proposed framework for family diagnosis represents the method evolved for facilitating the diagnostic process. Its general purpose is to assist the caseworker to reconstruct the healthy as well as the pathological processes of individual and family social functioning, as these may relate to the presence or absence of identified psychosocial disorders.

FRAMEWORK FOR FAMILY DIAGNOSIS

This framework pinpoints areas of social functioning and of interpersonal living, the nature of the individual characteristics of adult and child, and the kinds of historical data most frequently found relevant to the diagnosis of family disorders. The diagnostic scheme identifies two particular and important groupings: the first is designated "basic areas"; the second, more specific grouping is termed "major factors." Both are fundamental to the diagnostic scheme, with each deriving meaning from, and giving meaning to, the other.

---

[1] The first two in this series are: "A Classification of Psychosocial Disorders," Chapter IV, and the chapters on the four disordered family types.

1. FAMILY COMPOSITION
2. PSYCHOSOCIAL DISORDERS
     Level A and Level B disorder classifications
     External stress precipitating identification of disorder
3. FAMILY SOCIAL FUNCTIONING
   Child-rearing Functioning
     Parental Functioning
       Events and circumstances influencing parenthood
       Physical care provided child
       Love relationships encouraged in child
       Self-identity development encouraged in child
       Socialization measures and standards
     Child Development
       Events and circumstances influencing child development
       Early childhood (under 6 years)
         Love relationships to parents
         Self-identity development
         Socialization
       Latency and adolescence (6–12 years; 13–20 years)
         Love relationships to parents
         Love relationships to siblings
         Self-identity as manifested in home; in school; in sexual behavior
         Socialization
            friends
            social conformance in community
   Marital Functioning
       Events and circumstances
       Love relationship in marriage
       Self-identity maintained in marriage
       Socialization in marriage
         Helpful concern
         Problem-solving
   Financial Functioning
     Events and circumstances
     Income production
       Work situation
         skill and efficiency
         cooperativeness
         achievement incentive
     Income management
         emotional acceptance of provider role
         financial support undertaken
         planfulness and spending of income

4. INDIVIDUAL CHARACTERISTICS
   Adults
     Intelligence
     Physical condition
     Preferred ego defenses
     Emotional stability
   Child
     Physical condition
     Intelligence
     Emotional stability
       latency child
       adolescent
5. FAMILY OF ORIGIN
     Events and circumstances
     Continuity of contact between adults and own parent or parental
       substitutes
     Adequacy of financial support within adults' families of origin
     Emotional ties to own parents or parental substitutes
     Self-identity and identification
     Standards of socialization

BASIC AREAS

The five basic areas that comprise the framework for family diagnosis may be generally defined as follows:

1. *Family composition* denotes all persons who are members of the nuclear family group, as well as those persons living in the home who are related or nonrelated to the heads of the family by blood ties.

2. *Psychosocial disorders* encompass behavior and conditions that represent varying degrees of impairment in social functioning on the part of the family or individual. The two general types—Level A and Level B—and the five categories under which they are generally classified—child rearing, marital, financial, adult, and child—have been defined and discussed in Chapter IV.

3. *Family social functioning* refers to the attitudes and behavior displayed by adult and child members of the nuclear family in meeting the social and emotional demands of marital functioning, child rearing, and financial functioning.

4. *Individual characteristics* denote the individual's constitutional inheritance; his physical condition; his intellectual capacity, as determined by psychological tests; the preferred ego defenses (59; 98; 106) he characteristically employes; his emotional stability, as determined in accordance with the psychiatric classifications of the *Manual of Mental Disorders* of the American Psychiatric Association. In general, the same definitions apply to adult and child, with certain modifications with respect to the emotional stability of the latter, which are discussed in Chapter X.

5. *The family of origin* encompasses the family group in which the adult heads of the nuclear family were born and lived during their developmental years, or the substitute family in which they grew up. The history of the adults pertains to the series of events that transpired, the circumstances that prevailed, and the values and goals of the people who surrounded them in their original setting.

These basic area groupings designate the principal fields of inquiry from which will come the information necessary to compiling a family diagnosis. The principles followed in formulating these definitions derive from the concepts of family diagnosis that guided construction of the framework.

The central element in the frame of reference is the third basic area, "family social functioning." Conceptually speaking, the other four areas center around this nucleus and are diagnostically interpreted within its context. It is the center of gravity, so to speak. In other words, family composition, psychosocial disorders, individual characteristics, and the family of origin are thought of as fringe areas that encroach upon and thus add another dimension to family social functioning.

This does not necessarily imply that the factors identified within these other areas are of secondary importance, diagnostically, therapeutically, or in prognosis. Rather, they are significant for their implications with respect to the family's social functioning. From this perspective, these areas may represent a symptom of social dysfunction, its end result, one of many factors contributing to the social dysfunctioning of the family, or possibly all three.

Of a more specific nature is another important feature of this diagnostic scheme, the use of a "social setting" referent in formulating most of the area definitions. To a large extent, this applies also to the major factor criteria. This feature relates to one of the important concepts inherent in the diagnostic framework which presumes that there is a social situation in which an individual functions, to which he reacts, and which acts upon him. The guiding principles for identifying and evaluating family social functioning stem from this premise as discussed in Chapter I.

Referents

A look at the principal referents to which each area definition relates will provide the background for a closer examination of the specific implications of this social setting aspect of the framework.

The second area, relating to psychosocial disorders, encompasses behavior and conditions identified by the community's agencies, defined within the context of legally and socially determined sanctions and institutions. Thus its main social setting referent is what members of society are obliged to do according to law, and are expected to do, to support and conserve valued cultural patterns.

The areas of family composition, family social functioning, and family of origin history are described within somewhat different contexts. These consist of the structural form of the group with which the individual is identified; the particular milieu in which he lives and functions; and the specific psychosocial tasks which ordinarily are emphasized by our society for adult and child. In other words, the principal social setting referents are the psychosocial requisites of family functioning which stem from the nature of the family situation itself.

On the other hand, a social referent was not used in the same way in formulating definitions of individual characteristics. Rather, the criteria for this area encompass only the characteristics, inherited and acquired, which give adult and child their particular marks of individuality. These include constitutional inheritance, physical condition, intelligence, and personality structure, particularly the psychological processes. Certain of these attributes will have developed as a result of environmental stimulation. Regardless of these factors, it is nevertheless presumed that at any given point an individual, child or adult, possesses his own particular capabilities and incapacities, which in turn influence the way he will meet psychosocial demands arising from his environment.

Thus, these varying aspects of the social setting in which the family members live are implicit, in some form, in the referents to which the basic area definitions relate. The principles which guide the identification and evaluation of family patterns of social functioning reflect the integration of this concept with greater precision.

FAMILY SOCIAL FUNCTIONING

The key to understanding the processes of social functioning as here conceived is knowledge of the adaptive task that faces each individual family member, and an evaluation of how he meets it in relation to his developed capacities for doing so. In this diagnostic scheme, the tasks that face family members are those of the three family functions, in accordance with the psychosocial requisites which stem from there. The social functioning of the family and its members is observed and evaluated within this frame of reference, that is, within the context of the defined social tasks which stimulate specific, dynamic behavior reactions.

The term "developed capacities" requires elaboration. It presumes that each individual, according to the capabilities of his ego and the various possibilities of his social setting, selects a mode of behavior for meeting environmental demands. Moreover, this mode of behavior, in varying degrees of effectiveness, will satisfy the functional needs of the social setting and the individual's own physical needs, urges, desires, and pleasures.

Therefore, in its approach to the evaluation of social functioning this diagnostic scheme takes as a principle that different life situations can stimulate different aspects of the personality. That is to say, under certain external conditions noncharacteristic forms of behavior and degrees of ego mastery may occur in the same person. The specific form will depend upon the environmental situation itself, the problem presented for solution, and the individual's particular biological and psychological sensitivities to these. War neuroses are clear-cut examples of this phenomenon. The birth of a child, the illness of a father, the death of a spouse, the pressure from a highly critical employer, are among some of the situations that stimulate "changed," but nonetheless typical, behavior responses.

In the social situation of the family, however, as in any human group, the interaction of its individual members tends to set up circles of behavior and a chain of reactions. This is stimulated by a number of factors, one of the most important of which is the reciprocal nature of familial roles, wherein the *rights* of one family member become the *obligations* of another. It is on this basis, for example, that the child's developmental progress may be appropriately designated as an area of family functioning. That is to say, his right to protection and care becomes the duty of the parent.

The failure of one family member properly to fulfill his responsibilities thereby threatens another member's well-being, depending upon the reciprocal nature of their relationship. In this diagnostic scheme, the factors which characterize and give rise to the interpersonal behavior patterns of family members are best discerned and evaluated from the ways in which the reciprocal aspects of the functional roles are met. The detailed definitions of the family functions are formulated in these terms. The conscious and unconscious purposes underlying the interpersonal reactions also are inferred from the ways in which the reciprocal aspects of the family functional roles are met.

For the purposes of social casework practice the innumerable interpersonal patterns are limited to the following family relationships: parent to child; child to parent; child to siblings; father to mother; mother to father; husband to wife; wife to husband. These lines of demarcation do not disregard the fact that there is a constant ebb and flow of feeling between and among different family members at different times and in varying combinations. In fact, the possible combinations are almost endless. Therefore, both practical and diagnostic considerations required that the range be thus restricted in this framework.

MAJOR FACTORS

The area of family social functioning is, as already noted, the pivotal point on which all other elements of the diagnostic scheme ultimately converge. Of particular importance, therefore, are the major factors within this area, which delineate the range and specific nature of all three family functions. The major factors which bring each of these functions into focus are generally designated as: (1) events and circumstances; (2) love relationships; (3) self-identity; and (4) socialization. With minor exceptions these constitute the structural elements of the child-rearing, marital functioning, and financial areas. With certain adaptations, they also constitute the frame of reference for the family of origin history. The principal referents and the concepts underlying the use of these major factors in the family social functioning area require elaboration:

Events and circumstances. This factor refers to happenings that occur in the life of the family and social situations that prevail as significant influences in shaping the patterns of social adjustment in its members.

Love relationships. This factor generally embraces the basic qualities of strength and genuine emotion the individual has at his command for the formation of personal relationships; that is, his inner resources for giving and receiving affection, trust, and consideration, and for participating in a mature and adult sexual relationship.

Self-identity. This factor equates with the self-concepts and feelings of personal worth of the individual, his readiness to express native talents and to exercise initiative in the use of adaptive skills with a feeling of confidence consistent with his actual abilities.

Socialization. As here used, this factor denotes the moral, ethical, and social values of the individual, the independent judgment he exercises, the course of action he undertakes and responsibility he assumes for his personal acts, the respect he shows for the rights of others.

Although the particular emphasis of a single factor necessarily varies within the respective functional areas, each of these factors stems from generic conceptual bases. These concepts are best understood in their relevance to the diagnostic scheme by dealing, first, with the factors of events and circumstances and, second, with the three remaining factors—love relationships, self-identity, and socialization.

Events and Circumstances

Environmental strains, events, and social situations have always been considered by the social caseworker as factors that may possibly contribute to family dysfunctioning. Ordinarily, however, in most family diagnostic schemes these are not an integral part of the structural design. Rather, they are separately designated as "environmental factors." In this diagnostic framework, however, particular events and circumstances in the lives of adult and child family members are incorporated as a part of a framework of precisely defined family functions. Therefore, environmental factors are identified within, and evaluated in, their relevance to child rearing, marital functioning, and financial functioning. They are not considered separate entities nor do they constitute a "blanket" area to which "leftovers" may be relegated.

This treatment of environmental factors rests on a principle which originates in a previously developed concept relating to the varying social situations which can and usually do stimulate different aspects of the individual's personality. In other words, similar occurrences and events which do not become stressful situations for some families often create hardships for others. To a considerable degree this difference is a question of the capacities of family members for dealing with particular events and happenings. Therefore, the nature of these environmental factors, the particular areas of social functioning to which they relate, and the degree of dysfunctioning they create, are conceived to be the significant diagnostic considerations with respect to environmental factors.

Love Relationships, Self-Identity, and Socialization

Love relationships, self-identity, and socialization are such fundamental and familiar aspects of daily living that their diagnostic significance to family social functioning will be immediately obvious. In other words, if an individual is to get along in the world and to feel any pleasure in so doing, to love and be loved, meaningful personal relationships are necessary. A firm sense of himself as an individual is required for self-respect and for achieving the satisfactions which are gained by a productive person. A normally functioning conscience is requisite if one is to receive the consideration and protection of others.

By the nature of things, it is also obvious that most human needs can find expression and gratification only through relationships with other human beings. This is largely true whether the need is for loving and being loved, for maintaining a realistically founded sense of self-esteem, for protecting others, for being protected, or for any other reason. All of these involve the individual in interpersonal relationships, with their many facets. As here conceived, therefore, social functioning at the interpersonal level inescapably becomes an expression of the dominant emotional aims which motivate individual behavior. That is to say, person-to-person relationships and the interaction of groups inevitably reflect the sensitivities and predispositions contained within the personality structure of the individuals involved.

The choice of love relationships, self-identity, and socialization demonstrates the influence of these particular concepts of social functioning. In a more technical sense, they represent the attempt to introduce selected aspects of human motivation into the definition of family and individual social functioning. Illumination of the concepts on which these focal points are based further clarifies this aspect of the family diagnostic framework:

Love relationships. Object love versus self-love provides the conceptual base on which all definitions are formulated (18) with respect to love relationships of family members in the areas of child rearing and marital functioning. In the simplest terms, "object" love means love of another person which does not entirely supplant a normal degree of self-love. The genetic base of all such relationships is conceived as being rooted in infantile and early childhood relationships. Obviously, no one fully outgrows all the infantile characteristics of his first emotional ties. Thus remnants of these earlier attachments tend to persist, coloring to some degree the selection and the aims that perpetuate adult love. However, the greater the number of such infantile goals that persist with high intensity into adulthood, or beyond the normal developmental stage of childhood, the greater the likelihood of impairment of interpersonal relationships and integrated behavior.

Self-identity. As here used, the term relates to the individual's concept of himself as a person in his own right, manifested in self-reliance, a firm sense of appropriate sex identity, and pleasure in work achievement consistent with his actual abilities. The relationship between the acquired capacity for self-directive activity and for object relationships is, of course, well known from the point of view of personality development. Ideally, in adulthood the individual's self-concepts permit him to obtain narcissistic gratification in socially constructive or culturally valued work, as well as libidinal satisfaction in the sex act with an adult partner of the opposite sex. This is the conceptual base for self-identity definitions of social functioning in the parental functioning, child development, and marital functioning areas of the framework.

Socialization. For diagnostic purposes, socialization encompasses attitudes and behavior that denote the kind of social conscience the adult or child possesses. In other words, it embraces the wish to live in approximate conformance with the constructive cultural and social values of one's society, the individual's "wish" being based on an inner authority which automatically guides moral and ethical judgments and social behavior. The genetic roots of a normally functioning conscience are presumed to stem for the most part from parental standards of right and wrong which are taken over in childhood by a psychological process termed "internalization." This initially takes place as a result of the child's identification with the parent (19). Subsequently, the process is motivated by his wish to retain the parent's love and to protect his dependent status. At the same time, however, a child normally learns that he risks punishment, disapproval, or rejection if he does not do what his parents expect of him. A sense of guilt is thus developed which eventually acts as an inner authority to deter behavior that is punishable or disapproved. The superego thereby becomes an incorporate part of the personality, permitting the emergence of a social conscience which operates automatically (5; 69).

The psychological processes that result in the developed capacity for love relationships and a firm sense of self-identity and socialization are known to be closely interwoven. Well established also is the interdependence of the psychological and the social in achieving these evidences of personality development. Conceptually speaking, love relationships, self-identity, and socialization factors may be said to represent the social counterparts of particular aspects of personality growth. Therefore, it may be said that the principal referents for the specific social functioning criteria of the family functions are *psychosocial* in nature.

In general psychosocial terms, love relationships may be said to represent the manner in which the instinctual impulses (libido and aggression) have been deployed in the service of the ego; self-identity is a matter of ego-identity enabling the protection of the self; socialization denotes superego formation demanding that the ego take into account the rights of others in love relationships, achievement, and self-preservation.

X. INTERPRETATION OF THE DIAGNOSTIC FRAMEWORK

THE CHANCES of arriving at a sound family diagnosis are immeasurably increased when the social caseworker brings to this task a knowledge of what kinds of information will shed the greatest light on the causes of family dysfunctioning, and on the meaning of the context within which available data subsequently must be evaluated and synthesized. The diagnostic guides presented in this chapter are intended to provide this knowledge for the caseworker. Specifically, they make possible an informed approach to family diagnosis through knowledge of: (1) the kinds of data which should be sought; (2) the points of focus that should guide the selection; and (3) the general principles which should subsequently guide the interpretation and evaluation of selected data within the meaning of the framework for family diagnosis.

Family composition
Psychosocial disorders
Family social functioning
   Child rearing
      Parental functioning
      Child development
   Marital functioning
   Financial functioning
Individual characteristics
Family of origin

Emphasis will be given to identifying the information appropriate to each part of the framework. Frequent reference to the foregoing modified outline of the diagnostic scheme will assist in keeping the reader oriented to the basic structural elements of the framework.

FAMILY COMPOSITION

The purpose of this section is to enable the caseworker to make an evaluative description of the family structure. All children, whether dependent or over eighteen years of age, in or out of the home, are included. For example, a typical description of family composition might be: "The family consists of father, mother, and one six-year-old boy, who was adopted at the age of two months to replace immediately the parents' own son who died at the age of twelve years."

PSYCHOSOCIAL DISORDERS

This area is generally focused on two aspects of the psychosocial disorder identified by the agency social caseworker: classification of the disorder and the external stress that precipitates its identification.

Classification

"Psychosocial disorder" is one among several possible terms descriptive of psychosocial dysfunctioning, or the problems of a family and its members. As an aid to the systematic approach in diagnosis, all psychosocial disorders present in a family are classified according to the major categories, Level A and Level B, and their appropriate subgroups: adult; child; child rearing; marital; and financial disorders.

Previous Level A and Level B disorders should also be noted to make certain that significant events or conditions affecting the family's life will not be overlooked. For example, a history of hospitalization of a father or mother for mental illness, a previous Level A adult disorder, inevitably colors the immediate clinical picture whether the current problem is financial, marital, child rearing, or child development. It also is important to be alert to concurrent problems not specifically designated by the family as points of concern, but also needing identification.

These identified disorders should be considered in two groups: (1) those designated by the family itself as troublesome; (2) those designated by the caseworker or an outside source as troublesome, regardless of what the client considers to be the problem. There are two main reasons for making these distinctions. First, there are major differences in the nature of the therapeutic task in each instance. The family or client who recognizes the problem and spontaneously seeks help is more likely than those who do not do so to have a considerable degree of self-motivation toward its solution. When this occurs, the caseworker can proceed with the knowledge that he is on the same plane as his client; both know what they are working on and why. When outsiders see problems that are not readily avowed by the family, the caseworker has a completely different therapeutic task. He may have to employ considerable time in creating in the client the incentive to solve his own problems. In other words, the caseworker's task and immediate treatment objective are to soften defenses in the client that interfere with this goal. This effort may or may not succeed; the caseworker may or may not decide to attempt anything further until the total situation changes.

In the second place, the manner in which the adults view their problems, compared to what the caseworker or others may see, gives valuable diagnostic clues as to possible family types. The psychosocial disorders which are characteristically designated by the adult family members, as well as those which are overlooked, are quite distinctive and diagnostically significant within each.

Therefore, as an aid to diagnosis, it is advisable to be familiar with the typical psychosocial disorders to which any family is susceptible, and with the characteristic ways in which these disorders group themselves as points of family concern, or as factors incidental to this focus. The following Level A disorders and their occurrence in the four family types will illustrate the point:

Level A financial disorders are primarily typical of the inadequate family or the unsocial family. When such problems are present, the possibility that the family belongs to one or the other of these family types should always be considered, followed by careful evaluation of the total psychosocial pathology of the case under study.

Level A child-rearing disorders are most apt to occur in the unsocial family as neglect and child placement. In the egocentric family these disorders appear in therapeutic placement of a child; in the inadequate, occasionally neglect.

Level A marital disorders, separation and desertion, are most apt to occur in the inadequate or the unsocial family; divorce is characteristic of all family types.

Level A child disorders involving delinquency are most likely to be present among boys in the egocentric family; among both boys and girls in the unsocial family and, occasionally, in the inadequate family type. Psychotic illness of a child is more characteristic of the egocentric or unsocial family classes.

Level A adult disorders, consisting of antisocial acts committed outside the family, probably indicate the unsocial family type, although they may also take place within the family. However, when the adult's delinquent conduct is mainly acted out within the family itself, the possibility that the family is of the egocentric type should always be considered. Mental illness is a possible adult disorder in any family class, but if antisocial behavior is also present in an adult head, check the symptomatology of the unsocial family.

External Stress

External stresses or pressures refer to conditions or events (including the behavior of a family member) that precipitate a problem or crisis resulting in the family's voluntary or involuntary appearance at the social agency. These are differentiated from internal conflicts which may be stimulated by incidents of external stress.

The main point to determine is the typical environmental pressure that precipitates each of the identified psychosocial disorders in a family.

External stresses are of two types: (1) events or incidents that occur within the family setting; (2) incidents that occur outside the family setting. The latter are situations, conditions, or acts which come to the attention of a community agency or some outside persons. Such sources serve as precipitating agents in bringing the problem to a head. Although the family may well be aware of the disorder, its presence has not motivated them to do anything to alleviate it. Both types are abundantly illustrated by the four disordered family types.

Whatever event or condition mobilizes the family's concern in regard to any one of the psychosocial disorders and prompts them to seek agency help is quite distinctive from class to class, in type, degree, and duration. Comparative examples within the areas of child rearing will illustrate.

Stresses in the *perfectionistic family* may include physical or mental illness of the husband; child's night-wandering, interfering with parents' sex life; neighbor's or school's criticism of child (usually mild); temper outbursts by parent provoked by child's behavior; parent's equanimity on job disturbed by inability to cope with the child at home.

Stresses in the *inadequate family* may take the form of threats from relatives to bring neglect charges; school action because of truancy permitted by parent, or because of the maladjustive behavior of a mentally deficient child.

In the *egocentric family*, stresses may be suspension or expulsion of child from school; physical attack on children and police intervention; third or fourth running away from home, noted by others; school failure, noted by school; delinquent conduct, noted by school or by officers of the law.

In the *unsocial family*, such stresses may arise from a father's dislike of a stepchild, with demands that he be placed; children's apprehension for delinquency; the school's demands that parents take responsibility for child's truancy; child's bizarre behavior noted by school or other authorities.

The degree of the stress and the traumatic effect on the family are determined by considering what the average person would do under similar circumstances. For example, the average man can be exposed to the responsibilities of providing for a family without developing a psychosocial disorder, such as desertion at the time each child is born. In other words, it is not to be presumed that the environmental stress of providing for a family is extraordinary because several individuals react poorly to this responsibility. When such symptoms do occur, they generally denote that the individual is overreacting to a normal stress, and thus points to an area of vulnerability in the family member which impairs social functioning. Also, by suggesting the nature and source of the emotions that impair social functioning, it conveys some dynamic causal relationship between the symptom of disorder (desertion) and the particular precipitating stress (birth of child).

FAMILY SOCIAL FUNCTIONING

Clinical descriptions concerning family functioning pertain to: (1) the male and female heads of the family and/or substitute parents, with their own, adopted, or stepchildren; (2) their social functioning in child rearing, marital partnership, and financial responsibilities. Insofar as possible, data pertinent to these areas are systematically organized under four headings: events and circumstances; love relationship; self-identity; and socialization.

It is particularly important to be clear about the meaning of information relevant to "social functioning." This term refers to attitudes and behavior of the husband and wife and child which are directly observable, "seen" by, or verbally communicated to, the caseworker. These behavior phenomena, therefore, represent the conscious or preconscious aspects and purposes of social behavior in the main family functional areas defined in this text. Such psychosocial data must be clearly differentiated from the diagnostic conclusions that may be drawn from them. However, certain aspects of social behavior may also be recognized as ego defense mechanisms, character traits, or neurotic symptoms which are significant to the ultimate diagnosis. Also, as noted earlier, implicit in the term "social functioning" is the fact that every individual functions in a social milieu to which he reacts and which acts upon him.

Child-rearing Functions
PARENTAL FUNCTIONING

This aspect of family diagnosis pertains to the male and female partners as parents or to the parental substitutes. Data are organized under five topics: events and circumstances; physical care given to children; love relationship; self-identity; and socialization patterns communicated to the children by the parents.

In this area of family functioning, it is necessary to think of the parents' behavior with their children as responses to a series of social and emotional tasks which are inherent responsibilities of child rearing; namely, the totality of each child's developmental needs. The data basic to a clinical description of the parents' child-rearing practices need to be focused on two fundamental elements, each deriving from, and giving meaning, to the other: (1) the parents' emotional response to the child's need for love, dependence, and prestige; and (2) protective and educational measures introduced by the parent to assure the child's physical health, development of independence, self-control, and respect for the rights of others.

EVENTS AND CIRCUMSTANCES

The abnormalities or personal events in the lives of the parents which, in the sample studied, most frequently resulted in "emotional" separation of parent and child were: the parent's preoccupation with his own emotions, due to psychosis, severe psychosomatic symptoms, or an unsatisfactory marital relationship; and the identification of the child with an unhappy event.

PHYSICAL CARE

This area pertains to the actual measures used and the standards maintained by the parents in order to insure the physical well-being of their children. The information should provide the basis for an evaluatory description of the following aspects of the physical-care function: nutrition; personal hygiene; clothing; and physical health.

In general, it will be necessary to describe in specific qualitative and practical terms: (1) division of parental responsibility for physical needs of the children; (2) regularity of, and adherence to, schedules for meals and sleeping hours; (3) judgment exercised in selection and preparation of food; (4) consistency and methods of parental supervision with respect to the children's habits, needed medical care, and prescribed regimes.

Under normal circumstances, the father customarily provides the family's income. This gives the mother the necessary economic and emotional support to enable her to minister to the daily needs of the children. Variations from this pattern of responsibility may or may not indicate pathology. The answer will lie in the reasons for such variations. Therefore, it is important first to determine which parent carries primary financial responsibility and which one is responsible for the personal, physical-care function.

Of clinical interest here are data which focus upon: (1) the specific functions of physical care which the mother and father actually and personally do undertake; and (2) the areas of physical care which the parents unconsciously overlook, openly disregard, recognize but meet ineffectively, or consciously or unconsciously overemphasize.

LOVE RELATIONSHIPS

The emotional tie of parent to child is best determined by the type of love the parent expects to give to, and receive from, the child. It is important to know the ways in which, and the extent to which, the mother and father use their relationships with the child to encourage in him both a feeling of being loved and valued as a person in his own right, a gradual willingness to share with others, and, finally, the making of meaningful relationships without losing his basic family identifications.

The emotional bonds of parents to their children have many variations. However, in all instances, the question to be answered is: What does the parents' behavior tell about the emotional needs they are attempting to satisfy through their children? Dependency, for example? Narcissism? A need for possessions? A need for objects on which to vent their hostilities? Substitutes for adult sexuality? The difference between normal and abnormal behavior is, of course, a matter of degree.

SELF-IDENTITY

This area of parental functioning pertains to the methods usually employed by the father and mother to instill in the child a wish for self-reliance, as well as to the opportunities which they afford him for learning work habits and for play, both of which forward the development of adaptive skills. Among important clues are: the parents' reactions to signs of independence and aggressivity in the child; the status given to boys versus girls; the behavior considered appropriate to each; and the values placed on academic achievement.

The clinical description needs to concentrate on the methods employed by the parents to teach responsibility for personal hygiene, personal possessions, use of money, consideration for others, respect for, and cooperation among, siblings. It is desirable to know the premium the parents place on school attendance, academic achievement, and cooperation with teachers.

In both settings it is important to identify: (1) the areas which the parents choose to emphasize, overlook, deemphasize, or openly disregard; (2) the methods which they use to encourage the child's acceptance of habit training; (3) the opportunities afforded the child to become a person in his own right. Some parents may feel that all these factors are important but the standards they impose are beyond the child's ability to master comfortably. In contrast, others may overlook dishonesty about money but place a high premium on academic achievement.

SOCIALIZATION

Of clinical interest are the actual ways in which parents define privileges and limitations in social behavior and implement these standards. To be noted are: (1) the particular areas of social behavior that the parents consider important; (2) the behavior that they consider acceptable; (3) the methods used to make sure that the children live up to these standards; and (4) the conviction with which parents give rewards and punishment.

In relatively few instances does a parent have a single attitude toward every aspect of his children's behavior. More often than not, mixtures of seemingly contradictory patterns characterize parental practices. Certain parents may consciously *believe* that their children should be honest, should consider another's welfare, be responsible for their own acts, attend school, respect law and order; but at the same time these parents may not be convincing in teaching their children how to *act*. In other words, they unconsciously encourage in the child the development of a defectively functioning superego. Other parents may be very definite with respect to honesty in money dealings. Still others may forthrightly approve truancy but exact obedience in home tasks. Thus, the caseworker should be alert to the precise aspects of social behavior toward which the parents have psychosocially constructive attitudes, and those which they overlook or toward which they are frankly deviant.

CHILD DEVELOPMENT

Child development as part of family social functioning is based on a concept noted earlier; namely, that the reciprocal aspects of all familial relationships are such that the rights of one member become the obligation of another. This is particularly evident in child rearing.

The clinical description appropriate to this section relates to the behavior of children in the family which denotes their progress toward maturity. Information is generally classified under two headings: early childhood (through the fifth year); and latency and adolescence (six to twelve years; thirteen through twenty years). The criteria take into account the differences in ego integration and symptoms of behavior which are normal to the developmental stages of each of the three groupings.

The object is to describe the progress the child is making toward socialization by identifying and evaluating the appropriateness of his behavior according to his chronological age, the emotional and social tasks characteristic to his age level, and the social milieu in which he functions. Particular emphasis is placed on noting what behavior in the young child denotes normal progress and what warns of danger. Experience strongly suggests that the average social caseworker not only often overlooks the importance of securing such data, but also does not know what to look for or how to evaluate his observations. Either the worker's insufficient knowledge or a lack of skill in applying it to practice undoubtedly accounts for these omissions.

More often than not, data about children comes secondhand. This introduces an additional problem of possible bias. Information can come from direct observation by the caseworker, verbal communication with the parent, therapeutic interviews with the child, and from outside sources such as schools, clinics, and so forth. The parent is perhaps one of the most usual and important sources of information. Even though distortions may enter the picture, much can be inferred about the child's adjustment from the parent's description of what he thinks his child is, or ought to be, like. The caseworker's astuteness in recognizing what a parent tends to gloss over, emphasize, deemphasize, or avoid altogether, with respect to his relationship with his children, helps reduce the margin of error.

EVENTS AND CIRCUMSTANCES

In general, "external stress" within the context of child development concerns particular events or circumstances that significantly influence the course of the child's emotional and social growth. Factual data need to describe: (1) continuity of contact between child and his own parents; and (2) abnormalities of parent or parents and/or events of personal significance to them as these affect parental functioning.

"Continuity of contact" refers to whether the child has or has not been deprived of one or both parents. In general, one wants to know the events which cause separations that create stresses for the child. For example, mental illness of the parent or marital unhappiness may be external stresses insofar as the child is concerned, when they result in emotional separation of parent from child, although not in the deprivation of the parent's physical presence.

In other words, "events and circumstances" refer to environmental influences, insofar as the child is concerned, and may also concern the parent. As such, they act either as primary causes of emotional maldevelopment in the child or as secondary factors which compound already existing destructive parental attitudes.

In general, it is necessary to establish the relationship of these events to the child's current adjustment and his adaptive potential. Answers to the following questions will provide a sound base for a clinical evaluation of these external stresses in their significance to child development:

1. Which children in the family have had the continuous presence of both own parents? Of at least one parent?

2. If separations occurred, what were the reasons?
3. What was the age of the child at the time of the separations?
4. What substitute arrangements were made for the care of the child?
5. What were the duration and the multiplicity of separations?

Psychodynamically, an event or circumstance becomes traumatic to a child when he is either incapable of mastering the suffering and anxiety which the experience produces or cannot independently resolve the emotional conflicts created by it. The first situation is apt to result when the child's ego is normally weak and the event too overpowering for him to handle; the second, when he receives insufficient help from parental persons in handling some external threat to his integrity. Obviously, the younger the child, the weaker his capacity for overcoming the insecurity which such happenings engender. Therefore, the age of a child, the nature of events, and the help given by the parent need to be taken into account in determining the benign or destructive influences of such happenings.

EARLY CHILDHOOD

Through age five, the social world of a child is limited almost exclusively to his family. His actions inevitably mirror his mother's —or mother substitute's—expressions of love for him and her encouragement in his struggles for self-identification and for self-discipline. For this reason, these directly precipitating influences are incorporated into the framework for evaluating the behavior of the young child. These include: (1) the characteristic way in which the mother or her substitute responds emotionally to the child; and (2) the habit-training measures typically employed.

There are three areas of particular importance to consider in evaluating the course of the child's development: (1) love relationship, or behavior that denotes trust in the parents' love; (2) self-identity, or behavior that indicates gradual acceptance of toilet training, self-feeding, independence in dressing, and so forth; (3) socialization, or behavior that reveals spontaneous curiosity in play interests and friendliness with playmates. The behavior of young children observed in various families may not appear to vary greatly.

Thus it is important to delineate the associated precipitants in the environment which give rise to the child's behavior. However, behavior warns of dysfunction only if it persists beyond the age level for which it is a natural part of growth, or exists in a form and intensity which differ from the normal.

Love relationships. A child in this age group indicates security in his mother's love in a variety of ways. Normally, from birth, he is increasingly responsive to his mother's overtures of interest, gradually tolerates her temporary absence out of a trust that she will reappear, and progressively develops a liking for human contact in general. By the age of three and thereon, he knows members of his family by name and the relationship they bear to him as well as other persons with whom he has regular contact.

Among the possible signs of insecurity to be noted by the caseworker are; persistent crying, wakefulness, babyish clinging to the mother or her substitute, undue apprehension when she is out of sight, repeated outbursts of rage, poor appetite, and so on. The specific symptom will be determined by the particular points of sensitivity in mother and child relationship.

Self-identity. For the child through the fifth year, data should be focused on behavior that denotes the child's acceptance of self-feeding and sleeping schedules, his ability and wish to communicate verbally with the mother, the use of muscular skills, and so on. The extremes to watch for are precociousness, regressions, and marked delays in these areas. The first is less likely to be recognized because the average person may consider the child's surface adjustment to be desirable. Again, the precipitants in the environment which give rise to the behavior are among the most reliable indicators.

Socialization. Through the fifth year, "socialization" refers to the child's play interests and playmates. Data secured should supply information useful in describing clinically the spontaneity and curiosity the child displays in his imaginative use of toys and his interest in people other than himself and his mother.

With regard to play and friends, the caseworker needs to be alert to: (1) the child's lack of interest, inhibitions, or overconstriction in the use of toys; (2) alienation of other children either by over-shyness or by overactivity. These behavior reactions can appear in children from differing types of background, though the precipitating factors may not be identical. Therefore, if similar symptoms are to have any diagnostic meaning, these familial differences must be identified.

LATENCY AND ADOLESCENCE

Here, the purpose is to describe and evaluate the progress toward socialization of the older children of the family.

In this diagnostic scheme the major differences that characterize these periods as contrasted with earlier childhood are: the expanded environmental setting in which the latency and adolescent child functions; the ever-increasing integrative capacity of the ego and the consolidation of the superego. Both the advancing stages of personality development and the extended social milieu are taken into account in the criteria used for observation and evaluation.

In general, two social settings are involved—the family and the larger community. In the first instance, information needs to describe the behavior of the latency child and the adolescent with their parents and siblings, including the nature of their emotional attachments, the independence they have achieved from these familial figures, and the responsibility they assume for their own acts. Outside the family, social behavior and attitudes relate to adults and peers of both sexes. Information concerning behavior at school should include notations on their actual skills and academic achievement.

Love relationships. In the social setting of the family, the data will pertain to the emotional tie of the latency child or adolescent to his parents, or parental substitutes, and siblings. Data will be more easily secured and pertinent if some of the following questions are answered:

1. What qualities in the father and mother do boys and girls like, dislike, belittle, criticize, actually hate, overidealize?
2. Which qualities in the parent and/or the sibling do they consciously or unconsciously emulate?
3. What is the intensity of feeling, positive and negative, that char-

acterizes the child's relationship with the parents and with the siblings?

Sibling rivalries, of course, are common in all families. It is important to determine the intensity of these feelings, what areas are a point of competition, the extent to which the parents promote them.

Self-identity. Data regarding the home should indicate how the child cares for his possessions, attends to his personal hygiene, shows consideration for others, does his assigned tasks, handles money, and so on. Concerning the school, data will pertain to his interest in academic pursuits, school attendance, and cooperation with teachers and other school authorities.

In general, it is important to identify social responsibilities the older child meets without undue dependence upon the parent, except for guidance; which ones he meets by overreliance upon the parent; and the behavior technique he utilizes in so doing. This surface adjustment may best be evaluated by giving attention to three extremes:

1. Accomplished self-reliance, because of the parents' exaggerated premium on perfection
2. Pseudo self-reliance, due to lack of parental guidance; that is, from necessity
3. Limited self-reliance, because the parents provide no incentive for pleasure in self-mastery but encourage dependent goals.

In the sample studied, the academic achievement of the latency child and the adolescent was not as significant evidence of potential adaptive capacity for social adjustment as were the other factor areas. That is to say, a good school record did not consistently equate with the child's ability to make meaningful friendships with peers of both sexes, with his socially constructive use of abilities; and with the maintenance of relatively good relationships within the family. The following guides will help to clarify this aspect of child adjustment:

1. Child's attitude toward school attendance (readily accepts, is indifferent to, or markedly dislikes)
2. School behavior (cooperative or persistent misbehavior in classroom, on playground, or en route)

3. Academic achievement (above average, average, below average, or failing).

Important also is evidence of the young person's acceptance of his normal sex membership or sex identity. This will be seen mainly in the identifications he makes with persons of his own sex, including adults and peers. The predominance of male or female qualities which the boy or girl seeks to emulate provides an important diagnostic clue in evaluating this aspect of adjustment.

Socialization. This area pertains to: (1) the kinds of social relationships the latency child or adolescent forms with peers and adults of both sexes; (2) his approximate conformance to social behavior acceptable in the community.

Two general aspects provide focus for evaluating the child's relationships outside the family: (1) the range, constancy, and intensity of friendships; and (2) the qualitative aspects or types of friends preferred, and the characteristic ways in which the individual relates to them. For example, is he cooperative, considerate, trying to keep friendships? Or is he exploiting, negativistic, domineering, parasitic, cruel, possessive, patronizing? The particular emphasis, intensity, and nature of these interests will vary from latency to adolescence.

Certain children, for example, display a marked impairment in forming friendships through avoidance of close relationships with peers. Consequently, their friends are few, and any relationships tend to be short-lived. Another pattern is characterized by impulsive, striking-out, cruel and negativistic behavior of high intensity, with the child perhaps actively disliked. The possibility of mental retardation or organic brain impairment should never be overlooked in such instances. Avoidance of close relationships coupled with bizarre behavior may portend the possibility of psychotic illness.

Data on social conformance in the community should be focused on behavior that denotes the child's identification with the social institutions and the culture within which he lives—positive, indifferent, or negative. Two kinds of data are required. The first set pertains to the *type* of conformist or nonconformist behavior, such as, for example, overcompliance, shrewd, impulsive, striking-out behavior, becoming an object of exploitation, and so on. The second set refers to the *areas* of conformity or nonconformity as, for example, stealing, destruction of property, sexual molestation, promiscuity, truancy, and so on.

Behavior that forewarns of a negative identification with social custom should never be overlooked. In this regard it is appropriate to restate some principles and governing attitudes. Many people, particularly caseworkers, miss significant clues that indicate a child's lack of identification with the purposes and goals of our culture; that is, the right of the individual to be himself without endangering the welfare of himself or of others. Two biases may hamper objectivity. One grows out of the wish to understand rather than to condemn deviant behavior; the second arises from the vicarious gratification which may be derived from another's behavior which runs counter to social custom.

Both tendencies may be recognized in such rationalized statements as, "All children break the law," cut classes, tear up the neighbors' lawns, take the family car without permission, mistreat pets, and so on. These may be charged off as peccadilloes that will be outgrown, and therefore are inconsequential; or the caseworker may take outright pleasure in thinking that the child's actions "serve somebody right." Such behavior may well be a transitory phase of the latency child's or adolescent's growing up; it may also foreshadow more serious acts of violence against society. In differentiating the normal from the abnormal, the caseworker needs to be guided by a simple principle; namely, that while dislike of certain laws, rules, and regulations is understandable, this fact can never excuse open defiance of them and disregard for the welfare of others.

Thus, data concerning behavior of the child in the community attain clinical significance only as the type, the kind, and the number of areas of conformity or nonconformity are clearly identified. There is less likelihood of confusion between similar symptoms, in terms of etiology, when the symptom picture has also been related to the conscious or unconscious ethical standards which have been communicated by the parent to the child.

Marital Functions

The purpose here is to identify the type and intensity of the behavior and the emotional tie of the marriage partners, as these indicate their reciprocation in love relationship, self-identity, and socialization. As pointed out in previous chapters, marital behavior is only one among many factors to be considered in the collection and diagnostic evaluation of data with respect to total family functioning. In family diagnosis, as here conceived, the marriage partnership cannot be presumed to be healthy on the sole evidence that partners "get along," have shared interests and values, do not quarrel or otherwise exhibit dissatisfaction. It is necessary to discover also: (1) of what these values and interests consist; (2) their relevance to child-rearing and financial functioning and to the individual personality functioning of the partners themselves; and (3) whether or not they lead to a relatively stable social adjustment.

Therefore, in differentiating the normal from the abnormal features of the marriage relationship, such an assessment must also take into account how the developmental needs of the children, the parents' performance in providing for the family, the physical and mental health of the partners, and their social conduct at home and in the community are enhanced or interfered with.

LOVE RELATIONSHIPS

The term "love relationship" embraces the affectional and dependency ties that exist between the partners, especially those of tenderness, consideration, and loving care, and the overt sexual patterns. As previously noted, a person reacts differently to different people and to different situations, depending upon what the relationship or situation offers *to* him and demands *from* him. It is meaningless and insufficient to record that a male is "hostile and belittling." As applied to the love relationship of the marriage, the important thing is to know the precise way, and in what socially and emotionally defined context, these attitudes come to the fore.

SELF-IDENTITY

In this aspect of marital functioning it is important to know how and to what extent the partners use the marital relationship for supporting healthy self-concepts or as a vehicle for undermining mutual self-respect. The caseworker needs to identify the major areas of social or individual functioning within which the partners bestow confidence and/or disrespect, what these attitudes consist of, and the behavioral technique utilized. The self-identity aspect of the marriage is not only significant to the partners' self-esteem and social functioning, but it is also importantly related to the identification that the children are permitted, encouraged, or forbidden to make with an own parent.

SOCIALIZATION

This part of marital functioning pertains to a clinical description of how the marriage partnership fosters or discourages healthy superego functioning when physical illness, emotional disturbance, or delinquent conduct is present in one or both partners. Data required will relate to two major areas: helpful concern and problem-solving orientation.

Helpful concern. The focus here is on considerateness and realistic appraisal of the seriousness of the partner's problem and of his capacities for self-direction and self-observation in regard to its solution. Four possible extremes which interfere with considered action and corrective measures are: (1) unfounded confidence or overadaptation to the partner's needs; (2 "overlooking" for purposes of secondary gain; (3) retaliation and critical blame; and (4) obstructionistic tactics under the guise of "protection."

Problem-solving. Here, it is important to focus upon the partners' view of marriage as a process of continuous readjustment for each, with problems to be solved, not "got rid of." Four characteristics of any problem-solving process need to be taken into account: (1) the individual's awareness and scrutiny of the problem; (2) his evaluation of how he feels about it and how others feel about it; (3) his plan concerning its solution; and (4) the steps he takes to implement the solution.

A breakdown at any point in the sequence of these processes interferes with the end results. Four types of attitudes and behavior were found to be deterrents in marital problem-solving.

One is a lack of awareness of the problems and failure to evaluate the feelings about it, with the result that measures taken to resolve differences are undertaken impulsively, in all probability at the expense of someone else.

In another, overreliance upon the partner's support, guidance, help, and reassurance makes problem-solving difficult: "When my wife is upset, I am confused and uncertain"; "I want to be a good husband but I do not know how." As a result, discouragement, frustration, and postponement of decisions take place. There is awareness of a problem, but inability to scrutinize it truly. The feeling of being overwhelmed is recognized but not evaluated, and thus beclouds judgment and delays action.

Uncompromising, autocratic standards are also deterrents to considered judgment in the resolution of problems and to a stable marital relationship. One partner is expected to make continuous readjustments to the other's rigidity. This adherence to autocratically determined values often is based on the feeling that "to discuss problems is a sign of weakness." Action is considered mandatory. To avoid a feeling of "weakness" within himself, for whatever reason, such a partner also eliminates the possibility of valid compromise.

Of equal importance, also, are the kinds of values which are arbitrarily imposed, because to a great extent they determine the nature of the symptom picture and the consequences in social conduct. These specific values may mark the difference between the family in which standards may well be frankly antisocial in nature and the family in which such demands stem from more constructive social goals.

Lastly, for the extremely infantile or psychotic partner, one of the possible responses is absolute faith that the spouse will take care of everything. Such a person does not deny that a problem exists, but neither does he look at or evaluate how he feels about it. Another possibility may be withdrawal of interest because of anxious preoccupation with his own emotional life. He is neither aware of, nor concerned about, the family's problems but only with his own feelings. When such a partner is married to the type of person who acts on impulse, neither partner can act constructively in behalf of the other.

Financial Functioning

This aspect of family functioning provides the basis for the clinical description of how the family manages its financial affairs. Information is generally classified under two headings: (1) income production; and (2) income management.

By and large, health and welfare agencies specify what factual financial data they routinely require and how these should be recorded in order to be consistent with agency policies and functions. For the diagnostic framework, this section will supplement the information required by the agency in order to give a more comprehensive diagnostic interpretation of the family's work habits and management of its financial affairs.

INCOME PRODUCTION

There are two initial points of focus for this section: (1) designation of the partner who actually assumes the provider role; and (2) the agreement or disagreement which exists between the spouses concerning this division of labor. The second point becomes significant only as the values and circumstances that form the basis of agreement or disagreement also become known.

In relation to the work situation, three sets of data are important:

1. The actual skill and efficiency shown in meeting the requirements of the job
2. The partner's ability to cooperate with those with whom or for whom he works, or who work for him
3. The achievement, incentive, and realism of the partner's goals with respect to his or her actual abilities.

To a great extent, each of the three kinds of data gives meaning to, and derives it from, the other. In the study sample, demonstrated efficiency and cooperation on the job do not necessarily equate with a high degree of achievement incentive, a fact which can be noted in each of the four family types. On the other hand, a high degree of achievement incentive and realism with respect to actual abilities almost always resulted in good work habits and working relationships.

Included here are data that describe how the family heads plan to and actually do meet the financial needs of the family. The three kinds of data needed pertain to: (1) emotional acceptance of provider role; (2) financial support actually undertaken; and (3) planfulness in budgeting and spending income.

The specific nature of these three factors provides the explanation for the coexistence of a variety of financial and/or other psychosocial disorders in the family. Of the three factors, the one that ultimately gives the greatest coherence to the others is emotional acceptance of the provider role. This should be an initial point of evaluation. It refers to the male partner's avowed intention of undertaking the responsibility for supporting his family and finding the ways and means for doing so. Viewed within this context, the adequacy of funds supplied, the judgment exercised in anticipating needs, and the use of income in meeting these needs may be meaningfully evaluated.

To reach a sound diagnostic understanding of the reasons why one male partner supports his family and another does not, one of the surest insights will be found in his avowed intentions at the time of his marriage, irrespective of the subsequent course of events. Examples from the various family classes emphasize the diagnostic validity of this approach as a base from which to work out the significance of a myriad of problems—debts, dependency, nonsupport, desertion resulting in lack of funds, and so on.

ADULT CHARACTERISTICS

Data pertinent to this section relate to the adults of the family with respect to: (1) physical condition; (2) intelligence; (3) preferred ego defenses; and (4) emotional stability. The precise interpretation of many of these diagnostic data will require the expert skills of the related fields of psychology, medicine, and psychiatry. However, certain basic descriptive data must first be secured and tentatively classified by the caseworker until they are confirmed by the appropriate profession.

The caseworker will be concerned with how these conditions interfere with the adjustment of the individual and the family. In other words, the aim is to establish what causal relationship might exist between complaints or diagnosed disabilities and the type of family dysfunctioning that has been noted by the social caseworker.

PHYSICAL CONDITION

Physical illness, handicaps, organic brain disorders, accidents, operations, may or may not bear a direct causal relationship to the disordered symptom picture (135). However, their very presence inevitably influences the total familial atmosphere. Evaluation of their significance therefore provides additional diagnostic clues with reference to family functioning. To be noted are: (1) the nature of the physical disability; (2) the degree of disability for ordinary activity; (3) the cooperativeness of the patient in following a medical regime; and (4) the attitudes that others take toward the afflicted family member.

INTELLIGENCE

Native intelligence obviously has a bearing on social adjustment and is also an important factor in the determination of treatment goals. Mental deficiency, per se, does not necessarily equate with a poor social adjustment. However, the caseworker needs to be alert to the combination of mental deficiency and severe personality disorders in the same individual, which may make ordinary social tasks much more difficult for him to meet. In the sample studied, mentally deficient parents were occasionally found in the *unsocial family*. Interestingly enough, most families in this group were economically self-sufficient, and the husband was able to hold a job. The problem of mental deficiency was most clearly manifested in the parents' inability to cope with the problems of running a household and rearing children.

PREFERRED EGO DEFENSES AND EMOTIONAL STABILITY

Data concerning the preferred ego defenses and emotional stability of adults are gathered for their usefulness in determining what causal relationships exist between the family's ability to function socially and the capacity of the adult's personality for integrated behavior.

Identification of characteristic ego defenses and emotional stability (diagnosed psychiatric syndrome or mental disorder) is not an end in itself. The object of making these identifications is: (1) to locate the primary cause of psychosocial dysfunctioning; and (2) to make some determination of the adult's motivation and capacity to seek and use help in the solution of his problem. To do this effectively, it is necessary to recognize and understand the meaning of defensive reactions that assist, markedly interfere with, or inhibit the client in social functioning and the constructive use of casework service (40, p. 295). The focus most generally helpful in this regard centers on the following points:

1. How the adult defends himself against threats to his personality; that is, the customary ego defenses for dealing with ordinary and acute stresses
2. The order of severity and exaggeration of the ego defenses
3. The emotional areas in the adult's personality that precipitate the social dysfunctioning, or keep it alive; that is, how much the environment suffers due to the focus and mode of emotional discharge.

It may be possible to designate ego defenses and the aspects of personality functioning related to emotional stability by a conventional "personality type" classification or psychiatric syndrome, using the American Psychiatric Association's diagnostic terminology (10). However, a descriptive statement which suggests the answers to any questions is more useful to the caseworker.

Knowledge and understanding of the ego defenses and forces in the personality which precipitate a family disorder, or keep it alive, can mean the difference between wasted and productive treatment efforts. For these reasons, identification of the psychological factors is required.

The Child

These individual factors are organized under three topics: (1) physical condition; (2) intelligence; (3) emotional stability of latency children and adolescents. Although precise diagnosis requires confirmation from other professions, the possible presence of any of these disordered conditions needs to be noted, described, and tentatively classified by the social caseworker. Our primary concern is to establish any causal relationship that might exist between such impairments and the child's developmental progress.

PHYSICAL CONDITION

The relationship of the physical condition of the child to normal development and acquisition of adaptive skills needs no elaboration. Not only does the type of disability have a significant bearing upon the child's health and adjustment, but so also do the attitudes he acquires about his body as a result of disease or handicap. This is largely determined by the attitudes of those around him, particularly his mother (40, pp. 301–3).

Physical disabilities of every variety may occur in children of any family. Of importance to the social caseworker, however, are the ways in which the family copes with such problems. Although the criteria used here in arriving at the classification of families had no relationship to types of physical disability present in child or adult, the ways in which the physical disabilities subsequently grouped themselves, in the different disordered family types, posed some interesting questions that bear further examination in regard to the psychological components of, and predispositions to, certain diseases.

INTELLIGENCE

Intellectual capacity is more easily determined and confirmed in the child than in the adult, because of pediatric clinic and school records. It goes without saying that any symptom of maladjustment and/or maturative delays and/or school failure requires a check of the child's intellectual capacity and potential. In both the *inadequate* and the *unsocial families,* where such deficiencies were occasionally encountered in the sample studied, seemingly bizarre behavior in the mentally retarded children subsided considerably with appropriate training-school placement. This occurred for two reasons: (1) removal from an environment in which the parents were ill-equipped to deal with a mentally defective child; and (2) educational programs suited to the child's abilities and within his range of accomplishment.

EMOTIONAL STABILITY

In latency, as in other periods of childhood, multiple causes account for the development of emotional problems. The same unfavorable parental patterns which affect the years through five will, if unchanged, continue to create problems in latency.

The classifications found most useful in the analysis of case materials are those of Gerard (69, p. 193). These designate the more common difficulties of the latency period classified according to "realms of interference," not according to classical symptom categories or dynamic constellations:

1. *Infantile phenomena,* denoting marked developmental immaturity, are evidenced by thumb-sucking, anal or urine incontinence, excessive masturbation. Such symptoms are normal or only questionable for the child under five but are indicative of pathology beyond that age.

2. *Motor disorders* are indicated by excessive purposeless activity, hyperactivity with conduct problems, lack of concentrated effort, inhibition in use of hands and development of skills, rhythmic movements such as head-rolling, nail biting, rocking, tics, and stammering.

3. *Conduct problems* include a variety of behavior symptoms that interfere with social living at home, at school, or in the larger community. Children with such problems may avoid close relationships with adults or children; indulge in provocative conduct of an aggressive nature; steal, followed by self-punishing. They may tend toward destructiveness (including stealing) followed by behavior to avoid punishment; sadistic cruelty; sexual delinquency (although rare in latency); exhibitionism or "peeping," if compulsively repetitive.

4. *Common neuroses* include compulsions such as excessive cleanliness; phobias, such as fear of animals; and hysterical phenomena.

5. *Psychoses* denoting severe ego defects and the same mechanisms as in adult psychoses are indicative of a disturbed relationship to the mother.

Data with respect to psychic disturbances in the latency and the adolescent child need to be focused on identifying the presence or absence of such problems. Symptoms of such disturbances vary greatly from one age to another. For example, bed-wetting, temper outbursts, and genital exposure, normal in a two-year-old, become questionable for a five-year-old, and indicate increasingly serious pathology in latency, adolescence, and adulthood (69). It is obvious that expected or "normal" behavior at specific age levels must be taken into account in determining the presence or absence of psychic disorders in a child.

Data in regard to the adolescent pertain to psychic disturbances in the child and ordinarily require psychiatric diagnosis. However, descriptive information can and should be secured by the social caseworker. The object is to identify symptoms of psychopathology.

The line between normality and pathology is extremely difficult to draw. By definition, adolescence is an interruption of peaceful growth, and its symptoms resemble a variety of other emotional upsets. However, the psychic reactions in adolescence, formulated by Anna Freud (61, pp. 255-78), have been found useful in the analysis of sample cases. Arranged in order of increasing pathological disturbances, they represent the defenses used by the adolescent in his attempts to sever or to change his emotional ties to the parent or the parent person:

1. *Sudden withdrawal and transfer of ties from parent to others.* Instead of permitting a process of gradual emancipation from parents to take place, the affect, or emotional attachment for the parent, is withdrawn suddenly and altogether and transferred to someone outside the family. Whether the action undertaken by the adolescent is harmless, idealistic, antisocial, or criminal will depend upon the new attachments he elects to make.

New attachments may be formed for parent substitutes, provided the person selected is diametrically opposed in every respect, personally, socially, and culturally, to the parent. In this instance the emotion previously invested in the parent is transferred, more or less unchanged, to the new person.

"Leaders" in the age range between that of the parents and the adolescent may become the objects of new emotional ties. Passionate crushes on contemporaries, homosexual or heterosexual friendships, or attachments to adolescent gangs or groups are common possibilities.

2. *Reversal of affect.* Less outwardly conspicuous but more ominous inwardly is the reversal of the child's emotions toward the parent. Instead of displacing the emotional tie from the parent to an outsider—or, which is more likely, after having failed to do so —love is turned to hate, dependence to revolt, respect to contempt and derision. The adolescent imagines himself free, but to all intents and purposes he remains as securely tied to the parent as before. This adolescent's pathological development should be watched.

No positive pleasures are derived from these reversed relationship patterns. There is no room for independent growth or action, while compulsive opposition proves as crippling as compulsive obedience. The child continues his acting out in the family and remains uncooperative, hostile, and churlish. The clinical picture may also range from intense depression and tendencies toward self-abasement, turning the hostility against the self, to self-injury and suicide.

3. *Withdrawal of affect to self.* In this type of adolescent reaction, anxieties and inhibitions block the formation of new attachments outside the family. The affect, or felt emotion, remains within the self.

The adolescent may display any of the following symptoms: fantasies of major achievement or championship in one or more fields; suffering and persecution in Christ-like proportions, with corresponding fantasies of saving the world; hypochondriacal sensations and feelings of bodily changes. Clinically, these are all well known to be characteristic of the initial stages of psychotic illness.

4. *Regression.* At the extreme height of anxiety aroused by object ties, the adolescent's relations with the outside world may be reduced to the emotional state known as "primary identification" with the parental person, familiar in psychotic illness. This implies regressive changes in all parts of the personality.

Surprising changes of qualities, attitudes, and even outward appearance take place. These alterations in personality are betrayed in allegiances and identifications with other persons which represent a superficial, meaningless tie. Dominating the scene are projections, together with these identifications, which will reflect the nature of the personality change. Distinctions between external and internal world temporarily are negligible, accompanied by a state of confusion.

FAMILY OF ORIGIN

These are retrospective data pertaining to the adults' life experiences in the families into which they were born, or in which they grew up. The purpose of gathering such information is to gain further logical understanding of the current emotions and behavior of the male and female partners, in terms of their life experience. Requisite data encompass the following areas: (1) events and circumstances; (2) the continuity of contact with own parents or substitute parents; (3) adequacy of financial support afforded the family; (4) the nature and strength of emotional ties to own parents or parent persons; (5) the self-identity achieved through these parental identifications; and (6) socialization standards.

The characteristic way of meeting and dealing with both ordinary and extraordinary situations in the present is likely to derive from the many repetitions of a formula learned in the past. Current patterns are the end result of all factors which have shaped the life of the individual. Therefore, emphasis is laid not on a series of facts or events per se, nor on their accurate chronological listing alone. Focus is placed, rather, upon the adult's reactions to, and interpretation of, such happenings.

For example, the emotional climate in which each adult partner lived in his developmental years, the dominant forces that shaped his personality, the values, goals, and attitudes of the people who surrounded him, can explain the logic of his current emotions in the performance of his family functions more adequately than can the mere knowledge that he did or did not come from a broken home. Inferences can be drawn from the former kinds of data concerning the psychodynamic origins of current patterns of family behavior.

The history of the current social dysfunctioning of the family, its time of onset, and the nature of the behavior patterns will shed some light on the immediate factors which underlie it. It may be impossible, however, to organize or interpret these contemporary features in their true meaning without the help of certain information pertinent to the developmental history of the adults. This entails collecting retrospective data from the family heads themselves. Often other sources are required, such as family members, relatives, police officers, and professional workers.

A diagnostic formulation from the perspective of historical data as well as of current data immeasurably increases accuracy in the selection of appropriate treatment goals and influences the success of the therapeutic program. Examples in the sample studied clearly show this.

Those adults who as children were placed in foster homes or institutions, with no opportunity to experience enduring emotional attachments to a parent person, were observed to form shallow relationships in adulthood. They also possessed a weak "inner authority" or "conscience," were easily influenced, were easy prey to exploitation, and highly vulnerable to involvement in situations that led to desertion, neglect, nonsupport, and, in some instances, antisocial acts.

At the other end of the scale, the male partners whose own mothers were overindulgent and whose fathers were overpunitive also tended, upon reaching maturity, to engage in antisocial activity, disregard work rules, become alcoholic, fail to support their families, and resort to various kinds of overdependent, passive-receptive behavior.

Defective superego development was found to be characteristic of both, but the psychodynamic explanations were vastly different. In the first instance, the factors which gave rise to the pathology concerned deprivation; in the second, overindulgence. In both cases, in childhood it had not been worthwhile for this adult to abandon infantile goals, eventually to take responsibility for his own behavior. However, this lack of incentive derives from two different sets of etiological factors. Treatment goals formulated and implemented must reflect these diagnostically determined differences, even though the symptomatic behavior has many similarities.

XI. APPLICATION

CONCLUSIONS CONCERNING the usefulness of the classification of the four disordered family types inevitably derive from two sources:

1. The three demonstration projects, in which casework and psychiatric personnel applied the family classifications to project case loads and administrative use was made of such classified data
2. The author's predictive judgment concerning the usefulness of this process, based on relevant experience.

By the spring and summer of 1957 these findings were sufficiently complete to be tested in each of the three projects on a total of 672 cases. This experience, combined with the author's considered opinion, led to the following conclusions regarding the utility of these classifications.

For the Caseworker

Knowledge about, and use of, classifications of the four disordered family types may serve the following purposes:

1. Assist in problem identification, within a consistent classification scheme
2. Facilitate greater precision and perception in the collection of data
3. Increase accuracy in the evaluation of new data and those already on hand
4. Provide a supplementary aid to more adequate family diagnosis and treatment of psychosocial disorders.

There are several underlying factors here. First, psychosocial disorders, social behavior, and the individual condition of the family members specific to a case under study can be compared with similar data, identified and known to distinguish each of the disordered family types. This comparison, plus the use of the outline for family diagnosis, lends perspective and stimulates the selection and focusing of data with a distinct purpose in mind; namely, to circumscribe the area of trouble and thus discover the causes of the family's dysfunctioning. Second, the organization and the specific nature of the data pertaining to each family type illustrate the principle of interrelatedness in family diagnosis. This is exemplified in the psychosocial syndromes distinctive to each family class; for, viewed collectively, seemingly isolated factors assume their appropriate significance in relation to all factors and thus are explained. Third, the very necessity of classifying a case according to its family type provides the caseworker with a tentative working hypothesis upon which to proceed, prognosticate, and plan treatment.

In other words, the purpose behind the use of the disordered family types is *not* the classification as an end in itself, but the provision of a means for greater diagnostic accuracy. If classification by disordered family types is applied to the practice of casework in this manner, it will prove to be a valuable asset. The result will be more conducive to follow-up and reevaluation than to rigid, unimaginative reliance upon a formula. Moreover, the fear of relying too heavily upon a diagnostic formula such as the family classification was not a deterrent when applied to the CRA projects. Nor was there difficulty, at the other extreme, of inappropriate application of classified data as a substitute for independent thinking and use of the worker's own perceptive capacities. However, these are possible interfering factors, not uncommon in any profession dealing with human problems, and should be taken into account in the use of classifications such as these.

For the Casework Supervisor

The supervisor or casework director holds one of the most strategic functional positions in the agency with respect to implementing the integration of casework program and administrative procedures and policies. Whatever happens in the administrator's office, at the prac-

titioner level, and on boards of directors, is a result of the ebb and
flow among and between them. Integration of all three interests is
easier and more possible if the methods and criteria for measuring
and interpreting the needs of the agency's case load are not inconsistent with those useful in determining policy. One systematic
method for facilitating this exchange is to apply the classification
scheme for disordered family types to the total case load.

This has several advantages in the supervisory process itself, as
well as in the conduct of the casework program and in communication between the administrator and supervisor:

1. In administrative supervision, case assignments may be guided
by the probable nature of the case, suggested by the family type as
tentatively classified by the caseworker and/or confirmed by the
supervisor. This reduces guesswork in the distribution of case loads.

2. In the supervisory process, the family type thus serves as a
tentative hypothesis and a consistent base from which both caseworker and supervisor can evaluate, at the outset and in retrospect,
the reliability of judgments and weigh the significance of new materials.

3. In carrying out the casework program, the agency's case load
can be understood in terms of the probable nature and degree of
family dysfunctioning and the psychosocial disorders typical of the
respective family types.

4. When so classified, the case load is readily subject to review
and interpretation by the supervisor in a form useful to the administrator.

For the Administrator

During a fiscal year, some type of review or analysis of case loads
is always conducted by any agency that must depend upon its con-
stituency for financial support and sponsorship of program. There are
many ways in which an agency case load can be analyzed. The
classification of family types may serve the administrator in this
regard.

The administrator benefits from the end result of the classification which has been made at the practitioner and supervisory level.
Although he does not actually take part in the process, he must

accept its principles so that the methods of the system used are reflected in policies and procedures.

Insofar as the entire case load is classified by family type, the administrator is able to secure information concerning the various diagnosed conditions and psychosocial disorders that require one kind of service rather than another. The use of the classification as an integral part of these procedures, can provide additional material useful to community planners and administrators. It can tell them under what circumstances it is profitable to provide a specific kind of casework skill or other services for a particular family, the probable duration of the service, and the probable rehabilitative results.

Material from CRA's San Mateo County project report (33) illustrates the kind of information obtained and used for administrative purposes. The major focus of the project was disordered behavior classified as Level A.

Among 231 families classified by the project staff, 3 percent were perfectionistic; 33 percent, inadequate; 32 percent, egocentric; and 29 percent, unsocial family types.[1] This information told the project staff that in agencies dealing with youthful unsocial behavior, major and minor crimes, divorce, separation, desertion, and hospitalization for mental illness, the three main types of family dysfunctioning represented in the case loads are those with the more severe types of pathology. In fact, 61 percent were concentrated in the egocentric and unsocial family types, portraying pathology with distinctive characteristics. The rehabilitative potential, related to levels of treatment and psychosocial disorders present, thus became more meaningful.

This report also showed the psychosocial disorders present in 231 cases. Child-rearing disorders existed in cases in three family types —inadequate, egocentric, and unsocial—in about the same proportion: 99, 99, and 97 percent respectively. However, these would also be known to have particular characteristics within each family class. Financial or economic disorders, as in our sample, were concentrated in the inadequate family and the unsocial family. It would be easy to say, "This is not news. It is what we suspected all along."

It is not proposed here to go into all the implications of admin-

[1] In the report (33) these are referred to as types 2, 3, 4, and 5.

istrative reorganization that must accompany any integration of these new elements into an agency. However, as a result of its experience with the San Mateo project, that county incorporated into its permanent operations the complete set of procedures used in the CRA project.

It need only be stated here that to use the four disordered family types intelligently, the practitioner should be familiar with the concepts of family casework diagnosis, have a working knowledge of requisite data and the points of focus of basic areas of the diagnostic framework; namely, family composition, psychosocial disorders, child-rearing, marital, and financial functioning, and individual characteristics of adult and child family of origin history.

SYSTEMATIC PROCEDURES

Throughout Community Research Associates' entire experience the systematic use of five casework procedures has been considered a basic requisite, underpinning integrated planning and operation of the community's health and welfare services. The key procedures, noted in Chapter I, have been consistently pursued: identification of psychosocial disorders; diagnosis; prognosis; treatment planning; and evaluation. As these procedures developed in the experimental projects reported here, primary emphasis was given to their administrative value as a basis for planning treatment services, accounting for uniformly defined problems, assigning cases, and achieving efficient administrative methods of case control and evaluation.

Diagnostic Procedures

Whatever is done for the client who goes to the social agency is treatment, no matter what the caseworker may call it. A family or its individual members do not go to an agency for a diagnosis and they do not go to have their problems classified. They want something done to or for themselves or others that will put an end to their socially handicapped status. They submit to questioning as a necessary condition imposed by the caseworker in order to obtain the help they seek. Therefore, in a sense, for the client treatment precedes diagnosis. However, for the caseworker, it should not preclude diagnosis.

Two kinds of working processes are called for in meeting these requirements. One is the collection and organization of the necessary facts. The other is interpretation of the significance of the many diverse kinds of data in a way that lends coherence to the family's dysfunctioning.

COLLECTION AND ORGANIZATION OF DATA

The classification scheme used for organizing psychosocial data about the four family types represents the working outline followed for achieving a family diagnosis. It delineates the specific fields of inquiry within which data are to be interpreted and suggests the general types of data to be commonly noted:

> Family composition
> Psychosocial disorders
> Family social functioning
> Individual characteristics
>> Adult
>> Child
> Family of origin

A study of these major factor areas or specific fields of inquiry will suggest the requisite data upon which the next step will depend —diagnostic synthesis. The concepts and dynamics of social functioning implicit in the outline will facilitate organization and interpretation of data to this end. The general purpose is to encourage the caseworker to make an orderly approach to diagnosis and to record his findings systematically. For the most part, what will be recorded within each major factor area of inquiry will be partial descriptions. They must be fully enough recorded, however, so that they can be used as documentary illustrations to justify the diagnostic synthesis to follow.

DIAGNOSTIC SYNTHESIS

The purpose of the process of diagnostic synthesis is to identify and describe the maladjustment or handicapped status of the family and establish the causal relationships. The requisites and the results of this procedure determine subsequent processes: prognosis; treatment planning; and evaluation of both normal and abnormal features of the family's functioning based on accumulated data in the outline. The assets and potentialities must be taken into account as foundations upon which to build treatment. This part of the work should be organized into three parts: the maladjustment; the causal relationships; and the diagnostic summary. The formulation might consist of the following items:

The Maladjustment

1. *Current psychosocial disorders.* Identify basic problem as Level A and/or Level B; designate appropriate subcategories—child-rearing, marital, financial, child adult.

2. *Dislocation centers.* Indicate which of the following most aptly identify the locale of the maladjustment: (*a*) family functioning of adults; (*b*) social development of children; (*c*) intellectual, physical, or emotional stability of adult and/or child.

3. *Precipitating external stresses.* Describe the prevailing environmental situations in which the family or family member is immersed and the immediate events which have brought about the psychosocial disorders.

4. *Net results of existing maladjustment.* Understand the problem in terms of family dynamics: (*a*) how family members have tried to and are coping with it; (*b*) how they behave and react to this stress; (*c*) who, if anyone, takes the leadership in trying to solve the problem; (*d*) whether the attempt results in action appropriate to its solution or whether the action is ineffective. Indicate these manifestations from data in child rearing, marital relationships, income production, income management, child development.

Causal Relationships

The final step is to pinpoint the causative factors so far as this is possible. Here the worker brings into play all that he knows about the family from all sources, as well as what can be inferred, irrespective of where the client places his problem. The objective is to describe all factors in a chronological sequence of cause-and-effect relationship, indicating how the current disordered symptoms are related to all aspects of the maladjustment. Consideration should be given to the following five points in arriving at an evaluative judgment:

1. The external circumstance which *could* account for the problem the family faces and which could realistically be considered causative

2. The degree to which external or environmental factors in fact do interfere or cause trouble, thus contributing to the major problem
3. The attitudes, behavior, or internalized personal conflicts which could account for the problem
4. The degree to which attitudes, behavior, and internalized personal conflicts in fact do interfere or cause trouble, thus contributing to the major problem
5. The degree to which the family is relatively free from either external or internal problems, thus increasing the rehabilitative potential.

Diagnostic Summary

Try to indicate:
1. Family type designation—perfectionistic; inadequate; egocentric; unsocial.
2. The characteristic syndromes of the family type, and a brief description of their severity and extensiveness in the family under study. For example, try to indicate in what respects the picture suggests the unsocial family, and in what way it may suggest another.
3. If no clear classification can be made, what procedures would help clarify a diagnosis by family type?

Prognostic Procedures

All aspects of the diagnostic work-up, including collection and organization of data and the diagnostic synthesis, are undertaken for one major purpose intrinsic to the over-all objective of any agency —to determine the most effective treatment program for families under its care and how this can be implemented. Prognosis is actually one aspect of the diagnostic work-up, and it proceeds toward the same end. This is true irrespective of what subsequent administrative use may be made of prognosis—as a procedure in case assignments, in determination of services rendered, and so on. To require the caseworker to state an opinion concerning the extent to which the family's maladjustment or disordered status can be modified is one way of better implementing both the treatment and the administrative purposes. However, unless both purposes are accepted and understood by the caseworker, his prognostications will not serve the dual aims of this process.

The precise focus of a casework prognosis as introduced in all of CRA's experimental projects reflects a specific purpose. It is to be made and used for definite administrative and/or research needs related to the prevention and control of Level A psychosocial disorders: dependency; medical indigency; and disordered behavior. Therefore, the caseworker predicts the changes anticipated in the status of these disorders; namely, the expectation for (1) improvement, to denote movement toward the reduction of disorders in number or severity; (2) deterioration, to denote progressive worsening in the number of the family's disorders; or (3) no change, to denote arrestment of the disorder at approximately the same level as at the time of prognosis. Such predictions entail and depend upon the caseworker's perceptiveness and the soundness of his professional knowledge about the total family situation.

The focus of a prognosis can and will vary with the agency. From our experience we suggest the following principles:

1. Two types of prognosis should be made: (a) on the assumption that appropriate treatment resources are available; (b) on knowledge of treatment resources actually available.

2. The prognosis should be problem-focused on Level A psychosocial disorders for administrative purposes (on Level A and Level B for diagnostic purposes). Actually, the two cannot be separated as an intellectual process. As a procedure, however, they may be separated.

3. The prediction should relate to a specified time period.

4. Consistent criteria should be applied.

Prognoses are always made with reference to possible changes that may take place with respect to disorder already present in some family member. Thus:

Dependency, as denoted by the receipt of an assistance grant for food, clothing, and shelter, may be predicted in relation to financial functioning.

Indigent disability, or the presence of disabling physical conditions, may be predicted in relation to dependency *vs.* medical indigency only. Changes in extent of disabling conditions and achievement of rehabilitative goals may be expected.

Child-rearing disorders (neglect, placement, adoption) may be predicted in relation to child-rearing functioning.

Child disorders (delinquency, truancy, school dropout) may be predicted in relation to child development and individual character-istics of children.

Adult disorders (criminality, institutional commitment for mental disorders) may be predicted in relation to individual adult charac-teristics as well as to behavior in family functioning.

Unmarried parenthood may be predicted in relation to possibility of a new episode.

Other marital disorders (divorce, separation, and desertion) may be predicted in relation to marital functioning. A variety of criteria is applicable. Here, the focus is upon the possible mending of a marriage or prevention of its dissolution.

The accompanying table will be a useful guide in predicting the probable course of Level A psychosocial disorders within a twelve-month period:

PROGNOSTIC CRITERIA FOR LEVEL A DISORDERS

| Disorder | PROBABLE COURSE | | |
	Improvement	Deterioration	No Change
Dependency	Self-maintenance or decreased fi-nancial assistance	Increased finan-cial assistance	No appreciable change
Indigent dis-ability	Less serious ex-tent	More serious ex-tent	No appreciable change
	Complete or par-tial achievement of rehabilitative goals	Lack of achieve-ment of rehabili-tative goal	No appropriate rehabilitative goal possible
Child-rearing, child and adult disorders	Supervision to be discontinued; no new episodes expected	Additional epi-sodes expected	Supervision to con-tinue; no addi-tional episodes ex-pected
Unmarried parenthood		New episode ex-pected	No new episodes expected
Other marital disorders: di-vorce; legal sep-aration; desertion	Spouse expected to return	Separation and desertion epi-sodes to increase or be of longer duration; divorce	Static marital status

The prognosis should focus on the likelihood of modifying the dis-order identified and classified according to the above categories.

The following criteria will assist the caseworker to arrive at a professional opinion at the time of diagnostic work-up concerning the course of the disorder within some specified period of time:

1. *Cessation of the disorder* is anticipated and also that the cessation will be accompanied by a readjustment that is personally satisfying, socially constructive, and self-sustained. In other words, it is expected that new damaging symptoms will not replace the old symptoms that worsen or perpetuate some form of individual or family malfunctioning.

2. *Modification* of the behavior related to the psychosocial disorders is anticipated, both in intensity and extent, to the point that social functioning of family members is not markedly impaired, although recurrence is likely under the same conditions of stress. Periodic or sustained personal and/or practical help is required to maintain the adjustment.

3. *Arrestment* of the psychosocial disorder as a symptom of family dysfunctioning is anticipated. In other words, it will continue to impair social adjustment of the family members in the same areas and to the same degree as at the time of the diagnostic work-up.

4. *Worsening* of the psychosocial disorders is anticipated. They may extend to other areas and may move into the Level A category. Social adjustment in the areas noted at the time of diagnostic work-up will become increasingly more handicapping, not only to the individual family member but to others as well.

The foregoing prognostic guides for Level B psychosocial dis orders are adapted from the criteria for evaluation applied in the research project of this text.

Treatment Planning Procedures

For sound and practical administrative reasons, CRA, in its demonstration projects, uses the term "levels of social service" to denote the type of therapeutic program appropriate to the case. Three major levels are defined. However, for purposes of this text these have been designated Social Service I, II, and III. The principle purpose of the social service classification is to provide the supervisor and administrator with an objective basis on which to assess the general characteristics of the case load as these relate to the type of casework treatment required to meet the problems presented. It also facilitates appropriate case assignment and the use of resources within the agency and in the community.

Social Service I calls for the use of the most skilled professionally trained casework staff available. They must be competent to use all the accepted casework methods and techniques. Underpinning their skill must be an understanding of the dynamics of personality functioning and of interpersonal relations. Thus they must be able to deal with families and individuals who lack motivation and have conflicts or fears, including emotional disturbances, that interfere with social adjustment. However, this does not mean that all cases with such severe problems are necessarily assigned to this level of service. If the prognosis is poor even with the best service available, the case may be assigned to a lower level for a less intensive type of supportive activity.

Here as well as in the other divisions of service it is not assumed that classification of the case is rigid and fixed. The family may reach a level of greater stability as the result of a resolved crisis, such as the placement of a child, commitment of a mentally ill person, and so on. At periodic points, the service level classification is re-examined, and shifts are made in the light of changes that have occurred.

Social Service II includes mainly the supportive method of treatment. The worker should be personally mature, experienced, and skillful in dealing with a considerable variety of family needs, and have at his command the first three treatment techniques of this method: direct intervention; offers of information; advice and guidance. The Social Service II case is distinguished from that in Social Service I chiefly on the basis of the significance of diagnostic data and the degree to which emotional factors may be immediately or potentially destructive to the social functioning of the individual and his family.

Social Service III entails primarily financial assistance, determination of eligibility, and administrative functions of a technical or facilitating nature. These might include budgetary changes, help with moving, housing, medical services information, and referrals or other concrete and supportive aid. The primary casework skill required is that appropriate to the treatment techniques of direct intervention and offers of information. Cases that require Social Service III will be those whose major need is for financial or long-term agency supervision. Two types of situations would prevail under these conditions: (1) there would be reasonable evidence of stability in family and individual social functioning with an absence of current crises or potential disorders; (2) rehabilitative goals would not realistically be attainable. This does not mean that Social Service III cases have no problems but rather that such as do exist either do not currently affect the capacity for social functioning or are not amenable to treatment.

These three types of social services establish the criteria for case assignment and, of course, for a continuing evaluation of staff interest and of professional skills available and needed by the agency and the community.

Evaluation Procedures

Identification of the problems of a single case or of the entire agency case load on the basis of uniform definitions makes it possible actually to assess, and to analyze, in a precise and accountable way, changes in the problems which are the agency's primary concern and its reasons for being in business. Only by systematically and uniformly applying such a concept of evaluation is it possible for any worker, supervisor, or agency to make an intelligible and objective report.

As part of the diagnostic work-up, prognosis is made with respect to the probable course of identified Level A and Level B disorders. At stated intervals the status of each disorder is reexamined. In so doing, two different but related kinds of evaluation are accomplished. The first provides knowledge of whether the disorder has recurred, is the same, or is no longer present. The second is an evaluation of the accuracy of the prognosis, which obviously has a variety of implications with respect to the adequacy of the caseworker's understanding, need for more training, better supervision, and so forth. Recording is done in the same terms as those used in the diagnostic work-up; that is, the recording of the specific disorder present. By comparing the data recorded at evaluation with that recorded at the diagnostic work-up, the precise change or lack thereof can be ascertained.

Irrespective of the method of recording, the criteria for prognosis and for evaluation of change for a given disorder are necessarily the same. Therefore, the prognostic criteria contained in the outline for Level A disorders and for Level B disorders also apply at evaluation.

INTERPRETATION

In the projects, evaluation is limited to a determination of the status of *Level A psychosocial disorders*, as is prognosis. Outcome is expressed in terms of improvement, no change, or deterioration. These terms refer to the fact that the agency service necessary in connection with the problems is no longer being given, has decreased in volume, remains substantially the same, or has increased. In most instances there will be a correlation between improvement in family functioning and whether or not service is being given. Professional judgment about improvement in social functioning does not necessarily equate with the fact that casework supervision is no longer required by the family; nor does deterioration, as indicated by new episodes that necessitate casework supervision. Placement of a delinquent child in a treatment institution, for example, points to deterioration in the family's child-rearing capacity. But it may be the professional judgment of the caseworker that this placement will eventually assure an increase in the child's capacity for successful social functioning. Therefore, the changes recorded at evaluation must *also* be related to, and interpreted in the light of, the total disordered symptom picture and the family's actual social adjustment.

As was stated previously, evelution based on professional judgment, as defined for the caseworkers who filled out the schedules in the classification project of this research, did not differentiate

between Level A and Level B disorders. The outline used for recording these changes covered specific points.

1. *Personal and environmental* problems are defined as follows:

"Personal" means the attitudes and behavior which are the result
of inner conflicts and which are related to fundamental character
structure. They are within the individual, regardless of outside influence or factors. Such conflicts may be intensified by external
stresses but are not caused by them in a genetic sense. Examples
of personal problems are symptoms of psychotic behavior, obsessions,
chronic or acute depression, and so on. "Personal" also includes the
physical condition of family members.

"Environmental" means the behavior, attitude, or presence of other
persons, as well as practical circumstances which cause difficulty
in the family or family member's adjustment. Examples are: loss of
employment; alcoholism; sexual inhibition of partner; presence of
mother-in-law in home; presence of children; and so on.

2. *"Effect on family members"* refers to the character of the identified problems and their influence on the family's psychological and
social functioning. Problems listed should have their counterparts
in the recorded effect on the family. Examples are: "husband's drinking," listed as "personal and environmental"; and "absence from
work," "income irregular," and "quarreling with wife." A problem
listed may not adversely affect the family in all areas.

3. *"Problem treated"* refers to the treatment of problems listed.
"Yes" should be checked for each problem entered, if it was the focus
or part of the over-all treatment plan. If not, "no" should be checked.

4. *"Degree of recovery"* means the extent to which the adjustment
of the individual family member or of the family as a whole changed
in terms of behavior symptoms indicating problems listed and their
effect on the family, as entered. The changes may be due to casework
or to other factors, such as hospitalization, recovery from an illness,
placement of child, better employment, and divorce. The degree of
change noted, for the husband, wife, and other family members is
evaluated according to the four-point rating scale used for prognosis.

5. *"Personal and social adjustment of family,"* a composite picture
of the way in which the family as a unit is functioning at the end of

the case or project, consists of an evaluative description of the specific changes, personal and environmental, which have occurred in various areas of family adjustment, as well as the caseworker's comments as to the basic strengths and weaknesses of the family and its members. For example: "With the commitment of wife to a mental hospital, the tensions in the home have subsided; husband is working regularly, is less guilty about wife's commitment and visits to her are regularly scheduled. He needs continued emotional support from worker, but with clarification of his feeling of shame at having to commit his wife, he is increasingly able to function well as a father with two motherless children and a sick wife."

BIBLIOGRAPHY

1. Aarons, Z. Alexander, M.D. "Some Problems of Delinquency and Their Treatment by a Casework Agency," *Social Casework*, XL (1959), 254–62.

2. Ackerman, Nathan W., M.D. The Psychodynamics of Family Life. New York, Basic Books, Inc., 1958.

3. Aichhorn, August. "Some Remarks on the Psychic Structure and Social Care of a Certain Type of Female Juvenile Delinquent," in *Psychoanalytic Study of the Child*, III and IV (New York, International Universities Press, Inc., 1949), 439–88.

4. Alexander, Franz, M.D. "Personality Factors in the Environment," in Clyde Kluckhohn and Henry A. Murray, eds., Personality in Nature, Society, and Culture. 2d. ed. New York, Alfred A. Knopf, Inc., 1953.

5. Alexander, Franz, M.D. Our Age of Unreason. Rev. ed. New York, J. B. Lippincott, 1951.

6. Alexander, Franz, M.D. "The Development of the Fundamental Concepts of Psychoanalysis," in Franz Alexander, M.D., and Helen Ross, eds., Dynamic Psychiatry. Chicago, University of Chicago Press, 1952.

7. Alexander, Franz, M.D., and Louis B. Shapiro, M.D. "Neuroses, Behavior Disorders and Perversions," in Franz Alexander, M.D., and Helen Ross, eds., Dynamic Psychiatry. Chicago, University of Chicago Press, 1952.

8. Alexander, Franz, M.D., and Thomas S. Szasz, M.D. "The Psychosomatic Approach in Medicine," in Franz Alexander, M.D., and Helen Ross, eds., Dynamic Psychiatry. Chicago, University of Chicago Press, 1952.

9. Allport, Gordon W. Becoming. New Haven, Yale University Press, 1955.

10. American Psychiatric Association Mental Hospital Service. Diagnostic and Statistical Manual: Mental Disorders. Washington, D.C., the Association, 1952.

11. American Psychiatric Association Committee on Public Information. A Psychiatric Glossary. Washington, D.C., the Association, 1957.

12. Barrabee, Paul, M.D. "The Family as a Unit of Treatment in

Mental Health Therapy," *Marriage and Family Living*, XIX (1957), 182–86.

13. Bateson, Gregory. "Discussion," *American Journal of Orthopsychiatry*, XXX (1960), 263–66.

14. Beck, Samuel J. "The Families of Schizophrenic and of Well Children: Method, Concepts, and Some Results," *American Journal of Orthopsychiatry*, XXX (1960), 247–62.

15. Behrens, Marjorie L., and Nathan W. Ackerman, M.D. "The Home Visit as an Aid in Family Diagnosis and Therapy," *Social Casework*, XXXVII (1956), 11–19.

16. Benedek, Therese. "Personality Development," in Franz Alexander, M.D., and Helen Ross, eds., Dynamic Psychiatry. Chicago, University of Chicago Press, 1952.

17. Benedict, Ruth. "Continuities and Discontinuities in Cultural Conditioning," in Clyde Kluckhohn and Henry A. Murray, eds., Personality in Nature, Society, and Culture. 2d. ed. New York, Alfred A. Knopf, Inc., 1953.

18. Beres, David, M.D. "The Person and the Group: Object Relationships," in Marcel Heiman, ed., Psychoanalysis and Social Work. New York, International Universities Press, Inc., 1953.

19. Beres, David, M.D. "Viscissitudes of Superego Functions and Superego Precursors in Childhood," in *Psychoanalytic Study of the Child*, XIII (New York, International Universities Press, Inc., 1958), 324–51.

20. Bernard, Viola W., M.D. "Adolescence—Its Implications for Family and Community," in The Family in a Democratic Society. New York, Columbia University Press, 1949.

21. Blos, Peter. "Preoedipal Factors in the Etiology of Female Delinquency," in *Psychoanalytic Study of the Child*, XII (New York, International Universities Press, Inc., 1957), 229–49.

22. Blos, Peter. "The Contribution of Psychoanalysis to the Treatment of Adolescents," in Marcel Heiman, ed., Psychoanalysis and Social Work. New York, International Universities Press, Inc., 1953.

23. Boehm, Werner H. The Social Casework Method in Social Work Education. New York, Council on Social Work Education, 1959.

24. Bonaparte, Marie. Female Sexuality. New York, International Universities Press, Inc., 1953.

25. Bonnard, Augusta. "Some Discrepancies Between Perception and Affect as Illustrated by Children in Wartime," in *Psychoanalytic Study of the Child*, IX (New York, International Universities Press, Inc., 1958), 242–51.

26. Bossard, James H. S. Parent and Child Studies in Family Behavior. Philadelphia, University of Pennsylvania Press, 1953.

27. Bowlby, John, M.D. Child Care and the Growth of Love. London and Tonbridge, Whitefriar Press, Ltd.; reprinted in Pelican Books, 1955.

28. Bowman, Karl M., M.D., and Bernice Engle. "Mediolegal Aspects of Transvestism." *American Journal of Psychiatry*, CXIII (1957), 583–88.

29. Brenner, Charles, M.D. "The Nature and Development of the

Concept of Repression in Freud's Writings," in *Psychoanalytic Study of the Child*, XII (New York, International Universities Press, Inc., 1957), 19–45.

30. Brenner, Charles, M.D. An Elementary Textbook of Psychoanalysis. New York, International Universities Press, Inc., 1955.

31. Buell, Bradley. Is Prevention Possible? Eduard C. Lindeman Memorial Lecture. New York, Community Research Associates, Inc., 1959.

32. Buell, Bradley, and Associates. *Community Planning for Human Services*. New York, Columbia University Press, 1951.

33. Buell, Bradley, et al. "Reorganizing to Prevent and Control Disordered Behavior," *Mental Hygiene*, XLII (1958), 155–94.

34. Burritt, Bailey B. "Maintenance of Health: Exploring in New York," in The Family in a Democratic Society. New York, Columbia University Press, 1949.

35. Butler, Ruth M. "Mothers' Attitudes toward the Social Development of Their Adolescents: Part II," *Social Casework*, XXXVII (1956), 280–88.

36. Coleman, Jules V., M.D., et al. "A Comparative Study of a Psychiatric Clinic and a Family Agency: Part II," *Social Casework*, XXXVIII (1957), 74–80.

37. Community Research Associates. Classification of Disorganized Families. New York, Community Research Associates, Inc., 1953.

38. Davidson, Henry A., M.D. "Criminal Responsibility: the Quest for a Formula," in Paul H. Hoch, M.D., and Joseph Zubin, eds., Psychiatry and the Law. New York, Grune and Stratton, 1955.

39. Davis, Allison. "American Status Systems and the Socialization of the Child," in Clyde Kluckhohn and Henry A. Murray, eds., Personality in Nature, Society, and Culture. 2d. ed. New York, Alfred A. Knopf, Inc., 1953.

40. Deutsch, Felix, M.D. "The Application of Psychoanalysis to Psychosomatic Aspects," in Marcel Heiman, ed., Psychoanalysis and Social Work. New York, International Universities Press, Inc., 1953.

41. Deutsch, Helene. "The Significance of Masochism in the Mental Life of Women," in Robert Fliess, M.D., ed., The Psychoanalytic Reader, No. 38. London, Hogarth Press, Ltd., and Institute of Psychoanalysis, 1950.

42. Deutsch, Helene. "The Psychology of Woman in Relation to the Functions of Reproduction," in Robert Fliess, M.D., ed., The Psychoanalytic Reader, No. 38. London, Hogarth Press, Ltd., and Institute of Psychoanalysis, 1950.

43. Dollard, John. "The Life History in Community Studies," in Clyde Kluckhohn and Henry A. Murray, eds., Personality in Nature, Society, and Culture. 2d. ed. New York, Alfred A. Knopf, Inc., 1953.

44. Dollard, John. "Hostility and Fear in Social Life," *Social Forces*, XVII (1938), 15.

45. Dollard, John, et al. Frustration and Aggression. New Haven, Yale University Press, 1939.

46. Dollard, John. "Do We Have a Science of Child Rearing?" in The Family in a Democratic Society. New York, Columbia University Press, 1949.

47. Eliot, Martha, M.D., and Neota Larson. "Child Health in Relation to the Family," in The Family in a Democratic Society. New York, Columbia University Press, 1949.

48. Eller, C. Howe, M.D., Gordon H. Hatcher, M.D., and Bradley Buell. "Health and Welfare Issues in Community Planning for the Problem of Indigent Disability," American Journal of Public Health, XLVIII, No. 11 (1958), 1–49.

49. Erikson, Erik Homburger, M.D. "Ego Development and Historical Change," in Psychoanalytic Study of the Child, II (New York, International Universities Press, Inc., 1950), 359–96.

50. Erikson, Erik Homburger, M.D. "Growth and Crises of the Healthy Personality," in Clyde Kluckhohn and Henry A. Murray, eds., Personality in Nature, Society, and Culture. 2d. ed. New York, Alfred A. Knopf, Inc., 1953.

51. Erikson, Erik Homburger, M.D. Childhood and Society. New York, W. W. Norton and Co., Inc., 1950.

52. Fabian, Abraham A., M.D. "The Contribution of Psychoanalysis to the Child Guidance Unit," in Marcel Heiman, ed., Psychoanalysis and Social Work. New York, International Universities Press, Inc., 1953.

53. Family Service Association of America. A Comparison of Diagnostic and Functional Casework Concepts, Cora Kasius, ed. New York, the Association, 1950.

54. Family Service Association of America. Method and Process in Social Casework. New York, the Association, 1958.

55. Fenichel, Otto. Psychoanalytic Theory of Neurosis. New York, W. W. Norton and Co., Inc., 1945.

56. Flugel, J C. The Psycho-analytic Study of the Family. The International Psychoanalytical Library, No. 3. Ernest Jones, M.D., ed. London, Hogarth Press, Ltd., and Institute of Psychoanalysis, 1950.

57. Freedman, Lawrence Z., M.D. "Conformity and Noncomformity," in Paul H. Hoch, M.D., and Joseph Zubin, eds., Psychiatry and the Law. New York, Grune and Stratton, 1955.

58. French, Thomas M., M.D. "Personal Interaction and Growth in Family Life," in The Family in a Democratic Society. New York, Columbia University Press, 1949.

59. Freud, Anna. The Ego and Mechanisms of Defense. New York, International Universities Press, Inc., 1957.

60. Freud, Anna. The Psycho-analytic Treatment of Children. London, Imago Publishing Co., Ltd.; reprinted 1954.

61. Freud, Anna. "Adolescence," in Psychoanalytic Study of the Child, XIII (New York, International Universities Press, Inc., 1958), 255–78.

62. Freud, Sigmund. "The Predisposition to Obsessional Neurosis," in Collected Papers, Vol. II. London, Bradford, Hogarth Press, Ltd., and Institute for Psychoanalysis, 1950.

63. Freud, Sigmund. "Neurotic Mechanisms in Jealousy," in Collected

Papers, Vol. II. London, Bradford, Hogarth Press, Ltd., and Institute for Psychoanalysis, 1950.

64. Friedlander, Kate, M.D. "Psychoanalytic Orientation in Child Guidance Work in Great Britain," in *Psychoanalytic Study of the Child,* II (New York, International Universities Press, Inc., 1950), 343–57.

65. Friedlander, Kate, M.D. "Neurosis and Home Background," in *Psychoanalytic Study of the Child,* III (New York, International Universities Press, Inc., 1949), 423–35.

66. Geleerd, Elisabeth R., M.D. "A Contribution to the Problem of Psychoses in Childhood," in *Psychoanalytic Study of the Child,* II (New York, International Universities Press, Inc., 1950), 271–91.

67. Geleerd, Elisabeth R., M.D. "Some Aspects of Psychoanalytic Technique in Adolescence," in *Psychoanalytic Study of the Child,* XII (New York, International Universities Press, Inc., 1957), 263–83.

68. Geleerd, Elisabeth R., M.D. "Borderline States in Childhood and Adolescence," in *Psychoanalytic Study of the Child,* XIII (New York, International Universities Press, Inc., 1959), 279–95.

69. Gerard, Margaret W., M.D. "Emotional Disorders of Childhood," in Franz Alexander, M.D., and Helen Ross, eds., Dynamic Psychiatry. Chicago, University of Chicago Press, 1952.

70. Glueck, Sheldon, and Eleanor T. Glueck. Unravelling Juvenile Delinquency. New York, Commonwealth Fund, 1950.

71. Glueck, Sheldon, and Eleanor T. Glueck. "Working Mothers and Delinquency," *Mental Hygiene,* XLI (1957), 327–52.

72. Glueck, Sheldon, and Eleanor T. Glueck. "Early Detection of Future Delinquents," *Journal of Criminal Law, Criminology and Police Science,* XLVII, No. 2 (1956), 174–82.

73. Gomberg, Robert M. "Family Oriented Treatment of Marital Problems," *Social Casework,* XXXVII (1956), 3–10.

74. Gorer, Geoffrey. "The Concept of National Character," in Clyde Kluckhohn and Henry A. Murray, eds., Personality in Nature, Society, and Culture. 2d. ed. New York, Alfred A. Knopf, Inc., 1953.

75. Gray, Paul H., M.D. "Report on Preliminary Impressions of Four Family Types." New York, Community Research Associates, 1960; un published.

76. Greenacre, Phyllis, M.D. "The Childhood of the Artist," in *Psychoanalytic Study of the Child,* XII (New York, International Universities Press, Inc., 1957), 47–72.

77. Greenacre, Phyllis, M.D. "Further Considerations Regarding Fetishism," in *Psychoanalytic Study of the Child,* X (New York, International Universities Press, Inc., 1955), 187–94.

78. Greenacre, Phyllis, M.D. "Play in Relation to Creative Imagination," in *Psychoanalytic Study of the Child,* XIV (New York, International Universities Press, Inc., 1959), 61–80.

79. Guttmacher, Manfred S., M.D. "Diagnosis and Etiology of Psychopathic Personalities Perceived in Our Time," in Paul H. Hoch, M.D., and Joseph Zubin, eds., Current Problems in Psychiatric Diagnosis. New York, Grune and Stratton, 1953.

80. Hamilton, Gordon. Theory and Practice of Social Casework. 2d ed. rev. New York, Columbia University Press, 1951.

81. Harris, Irving D. "Discussion," *American Journal of Orthopsychiatry*, XXX (1960), 271–75.

82. Hartmann, Heinz, M.D. "Comments on the Psychoanalytic Theory of the Ego," in *Psychoanalytic Study of the Child*, V (New York, International Universities Press, Inc., 1950), 74–96.

83. Hartmann, Heinz, M.D., Ernst Kris, and Rudolph M. Loewenstein, M.D. "Comments on the Formation of Psychic Structure," in *Psychoanalytic Study of the Child*, II (New York, International Universities Press, Inc., 1950), 11–37.

84. Hartmann, Heinz, M.D., Ernst Kris, and Rudolph M. Loewenstein, M.D. "Notes on the Theory of Aggression," in *Psychoanalytic Study of the Child*, III and IV (New York, International Universities Press, Inc., 1946), 9–36.

85. Hartmann, Heinz, M.D., Ernst Kris, and Rudolph M. Loewenstein, M.D. "Comments on the Formation of the Psychic Structure," in *Psychoanalytic Study of the Child*, II (New York, International Universities Press, Inc., 1950), 11–39.

86. Heiman, Marcel, M.D., ed. Psychoanalysis and Social Work. New York, International Universities Press, Inc., 1953.

87. Hill, Reuben. "Social Stresses on the Family," *Social Casework*, XXXIX (1958), 139–58.

88. Inkeles, Alex. "Some Sociological Observations on Culture and Personality Studies," in Clyde Kluckhohn and Henry A. Murray, eds., Personality in Nature, Society, and Culture. 2d. ed. New York, Alfred A. Knopf, Inc., 1953.

89. Jacobson, Edith, M.D. "Normal and Pathological Moods: Their Nature and Functions," in *Psychoanalytic Study of the Child*, XII (New York, International Universities Press, Inc., 1957), 73–113.

90. Jenkins, Richard L., M.D. Breaking Patterns of Defeat. Philadelphia, J. B. Lippincott, 1954.

91. Jenkins, Richard L., M.D. "Motivation and Frustration in Delinquency," *American Journal of Orthopsychiatry*, XXVII (1958), 528–37.

92. Jessner, Lucie, *et al.* "Emotional Impact of Nearness and Separation for the Asthmatic Child and His Mother," in *Psychoanalytic Study of the Child*, X (New York, International Universities Press, Inc., 1955), 353–75.

93. Johnson, Adelaide M., M.D. "Sanctions for Superego Lacunae of Adolescents," in K. R. Eissler, ed., Searchlights on Delinquency. New York, International Universities Press, Inc., 1948.

94. Johnson, Adelaide, M., M.D., and Mary E. Griffin, M.D. "Some Applications of Psychoanalytic Insights to the Socialization of Children," *American Journal of Orthopsychiatry*, XXVII (1958), 462–74.

95. Jones, Ernest, M.D. Miscellaneous Essays. Essays in Applied Psychoanalysis, Vol. I. London, Hogarth Press, Ltd., and Institute of Psychoanalysis, 1951.

96. Jones, Ernest, M.D. Essays in Folklore, Anthropology and Reli-

gion. Essays in Applied Psychoanalysis, Vol. II. London, Hogarth Press, Ltd., and Institute of Psychoanalysis, 1951.

97. Kephart, William M. "Some Knowns and Unknowns in Family Research: a Sociological Critique," Marriage and Family Living, XIX (1957), 7–24.

98. Klein, Emanuel, M.D. "The Psychoanalytic Concept of the Ego and Its Functions," in Marcel Heiman, ed., Psychoanalysis and Social Work. New York, International Universities Press, Inc., 1953.

99. Klein, Emanuel, M.D. "Psychoanalytic Aspects of School Problems," in Psychoanalytic Study of the Child, III and IV (New York, International Universities Press, Inc., 1949), 391.

100. Kluckhohn, Clyde. "Variations in the Human Family," in The Family in a Democratic Society. New York, Columbia University Press, 1949.

101. Kluckhohn, Florence Rockwood. "Dominant and Variant Value Orientations," in Clyde Kluckhohn and Henry A. Murray, eds., Personality in Nature, Society, and Culture. 2d. ed. New York, Alfred A. Knopf, Inc., 1953.

102. Kris, Ernst. "Roots of Hostility and Prejudice," in The Family in a Democratic Society. New York, Columbia University Press, 1949.

103. Kris, Marianne, M.D. "The Use of Prediction in a Longitudinal Study," in Psychoanalytic Study of the Child, XII (New York, International Universities Press, Inc., 1957), 175–89.

104. Kubie, Lawrence S., M.D. "The Concept of Normality and Neurosis," in Marcel Heiman, ed., Psychoanalysis and Social Work. New York, International Universities Press, Inc., 1953.

105. La Barre, Weston. The Human Animal. Chicago, University of Chicago Press, 1954.

106. Lample-DeGroot, Jeanne, M.D. "On Defense and Development: Normal and Pathological," in Psychoanalytic Study of the Child, XII (New York, International Universities Press, Inc., 1957), 114–26.

107. Leavell, Hugh R., M.D. "Professional Interplay for Family Health," in The Family in a Democratic Society. New York, Columbia University Press, 1949.

108. Levine, Maurice, M.D. "Principles of Psychiatric Treatment," in Franz Alexander, M.D., and Helen Ross eds., Dynamic Psychiatry. Chicago, University of Chicago Press, 1952.

109. Levy, David M., M.D. "Animal Psychology in Its Relation to Psychiatry," in Franz Alexander, M.D., and Helen Ross, eds., Dynamic Psychiatry. Chicago, University of Chicago Press, 1952.

110. Lidz, Theodore, M.D., et al. "The Intrafamilial Environment of Schizophrenic Patients: II, Marital Schism and Marital Skew," American Journal of Psychiatry, CXIV (1957), 241–48.

111. Litvak, Eugene. "Divorce Law as Social Control," in Norman W. Bell and Ezra F. Vogel, eds., The Family. Glencoe, Ill., Free Press, 1960.

112. Lutz, Werner A. Concepts and Principles Underlying Social Casework Practise. Monograph III. Washington, D.C., National Association of Social Workers, 1956.

113. Maas, Henry S. "Discussion," *American Journal of Orthopsychiatry*, XXX (1960), 266–71.

114. Mahler, Margaret S., M.D., and Bertram J. Gosliner, M.D. "On Symbiotic Child Psychosis," in *Psychoanalytic Study of the Child*, X (New York, International Universities Press, Inc., 1955), 195–212.

115. Mead, Margaret. Sex and Temperament in Three Primitive Societies. New York, Morrow and Co., 1935.

116. Mead, Margaret. Male and Female. New York, Morrow and Co., 1949.

117. Mead, Margaret. "Social Change and Cultural Surrogates," in Clyde Kluckhohn and Henry A. Murray, eds., Personality in Nature, Society, and Culture. 2d ed. New York, Alfred A. Knopf, Inc., 1953.

118. Mead, Margaret. "Administrative Contributions to Democratic Character Formation at the Adolescent Level," in Clyde Kluckhohn and Henry A. Murray, eds., Personality in Nature, Society, and Culture. 2d ed. New York, Alfred A. Knopf, Inc., 1953.

119. Mead, Margaret. "Some Relationships Between Social Anthropology and Psychiatry," in Franz Alexander, M.D., and Helen Ross, eds., Dynamic Psychiatry. Chicago, University of Chicago Press, 1952.

120. Meerloo, Joost, M.D. "The Contributions of Psychoanalysis to the Problems of the Aged," in Marcel Heiman, ed., Psychoanalysis and Social Work. New York, International Universities Press, Inc., 1953.

121. Menninger, Karl A., M.D. A Manual for Psychiatric Case Study. New York, Grune and Stratton, 1952.

122. Meyer, Carol H. "The Quest for a Broader Base for Family Diagnosis," *Social Casework*, XL (1959), 370–76.

123. Mitchell, Celia Brody. "Family Interviewing in Family Diagnosis," *Social Casework*, XL (1959), 381–84.

124. Mittelmann, Bela. "Motor Patterns and Genital Behavior: Fetishism," in *Psychoanalytic Study of the Child*, X (New York, International Universities Press, Inc., 1955), 241–63.

125. Mogey, J. M. "The Family in England," *Marriage and Family Living*, XVI (1954), 319–25.

126. Mohr, George J., M.D., and Marie A. Despres. The Stormy Decade: Adolescence. New York, Random House, Inc., 1958.

127. Mooney, Robert D., M.D. "The Meaning and Significance of Family Health," *Marriage and Family Living*, XIX (1957), 131–41.

128. Murphy, Gardner, M.D. "New Knowledge about Family Dynamics," *Social Casework*, XL (1959), 363–70.

129. Murray, Henry A., and Clyde Kluckhohn. "Outline of a Conception of Personality," in Clyde Kluckhohn and Henry A. Murray, eds., Personality in Nature, Society, and Culture. 2d ed., rev. New York, Alfred A. Knopf, Inc., 1953.

130. National Resources Planning Board. Security, Work, and Relief Policies. Washington, D.C., United States Government Printing Office, 1942.

131. Neubauer, Peter B., M.D. "The Psychoanalyst's Contribution to

the Family Agency," in Marcel Heiman, ed., Psychoanalysis and Social Work. New York, International Universities Press, Inc., 1953.

132. Nimkoff, M. F. "The Family in the United States," *Marriage and Family Living*, XVI (1954), 390–96.

133. Nunberg, Herman, M.D. Principles of Psychoanalysis. New York, International Universities Press, Inc., 1955.

134. Parsons, Talcott. "Age and Sex in the Social Structure of the United States," in Clyde Kluckhohn and Henry A. Murray, eds., Personality in Nature, Society, and Culture. 2d ed. New York, Alfred A. Knopf, Inc., 1953.

135. Parsons, Talcott. "Illness and the Role of the Physician: a Sociological Perspective" in Clyde Kluckhohn and Henry A. Murray, eds., Personality in Nature, Society, and Culture. 2d ed. New York, Alfred A. Knopf, Inc., 1953.

136. Parsons, Talcott, and Robert F. Bales. Family Socialization and Interaction. Glencoe, Ill., Free Press, 1955.

137. Peller, Lili E. "Incentives to Development and Means of Early Education," in *Psychoanalytic Study of the Child*, II (New York, International Universities Press, Inc., 1950), 397–415.

138. Philip, A. F., and Noel Timms. The Problem of the Problem Family. London, Family Service Units, 1957.

139. Pollak, Otto, and Ralph Ormsby. "Design of a Model of Healthy Family Relationships as a Basis for Evaluative Research," *Social Service Review*, XXXI (1957), 369–76.

140. Pumphrey, Muriel W. "Mary Richmond's Process of Conceptualization," *Social Casework*, XXXVIII (1957), 399–406.

141. Richmond, Mary E. Social Diagnosis. New York, Russell Sage Foundation, 1917.

142. Ripple, Lillian, and Ernestina Alexander. "Motivation, Capacity and Opportunity as Related to the Use of Case Work Service: Nature of Client's Problem," *Social Service Review*, XXX (1956), 38–54.

143. Ripple, Lillian, and Ernestina Alexander. "Motivation, Capacity and Opportunity as Related to the Use of Case Work Service: Nature of Client's Problem," *Social Service Review*, XXX (1956), 172–93.

144. Ruben, Margaret. "Delinquency, a Defense Against Loss of Objects and Reality," in *Psychoanalytic Study of the Child*, XII (New York, International Universities Press, Inc., 1957), 335–55.

145. Sandler, Anne-Marie, *et al.*, with an introduction by Anna Freud. "Inconsistency in the Mother as a Factor in Character Development: a Comparative Study of Three Cases," in *Psychoanalytic Study of the Child*, XII (New York, International Universities Press, Inc., 1957), 209–25.

146. Schelsky, Helmut. "The Family in Germany," *Marriage and Family Living*, XVI (1954), 331–35.

147. Shyne, Ann W., and Leonard S. Kogan. "A Study of Components of Movement," *Social Casework*, XXXIX (1958), 333–42.

148. Simcox, Beatrice R., and Irving Kaufman, M.D. "Handling of

Early Contacts with Parents of Delinquents," *Social Casework*, XXXVII (1956), 443–50.

149. Sneider, David M. "The Social Dynamics of Physical Disability in Army Basic Training," in Clyde Kluckhohn and Henry A. Murray, eds., Personality in Nature, Society, and Culture. 2d ed. New York, Alfred A. Knopf, Inc., 1953.

150. Sobel, Raymond, M.D. "The Contribution of Psychoanalysis to the Residential Treatment of Adolescents," in Marcel Heiman, ed., Psychoanalysis and Social Work. New York, International Universities Press, Inc., 1953.

151. *Social Security Bulletin.* October, 1959.

152. Spitz, René A., M.D. "Hospitalism," in *Psychoanalytic Study of the Child*, II (New York, International Universities Press, Inc., 1950), 113–17.

153. Stockard, C. H. Physical Bases of Personality. New York, W. W. Norton and Co., Inc., 1931.

154. United States Department of Commerce. Bureau of the Census Statistical Abstract of the United States, 1961. Washington, D.C., United States Government Printing Office, 1961.

155. United States Department of Labor. Bureau of Labor Statistics Special Labor Force Report No. 13, "Marital and Family Characteristics of Workers, March, 1960." Washington, D.C., United States Printing Office, 1960.

156. Waelder, Robert. "The Scientific Approach to Casework, with Special Emphasis on Psychoanalysis," in Clyde Kluckhohn and Henry A. Murray, eds., Personality in Nature, Society, and Culture. 2d. ed. New York, Alfred A. Knopf, Inc., 1953.

157. Weiss, Edoardo, M.D. "History of Metapsychological Concepts," in Franz Alexander, M.D., and Helen Ross, eds., Dynamic Psychiatry. Chicago, University of Chicago Press, 1952.

158. Weiss, Viola W. "An Application of Social Science Concepts to Family Diagnosis," *Social Casework*, XL (1959), 377–80.

159. Weiss, Viola W., and Russell R. Monroe, M.D. "A Framework for Understanding Family Dynamics: Part I," *Social Casework*, XL (1959), 3–9.

160. Weiss, Viola W., and Russell R. Monroe, M.D. "A Framework for Understanding Family Dynamics: Part II," *Social Casework*, XL (1959), 80–87.

161. The World Almanac. New York, *World-Telegram and The Sun*, 1960.

INDEX

"Acting out," and crime, 106; in narcissism, 224; adult, in unsocial family, 273

Adolescence, and social identity, 66 ff.; ambivalence in, 78; problems of, in perfectionistic family, 126 ff.; inadequate family, 168 ff.; egocentric family, 203 f.; psychic disturbance of, 226 f.; unsocial family, 253; psychotic disturbance of, 278 ff.; diagnostic data re, 316 f.; friendships, 318

Adolescent(s), and sex, 38 f.; personality development, 66 ff.; and personal relationships, 67 f.; role diffusion, 68; psychic disturbance, 142 ff., 329 ff.; inadequate family, 183; egocentric family, 208 f.

Adoption, in egocentric family, 198

Adult(s), demands of society upon, 34 ff.; emotional maturity, 68 f.; attitude toward problem-solving, 305

Adult characteristics, in perfectionistic couple, 138 ff.; of marital partners in inadequate family, 179 ff.; egocentric family, 222 ff.; unsocial family, 272 ff.; and problem-solving, 321 f.; data re, 324 ff.

Adult disorders, prognoses for, 22, 24 ff.; defined, 95; levels of, 105 ff., 306; perfectionistic family, 117; inadequate family, 158 f.; egocentric family, 196; unsocial family, 236 f.; prognosis, 342

Affect, in psychic disturbance of adolescence, 227 f.; reversal of, 280, 330; withdrawal by adolescent to self, 330

Affection, distorted, patterns of, 113; see also Love relationships

Aged, the, family association, 47 f.

Agencies, participation of, 7 ff.; quota of schedules, 10 f.; identification of psychosocial disorders, 95 ff.; voluntary, 97 f.; governmental, responsibilities, 97 ff.; family service, sample cases, 104; psychosocial disorders and, 17 f.; sociolegal, and unsocial family, 245 f.; administrator, use of diagnostic classifications, 335 ff.

Aggression, controlled, and discipline, 81; eroticized, 201; adolescent, 209 f., 214 f., 259 f.; see also Hostility

Allergy, 224 f.

Ambivalence, 78 f.; parental, 120, 124; and self-identity, 134 f.; in tie to mother, 153; re child bearing, 197; toward marital partner, 262; adolescent, 278

American Psychiatric Association, 326

Anxiety, of child, in love relationships with parents, 124, 249; and sex, 134

Asthma, 224 f.

Authority, defiance of, by children, 108; social, unsocial family and, 245

Autism, 250

"Badness," sense of, 63

Behavior, psychosocial disorders and, 17 ff.; patterns of, in basic areas, 19 f.; symptomatic, 20; prognosis, 26; family patterns, 26 f.; adherence to patterns of, 40; psychosocial aspects, 59 ff.; psychotic, and social

Behavior (*Continued*)
    identity, 68; forbidden, 81 f., 99,
    122, 126; restricted, 99 f.; and con-
    ditions, identification and determi-
    nation of, 104; provocative, as de-
    fense, 129; symptoms, in inadequate
    family, 166 f.; compensatory, 193;
    egocentric family, 204 f., 221; un-
    social family, 234 f., 245 f.; in la-
    tency and adolescence, 256 f.; in
    defective superego development,
    258 f.; passive, nonantagonistic, in
    unsocial adolescents, 258 ff.; in
    marital partner, 267; unsocial fam-
    ily, 269
Behavior, antisocial, 319
Behavior, social, *see* Social functioning
Behavior disorders, classification,
    98 ff.; socially incompatible, 106;
    adolescent, 142 f.; inadequate fam-
    ily, 183; wife's family of origin, 192;
    egocentric family, 225 f.; in latency,
    328
Bodily injury, young child's fear of,
    250 f.
Boy(s), identification with parent,
    56 f., 126 ff.; discipline of, 81 f.;
    and parental oversensitivity, 120;
    social adjustment, 130; perfection-
    istic family, 143 f.; effect of over-
    strict upbringing on adult sexuality,
    186; and fear of "genital harm,"
    251; sexual behavior, 259; infantile
    phenomena in latency, 277; unso-
    cial family, 279

Career, marriage and, 52 f., 58; *see
    also* Wife, employed
Cases, selection of, 9 f.
Casework, family, use of date, 6;
    schedule, 10 f.; duration of contact,
    12; systematization of procedures,
    18 f., 337 ff.; marital difficulties,
    50 f.; family diagnosis framework as
    tool for, 290 ff.; skilled, professional,
    344
Caseworkers, selection of, 7; case load,
    10 f.; guide to social dysfunction-
    ing, 70 ff.; understanding of parents,
    73; assistance to parent in child-
    care problems, 74 f.; and classifica-
    tion of psychosocial disorders, 102;
    and unsocial family, 247; therapeu-

tic objective, 305; use of diagnostic
    classifications, 333 f.; qualifications,
    344
Casework supervisor, 9 f.; use of diag-
    nostic classifications, 334 f.
Causal relationships, in family disor-
    ders, 339 f.
Census, marital statistics, 47
Chapin, F. Stuart, 15, 28
Character, growth of, 60 ff.
Characteristics, individual, definition
    of term, 294; *see also* Adult char-
    acteristics
Child (children), age of, in selected
    families, 10; prognosis re develop-
    mental progress, 23; demands of so-
    ciety upon, 34 f.; fundamental
    growth processes, 60 ff.; oedipal pe-
    riod, 64, 207; development of self-
    mastery, 64 f.; and adult preroga-
    tives, 65; parental adjustment to
    advent of, 73 f.; factors in de-
    velopment of, 77 ff.; age level and
    regression, 79; as "equals," 83; rec-
    ognition of inferiority, 84, 243 f.;
    barriers to developmental growth,
    113 f.; training, 119 f., 167 f. (*see
    also* Toilet training); love relation-
    ships, and age and position in fam-
    ily, 124; excessive demands on, 129;
    perfectionistic family, 141 ff.; in-
    adequate family, 160; handicapped,
    attitude toward, 161, 167 f.; ego-
    centric family, 200 ff.; exploitation
    of parent, 209 f.; relationships with
    peers or adults, 214; unsocial fam-
    ily, 240 ff.; babyish behavior, 249;
    effect on, of mother's indifference,
    251 f.; behavior in the community,
    318 f.; diagnostic data re, 326 ff.;
    see also Parent-child relationship
Child bearing, ambivalence re, 197
Child care, inadequate, 113; egocen-
    tric family, 199 f., 233; unsocial
    family, 239 f.; *see also* Physical care
Child characteristics, in inadequate
    family, 182 ff.; egocentric family,
    224 ff.; unsocial family, 276 ff.
Child development, in perfectionistic
    family, 123 ff.; inadequate family,
    165 ff.; egocentric family, 205 ff.;
    unsocial family, 246 ff.; clinical de-
    scription, 312 f.

Child disorders, 22; defined, 95; levels of, 107 ff.; perfectionistic family, 116; inadequate family, 157; egocentric family, 195; unsocial family, 235 f.; Level A, 306; prognosis, 341

Childhood, traumatic experiences, 73; ambivalence in, 78; perfectionistic family, 123 f., 147; "internalization" process, 301; *see also* Adolescence; Latency

— early: inadequate family, 106; perfectionistic family, 123; egocentric family, 206 ff.; unsocial family, 248 ff.; evaluation of data re, 314 f.

Child neglect, *see* Neglect

Child placement, *see* Placement

Child-rearing functions, 44 ff.; American attitudes, 55 f.; parental memories and, 72 f.; physical care (*q.v.*), 74 f.; perfectionistic family, 110, 117 ff., 147 f.; psychosocial disorders and, 111 ff.; distorted application of concepts, 121 f.; inadequate family, 159 ff.; egocentric family, 197 ff.; unsocial family, 237 ff.; diagnosis, 308 ff.

— disorders: defined, 95 f.; inadequate family, 156 f.; egocentric family, 194 f.; unsocial family, 235; Level A, 306; prognosis for, 341

Choice, independence of, 37 f.; of mate, 50

Classification, of disordered family types, 29 ff.; testing of, 32; of psychosocial disorders, 95-114; diagnostic, application of, 333-48

Cleanliness, child's attitude toward, 211

Common law marriage, 41

Community, social casework, 6 f.; and rehabilitation program, 19; social conformance in, 318 f.; *see also* Environment; Society

Community Research Associates (CRA), 5 ff.; report, 28; projects, 32, 47; experiments on Level A disorders, 104 f.; San Mateo project, 106, 111 f., 336; Washington County project, 110; casework procedures, 337 ff.; levels of social service, 343 ff.

Compatibility, areas of, in marital relationship, 13 f.

Concern, helpful, for spouse, 220, 267, 321

Confidence, emotional withdrawal of, 135

Conscience, development of, 64 f., 80 ff., 301 f.

CRA, *see* Community Research Associates

Creative activity, and the family, 48; and child rearing, 76 f.; and sex energies, 133

Crime, distinction between major and minor, 105; unsocial family and, 237, 246; *see also* Behavior, antisocial

Culture, American, trends in, 38 ff.

Data, areas covered by, 7 f.; quantitative aspects, 11 f.; types and analysis of, 11 ff.; diagnostic framework, 19 ff.; clinical analysis, 26 ff.; classified framework, 102 f.; selection and interpretation of, 303 ff.; collection and organization of, 338; diagnostic summary, 340

Dating, adolescent, 38 f.

Debts, family, 110; inadequate family, 179

Decision-making, in inadequate family, 163 f.; dependency on others, 187, 191; of egocentric husband's parents, 229 f.; unsocial family, 289

Defense mechanisms, 62; ego, 139; of marital partners in unsocial family, 266; adolescent, 278 f.; *see also* Ego defenses

Definitions, of psychosocial disorders, basis of, 103 f.

Delinquency, and role diffusion, 68; juvenile, 107 f.; inadequate family, 170; egocentric family, 195, 213; unsocial family, 200, 273; sexual, in latency, 277 f.

Dependency, agencies and, 97; legal definition, 109; and self-reliance, 169; financial, 178 f.; parental, in decision-making, 187; of wife, 191 f.; parasitic, in latency and adolescence, 253 f.; passive-receptive, 273 f.; passive, overcompensation for, 283; prognoses re, 341

Desertion, by parent, 188

Devaluation, personal, in marital partners of unsocial family, 265 f.

Diagnosis, see Family diagnosis

Discipline, in child rearing, 56 f.; acceptance of, 80; perfectionistic family, 122; in husband's family of origin, 145; inadequate family, 163 f.; unsocial family, 242; severe, 249; overpunitive father, 288

Divorce, cultural attitudes toward, 48 f.; rate, 49; restrictions on, 97; inadequate family and, 165; and new family units, 205 f.

Dysfunctioning, social, 17, 96, 98 f., 334; psychosocial, 21 ff.; see also Psychosocial disorders

Eating, overemphasis on, 200

Education, regulations re, 100; see also School

Ego, stage of development, and regression, 79; disturbances in development of, 253 ff.

Ego defenses, 139 f.; of marital partners, 180 f.; adult, 223, 273 f.; of husband, unsocial family, 270 f.; data re, 325 f.

Egocentric family, 193-233; stresses in, 307; percent of cases, 336

Emotional maturity, 68 f.

Emotional stability, of marital partners, 26; adolescence and, 66 f.; perfectionistic family, 140 f.; inadequate family, 182; adult, 223 f., 325; unsocial family, 274 f.; of child, data re, 328 ff.

Emotions, attitudes and love relationship, 132 f.

Environment, stresses of, 299, 306 ff.; problems of, defined, 347; see also Community

Epidemiology, of psychosocial disorders, 102

Equality of the sexes, 38, 51 f.

Erikson, Erik H., 36

Ethnic characteristics, 11

Etiology, and classification, 103

Evaluation procedures, 345 ff.

Events and circumstances, perfectionistic family, 123; inadequate family, 165 f.; egocentric family, 205 f.; unsocial family, 237 f.; definition of

term, 298 f., 309; interpretation of, 313 f.

Exhibitionism, egocentric, 218

Exploitation, by marital partner, 268

External stresses, 306 ff.; in child development, 313

Family, functional capacity and marital relationship, 14; areas of social functioning, 16 f.; dissolution, 22, 26; basic aspects, 41 ff.; structure of, 46 ff.; malfunction and divorce, 49; leadership, 52; functioning, healthy, 69-90; broken, and substitute arrangements, 248; composition, 293, 304; personal and social adjustment, definition of, 347 f.

— disorders: diagnostic classification, 5 ff.; classification of types, 7, 28 ff.; numerical distribution of types, 31; psychosocial disorders (q.v.), 110 ff.; and levels of social service, 343 ff.

"Family Casework Diagnosis," 6

Family diagnosis, approach to, 5-32; areas of analysis, 8; defined, 18; framework, 19 f., 96, 290-303; original classification of 100 families, 23 ff.; basic areas, 293 ff.; major factors, 298 ff.; interpretation of framework, 303-32; procedures, 337 ff.; diagnostic synthesis, 338 f.

Family members, prognoses re, 22 f.; "bilateral," 47 f.; acceptance of father's leadership role, 71 f.; identification among, 71 f.; love relationships (q.v.), 75 ff.; adaptive task, 296 f.; definition of problem effects, 347; see also Individual

Family of origin, perfectionistic, 144 ff.; inadequate, 184 f.; egocentric, 227 ff.; unsocial, 280 ff.; definition of, 294; data re, 331 f.

Family Service Association of America, 10

Father, parental responsibility, 44 f.; as family head, 71; role in child care, 74; and parenthood (q.v.), 76 f.; and family discipline, 81 f.; lenient, 119; effect of absence of, 123, 230 f.; identification with, 127; egocentric family, 197; assumption of maternal role, 239 f., 252; exploi-

tation of sexual differences in children, 244; attitude toward, in unsocial family, 255; seduction of daughter, 277 f.; overpunitive, 288
Father-daughter relationship, 57, 277 f.
Father-son relationship, in perfectionistic family, 143 f.; in husband's family of origin, 281 f.
Fears, irrational, of children, 108
Fetishism, 217
Financial disorders, 21; term, 195; egocentric family, 195 f.; unsocial family, 236, 271 f.; Level A, 305 f.
Financial functioning, family, 45 f., 58 f., 89; responsibility in, and the child's allowance, 83; in stable marriage, 89 f.; levels of disorders, 109 f.; perfectionistic family, 117, 137 ff.; in husband's family of origin, 144 f., 185, 228, 281; perfectionistic family of origin, 150 f.; inadequate family, 158, 177 ff.; of wife's parents, 189, 231, 287; egocentric family, 221 ff.; unsocial family, 269 ff.; data re, 323 f.
Flirtation, well-adjusted marriage and, 86 f.
Food, infant's attitude toward, 61
Freud, Anna, 329
Freud, Sigmund, 42, 59
Friends, adolescent, 130, 142, 279, 318; children of egocentric family and, 212, 214; restriction of, 243
Frigidity, sexual, 288
Frustration, child and, 63; in infant development, 63; parental, 75 f.; and adult immaturity, 266

"Genital harm," 250 f.
Gerard, Margaret W., 328
Germany, Nazi, 46
Girl, role in premarital relationship, 38 f., 55; identification with parent, 56 f., 126 ff.; discipline of, 81; parental oversensitivity toward, 120 f.; self-identity, 128 f.; social adjustment, 130; in inadequate family, 184; effect on, of emotional and physical neglect, 190 f.; mother's identification with, 202; and fear of "genital harm," 251; unsocial family, 254 f., 279; sexual behavior,

259; see also Father-daughter relationship; Mother-daughter relationship
"Good," experience of, 63
Grandmother, maternal, of egocentric wife, 233
Guilt, child's manifestations of, 126

Handicapped, the, society and, 35; see also Physical disability
Hartley-Salmon Child Guidance Clinic, 32
Homosexuality, 42; adolescent, 279
Hostility, in parent and child, 78 f.; perfectionistic family, 118 f.; as a response to excessive demands, 129; repressed, 187; overrepression of, 203; egocentric parents, 204; to parent, 209 f.; parental, in unsocial family, 240 ff.; child's, toward mother, 249; in latency and adolescence, 256 f.; pattern of, in wife's family of origin, 287 f.; see also Aggression
"Hours," family rules re, 83 f.
"House rules," 83
Housing, unsocial family, 240
Husband, psychosocial syndrome, 29 f.; financial functions, 45 f.; occupational status, 52, 58; sexual potency, 55; social relationships, 58 f.; role of, in love relationship, 86 f.; as provider for family, 89 f., 137 f., 216; defense mechanisms, 139, 180 f.; inadequate family, 171 f., 180 f.; and wife's preoccupation with children, 199; unsocial family, behavior disorders, 237, 262 ff., 270; wife's emotional investment in, 238; assumption of maternal role, 263, 269; see also Father
— family of origin, structure of, 144 ff.; inadequate, 180, 184 ff.; egocentric, 227 ff.; unsocial, 280 ff.; data re, 331 f.

Identification, in child's development, 61 f.; family, 71; of parent with child, 75 f.; of psychosocial disorders, 101 ff.; of adults with parents, 118; of child with parents, 126 ff.; with mother, 127 f., 253 f.,

Identification (*Continued*) 283; of mother, in egocentric family, 197 f.; maternal, 202

Illegitimacy, state and, 45 f.; reactions to, in unsocial family, 241; prognosis re, 342

Inadequate family, 156-92; compared with unsocial family, 30 f.; stresses in, 307; percent of cases, 336

Incest, 41 f.; with stepdaughter, 202

Income production and management, 89 f.; perfectionistic family, 137 f.; inadequate family, 177 ff.; egocentric family, 221 f.; unsocial family, 269 ff.; data re, 323 f.

Incompatibility, in marital axis classes, 14

Independence, *see* Self-identity

Indigent disability, levels of, 109 f.; prognoses, 341

Individual, healthy social functioning, 15 f.; and his society, 33 ff.; American, concepts re, 36; and changing social values, 40 f.; pressures re behavior of, 96 ff.; psychosocial disorders, 105 ff.; "developed capacities," 296; relationships, 300 f.

Infant, defenses, 62; development of, 62 ff.

Infantile phenomena, in latency, 328

Infantilization, of young child, 249 f.

Insecurity, child's manifestations of, 125; early childhood, 206, 315

Intelligence, perfectionistic family, 138; of adults in unsocial family, 272; of children in unsocial family, 276; adult, data re, 325 f.; of child, 327 f.

Interpretation, of treatment evaluations, 346 ff.

Intervention, and levels of disorder, 104; sociolegal, sabotage of, 245 f.; of marital partner to prevent corrective measures, 267

— protective: and psychosocial disorders, 100 f.; and mental illness, 105, 348; and dependency, 109; egocentric family, 220

Introjection, as psychic mechanism, 62

Jealousy, of sibling, 79 f.; in love relationships, 133; in marital relationship, 261 f.

Juvenile delinquency, *see* Delinquency

Labor, division of, in family, 58

Latency, developmental problems, 126 ff.; psychic disturbance in, 141 f., 225 f., 277 f.; inadequate family, 168 ff.; disorders, 183; egocentric family, 203 f., 208 ff., 277; unsocial family, 253; overreliance on mother, 258; diagnostic data re, 316; data re disturbances in, 328

Laws, on unacceptable behavior or conditions, 97

Leadership, family, 52, 71

Love, sole recipient of, 75 f., 263; adult, child as substitute for, 201 f.

Love relationships, family, 75 ff.; inadequate family, 106 f., 161 f.; unhealthy forms of, with child, 113; perfectionistic family, 120 f., 124, 127 f.; in husband's family of origin, 145 f., 186, 228, 282 ff.; in wife's family of origin, 151 ff., 189 ff., 231 f., 287 f.; latency and adolescence, 168, 209 ff., 253 ff., 316 f.; parent-child, in egocentric family, 200 ff.; early childhood, 206, 248 ff., 315; unsocial family, 240 ff.; definition, 298 ff.; diagnostic data re, 310

— marital, 86 ff., 171 ff.

— sole recipient syndrome, 75 f., 263; well-adjusted, 86 f.; perfectionistic family, 131 ff.; inadequate family, 171 ff.; egocentric family, 215 ff.; unsocial family, 261 ff.; definition of, 320

Magic formula, for problem-solving, 176

Maladjustment, in family functioning, data re, 339

— social, 234 f.; factors in, 33 ff.; of children, 108

Manic depressive reaction, 275

Marital axis, as key to research program, 7 f.; casework analysis of data, 12 ff.

Marital disorders, term, 96; egocentric family, 195; unsocial family, 236; prognosis, 342

Marital functioning, 43 f.; well-adjusted family, 84 ff.; levels of psychosocial disorders in, 110 f.; perfectionistic family, 116, 130 ff.; inadequate family, 158, 171 ff.; egocentric family, 215 ff.; unsocial family, 260 ff.; interpretation of data re, 320 ff.

Marital partners, criteria for selection of cases, 10; approach to marriage, 50; newly wed, agency cases, 51; exchange of roles, 54, 269; sexual adjustment, 55; biological and psychological differences, 71; well-adjusted, 85 ff.; incipient psychosocial disorders, 101 f.; goals, 117; perfectionistic, 131; overidealization and devaluation, 174 f.; attitude toward child-rearing disorders, 194; devaluation of one another, 219; effect of tenuous emotional ties, 250; attitude toward giving and receiving love, 261 f.; unsocial family, reaction to sexual act, 264 f.; withdrawal of interest, 268; interpretation of data re, 322 f.; see also Husband; Parents; Wife

Marital status, of families studied, 11

Marriage, cultural attitudes toward, 39 f.; legal, 41; functions of, 48 ff.; plural, 49 f.; legal and other sanctions re, 50; ideals and realities, 50 f.; goals of, 54; preparation for, 85; stable, and problem-solving, 88 ff.; termination of, 111 (see also Divorce)

Masochism, 71, 274

Maturity, sexual, 38; biological and emotional, 66 ff.; physical, 119; reluctance to attain, in adolescence, 227

Men, role in society, 37; and sex relationships, 39

Mental deficiency, in children, 276 f.; and adolescent behavior, 280

Mental illness, 105; prognosis re, 25; of children, 108; of wife, 348

Mental retardation, inadequate family, 183

Methodology, 14 ff., 19 ff.

Money, teaching the value of, 83

Monogamy, 49

Monroe, R. R., see Weiss, V. W.

Mother, parental responsibility, 44 f.; role in child care, 74; loss of freedom in child rearing, 76 f.; and family discipline, 81 f.; overrigidity, 119; identification with, 127 f., 253 f., 283; egocentric family, 197 f.; breaking of emotional tie to, 211; inconstancy of love, 241; overdevotion, 242 f.; see also Wife

Mother-daughter relationship, reactions, 152; egocentric family, 233; unsocial family, 288 f.

Mother-son relationship, 56 f., 122; egocentric family, 201 f., 228; effect of, on adult male, 282 f.

Motor disorders, in latency, 328

Narcissism, 132; in egocentric marital partners, 218, 223 f.

Needs, gratification of, 17, 29 f.; emotional, 75; insatiable, and frustration, 266

Neglect, of child, 249; defined, 112; inadequate family, 161; emotional and physical, 190 f.; egocentric family, 233

Neuroses, in latency, 328

Occupational status, 53, 137; inadequate family, 177 f.; egocentric husband, 222; see also Work

Oedipal: complex, 42; period, 64, 207; conflicts, 149

Opportunism, in marital functions of egocentric family, 215 f.; in marital relationship, unsocial family, 261 ff.

"Oral optimists and pessimists," 61

Ormsby, Ralph, see Pollak, Otto

Overaggression, self-centered, in adolescents, 254 f.

Overcompensation, maternal, 139 f.

Overdevotion, parental, 241 f.

Overidealization, of marital partner, 174

Overindulgence, parental, 190, 287 f.

Overprotection, 114, 199, 203

Oversensitivity, 120 f.

Oversubmissiveness, in decision-making, 230

Parent(s), identification with offspring, 75 f.; well-adjusted, and child rearing, 77 f.; regulation of behavior, 82; financial responsibility, 83; separation from, 112 f., 149, 188 f., 231, 247 f., 284, 313 f.; dis-

Parent (*Continued*)
torted direction and guidance of child, 113; perfectionistic family, 117 ff.; inadequate family, 159 ff.; emotional dependence on children, 160 ff.; egocentric family, 197 ff.; reversal of roles, 244; sexual indiscretion in child's presence, 249; overreliance on, 256; submissive and overindulgent, 282 f.; child-rearing function (*q.v.*), 308 f.; attitude toward social behavior, 311 f.; withdrawal of ties from, 329 f.; *see also* Father; Mother; Substitute parent(s)

Parent-child relationship, 56; severing of ties, 66 f., 165, 183 f., 205, 227, 247, 260, 278 f.; in well-adjusted family, 72 ff.; and child rearing (*q.v.*), 72 ff.; and sex education, 82; distortions of, 113 f.; perfectionistic family, 124 f., 127 f.; emotional ties, 142 f.; inadequate family, 160; husband's family of origin, 186; love-relationship syndromes, 200 ff.; egocentric family, 209 ff., 218; eroticized, 210 f.; unsocial family, 239 ff.; indecisiveness and overpunitiveness, 245; continuity of contact, 313 f.; psychic disturbances, 329 ff.

Parenthood, attitudes toward, 44 f.; responses to, 72 ff., 159 f.; desire for, and adjustment to, 73 f.; reactions to, in perfectionistic family, 117 ff.; rejection of, 197; reaction to, in unsocial family, 237 f.; illegitimate, prognosis, 342

Pathology, in perfectionistic family of origin, 149

Peers, relations with, 214, 258 f.; *see also* Friends

Perfectionistic family, 115-55; stresses in, 307; percentage of, 336

Personal devaluation, 135

Personality, development, 66 ff.; integration and socialization of, 70 f.

Personality traits, perfectionistic couple, 139 f.; unsocial family, 272 ff.; *see also* Adult characteristics; Child characteristics

Personal problems, defined, 347

Physical condition, in inadequate family, 160 f., 179 f., 182; egocentric family, 222 f.; unsocial family, 270, 272; diagnostic information re, 309; data re, 325; of child, 327

Physical disability, 107, 138; of children, 108 f., 199 f., 224 f.; *see also* Handicapped, the

Physical growth, 60

Placement, 112; and Level A disorders, 25; agencies and, 97; provisions for, 99 f.; egocentric family and, 194; effect of, 284, 332; evaluation and interpretation of, 326

Play, 126

Playmates, 126

Pollak, Otto, and Ralph Ormsby, "Design of a Model of Healthy Family Relationships," 6

Possession, child as, 201

Pregnancy, illegitimate, 184, 238

Premarital orientation and planning, 85 f.

Premarital relationships, 39

Prestige conflicts, 214 f.; adolescent, 130, 259

Privacy, need for, 82 f.

Problems, range of, 10; marital axis, categories of, 13 f.

Problem-solving, marital, 321 f.; in stable marriage, 88 f.; perfectionistic family, 135 f.; inadequate family, 175 ff.; egocentric family, 220 f.; unsocial family, 267 f.; caseworker's help in, 305

"Problem treated," definition of term, 347

Prognosis, as a research tool, 20 ff.; classification of 100 families, 23 ff.; procedures for, 340 ff.

Projection, as defense mechanism, 62; and unsatisfactory sex identity, 88; of blame, on marital partner, 268

Promiscuity, in mother of unsocial family, 246; as exploitation, 288

Psychic disturbance, in latency and adolescence, 141 ff.; of children in inadequate family, 183; *see also* Psychosocial disorders

Psychopathology, of adult disorders in unsocial family, 236 f.

Psychosexual development, arrestment in, 172 f.

Psychosis, in family member, 107; in egocentric adults, 224; adolescent potentiality for, 257; unsocial family, 273, 277 f.; in latency, 329; initial stages in adolescent, 330

"Psychosocial," definition of, 95

Psychosocial disorders, Level A, 17 f., 20 ff., 103 ff., 342 f.; Level B, 17 f., 103 ff., 115 ff.; classification, 20, 95-114, 304 ff.; "forced evasions," 100 f.; family, 109 ff.; perfectionistic family, 115 ff.; inadequate family, 156 ff.; egocentric family, 194 ff.; in sexual role, 217 f.; unsocial family, 234-89; definition of, 293; in family types, 336 f.

Psychosocial functioning, in family diagnosis, 29 ff.; see also Dysfunctioning, psychosocial

Reading problems, 143

Recovery, degree of, definition of term, 347

Referents, of basic areas in family diagnosis, 295

Regression, 125; parental attitude toward, 79; adolescent, 184, 330 f.; in latency, 226; into psychosis, 273

Rehabilitation, 18 f., 98; planning, 291; see also Treatment

Rejection, by parents, 81

Relationships, interpersonal, 300 f.; see also Friends; Love relationships; Parent-child relationships

Religious affiliation, 11, 46

Remarriage, divorce and, 49

Repression, in marital partners, perfectionistic family, 139 f.; as ego defense, 180 f.; in adolescence, 227

Research project, objectives, 5 ff.; resources and setting, 7 ff.; training, 8 f.; reformulated concepts, 15 ff.; tools, 19 ff.; see also Community Research Associates

Resistance, to decision-making, 229 f.

Responsibilities, distorted reactions to, 107 f.

Sado-masochism, in egocentric couple, 219

Sampling, methods, 9 f.; 100-case, 19 ff., 23 f., 26 f.; numerical distribution of types, 31

Sanctions, legal, on behavior, 99 ff.

Schizophrenic reaction, 275

School, child's acceptance of, 65 f.; failure in, 108; perfectionistic family and, 129; inadequate family and, 163; attitude toward, 169; egocentric family and, 204, 212; unsocial family and, 257 f.; child's attitude toward, 317 f.

Seductiveness, parental, 200 f., 208 f.

Self-centeredness, overaggressive, in adolescents, 254 f.

Self-confidence, development of, 62 f., 114

Self-determination, 36 f.

Self-direction, growth in, 63 f.

Self-esteem, lack of, in latency and adolescence, 257 f.

Self-identity, in well-adjusted family, 77 ff.; maintenance of, in marriage, 87 f.; of children, 121 f., 125; in latency and adolescence, 128 f., 169, 211 ff., 253 ff., 317; of perfectionistic couple, 134 f.; in husband's family of origin, 146 f., 187, 229 f., 284 f.; in wife's family of origin, 155 f., 191 f., 233 f., 288 f.; inadequate family, 162 f., 167 f., 174 f.; and separation from parents, 188; egocentric family, 203 f., 218 f.; early childhood, 206 f.; unsocial family, 243 f., 251 f., 265 f.; definition, 298, 301; interpretation of data re, 310; of marital partners, data re, 321

Self-mastery, development of, 64 f., 78

Self-reliance, hindrances to development of, 119; premature, 164 f., 206 f.; delayed, 252; child-training in, 311; degree of, 317

Sex, in American culture, 37 ff.; and the family system, 41 ff.; social regulation of, 43 f.; differentiation, in marriage, 51; premarital relationship, 55; well-adjusted marital partners and, 86 f.; relations, of perfectionistic family, 131 ff.; attitudes of wife's parents to, 152 f.; wife's attitude to, 160, 181 f.; inadequate family, 171 ff.; parent-child attachment, 210; abnormalities in object of, 217; deviant forms of, in egocentric family, 217 f.; unsocial family, 244, 259, 264 f.; behavior in latency and adolescence, 318

Sex education, by parents, 82

Sex identity, achievement of, 38, 285; maladjustment in, 88; in egocentric parents, 197; hindrances to, in unsocial family, 244

Sibling, birth of, 79 f., 125

Sibling rivalry, 42, 317; perfectionistic family, 128; egocentric family, 212; in latency and adolescence, 253

Sleep, disturbances of, in young child, 251

Social determination, processes of, 96 ff.

Social functioning, 296 f.; healthy, 15 f., 81 ff.; family, areas of, 16 f.; determinants of, 33-69; and psychosocial disorders, 95 ff.; maladjustment of children to, 108; parental overemphasis on, 121; and ego defenses, 180 f.; defined, 293, 308; judgment re improvement in, 346; *see also* Dysfunctioning, social

Social identity, acquisition of, 66 ff.

Socialization, degree of, 70 f.; of child, 80, 207 f., 252, 315 f.; well-adjusted family, 81 ff.; aspects of, 84; in stable marriage, 88 f.; incompetent practices in child rearing, 114; perfectionistic family, 122, 125 f., 135 f.; of adolescents, 130; husband's family of origin, 148, 187, 230, 285; wife's family of origin, 155, 192, 233, 289; inadequate family, 163 ff., 167 f., 175 ff.; in latency and adolescence, 170, 212 ff., 258 ff., 318; egocentric family, 204 f., 219 ff.; unsocial family, 245, 267 ff.; definition, 298, 301; diagnostic data re, 311 f.; marital, data re, 321

Social planning, preventive, 102 f.

Social Security Act of 1935, 109

Social setting, as referent, 295

Social work, professional schools, 7; service levels of, 343 ff.; *see also* Casework

Society, values and standards, 33 ff.; change in values, and the individual, 40 f.; attitudes toward marriage, 43 f.; demands upon the individual, 95 ff.; sanctions re behavior, 96 ff.; *see also* Community; Environment

Sociolegal intervention, unsocial family and, 245 f.

Standard of living, inadequate family, 178 f.

Stepchild, in egocentric family, 201 f.

Stepfather, seduction by, 211; unsocial family, 243

Stepmother, parent-child relationship, 151 f.

Stepparent, 149 f.

"Substitute family," 47 f.

Substitute parents, 149, 284; and teaching of social behavior, 163 f.; inadequate family, 165; egocentric family, 231; unsocial family, 239; relatives as, 286; transfer of ties to, 329 f.

Superego, in adolescence, 67 f.; development of, 80 f.; overrigid, 122; defective, 258 f., 273, 332; *see also* Conscience

Temper tantrums, 79, 206

Thumb-sucking, 250

Toilet training 82 f., 125 f.; egocentric family, 200; precocious, 252

Treatment, in social dysfunctioning, 98 f.; research needs, 101 ff.; prognosis and, 340 f.; planning procedures, 343 ff.

Unsocial family, 29 f., 234-89; compared with inadequate family, 30 f.; stresses in, 307; percent of cases, 336

United States, cultural trends, 35 ff.; the family in, 46 ff.

Urban middle class, 46

Value, egocentric, in parenthood, 238

Value scale, for problem areas, 13 f.

Weiss, V. W., and R. R. Monroe, "A Framework for Understanding Family Dynamics," 6

Wife, domestic role, 52 f.; attitude toward household tasks, 52 f.; career, 53 f.; role of, in love relationship, 86 f.; attitude toward sexual act, 134, 153 f.; family of origin, 148 ff., 188 ff., 230 ff., 286 ff., 331 f.; inadequate family, 172 ff., 181 f.; employed, 221 f., 240, 269; unsocial family, 237, 240, 262 ff., 274; mental illness, 348

Withdrawal, protective, of adolescents, 255

Women, role in society, 37; sex relationships, 39; role in marriage, 52 f.; emancipation of, 53 f.

Work, psychosocial disorders and, 110; attitude toward, 145, 221, 269 f.; habits of husband's parents, 221, 281 f.

Workshops, 9